Public Spheres, Private Lives in

Modern Japan, 1600–1950

Essays in Honor of

Albert M. Craig

Harvard East Asian Monographs 238

Essays in Honor of

Albert M. Craig

Public Spheres, Private Lives in

Modern Japan, 1600–1950

Edited by
Gail Lee Bernstein, Andrew Gordon,
and Kate Wildman Nakai

Published by the Harvard University Asia Center
Distributed by Harvard University Press
Cambridge (Massachusetts) and London, 2005

Printed in the United States of America

The Harvard University Asia Center publishes a monograph series and, in coordination with the Fairbank Center for East Asian Research, the Korea Institute, the Reischauer Institute of Japanese Studies, and other faculties and institutes, administers research projects designed to further scholarly understanding of China, Japan, Vietnam, Korea, and other Asian countries. The Center also sponsors projects addressing multidisciplinary and regional issues in Asia.

Library of Congress Cataloging-in-Publication Data
Public spheres, private lives in modern Japan, 1600–1950 : essays in honor of Albert M. Craig / edited by Gail Lee Bernstein, Andrew Gordon, and Kate Wildman Nakai.
      p. cm. -- (Harvard East Asian monographs ; 238)
   Includes bibliographical references and index.
   ISBN 0-674-01651-3 (cloth : alk. paper)
      1. Japan--History—1868– 2. Japan--History--Tokugawa period, 1600–1868.
I. Craig, Albert M. II. Bernstein, Gail Lee. III. Gordon, Andrew, 1952– IV. Nakai, Kate Wildman. V. Series.
   DS881.9.P83 2005
   952--dc22

                                                                2005008900

Index by Anne Holmes of EdIndex

⊗ Printed on acid-free paper

Last figure below indicates year of this printing
14 13 12 11 10 09 08 07 06 05

Contents

Figures and Tables

Figures

Tables

Contributors

GAIL LEE BERNSTEIN is Professor of History and East Asian Studies at the University of Arizona. She is the author of *Japanese Marxist: A Portrait of Kawakami Hajime, 1879–1946*, and *Haruko's World: A Japanese Farm Woman and Her Community* and editor of *Recreating Japanese Women, 1600–1945*, and (with Haruhiro Fukui) of *Japan and the World: Essays in Japanese History and Politics in Honour of Ishida Takeshi*. Her forthcoming book narrates the three-hundred-year history of a Japanese family.

MARY ELIZABETH BERRY is Professor of History at the University of California, Berkeley. She is the author of *Hideyoshi* and *The Culture of Civil War in Kyoto*. Her contribution to this volume distills portions of a monograph—*Information and Society in Early Modern Japan*—that deals with many genres and texts of what she calls "the library of public information." The concluding chapter explores the notion of early modern "nationhood," a *leitmotif* in the essay appearing here.

JOHN W. DOWER is Ford International Professor of History at the Massachusetts Institutes of Technology. He is the author of *War Without Mercy: Race and Power in the Pacific War*; *Empire and Aftermath: Yoshida Shigeru and the Japanese Experience, 1878–1954*; and *Embracing Defeat: Japan in the Wake of World War II*, which won numerous prizes. His primary research interests are modern Japanese history and U.S.-Japan relations. He has broken new ground in the use of visual materials and other expressions of popular culture in examining Japanese and U.S.-Asian history.

STEVEN J. ERICSON is Associate Professor of History and chairs the Asian and Middle Eastern Studies Program at Dartmouth College. He has authored *The Sound of the Whistle: Railroads and the State in Meiji Japan* and is co-editing a conference volume on the history and legacy of the Portsmouth Peace Treaty. He includes among his research interests the Matsukata financial reform, the Russo-Japanese War, and business deconcentration during the U.S. occupation of Japan.

HARALD FUESS works at Sophia University in Tokyo. He grew up in France and Germany, studied at Princeton, Tokyo, and Harvard Universities, and taught Japanese history, culture, gender, and business in the United States, Germany, and Japan. He edited *The Japanese Empire in East Asia and Its Postwar Legacy* and authored *Divorce in Japan: Family, Gender, and the State, 1600–2000*. His current book-length research project is on the history of Japanese beer.

TIMOTHY S. GEORGE is Associate Professor of History at the University of Rhode Island and taught at Harvard University in 1997–98 and 2004–5. He is the author of *Minamata: Pollution and the Struggle for Democracy in Postwar Japan*, editor and co-translator of Harada Masazumi's *Minamata Disease*, and coauthor (with John W. Dower) of *Japanese History and Culture from Ancient to Modern Times: Seven Basic Bibliographies*.

ANDREW GORDON is Lee and Juliet Folger Fund Professor of History at Harvard University. He has written books on the history of labor and management in nineteenth- and twentieth-century Japan and on the politics of labor in the prewar era. He is currently studying the emergence of Japan as a mass consumer society in the twentieth century, with particular focus on the sewing machine.

Kʏᴜ Hʏᴜɴ Kɪᴍ is Associate Professor of Japanese History at University of California, Davis. He is the author of *The Age of Visions and Arguments: Parliamentarianism and the National Public Sphere in Early Meiji Japan*, which examines the transformation of the public sphere in response to proliferation of the parliamentarian discourse in late nineteenth century Japan. He has also written articles on Korean and Japanese popular culture: "Horror as Criticism in *Tell Me Something* and *Sympathy for Mr. Vengeance*" and "Girl (and Boy) Troubles in the Animeland: Exploring Representations of Gender in Japanese Animation Films." His current research projects include the intellectual history of Korean "collaboration" with the Japanese colonial empire in 1930s and 1940s and the postcolonial discourse in contemporary Korean cinema.

Bᴀʀʙᴀʀᴀ Mᴏʟᴏɴʏ is Professor of Japanese History and Director of the Program for the Study of Women and Gender at Santa Clara University. She has published numerous articles on women's rights movements in Japan and Asia, including "Women's Rights, Feminism, and Suffragism in Japan," which won the Ridge Prize of the Western Association of Women Historians. She is the co-editor (with Kathleen Uno) of *Gendering Modern Japanese History* and co-author of a biography of Ichikawa Fusae and a history of modern East Asia.

Kᴀᴛᴇ Wɪʟᴅᴍᴀɴ Nᴀᴋᴀɪ completed her Ph.D. at Harvard in 1972. After holding teaching posts at Harvard and the University of Oregon, she moved in 1980 to Sophia University, Tokyo, where she is Professor of Japanese History in the Faculty of Comparative Culture. Since 1997 she has also served as editor of *Monumenta Nipponica*. A specialist in premodern intellectual history, she is the author of *Shogunal Politics: Arai Hakuseki and the Premises of Tokugawa Rule*. The Japanese translation of her study of Hakuseki was awarded the Watsuji Tetsurō Culture Prize for 2002.

PATRICIA SIPPEL is Associate Professor of Japan Studies at Toyo Eiwa University in Yokohama, Japan. Her research focuses on Japan's economic and political history since the early modern era. Her doctoral dissertation was "Financing the Long Peace: The Agricultural Tax in the Bakufu Domain" (Harvard, 1994). Publications include "Mapping the Tokugawa Domain from 1590 through the Early Nineteenth Century" and "Abandoned Fields: Negotiating Taxes in the Tokugawa Domain." She is currently working on the history of copper mining in the Tohoku region.

KERRY SMITH is Associate Professor of History at Brown University and the author of *A Time of Crisis: Japan, the Great Depression and Rural Revitalization*. His current research explores the social and cultural histories of the 1923 Kantō Earthquake.

SEE HENG TEOW is Associate Professor of History at the National University of Singapore. He is the author of *Japan's Cultural Policy Toward China, 1918–1931: A Comparative Perspective*. He is currently researching various aspects of Japan's relations with Southeast Asia from the 1870s to 1945, including Japanese interactions with Southeast Asian Chinese communities. He is also working on recent initiatives by Japan and Southeast Asian countries regarding East Asian regionalism and economic integration.

Public Spheres, Private Lives in

Modern Japan, 1600–1950

Essays in Honor of

Albert M. Craig

Introduction
Gail Lee Bernstein, Andrew Gordon,
and Kate Wildman Nakai

This volume results from a two-day symposium held in 1999 to honor the eminent historian of Japan Albert M. Craig on his retirement after forty years of teaching at Harvard University. All the contributors received their Ph.D. degree under Professor Craig's direction. Because the symposium was organized to showcase the participants' diverse research interests—a testament to their mentor's own scholarly breadth—it was not centered around a particular topic or theme. A substantial number of the papers, however, shared a common focus on the relationship, broadly conceived, between state and society in modern Japan. These papers became the eleven chapters in this volume. Together, they explore the process of carving out, in discourse and in practice, the boundaries delineating the state, the civil sphere, and the family in the period from 1600 to 1950.

One major theme addressed in the volume is the demarcation of relations between the central political authority and local ommunities. Although this is the particular concern of the four chapters in Part I, it figures in other contributions as well. Focusing on the early modern period, Mary Elizabeth Berry describes how a "quiet revolution in knowledge" contributed to the formation of the sense that "Japan" was a nation. Detailed maps, gazetteers, travel guides, itineraries, and pictorial surveys conveyed not only a spatial sense of nation but also a long, putatively common history. The "public information" library circulating in the Tokugawa period helped merge the "landscape of power" with the "landscape of culture" in graphic images that contributed to the growing perception of the country as a coherent unit.

The dissemination of other information in popular forms furthered the envisioning of Japan as a "geobody" ruled by a "national governing fraternity." "Military Mirrors" (*bukan*), books containing data on the daimyo, helped the shogunate to construct and project its power throughout the realm. Like national maps, these rosters of politically significant figures cast them as both local lords and a "national constellation of authority" by portraying the scale and scope of their work.

Maps and the Military Mirrors also carried messages about the relationships between regional and central institutions, or between rulers and ruled. National maps, for example, depicted the daimyo as the "irreducible units of local power and local meaning" while omitting villages as named entities. Behind this depiction of power relationships, however, lay other traditions not immediately apparent in such nationally oriented visual representations. These included structures of village self-rule and patterns of mutual expectations and responsibilities connecting the governing authorities with localities below the level of the provincial military ruler.

One link in the relationship between higher levels of government and local communities was *chisui*, "river management," which became a significant aspect of early state-building efforts. The call for flood-control measures might begin in local communities, but such projects required the assistance of the ruling elite. Patricia Sippel's study in Part II of the expensive, technologically challenging, and often dangerous hydraulic engineering works undertaken in the Nōbi plain reveals a pattern of mutual accommodation of state and local interests that continued from the Tokugawa era to modern times. Local and regional leaders looked to the shogunate to exercise leadership by providing money, technical support, comprehensive flood-control plans, and mediation of conflicting local claims. Although the results often did not satisfy the parties directly concerned, a "convergence of interests between village communities dependent on farming and a government dependent on agricultural tax revenues" brought government and villagers to work together "to impose their will on rivers."

Meiji-era efforts to establish a stronger central government after the overthrow of the Tokugawa in 1868 inevitably raised questions about the proper relationship between the new "imperial" government and local groups and interests at the prefectural and village levels. As Berry reminds us, the "gravitational pull of the center" had remained "curiously unemphasized" in the Tokugawa period. While leaders in Tokyo attempted to carve out new political boundaries and redesign administrative units throughout the country, various subject-citizens of the emerging nation-state sought means to voice their concerns and defend local interests. The chapters by Kyu Hyun Kim and Timothy S. George address aspects of this effort in the late nineteenth and early twentieth century.

Moves to demarcate the boundaries of central and regional jurisdictions, and of state and society, in the course of constructing a modern nation contributed to a public discourse that drew on Western political ideas as well as longstanding assumptions about political legitimacy, authority, and responsibility. One of the most significant political ideas debated in early Meiji Japan was *chihō bunken* or *chihō jichi*—local autonomy or local self-government—terms containing notions that resonate with the more recent concept of civil society.[1]

Meiji-era debates over the meaning of "local" and "autonomy" gave rise to diverse conceptions of the polity. The Meiji government itself, as Kim notes, believed that involving the general public

---

1. We gratefully acknowledge Frank Schwartz's chapter "What *Is* Civil Society?" in *The State of Civil Society in Japan*, ed. Frank J. Schwartz and Susan J. Pharr (Cambridge, Eng.: Cambridge University Press, 2003), for helping to clarify the multiple meanings of this ambiguous term. We use it here in a broad sense to refer to activities occurring in the space between the family and the state. Social actors include members of political parties, voluntary organizations, newspapers, citizens' movements, labor unions, and so on. Local self-government, according to certain theorists, is also included in the broad definition of civil society, although Tocqueville posited a separate "political society" between the state and civil society, in which citizens' involvement in politics occurred. Whether the market economy should be considered a part of civil society is subject to dispute. Civil society assumes a realm of free public debate and limited government.

in a limited way in the affairs of state would facilitate the implementation of government policies at the local level. Popular Rights activists in the 1870s and 1880s went further. They saw local autonomy not only as a link between local and national participation in political institutions but as a right and a necessary step toward the democratization of Japan's political system.

The contours of local rule, however, remained contested ground in the various administrative plans, political tracts, and philosophical treatises penned by bureaucrats and political reformers of the period. "Local rule," for example, could mean operating under the supervision of the prefectural governors (newly appointed by the central government), who had replaced the daimyo, or it might refer to the functions assigned village- and county-level assemblies composed of local leaders; it might even connote preservation of the traditional role of village heads. One of the most important ideologues of the early Meiji government, Inoue Kowashi, argued that self-rule at the village level as it had developed under the Tokugawa system had established the "foundations of modern local self-government."

Local elites, however, were not satisfied by such assumptions about local autonomy. They disagreed with officials who held that local self-government was "not about allowing the people to handle the tasks of government directly." Concerns about being excluded from national decision-making led some local elites to try to claim greater powers for the newly established prefectural assemblies or to become involved in political parties. Popular Rights activists argued that local autonomy could be realized only if representatives of the community were empowered to participate actively in a national parliament.

The concept of local autonomy also figured prominently in the thought of Fukuzawa Yukichi, the famous Meiji educator and popularizer of Western learning. Distinguishing between "political power" (seiken) and "administrative power" (chiken), he opposed any model of government that weakened the political power of the center. At the same time, he argued that the state "should not impair the natural development of social forces by insisting on the expansion of its administrative powers," and he advised against the state's "intervention into the private spheres of the people's lives either to protect them or to prohibit or suppress them."

Local autonomy, as conceived by Fukuzawa, was necessary to preserve the distinction between the political power reserved for the national unit and the administrative power that should be exercised locally. It also was crucial for fostering the independence and public spirit requisite in the citizens of a sovereign, civilized nation. One potential locus of civic life existed, he held, in the traditional village community. The "Japanese people," he wrote in regard to the pre-Meiji period, "even though unable to exercise political power, had long practiced autonomy in the public affairs of local regions and successfully resisted intervention from the state." He favored allowing local residents to administer their own lives, debate state policies, and thereby complement the activities of the state. "Public and private interests will then find their point of convergence."

Kim's chapter highlights the fluidity of the boundaries between state and society in early Meiji discourse. Thinkers and activists were not only or even mainly concerned to wall off an autonomous realm of civil society from the state. At the same time, a lively debate ensued over where to locate local rule and how much local autonomy, political power, and popular political participation to allow and to whom to allocate it. The disputes that arose when local political leaders tried to implement ideas of self-rule after the promulgation of the Meiji Constitution in 1889 exposed the continuing tensions between the central government's version of that term and their own.

Readers can observe a desire to join state and society in a common cause in Timothy George's analysis of Diet representative Tanaka Shōzō, a former village head, Popular Rights activist, and prefectural assemblyman. Like Fukuzawa, Tanaka hoped for a cooperative relationship between government and the people. Tanaka, however, also defined the government's responsibilities toward citizens to include state protection and relief. When operations of the privately owned Ashio mine poisoned rivers and caused flooding that ruined villagers' agricultural lands, Tanaka called on the government to protect the people's property, provide relief for victims, and impose controls on pollution. His demands reflected assumptions about the role of government similar to those held by the Nōbi plain villagers described by Sippel. What was new was the much higher degree of politicization. Frustrated with the Diet's failure to act, Tanaka turned to unofficial, voluntary civic organizations, which, by the turn of the twentieth century, had been functioning for two decades. Newspapers, political discussion groups, and political parties proved capable of galvanizing support from a wide array of emergent political actors: women's groups, Christian and Buddhist associations, university students and faculty, journalists, socialists, and labor organizers. But Tanaka also relied on the dramatic, tension-filled ultimate resort of traditional village protests—a direct appeal to higher authority, in this instance, none other than the emperor.

In Tanaka's impassioned defense of the Ashio mine victims, George finds a vision of an alternative form of political modernity for Japan. This vision called for a "viable, constitutional, civil society," one in which everybody, including the emperor, practiced "harmonious cooperation" as enjoined by natural law—the "constitution of the universe." This formula implied that ministers should be responsible not only to the emperor but also to the people. George argues that Tanaka grasped the central concept of constitutional government: that government should be accountable and operate under the rule of law. At the same time, Tanaka's vision of a polity based on the people and village communities was also rooted in his own origins. Like local notables of old, he "identified with and acted on behalf of the villagers of his home area."

The notion of "harmonious cooperation" suggested not only that ultimately "the people were the owners of the nation, and therefore they were the masters of the government officials, who were their employees," but also that the government was responsible for the people's well-being. The links to the familiar Confucian vocabulary of "benevolent rule," as well as Tanaka's references to harmony between the natural order and human society, indicate to George that his political thought "looked both ahead and behind."

Kerry Smith, too, explores understandings of the proper relationship between local communities and the central government and examines how these were realized in practice in contemporary relief and revitalization projects in the 1930s. Although rural economic reform was understood "essentially [as] a local effort," and reformers emphasized community-wide solutions, initiatives to revitalize rural communities were, he finds, accompanied by efforts to gain central government assistance.

Aid from the Ministry of Agriculture and Forestry contributed to recovery programs in the countryside during the Depression years. The forging of relief and reform policies nevertheless was not the work of bureaucrats and politicians alone. A "diverse array of farmers' organizations, spokespersons for landlords and other local notables, and everyday farmers, all demand[ed] a say in how the countryside was to be rescued." The rural reform schemes described by Smith reveal, once again, the existence of rural activists "skilled in using the power of the state to help implement their vision of an ideal society." This coming together of local and state initiatives is reminiscent of the sometimes ironic "convergence of interests" that Sippel finds in water-management projects as early as the Tokugawa period. It also echoes the vision of "harmonious cooperation" voiced by Tanaka at the end of the nineteenth century.

These chapters by Kim, George, Smith, and Sippel demonstrate that both mutuality and tension characterized the increasingly complex relationships between central government institutions and local communities. To be sure, fending off central government encroachment, domination, or exploitation was always a concern of local communities. An equally important concern, however, was enlisting the assistance of the state. Local elites worried that Tokyo would neglect or overlook their community in allocating relief or development funds vital to their region's wellbeing and growth. Some individuals discussed in these essays and in the chapter by Barbara Molony in Part III also sought to mobilize the state to defend themselves against deleterious impacts of the market economy. Issues of local autonomy in modern Japan, therefore, were not inevitably framed in terms of a confrontational relationship: prefectures did not demand "states' rights," and not everybody agreed that the government was best which governed least. Rather, local leaders and reformers alike sought a mutually beneficial mix of autonomy and aid, participation and noninterference, rights and protection.

Although the debates over local autonomy and civic life were shaped by traditional assumptions regarding the role of government, they also reflected new intellectual currents originating from the West. Fukuzawa Yukichi's vision of an autonomous civic sphere was grounded in his reading of John Stuart Mill and Alexis de Tocqueville, and Tanaka Shōzō drew inspiration from Jean-Jacques Rousseau and European constitutional thought as well as Mencius. Molony draws attention to Christian and socialist influences, among others, that shaped the discourse on "women's rights" in the late nineteenth century. The impact of foreign influences is visible in areas other than ideas and political institutions, however. The assimilation of foreign technology had equally far-reaching consequences. The two chapters in Part II focus on aspects of the incorporation of technological advances, a phenomenon that also illustrates the interweaving of public and private initiatives.

One remarkable aspect of Japan's efforts to master advanced material technology is the degree of expertise available in the early Meiji period, despite the long ban on contact with the West. The precision of the specifications set by state railway officials in their negotiations with European and American locomotive manufacturers in the late nineteenth century, like the detailed observations on Jacquard weaving made by members of the Iwakura Mission on their tour of Lowell mills in the early 1870s, illustrate considerable technical understanding.[2] What explains this successful acquisition of modern technology?

The studies in this volume cannot provide a definitive answer to this central question in modern Japanese history, but they do suggest continuities in the role of government, the availability of both community and private energies and initiatives, and a faith in technology. Throughout the Tokugawa period, the kind of large-

---

2. This point was made by Martin Collcutt at the 1999 symposium. See chapter 20 of his translation of the first volume of Kume Kunitake, *Bei-Ō kairan jikki*, translated as *The Iwakura Embassy, 1871–1873: A True Account of the Ambassador Extraordinary & Plenipotentiary's Journey of Observation Through the United States of America and Europe* (Chiba, Japan: The Japan Documents, 2002).

scale, state-directed engineering enterprises examined in Patricia Sippel's chapter on flood-control projects had engaged government officials and villagers alike. The Tokugawa bakufu maintained a corps of engineers who built land- and water-transportation systems of considerable complexity.

The dissemination of the practical learning needed to adopt and apply technological innovations was facilitated by a high rate of literacy, the result of the widespread establishment of schools in early modern Japan, and by a boom in commercial printing. The Tokugawa period, as Berry describes it, was an age of information. The publication of books with concrete, useful, and ever-changing information affirmed the "knowability through observation of worldly phenomena." Not only detailed maps but manuals on farming, instructional texts on brewing, and, by the end of the era, Dutch treatises on gunnery became part of this store of useful information.

The new element in the Meiji period was the role of Western technical advisors in technology transfer. Dutch engineers introduced new methods of river reconstruction and erosion control, and German, American, and British engineers assisted in the mastery of locomotive manufacture. In the 1870s, petitions from local leaders in the Nōbi plain area for central government support of water-management projects included a request for foreign—specifically Dutch—expertise. Even when a Dutch-style river-transportation system failed to prevent the breaching of dikes, the loss of confidence in Dutch technological expertise did not undermine faith in the "power of technology to shape and control Japan's physical and human environment" in the early modern and modern eras.

Central government support and the initiative of private individuals alone were not the sole factors in Japan's rapid incorporation of new technology. As Steven Ericson's study of the importing of locomotives demonstrates, an important element in the process of technology transfer in the Meiji period was aggressive marketing by Western producers and the competition among them. Nevertheless, Ericson also emphasizes the critical role of state intervention in Japan's rapid shift to self-sufficiency in locomotive manufacturing. The state-owned national railways constituted "by far the largest concentration of technical skill in all of Japan," Ericson writes, and their technicians achieved a high level of expertise in locomotive production, thanks, in part, to the on-the-spot training they had received from Western manufacturers. They passed their expertise to private Japanese manufacturers, thus "nurtur[ing] domestic private builders . . . by furnishing vital technological assistance and leadership."

The chapters in Parts I and II describe efforts of government officials, local leaders, and individual reformers to define state-local relations. Those relations encompassed multiple intersections of public power and private initiatives. Ordinary citizens from many walks of life engaged with the state bureaucracy and politicians in promoting economic development, social reform, and technology transfer and in reshaping various spheres of intellectual and material life under the impact of new influences from abroad. Another important dimension of the formation of modern Japanese society—the private sphere and its articulation with political authority—is the focus of Part III. What were the norms and expectations of the state's role in gender relations and family life? Were these arenas in fact private? The definition of "private" itself warrants closer scrutiny.

By the last decade of the nineteenth century, the central government had made significant inroads into family life. The political system encoded in the 1889 Constitution and accompanying documents deliberately blurred the boundaries between national goals and private life in order to foster nationalist loyalties. The ideology of family-state nationalism heavily politicized and intruded on the institution of the family. The Civil Code of 1898 reinforced a patriarchal model of the family, and the Ministry of Education's slogan of "good wife, wise mother" likened married women's performance of domestic functions to a public duty. At the same time, the Police Security Regulations of 1890 barred women from attending political meetings or joining political organizations. From top to bottom, the formal political system and civic life were gendered male.

Feminists in the Meiji period nevertheless struggled to create a place for women in social spheres outside the family and to gain equality within it. Barbara Molony notes that Meiji-era feminists viewed women's education as the prerequisite for achievement of these goals. Intellectual and moral cultivation would enable women to be worthy of respect as individuals and thus capable of contributing to civic life and deserving of rights. "Respect for women's personhood and recognition of women as subjects were central goals of rights advocates in the 1890s." The elevation of women's political and social status also depended on abolishing certain customs, such as concubinage and prostitution, that, Meiji feminists argued, undermined women's dignity and equality.

By the interwar period, thanks in part to education, women of all classes had become more visible in society—in offices and factories, in department stores and cafes, in literary magazines and women's associations. Yet they lacked political rights. With the structure of the state more firmly established, feminists in the Taishō period recognized that education alone was insufficient to assure them access to national life and intensified their political efforts. But they changed their strategy and tried to enlist the state's power for the protection of women. In particular, women "shifted the discourse from wifehood to motherhood" and demanded state-legislated maternity benefits and other assistance to mothers. They also sought protection from oppressive economic conditions that led to the injury and deaths of women and children. Feminists thus came to "accept the state as a fixed institution capable of protecting rights . . . as well as of denying rights."

Once again, we see expectations of governmental assistance playing an important role in political discourse. Like other groups discussed in this volume, female activists, with few exceptions, did not attack the state or question its legitimacy. Nor did they view calls for protection by, and inclusion in, the state as incompatible. Rather, they campaigned for political rights whose meaning extended to both participation in the political process and state assistance. "Civil rights and gender-based protections," as Molony writes, "were two sides of the same coin." In the 1930s, however, when "overt suffragism was risky" and concepts of individual rights potentially subversive, "feminists increasingly formulated rights as protections." At the same time, social causes benefiting women or families, such as consumer movements or campaigns for welfare aid to single mothers and children, continued to engage women in political activity that, even in the absence of suffrage, served to "inject feminine values into a masculine political system."

Even as vibrant debates over women's rights, responsibilities, and needs as subject/citizens and as mothers found expression in public forums, a quiet revolution in family life was taking place outside government circles. In the early twentieth century, women's magazines, advice books, and journals devoted to early childhood education occasionally dealt with the topic of the role of fathers in family life. Although state officials linked effective child rearing by women to the larger benefit of the nation, the state did not form a significant point of reference in this urban, middle-class discourse on parenting. Rather, Harald Fuess finds that, at least among the group of intellectuals he studied, parents expressed their own individual and often diverse views on their domestic duties in personal terms unrelated to nationalist ideology. Moreover, the picture that emerges from these parental self-reflections shows a domestic ideal of conjugal families in which husbands viewed the home not as a man's castle but as "women's kingdom."

This validation of the centrality of women's roles within the family suggests that, by the 1920s, middle-class women had to a considerable degree achieved the respect and equality within the home that they had fought for throughout the Meiji period. In contrast, urban white-collar fathers, in popular discourse if not in practice, had lost much of their patriarchal authority. Indeed, the middle-aged urban professionals contributing in the 1910s to *Fujin no tomo*, a leading women's magazine, described interactions with their children predominantly in terms of leisure and companionship, calling themselves not disciplinarians and patriarchs but "play partners" for their children and "assistants" and "discussion partners" for their wives. By the 1920s fathers evinced interest in their children's education as well. In general, however, urban middle-class men appear to have left, or entrusted, to their wives the responsibility not only for household management but also for the important and onerous tasks and duties of child rearing and early socialization at a time when women in increasing numbers were also becoming more involved in political activities and wage-paying work outside the home. These trends reveal important changes in women's relations to both the state and their husbands. On the one hand, mothers had taken central stage in the care of their children and the management of their homes. On the other hand, Fuess suggests, women may have achieved "domestic autonomy at the price of turning the home into a place of feminine work and masculine leisure."

If women as a group were acquiring a greater voice in family and civic life, they were also assuming a greater burden of work. This social reality did not escape the eyes of reformers in either urban or rural Japan. Rural women, who, as Kerry Smith notes, played a central role in rural revitalization in the 1930s, complained that although they had gained new community and domestic managerial roles (and presumably greater recognition of their importance), they also carried an excessive weight of responsibilities.

The exploration of women's expanding and increasingly more visible roles both inside and outside the household reveals how they managed to create their own spheres of influence within family and political systems that were legally patriarchal. Gail Bernstein's study of the social network of kin created by the well-educated married sisters of one family, beginning in the interwar period and maintained into contemporary times, shows how "kin work was gendered," with middle-class urban women doing the greater share of it.

The family network provided an alternative source of protection and welfare and also a social arena outside the conjugal unit for women charged with the main responsibility for child care. The middle-class women in Bernstein's study neither worked outside the home nor engaged in political activities in either the interwar or immediate postwar years; yet through the family network, they "gained access, albeit limited and indirectly, to the public or outside 'men's world.'" It is hard to say whether women assumed a greater role in family life by default, due to middle-class men's preoccupation with their jobs, or by design, as a conscious effort of their own to enhance their position and well-being. A mix of factors was probably at play, including the impact of the feminist discourse and practice described by Molony and the changes in ideas about the father's function within the home as outlined by Fuess and Bernstein.

It was not only in the area of family relations and the position of women that the modern state impinged, directly or indirectly, on the lives of individuals. The goal of building a strong and rich nation led the Meiji government to emphasize the creation of a powerful military and to seek to expand Japan's influence overseas. The two chapters in Part IV explore some dimensions of this aspect of Japan's modern state-building experience. Focusing on what has been termed Japan's cultural imperialism toward China between the 1890s and 1930s, See Heng Teow examines the activities of the Cultural Affairs Division of Japan's Ministry of Foreign Affairs, which, in the 1930s, sponsored a wide variety of medical, scientific, and humanistic activities in China. The motives behind such activities, as unraveled by Teow, were "a blend of ethnocentrism, moralism, and idealism." One motive was certainly to promote Japan's role as "cultural leader of East Asia" vis-à-vis the Western powers, who were energetically spreading their own culture along with their material technology. Cultural assistance to China thus helped justify "Japan's status as the only major Asian power, and enhance[d] Japan's national prestige on the international scene."

Such prestige, like ideals of harmonious cooperation and the benevolence of the emperor, had little meaning in the chaos and poverty of defeated and occupied Japan. Instead, cartoonists and popular games parodied wartime slogans such as "one hundred million, one heart." As John Dower writes, "yesterday's heroes, both military and civilian, . . . had become today's goats." The most popular explanation of how the Japanese had become "embroiled in such a disastrous war" was that they had been "deceived." From this explanation, "it followed that the people as a whole had to take care never again to be misled by their leaders." This observation, in turn, Dower suggests, fostered the conclusion "that the best way to do away with irresponsible leaders was to create a genuinely open, rational, 'democratic' society." But Dower's analysis suggests as well how difficult it can be to turn cynicism into commitment toward civic, or other, goals. The satirical spirit presents all sorts of authority as bankrupt, from the state bureaucracy and, of course, the military to parents or husbands. Rampant egoism and a self-seeking quest for survival emerged as dominant themes in the aftermath of defeat.

Dower also notes, however, the return of business and political leaders who reiterated their faith in technology and in strong state input into economic planning as the foundations of Japan's recovery. Was the spirit of mocking misery a passing phenomenon of a desperate moment, when authority had lost credibility, or a constant current in Japanese cultural life, or even a combination of the two? Was the government being mocked because it had failed to do what it ought to have done? Or were people indeed questioning the long-held wisdom of expecting the state to play the role of protector, while asserting their independence from it?

Answers to such provocative questions concerning the postwar period fall beyond the historical parameters of this volume. Their treatment awaits the work of others, among whom, we may hope, will be doctoral students fortunate to obtain guidance as dedicated as that which the students of Al Craig were privileged to receive.

PART I

State and Community

CHAPTER ONE

Conventional Knowledge in Early Modern Japan

Mary Elizabeth Berry

By the end of the seventeenth century, commercial publishers in Japan had put into circulation an enormous body of material I call "public information." Ranging prodigiously in content and function, the material includes, for example, maps, atlases, encyclopedias, dictionaries, rural gazetteers, urban directories, calendars, almanacs, travel literature, personnel rosters, biographical compendia, manuals of work, manuals of play, guides to commerce and local products, and numerous instructional primers. Although this very variety has disposed scholars to treat particular types of text discretely, genre by genre, the collective archive nonetheless shares revealing common features.[1] Each of its parts concentrates on "information"—on the generally factual and verifiable details of contemporary, and typically mundane, experience. Each is premised, too, on dual notions of the "public." As systematic reports on the human environment, the texts posit a public of open, intelligi-

---

1. For bibliographic categories in use in the early modern period, see Shidō bunko, ed., *(Edo jidai) Shorin shuppan shoseki mokuroku shūsei* (Collection of catalogues of printed material of booksellers [of the Edo period]) (Tokyo: Inoue shobō, 1962–64), 3 vols. For the categories of modern scholarship, see, e.g., the taxonomy of Kinsei bungaku shoshi kenkyūkai, ed., *Kinsei bungaku shiryō ruijū* (Classified collection of literary sources of the early modern period) (Tokyo: Benseisha, 1972–79), 157 vols.

ble practice that can be made the object of impersonal scrutiny and aggregate analysis. As commercial commodities addressed to anonymous readerships, the texts posit a public of permeable audiences that can be bound alike by mutual interests and encompassing frames of reference.

From the vantage of the medieval era, the emergence of public information during the seventeenth century represents a quiet revolution in knowledge, one that separates the early modern period from all earlier time in Japan. Certainly there were precedents for some of the material, particularly in the classical period when an ambitious state produced a national map as well as a number of gazetteers, encyclopedias, and biographical compilations. Then, and throughout the medieval period, we also find dictionaries, genealogies, calendars, and primers. Still, the difference of the early modern sources is fundamental and sweeping.

It derives most clearly from commercial printing and the resulting leaps in both the scope and the circulation of textual matter. It derives, too, from an emphatic, seemingly omnivorous empiricism that drove investigators to timely investigations of myriad subjects. The ethnographer Hitomi Hitsudai, for example, informed readers that he had spent 30 years in the field before classifying and assessing 442 local foodstuffs in *The Culinary Mirror of the Realm* (published in 12 fascicles in 1697).[2] Similarly, the agronomist Miyazaki Yasusada introduced *The Complete Book of Farming* (published in 11 fascicles in 1697) by discussing his 30 years of research on 145 crops in sixteen provinces.[3] Other observers combined similar claims to witness with relentless parades of detail to put in order the physical landmarks of Edo (292 in 22 categories); the leading merchants and craftspeople of Kyoto (over 700 in 166 categories); the types of work pursued in the realm (almost 500 in 7 categories); its chief products and manufactures (1,823 and counting); and any number of other phenomena, from transport arteries to medical practices,

---

2. Hitomi Hitsudai, *Honchō shoku kagami* (The culinary mirror of the realm), ed. Shimada Isao (Tokyo: Heibonsha, 1976–81), 5 vols.

3. Miyazaki Yasusada, *Nōgyō zensho* (The complete book of farming), in *Nihon nōsho zenshū* (Compendium of works on farming in Japan), ed. Yamada Tatsuo and Iiura Toku, vols. 12–13 (Tokyo: Nōsangyoson bunka kyōkai, 1978).

from mortuary monuments to marriage customs.[4] Information swelled, in short, as outsiders crossed the boundaries of place and station to explore in action a manifold reality.

Yet however critical the market orientation and restless inquiry that animated the new information library, it stands most formidably apart from antecedents in its holistic and taxonomic modes of analysis. Not only do the texts affirm the knowability through observation of worldly phenomena, they presume the coherence of those phenomena within comprehensive schemes of interpretation, frequently national schemes. Indeed, the facility of the texts with totalizing conceptions of space and society has, for anyone accustomed to the fracture of medieval sources, real shock value. And nowhere is this clearer than in maps.

Again and again early modern cartographers captured in legible, universal categories the nation, its highways and circuits, and its monster cities. Projecting visual images of connection and a common vocabulary of power and culture, they produced frameworks for thinking about the place variously called Nihon, Dai Nihon, Honchō, Yamato, and Wagakuni. Late classical and medieval cartographers, by contrast, captured isolated parts of a fragmented world in maps that focused invariably on small units of landholding and depended remorselessly on local terms of reference. Although they occasionally made copies of an early classical map of the country, these cartographers left no large area maps of their own—not even of the capital of Kyoto—to orient the medieval viewer (whether prince or martial governor) in a realm beyond the individual proprietary holding.[5]

---

4. For the landmarks, see *(Zōho) Edo sōkanoko meisho taizen* (The great dappled fabric of Edo: [expanded] omnibus of famous places), in *Edo sōsho* (Anthology of writings on Edo), ed. Edo sōsho kankōkai, vols. 3–4 (Tokyo: Meichō kankōkai, 1964); for the workers, *Kyō habutae* (The Kyoto brocade), in *(Shinshū) Kyōto sōsho* ([Revised] Anthology of writings on Kyoto), ed. Shinshū Kyōto kankōkai, vol. 2 (Kyoto: Rinsen shoten, 1976); for employments, *Jinrin kinmōzui* (The encyclopedia of humanity), ed. Asakura Haruhiko, Tōyō bunko, 519 (Tokyo: Heibonsha, 1990); for the products, Matsue Shigeyori, *Kefukigusa* (Feather-blown grasses), ed. Katō Sadahiko (Tokyo: Yumani shobō, 1978–80), 2 vols.

5. For surviving maps made before 1600, see Nishioka Toranosuke, *Nihon shōen ezu shūsei* (Collection of estate maps of Japan) (Tokyo: Tōkyōdō, 1976, 1977), 2 vols.; and Tōkyō daigaku shiryō hensanjo, ed., *Nihon shōen ezu shūei* (Collected

Nor do we find counterparts in the medieval archive to other synoptic texts of early modernity—to the charts of shogunal administration, for example, which listed with copious formulaic notes every single daimyo of the nation as well as every significant officeholder in the Tokugawa bureaucracy (about 2,000 of them, both central and local, lined up under 230 and more job titles).[6] Just as remarkable were national gazetteers, such as *The Ten-Thousand Leaf Record of Japan's Provincial Flowers* (published in 1697 in 21 fascicles and 2,300 pages), where readers found each province parsed uniformly as part of a coherent union. Arranged in geographical order, every province was a composite of its districts, geographical features, annual production totals, chief crops and manufactures, principal temples and shrines, famous places, castellans and official personnel, and much else.[7] Systematic analysis of provinces extended, moreover, to systematic analysis of cities. The great urban directories of the seventeenth century identified virtually all streets, neighborhoods, landmarks, religious institutions, elite residences, commercial firms, ritual events, notable art objects, and historical remains.[8] Perhaps most indicative of the reach for wide and categorical mastery of worldly affairs were the family en-

---

reproductions of estate maps of Japan) (Tokyo: Tōkyō daigaku shuppankai, 1988–2002), 5 vols. A good sample of early modern maps appears in Nanba Matsutarō, comp., *Nihon no kochizu* (Old maps of Japan) (Osaka: Sōgensha, 1969); Akioka Takejirō, comp., *Nihon kochizu shūsei* (Collection of old maps of Japan) (Tokyo: Kajima kenkyūjo shuppankai, 1971); and Unno Kazutaka et al., comps., *Nihon kochizu taisei* (Compilation of old maps of Japan) (Tokyo: Kōdansha, 1974). The relationship between extant maps and the full range of cartographic practice in classical and medieval Japan is a vexed matter that I address at length in "Aratana seiji bunka no tanjō" ("Maps Are Strange; Mapmakers Are Strangers"), in *Chizu to ezu no seiji-bunkashi* (*Mapping and Politics in Premodern Japan*), ed. Kuroda Hideo, Sugimoto Fumiko, and Mary Elizabeth Berry (Tokyo: Tōkyō daigaku shuppankai, 2001), pp. 137–84 (English titles given in publication).

6. For an extensive selection of texts, see Hashimoto Hiroshi, ed., *(Kaitei zōho) Dai bukan* ([Revised and expanded] Anthology of Military Mirrors) (Tokyo: Meicho kankōkai, 1965), 3 vols.

7. *(Nihon) Kokka man'yōki* (The ten-thousand leaf record of [Japan's] provincial flowers), facsimile edition in *Kohan chishi sōsho* (Anthology of early printed geographical writings), ed. Asakura Haruhiko (Tokyo: Sumiya shobō, 1969–71), 4 vols.

8. See, e.g., the *Kyō habutae* and the *Edo sōkanoko meisho taizen*, cited in note 4.

cyclopedias, such as *Everybody's Treasury*, which offered digests of basic knowledge for basic readers.[9] Handily cannibalizing more specific sources, they gathered together concise lists of emperors, courtiers, major abbots and abbesses, martial rulers, provinces and productivity figures, highways and post stations, famous places, famous products, and rituals and festivals across the country. They also included chronologies, almanacs, dictionaries, and guides to the polite arts, pre-eminently poetry and letter writing.

By thinking generally rather than discretely about these texts of public information, we begin to trace a revolution of several parts. The data collection itself needed not only an empiricist and eclectic curiosity but an assumption of free access to a public domain of investigation. Most important, it required both the classifying mind that ordered findings and the body of conventions that made order intelligible. So, too, the circulation of data among open audiences of consumers needed not only a commercial medium of distribution but an assumption of public entitlement to self-knowledge. Most important, it required both the communal investment in information that prompted people to buy books and the facility with conventions that made their content understandable. Although diffuse, these transformations converged in language—in the formulation of tropes of communication, binding writers and readers, which situated data in a universe of shared labels and meanings. The appearance of such master conventions is the hallmark of the new information library and suggests the emergence of that fugitive source of collective identity we call common knowledge. Insofar as the conventions were used repeatedly to organize a national experience, they also offered foundations for a national identity. Locating parts within a whole, making a society visible to itself, the language of the new information culture conspired in the integration, and thus the creation, of a Japan.

The shift in mind from particular to integral thought had a great deal to do with the explosion, especially after 1640, of commercial

---

9. *Banmin chōhōki* (Everybody's treasury), facsimile edition in *Kinsei bungaku shiryō ruijū: sankō bunken-hen* (Classified collection of literary sources of the early modern period: reference work series), vol. 10, ed. Kinsei bungaku shoshi kenkyūkai (Tokyo: Benseisha, 1977).

printing. Based in swiftly expanding cities with mounting concentrations of literate consumers, the publishing industry linked enterprising writers and readers, stimulating appetites for more, and novel, material. The volume and variety of the information texts came with the market. And as popular publication transcended social boundaries, it encouraged those attitudes of connection—those wide gazes at collective experience—that most deeply characterize the information library.[10]

Yet both the foundation and the model of change were established earlier, more dramatically, not by the market but by a nascent state. The information culture is inextricably linked with the universal surveys—cadastral and cartographic—pursued with remarkable tenacity by new hegemons during the long transition from war to peace between about 1580 and 1640. Imperfect in execution, the surveys nonetheless conceived Japan in integral tropes while habituating officials and residents alike to investigation. They objectified land and society as domains of impersonal scrutiny. And they demonstrated that both could be assessed in the aggregate. In the process of their work, surveyors reconfigured in common categories a world understood since the late classical period in the multiform terms of local practice.

The genius of cadastral registration lay, first, in the definition of the target. Surveyors took as their object individual agrarian settlements that were uniformly designated as "villages" (*mura, gōson*) and thus detached, at least for registration purposes, from tortuously complex histories and conditions of local rule. Then they proceeded to measure fields and harvests (more or less fully) according to (more or less) standard measures. The totals were converted, by formula, into statements of gross productive value expressed in terms of a rice equivalent. Thus, for example, an assessment for "Yanagi village" of 3,000 *koku* would indicate that its lands and crops had been assigned a total productive value

---

10. For excellent discussions of printing, see Peter F. Kornicki, *The Book in Japan* (Leiden: Brill, 1998); and Henry D. Smith II, "The History of the Book in Edo and Paris," in *Edo and Paris: Urban Life and the State in the Early Modern Era*, ed. James L. McClain, John Merriman, and Ugawa Kaoru (Ithaca, N.Y.: Cornell University Press, 1994), pp. 332–52.

equivalent to roughly 15,000 bushels of rice (1 *koku* equals about 5 bushels). In effect, the cadastral surveys abstracted a physically intricate, politically riven landscape into integers.[11]

There are mysteries at the heart of this project, not least the motives of military leaders who detached themselves from the local meanings of land to reimagine resources in raw numbers and uniform classifications. The radical reorientation depended, I believe, on radical deracination. It was a product of war, which both alienated military leaders from place and disposed them to institutional modes of rule. Especially during the late stages of conflict attending the Toyotomi and Tokugawa conquests, warlords became transients—accustomed to perpetual motion by far-flung campaigns and the transfers that propelled almost all of them from one domain to another. And physical dislocation was accompanied by the social upheaval—betrayals by vassals, rural uprisings, urban lawlessness, sectarian battles—that encouraged daimyo cooperation with the surveillance and disciplines of the emerging state. Local lords came to enforce, for their own protection, national controls on arms, movement, residence, employment, and religious affiliation. In the formulas and tropes of the cadastral surveys we find the imagination of victors who had learned to level into categories a public of subjects.[12]

---

11. For a convincing demonstration of the limitations, errors, and reliance on local initiative that attended cadastral registration, see Philip Brown, *Central Authority and Local Autonomy in the Formation of Early Modern Japan* (Stanford: Stanford University Press, 1993). I am concerned here, however, not with the execution but the conception of a project that had, by the time of Hideyoshi's death in 1598, generated rough productivity figures for much of the country and, in consequence, a framework for thinking systematically about the polity and the economy. The literature on the surveys is enormous; for a good recent discussion, see Akizawa Shigeru, "Taikō kenchi" (Hideyoshi's cadastral surveys), in *Iwanami kōza Nihon tsūshi, Kinsei 1* (The Iwanami lectures on Japanese history, the early modern period 1), ed. Asao Naohiro et al. (Tokyo: Iwanami shoten, 1993).

12. For the frequent transfers of the daimyo and their relations with the central power, see Fujino Tamotsu, *(Shintei) Bakuhan taiseishi no kenkyū* ([A revised] Study of the history of the bakuhan settlement) (Tokyo: Yoshikawa kōbunkan, 1975); and Harold Bolitho, "The *Han*," in *Cambridge History of Japan*, vol. 4, *Early Modern Japan*, ed. John W. Hall (Cambridge, Eng., and New York: Cambridge University Press), pp. 183–234.

We also find a complex legacy. The practical applications—from conscription and taxation to the apportionment of samurai stipends and daimyo domains—were essential to the new polity. So, too, were the effects of statist indoctrination. The surveys schooled thousands of officials and far larger numbers of local headmen and assistants in (broadly) standard practices and terminology. Yet the habit of investigating and being investigated had richer repercussions. The surveys set both a precedent for wide public examination and a style of inquiry—empirical, categorical, impervious to boundaries—that organized the information culture. Not coincidentally, the authors of the information texts tended to come from the ranks of samurai officials. These were the roving agronomists, geographers, ethnologists, and compilers of travel materials who had been trained in observation and accustomed, by transfers and demobilization in cities, to a certain homelessness. Often underemployed by their lords but educated to an ethic of service, they continued to cross boundaries in pursuit not just of official data but of general learning. They also began to write for publication (and sometimes for profit) to instruct and entertain a public audience.[13]

When they did so, these investigators relied for communication on devices that were becoming the tropes of union. They anchored their material in the language of nation, province, village, famous place, castle town, city, agrarian productivity, highway, barrier, post station, and martial lord. And in these tropes, in the construction of commonplaces for national geography, lies the great legacy of the cadastral surveys. It was cartographic surveys, rather than cadastral surveys, that created durable frames for spatial and social understanding. But it was the breakthroughs of the cadastres, with

---

13. Prominent samurai authors of the information texts include, for example, Hitomi Hitsudai (*Honchō shoku kagami*), Kaibara Ekiken (*Yamato honzō* and many other titles), Kurokawa Dōyū (*Yōshū fushi*), Miyazaki Yasusada (*Nōgyō zensho*), and Nishikawa Jōken (*Chōnin bukuro* and many other titles). For discussion of the peacetime transformation of fighting men, see Eiko Ikegami, *The Taming of the Samurai* (Cambridge, Mass.: Harvard University Press, 1995). For an excellent discussion of the philosophical environment of samurai (and other) thinkers, see Tetsuo Najita, *Visions of Virtue in Tokugawa Japan* (Chicago: University of Chicago Press, 1987), pp. 18–59.

their seminal formulation of "village" and "productivity total," that made mapmaking possible.

Initiated by Toyotomi Hideyoshi in the late sixteenth century and conducted on four occasions by the Tokugawa shogunate in the seventeenth century, the national cartographic surveys again put huge numbers of officials and assistants in the field—this time to plot physical and social topography in standard categories. The resulting maps of the provinces and the nation served as the basis of commercial cartography for two centuries. Details might change and emphases might vary, but the conception remained astonishingly consistent.[14] So, too, official maps created the analytical conventions that organized the information library. Often geographical in subject and almost invariably concerned with the spatial dimensions of experience, the information texts hung on a cartographic scaffold. It was the rudiment of cultural literacy.

In the remainder of this chapter, I turn first to official maps to explore both their message—the high story they told early modern audiences about land and power—and the source of their lasting influence. They put across a simple, coherent Japan that was nonetheless legible at several different levels; for embedded in singularly lucid tropes was a complex spatial politics. Then I pursue the subject of land and power through a second genre, the "Military Mirrors," which catalogued the full compass of Tokugawa officialdom in popular printed editions. The change in genre permits us to track the affinities of the information texts even as it exposes the mutations in their content that challenged static worldviews.

---

14. See note 18 for the foundational scholarship on the official cartographic surveys and note 5 for compilations containing the commercial maps based on them. Although much official cartography remained secret, the shogunate shared such important works as the Keichō survey and Hōjō Masafusa's maps of Edo with publishers. On the innovative rather than derivative contributions of publishers to mapmaking, see Marcia Yonemoto, *Mapping Early Modern Japan* (Berkeley: University of California Press, 2003), pp. 13–43. Ronald Toby finds commercial practice largely independent of, or parallel to, official practice; see his "Kinseiki no 'Nihonzu' to 'Nihon' no kyōkai" ("Mapping the Margins: The Boundaries of 'Japan' in Early-Modern Cartography"), in *Chizu to ezu no seijibunkashi*, pp. 79–102 (English title in publication). The categorical conception of space, however, remains inextricable from the prototypical surveys.

What initially seems clearest in the Mirrors, for all their steadily more staggering detail, is a basic fidelity to the cartographic conception of power. Such consistency in a genre both long-lived and attractive to competitive firms suggests that official maps served two functions for the authors of the Mirrors and, indeed, the greater number of information texts. On the one hand, official surveys defined prototypes for imagining the nation. On the other hand, they provided a normative prescription for analysis. Thus even as investigators continued to generate material, they also continued to deliver data within familiar ideological categories. Their vision of Japan remained, at least on the surface, a conservative one of hereditary martial rule over rice-producing villages.

Here, then, is an irony. From the vantage of the medieval era, the information library represents change of a quietly revolutionary order. From the vantage of the nineteenth century, the information library looks anything but revolutionary. Texts like the maps and the Mirrors changed rather little over the course of two hundred years and more. If they were ever thicker and always up to date, many later editions would have been recognizable to their original formulators. Learning clearly expanded while its social frames appeared steady.

Social frames were certainly unsteady in fact. They were also under assaults that ranged, in the domain of letters, from parody to graffiti to academic invective. Assault was most pervasive in fiction and drama, where a guise of make-believe helped sanction long, disturbing looks at a society that made no (official) sense. Nonetheless, the information library remained a seemingly safe place. Here alternative frameworks did not openly reorganize data, social knowledge did not shift seismically to social commentary, investigation did not move into news gathering.

The absence of overt challenges to convention gives pause, for the promise of skepticism, which may seem inherent to investigation, appears lost. We might look for explanation to censorship laws, particularly those umbrella statutes that forbade discussion of the military houses and unusual contemporary events. They do seem to have constrained the circulation of broadsheets, the ephemeral reports of scandals and natural disasters hawked occa-

sionally on the street from the late seventeenth century as the closest things to newspapers in early modern Japan.[15] Yet there is little
evidence that the statutes, vague and erratically enforced in any
case, frustrated innovation among investigators, who hardly seem
to have tested them. As far as we know, they never attempted to
assemble for publication such licit but sensitive information as
shipping schedules, exchange and lending rates, and commodity
costs. Nor did they veer toward social analysis by collecting information about rents, or the seasonal migration of labor, or
manufacturing volumes, or food consumption. And they emphatically declined to introduce surprises into the endlessly revised sta-
ples of the information library. Right until the end of the shogunate, maps of Edo continued to locate every daimyo mansion
while consigning commoner wards to blank white space—never
the reverse.[16]

It is the defining power of conventions, of course, that they
frustrate any radical revision of their underlying premises by making them virtually unthinkable. Remapping Edo to concentrate on
commerce or remapping the nation to focus on sea routes to foreign ports (for example) would have required not so much new
knowledge as new ideologies. Thus the conservatism of the information texts bears testimony, perhaps perversely, to the durable
genius of the prototypes. Once established by a remarkable integral vision, the conventions of the maps and such sister sources as
the Mirrors fixed relations and meanings convincingly enough to
absorb stress and conceal contradiction. Here was the revolution,
away from medieval fracture, that projected collective identities.

But this awful feat hardly precluded trouble. In the very pliabil-
ity and versatility of their messages, national maps enabled subversive readings. And in the very accretion of their data, other texts
confounded clear interpretation. If urban cartography concen-
trated on social hierarchy and elite privilege, urban directories

15. For discussions of censorship, see Kornicki, *The Book in Japan*, pp. 320–61;
and Munemasa Isoo, *Kinsei Kyōto shuppan bunka no kenkyū* (A study of the publishing culture of early modern Kyoto) (Kyoto: Dōmeisha, 1982), esp. pp. 54–56.

16. For a masterful survey of Edo maps, see Iida Ryūichi and Tawara Motoaki,
Edozu no rekishi (The history of Edo maps) (Tokyo: Tsukiji shokan, 1988), 2 vols.

celebrated markets, money, and commoner expertise. The sheer volume of factual observation about the city's functions dislodged, without dissolving, any singular framework of understanding. So, too, the multiplying entries in the Mirrors exposed conflicting notions about public administration, juxtaposing against the hereditary dominion of daimyo houses the professional service of a competitive bureaucracy. Even as seemingly stable frames continued to buttress the polity, the information texts opened fissures of change. Here was the incremental shift, away from stasis, that projected social reinvention.

Maps

The world that early modern maps put in order was extravagantly disorderly. During the last years of the sixteenth century, Toyotomi Hideyoshi had constructed a rough model for political alliance, which depended on the submission of local territorial lords to the authority of a central hegemon. But when the Tokugawa began their first cartographic survey of the nation around 1605, there was no certainty about the durability of the model and enormous confusion over the roles and identities of the players. The convulsive process of union unfolded over two more generations as the Tokugawa consolidated their hold on the shogunal title and defined the status of subordinate lords. Very gradually, the meaning of "daimyo"—for centuries a fugitive term more evocative than exact—narrowed to something (reasonably) specific. It came to designate a martial leader, explicitly invested by the shogun with lands assigned a minimum productive value of 10,000 *koku*, who exercised a contingent local rule in exchange for service. Established over time by practice and by law, service included obedience to the shogun's statutes, periodic attendance at the shogun's capital in Edo, and the maintenance of armies for the shogun's use.[17]

---

17. The essential definition of the daimyo in terms of landed revenue appears in the second article of a memorandum (*oboegaki*) of 1635, which defines the basic charges of the Tokugawa senior councilors. See, e.g., Kodama Kōta, ed., *Shiryō ni yoru Nihon no ayumi: kinsei-hen* (Japanese history through documents: early modern series) (Tokyo: Yoshikawa kōbunkan, 1969), p. 71. For the broader normalization of shogunal-daimyo relations, see Irimoto Masuo, *Tokugawa sandai to bakufu*

This clarification was a minor miracle, achieved across years of violence that constantly altered the numbers and distribution of a changing cast of characters. Even as the polity began to quiet around 1640, the daimyo who survived the transition to peace remained profoundly divided in wealth, armed power, and relations with the shogunal house. Their domains, still subject to reassignment and redistribution, were sometimes scattered and often intermixed with lands assigned to other parties (including the shogun himself as well as the nobility and religious establishment). And the administration of those domains varied considerably in a settlement that lacked anything like a job description for its leaders.

But creating cartographic sense out of a polity still in formation was a graver task still than defining the daimyo. In attempting it at all, Tokugawa Ieyasu (barely into his first year as shogun and under challenge from the Toyotomi loyalists) did something as daring as it was prescient. His administration used maps to prefigure political stability by normalizing a nascent view of space and power. The legacy of the cadastral surveys was indispensable. But it was not everything.

Figure 1.1 is a map of Echizen, completed in 1606 in response to the first Tokugawa call for cartographic surveys, that illustrates the decisions and directions of official cartography.[18] Here, and throughout official maps, the province is the principal frame of cartographic analysis, a decision we might take (for the moment) as a pragmatic one. Defined in the classical period as the major units

---

seiritsu (The first three Tokugawa generations and the establishment of the bakufu) (Tokyo: Shinjinbutsu ōraisha, 2000).

18. For the foundational work on the original and subsequent Tokugawa surveys, see Kawamura Hirotada, *Edo bakufu-sen kuniezu no kenkyū* (A study of the provincial maps compiled by the Edo bakufu) (Tokyo: Kokon shoin, 1984); and idem, *Kuniezu* (Provincial maps) (Tokyo: Yoshikawa kōbunkan, 1990). For critiques, see Kuroda Hideo, "Kan'ei Edo bakufu kuniezu shōkō" (Thoughts on the Kan'ei-period provincial maps of the Edo bakufu), *Shikan*, no. 107 (1982): 47–62; and idem, "Kuniezu ni tsuite no taiwa" (A dialogue on provincial maps), *Rekishi hyōron*, no. 433 (1986): 27–39. See also Sugimoto Fumiko, "Kuniezu kenkyū no ichi to kadai" (Situating and framing research on provincial maps), *Nihon rekishi*, no. 529 (1992): 84–94; and idem, "Kuniezu" (Provincial maps), in *Iwanami kōza Nihon tsūshi, Kinsei 2*, pp. 303–25.

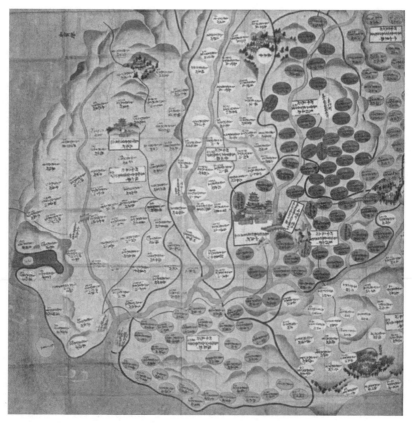

Fig. 1.1 *Map of Echizen Province*, compiled by order of the Tokugawa shogunate in 1606. Detail of northern districts in a map measuring 272.5 x 228.5 cm. Matsudaira Collection, Fukui Prefectural Library, manuscript.

of internal administration, the 66 provinces had lost their salience to governance but remained conventional geographical markers. Unlike the volatile domains of the daimyo, they also had approximately understood boundaries. In the Echizen map, as in its counterparts, the province is subdivided into districts (another classical convention), identified in this case by both purple boundary lines and small boxes containing labels: each specifies the name of the district, its total registered productivity, and the total number of villages within it. Against this background of province and districts, the map portrays a host of villages, 563 in all, each identified by an oval icon (color coded by district) that contains more labels: the name of the village and its total registered productivity. The large castle town of Kitanoshō and two lesser castle towns are marked pictorially, as are a number of temples and shrines. Finally, the Echizen map colors mountains with a green wash, waterways with blue lines, and roads with red lines.

The marvelous simplicity of this map derives partly from disciplined choices about the representation of physical topography. Provincial cartographers were clearly concerned with coastal surveying and sufficient land measurement to produce maps very roughly to scale. They were concerned, too, with plotting logistically important waterways and roads. Otherwise they represented only gross distinctions between lowland and mountain without close attention to land types and uses (which did remain important in village cartography). By reducing topographical detail, mapmakers made the social and political relations of land—not the land itself—their subject.

Cartographic simplicity thus had to derive in great measure from brilliantly clear and reductive treatments of the social-political order. The prime strategy was erasure of all fraught boundaries. Within the old cultural frames of province and district, the Echizen map converts local settlements into uniform ovals uniformly designated as villages. Apparently equal in gravity, each is reduced to a name and a general location. Each enters the realm of production and power with the further notation of its assessed yield. Perpetually vexed details—internal and external borders, the distribution of resources and privileges—are elided here to be consigned to cadastres, tax documents, and small-area cartography.[19]

This masterful solution to the problem of depicting local settlement was a gift of the cadastral surveys. The next leap was trickier.

---

19. Detailed representation of village topography did continue in maps of small areas. See, e.g., Sugimoto Fumiko, "Chiiki no kiroku" (Local records) in *Chiikishi to wa nani ka?* (What is local history?), ed. Hamashita Takeshi and Karashima Noboru (Tokyo: Yamakawa shuppan, 1997), esp. pp. 381–85; Igarashi Tsutomu, "Mura ezu ni miru kinsei sonraku no seikatsu sekai" (The world of early modern village life as seen in village maps), in *Ezu no kosumoroji* (The cosmology of maps), ed. Katsuragawa ezu kenkyūkai, 2: 92–111 (Tokyo: Chijin shobō, 1988–89); and Kimura Tōichirō, *Kinsei mura ezu kenkyū* (A study of early modern village maps) (Tokyo: Komiya shoten, 1962).

Attention centers in the Echizen map on castle towns, which are accorded visual privilege through the use of both conspicuous icons (including pictures and abbreviated street layouts) and prominent labels, which indicate the name of the town, its daimyo occupant, and the registered productivity of his domain. Once again, boundaries disappear. By identifying the daimyo with his headquarters and its resources rather than a demarcated territory, the map creates a radiant conception of power. Dominion is associated with an urban node: flowing inward is the wealth signified by the productivity totals of villages; radiating outward, without fixed limits, is the authority of the castellan.

Those productivity totals are the link between castellan and village. Daimyo control of the village is implicit in the standardized valuations that evoke the presence of official inspectors. It is explicit in the juxtaposition of the comparatively small yields from individual villages with the aggregate totals of daimyo wealth. Some early maps link villages to castle holders more emphatically by marking the oval icons with colors or characters keyed to particular daimyo.[20] No markings, however, link villages to other proprietors—to daimyo vassals or collaterals, for example, or courtly and religious elites.

Obliterating minor or derivative land claims, the provincial maps tell a single, elegant story. Within an enduring topography of mountains, valleys, and rivers, the land supports a vast, seemingly timeless society of villages—each known, located, and named; each productive in standardized terms that convey membership in the polity and relationship to the centers of power and prestige. These centers are important castle cities—each known, located, and named; each headed by a daimyo whose authority is expressed by agrarian harvests and radiant throughout the society producing them. The maps either expunge everything mutable (boundaries, village details) or situate variables within stable frameworks. Thus, an individual productivity total might change without disturbing the conventions of land valuation; a village might appear or disappear without disturbing the array of ovals; a daimyo might be replaced, his domain altered in size, and even a castle headquarters re-

---

20. Kawamura, *Edo bakufu-sen kuniezu no kenkyū*, chart following p. 68.

located, without disturbing the categories of daimyo and castle town. Seeming fixity transcends volatility because the classifications of the map—village, castle town, productivity total, daimyo—define so adeptly the spatial constants that they can absorb changes as superficial.

But, of course, those classifications are the black magic of cartography. They belong not to a transparent reality but to the politics of mapmakers. Everywhere animating the Echizen map is the mind of hegemons who were learning to detach power from territorial boundaries, abstract authority into castle nodes, and level agrarian society into revenue-generating units. Their clarity of vision seemed to defy upheaval even as it was a product of upheaval. Wrenched out of both the corporate relations of the late medieval era and the lord-vassal relations that centered on specific landholdings during the era of warring states, surviving conquerors thought structurally about resources and their control.

Tokugawa maps are something more, however, than anatomical sketches of martial power. They contain an integral conception of culture that helps explain their persistence as models of geographical thought. Figure 1.2 reproduces a national map first assembled by the shogunate in the 1630s on the basis of continuing provincial surveys.[21] Initially striking is its resemblance to the national map first drafted in the classical period and occasionally reproduced in the medieval era (see Fig. 1.3). The classical archetype, attributed to the monk-engineer Gyōki (688–749), is an extremely precocious representation of a holistic spatial politics. Presumably using coastal and hilltop sightings, the drafters created a recognizable outline of the three major islands and then imposed on it a statist story: extending from the central capital, named and bounded provinces express an administrative union that is elaborated by the

---

21. Kawamura (ibid., pp. 283–308) argues that this map was based on Kan'ei surveys conducted in 1633–36 and then amplified in 1638–39; Kuroda ("Kan'ei Edo bakufu kuniezu shōkō"), who finds mapmaking efforts from the Genna to Shōhō periods (1615–47) more continuous and cumulative than discrete, inclines toward a later dating of national maps. I am concerned here not with chronology but the conception of the nation that emerges graphically in this map and remains consistent throughout official cartography.

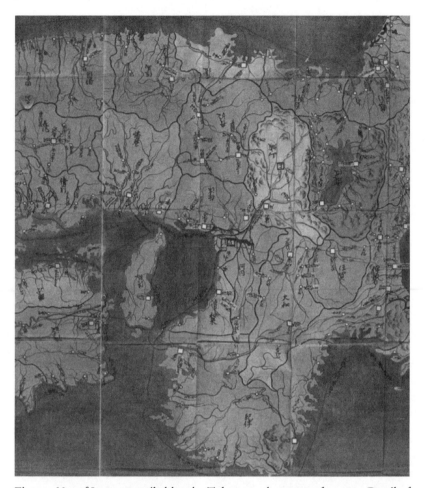

Fig. 1.2 *Map of Japan*, compiled by the Tokugawa shogunate after 1639. Detail of
the area surrounding Kyoto and the home provinces (including the Kii Peninsula,
Awaji Island, and part of Shikoku) in a map measuring 370 x 433.7 cm. Provinces
are marked by different colors, highways and waterways by red lines, castle towns
by white squares (and grey tags with details on individual daimyo), and other important sites with white circles. National Diet Library, manuscript.

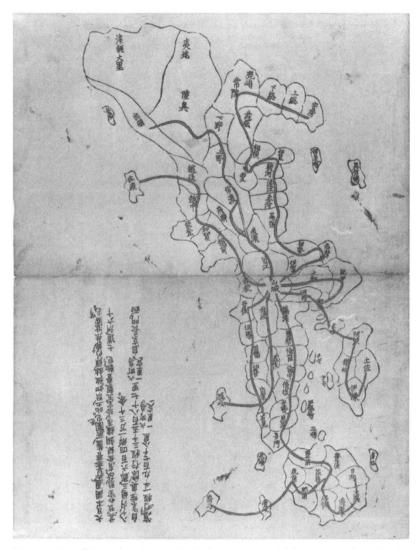

Fig. 1.3 *Map of Japan*, based on a classical prototype, which was reproduced in the medieval encyclopedia *Shūgaishō* and printed in an early seventeenth-century version of that text. Labels are oriented to the northeast, and the colophon is oriented to the southwest (and thus here appears to be upside down), in a map measuring 27.5 x 17.5 cm. National Museum of History and Ethnography, woodblock print.

penetration of a national highway system.[22] So, too, the Tokugawa map centers on the classical capital of Kyoto, retains the provincial boundaries, and emphasizes the highway arteries. It plots a new polity—issuing from Edo and unaffected by the provincial system—within the structures of an old order.

These choices had little to do, I think, with either failures of vision or pragmatic compromises. However useful to local surveyors as preliminary units of analysis, provinces could easily have been erased on national maps. Just as easily, and in conformity with realities of scale, the center of gravity could have been shifted eastward. The decisions consequently appear deliberate. Benedict Anderson draws our attention to a likely source of inspiration when he observes that "the colonial regimes [of nineteenth-century Southeast Asia] began attaching themselves to antiquity as much as conquest." They drew "'historical maps,' designed to demonstrate, in the new cartographic discourse, the antiquity of specific, tightly bounded territorial units" and then laid claim to that ancient territorial dominion as the heirs or guardian—rather than the conqueror—of the tradition.[23] A similar appropriation seems to have occurred in Tokugawa cartography. The shogunate did not so much copy as revive the Gyōki-style image to legitimate its own polity. By linking land to ancient names (embedded in the imagery of art and the nomenclature of official titles) and by reaffirming the centrality of an old imperial capital to a cultural order of provinces, the Tokugawa insisted on the (fictive) integrity of the nation and the (imagined) continuity of its history. Concealing the newness and violence of Tokugawa rule, the map situated the polity within a perduring framework and thus represented the rulers themselves as custodians of an enduring tradition.

---

22 . For discussion of the "Gyōki-style" maps, see Iwahana Michiaki, "Gyōkizu—saikō no Nihonzu" (The Gyōki map—the oldest map of Japan), in *(Kaitei zōho) Chizu to bunka* (Maps and culture [revised and expanded]), ed. Hisatake Tetsunari and Hasegawa Kōji (Tokyo: Chijin shobō, 1993). See also Kuroda Hideo, "Gyōki-teki 'Nihonzu' to wa nani ka?" ("Just What Is a Gyōki-Style Map?"), in *Chizu to ezu no seiji-bunkashi*, pp. 3–77 (English title in publication).

23. Benedict Anderson, *Imagined Communities* (London and New York: Verso, 1996 [1983, 1991]), pp. 174–75.

Messages of continuity and custodianship were reiterated in the cartographic representation of *meisho*—notable sites such as imperial mausolea, old battlegrounds, scenic landmarks, and important sanctuaries. Just as the Echizen map marked temples and shrines, so successive mapping efforts would mark increasing numbers of places accorded sacred and historical meanings. The landscape of power merged with the landscape of culture in graphic images that took many discrete phenomena—castles, old capitals, shrines, famous mountains—and then juxtaposed them in a common geobody.

They were not simply juxtaposed, however. They were connected. A background feature of provincial maps, transport became a pronounced feature of national maps. Fords, ferry routes, mountain passes, highways and low roads, ports, and post stations—all were entered to imply the accessibility of each locale in a country where frontiers had seemingly been vanquished and integration achieved. Far more elaborately than the highway system of the classical prototype, the arteries of Tokugawa cartography appear to bind and penetrate every space.[24]

What disappears from the national map is the village: the 563 ovals of Echizen, and the tens of thousands of similar ovals in other provinces, are gone. Something had to go, of course, to make space legible. But the ease of this particular sacrifice suggests the distillation of the village into a productivity total that could simply be absorbed into the aggregate wealth of the local daimyo. It also suggests that those daimyo—represented on the national map by name, title, castle town, and the registered value of their domains—were the irreducible units of local power and local meaning. Again, the cartographic choice was hardly inevitable. The daimyo who were prominent on provincial maps might have been variously diminished on national maps. Their names might have been either effaced or consigned to legends; their castle towns either evoked by a few exemplary centers (held by the Tokugawa and their collaterals) or reduced to icons without labels; and their investitures concealed in productivity figures expressed solely in provincial totals.

Yet rather than diminishing the daimyo, Figure 1.2 amplifies them both as local lords and as a national governing fraternity. The

---

24. Kawamura, *Edo bakufu-sen kuniezu no kenkyū*, pp. 96–97, 286–308.

elimination of villages leaves the castellans alone to define local society. But it also lifts them out of purely local economies into a national constellation of authority. The standardized icons and labels
of the daimyo construct a body of peers—each with a headquarters
and a title and a vested domain—who collectively define authority.
The naming of the daimyo carries a similar dual message. It identifies place with person, hence tempering an institutional order with
the claims of history, genealogy, and personal ambition. But it also
converts an otherwise abstract polity into a convincing reality:
every one of the hundreds of identifiable lords—each dangerous
and proven in war—has now taken his place in an orderly whole
bigger than himself.

The gravitational pull of the center, however, remains curiously
unemphasized. Tokugawa power is implicit in the prodigious information and overarching classifications of the map. It is intimated in the slight exaggeration of shogunal castle towns and the
ubiquity of the Matsudaira surname (the former family name of
the Tokugawa, which was bestowed not only on collaterals but on
a large number of unrelated houses as well). Yet we find no mention of the shogun's vast holdings, no effort to orient the eye on
Edo. The result is to foreground the collective presence of the daimyo and thus imply rather than explicate the control of the shogunate. Security concerns as well as an ideological commitment to
corporate rule may lie behind this concealment. There also appears
to have been a cartographic decision to insinuate the shogunate,
without jarring emphasis, into a portrait of complex balance.[25]

In effect, the map fabricates a union of past and present, power
and culture, center and locale, institution and person, nature and
artifice, Kyoto and Edo. The ancient province situates the new
domain; the historical landmark enriches a landscape of castle
towns; the profile of local rule conforms to a national pattern; the
particular man administers resources calculated by formula; the
binding highway vanquishes a ragged terrain; the imperial capital
tethers an eastern shogunate to the west. This entangling of mes-

---

25. In addition to the security concerns explored by Kawamura, the muted
representation probably reflects both a nominal deference to the throne and a
habit of concealment.

sages creates a seductively thick realm of meaning. Some might read the map, quite dutifully, as a statement of cohesion in which all parts enhance one another. Others might variously concentrate on cities or transport or agrarian yields or martial power or imperial history or points of local pride. But the very mixing of messages within a simple cartographic structure gave the map a seeming truthfulness that allowed it a two-hundred-year run in the geographical imagination.

Not coincidentally, the map also defines the properties of nation. "Japan" is the place constituted by the provinces and highways of the imperial state; the daimyo, castle towns, and registered productivity totals of the Tokugawa polity; and the "famous places" of a long, putatively common experience. Culture, power, and history fuse here to create the national space. Implicit, too, is a certain presumption that "Japan" is a place where rice agriculture—the standard for evaluating productivity—establishes economic and social foundations. These properties certainly constitute a territory, although not one conceived in purely territorial terms. Land itself, unmarked by culture and power and history, was never the subject of early modern cartography until the inspired maverick Inō Tadataka (1745–1818) undertook strictly topographical surveys in the nineteenth century. Breaking from a culturalist conception of space, Inō fused nation with territorial definition.[26] The overwhelming message of early modern cartography, however, was that Japan was a landscape made of time.

Military Mirrors

Just as space had thick meanings on official maps, so, too, did daimyo. Each was constructed of seven conventional parts: a personal name, a family name, a courtly title, a provincial location, a specific castle town, a productivity total for the domain, and (in many cases) a family crest.[27] And each of these parts intimated a some-

---

26. Sugimoto, "Kuniezu kenkyū no ichi to kaidai," esp. pp. 89–91; idem, "Kuniezu," esp. pp. 320–23.

27. Although striking in the late seventeenth-century national maps of Ishikawa Ryūsen, this combination of attributes, with prominent treatments of the crests, is particularly conspicuous in the urban cartography of Edo.

what different identity. The daimyo was, at once, a particular man; the head of a martial house; an honorary aristocrat within the ancient imperial system; a local governor within the classical, Kyoto-centered order of provinces; a castellan within the shogunal, Edo-centered order of command; a territorial lord in control of agrarian wealth; and a subject of public display through heraldic insignia. Following the cartographic surveys, the attributes that forged these compound identities became matters of common knowledge as publishers continued to recycle the information in commercial maps, gazetteers, urban directories, guidebooks, dictionaries, and family encyclopedias. There was nothing secret about it.

The fullest, most current representations of the daimyo appeared in books typically called *bukan*, or Military Mirrors, which were published regularly after 1643.[28] Early versions stuck close to the cartographic categories of identity, listing each daimyo, in descending order of wealth, with the seven principal attributes as well as the address of his major residence in Edo and the name of his chief deputy there. Direct and utilitarian in approach, they were doubtless intended, in the main, for military men themselves. Indeed, military men probably put together the forerunners of the genre sometime after 1635 when the shogunate required that most daimyo be present in Edo for specified terms of annual service and retain permanent residences there for their wives and heirs. In 1642 the order was extended to all daimyo. The ensuing mass movement to Edo threw into contact and commotion a military elite both ill-acquainted and in flux. "The martial holdings of the realm are hard to fix," wrote a Tosa official in Edo, "for year by year individuals suffer from disinheritances, attainders, succession failures, and both increases and transfers in domain."[29] In a situation of forced proximity and routine ceremonial encounter, self-appointed chroniclers like the Tosa official appear to have assembled the first daimyo catalogues in an effort to get things straight.

Commercial publication of the catalogues in the 1640s suggests a continuing demand for information among military men who,

---

28. See the source cited in note 6.

29. Quoted in Fujizane Kumiko, "Bukan no shoshigakuteki kenkyū" (A bibliographical study of the Military Mirrors), *Nihon rekishi*, no. 525 (1992): 48–49.

apart from lively curiosity about their kind, were obliged to recognize and conduct business with one another (hence the prominence of crests and the notes about addresses and major deputies).
Rather quickly, however, the basic rosters developed into something more elaborate. From the 1670s, compilers of multivolume
Mirrors began adding details in what would eventually grow to 44
categories. Most of these additions amplified the personal and family profile of each daimyo. They specified his courtly rank as well
as his courtly title; sometimes his age; the identities of his father,
mother, heir, and consort; the names and revenues of increasing
numbers of major retainers; his genealogy (with notes on prominent ancestors); his ancestral and clan names; the locale of the ancestral home; and the name of the family mortuary temple. A second significant group of additions concerned the daimyo's life in
Edo. Entries included the locations of his primary and secondary
and tertiary residences there; the schedule of his annual attendance
on the shogun; the distance he traveled to reach Edo, and sometimes the route; the list of gifts he presented to the shogun; and the
name of the room in Edo castle where he was received. One more
group of conspicuous additions attended to insignia. Successive
Mirrors introduced sketches not just of principal crests but of alternative crests, lances and other processional regalia, horse fittings,
and sails.[30]

This steady expansion of the Mirrors was stimulated, certainly,
by competition. By the last decades of the seventeenth century,
over ten firms lured consumers with varying formats, new details,
and adamant claims to accuracy. They vaunted their material with
splendid titles—*The Military Mirror of the Realm, The Military Mirror of the Great Peace, The Complete Military Mirror*—and assurances
of up-to-date improvements on the editions of rivals. Noting that
information could change daily, some publishers promised to enter
handwritten emendations in the Mirrors for readers unable to wait
until the next printing.[31] Competition narrowed in the eighteenth
century, when internal and shogunal regulation of the publishing

---

30. See the table describing changes and additions over time in ibid., pp. 56–57.
31. See, e.g., the closing remarks of the *Seikyoku Edo kagami* (Kanbun 12), in
Dai bukan, 1: 132.

industry assigned control of the Mirror market to two firms, Suharaya and Izumojiya. Even so, they continued to revise and extend coverage in editions with annual runs numbering in the tens of thousands.[32]

Just who was consuming this vast output, and consequently driving the need for new packaging, is not clear but not entirely mysterious either. Military men must have remained the prime audience and certainly one large enough (numbering, with their families, up to 500,000 in Edo alone) to sustain vigorous production. Presumably important, too, was the great audience of commoners who depended on military trade and thus had immediate interests in such matters as travel schedules, the location of daimyo residences, and the identity of their staffs. Readers simply curious about their betters probably became a target of publishers as well and doubtless made up the larger part of the huge secondary audience served by used book dealers and peddlers. Countless discards, I imagine, got handed down to servants or passed off as souvenirs.

Yet for all its new kinks, the message put across to these disparate consumers became a peculiarly static one. The early Mirrors had the punch of news, since they tracked the ups and downs of lords who might not last the year. We may wonder, then, over the complicity in their publication of the shogunate—which was either passively content to see the rosters circulate or actively cooperative in their compilation. The detail and consistency of the daimyo lists point to cooperation. And the general thrust of the presentation suggests a motive. In the Mirrors, as in the official maps that the shogunate selectively released to commercial printers, readers could find edifying images of the polity. It was complete and universal, covering all the great lords of the realm. It was coherent in structure, combining in each daimyo the authority of house, history, imperial prestige, shogunal appointment, and local rule. And it was united in power, assembling in the Tokugawa capital every confederate of the Great Peace. Small matter that those confederates could change by the day. A big system,

---

32. Kornicki, *The Book in Japan*, p. 211.

the Mirrors seemed to insist, held things together—a piece of propaganda critical to a shogunate still in trouble in the 1640s, when memories of the Shimabara rebellion of 1637 stirred fears of resumed violence.

With the gradual normalization of the peace, an already strong message about a stable system became all the stronger, overwhelming any real newsworthiness in the Mirrors. Crammed as they were with novelties and the vicissitudes of biography, the Mirrors seemed to be about change. In fact, they increasingly told a story about continuity, even predictability, in what had emerged as a fixed, closed, and hereditary elite. The heavy gravity of the daimyo was the subject of Mirrors, which thickened the attributes of honor laid out on the maps. Thus the eminence of the house, which came to subsume the individual man, was emphasized in entries focused on succession—on the daimyo's long genealogy, the names and titles of his father and his heir, the pedigrees of his mother and his consort, the mortuary temple of his line. The history of the house was recovered, too, in notes indicating the daimyo's original family name (in the event that adoption or induction into the Matsudaira house had obscured it), the locale of the family's wartime rise to fame (in the event that domainal transfer had moved successors elsewhere), and the clan of origin (usually Fujiwara, Tachibana, Taira, or Minamoto).[33]

The entry of clan names situated the daimyo in deep time (for all dated to the classical period) as well as aristocratic frames of prestige (for all derived from noble houses). Conveyed, too, by notes on the daimyo's courtly rank and title (and occasional mention of his residence in Kyoto), this monarchical connection attached the martial lord to an alternative realm of authority that even casual readers knew something about. Basic reference works, like the all-purpose family encyclopedias, included lists of the emperors; the current occupants and officials of the imperial palace; the heads of aristocratic houses and their incomes; the princely abbots and abbesses; and the imperial era names. Such information

---

33. See, e.g., the daimyo entries in *Gorin bukan* (Kan'ei 2), in *Dai bukan*, 1: 329–63.

assumed primacy of place in the encyclopedias over lists of military leaders, intimating both the distinction and the superiority of monarchical authority.[34]

Yet in their portraits of diffuse honor, the Mirrors also attached the daimyo firmly to the Tokugawa shogunate. Muted in maps, the presence of the shogun himself was sometimes muted in the Mirrors as well. The catalogues might open with material on the shogun (the Tokugawa crest, the family genealogy, the names of the incumbent head and his heir), but they might also dispense with it entirely, as if in deference to persons exalted past mention. Shogunal power was nonetheless everywhere apparent—in the prominence of the Tokugawa collaterals who led the daimyo roster, the conspicuousness of the Matsudaira surname, and the Edo-centrism of the whole project. Fastidiously noting the locations and staffs of military mansions in the capital, the Mirrors converted the daimyo into men of Edo who were there, implicitly, to attend upon their lord in his castle. Successive editions brought the ritual of attendance to the surface, with, as noted above, expanding information on schedules and conduct.

Such details conjure mental pictures of the daimyo in action and are thus startling in catalogues otherwise given over to what a daimyo *is* rather than what he *does*. But these things may have been the same. The ceremonial attendance of the daimyo on the shogun—at the right time, in the right room, with the right gifts—was both expression and confirmation of his privileged status. He enacted who he was. Being a daimyo, with its lapidary layers of significance, seemed to be his job. The point is suggested again by the increasing attention in the Mirrors to daimyo regalia. Once confined to the primary household crest, illustrations expanded to include secondary crests; the lances, spears, standards, and decorative umbrellas carried in processions; and the various insignia used on uniforms, ships, sails, and horses. This array of visual signs—hardly necessary for simple identification—implies parading and watching. It implies that the daimyo manifested his honor in rich regalia and then per-

---

34. The *Banmin chōhōki* (see note 9 above), for example, contains not only extensive information on the court and aristocratic families but also a list of aristocratic titles.

formed that honor in flamboyant marches. Display on the streets appears to be the public counterpart to the enactment of status undertaken for closed audiences within Edo castle. And, indeed, the occasions for display were many, most of them carefully scheduled and announced. Daimyo proceeded to and from Edo each year. When in the capital they processed to the shogunal residence, the Tokugawa mortuary temples of Zōjōji and Kan'eiji, and one another's mansions. They also marched their companies with some regularity to the Tokugawa temple and shrine complex at Nikkō. They were men not only of Edo but of the streets.

In their fulsome treatment of regalia, the Mirrors effectively present themselves as field guides to the birds. Instead of addressing insiders with increasing amounts of practical information (concerning the size of daimyo retinues in Edo, say, or the names of their principal purveyors), they seem to address an audience of spectators with lengthening inventories of both symbols and honors. The symbols invite informed watching, the honors provide the incentive to watch. Here, the Mirrors say, is a big creature: a wealthy castellan, descendant of an ancient house, continuing link in an eminent family chain, bearer of aristocratic title, lord in the shogunal circle of prestige. He is important in his very being. Look at him.

This identification of the daimyo with his symbols and honors made him into an icon—a figure of parade and public consumption. Certainly his person mattered in the Mirrors, although in the context of the family dramas of birth and marriage and succession. Individual detail inflected a predictable story. Certainly, too, variation among the daimyo mattered in the Mirrors. In a fashion doubtless delectable to cognoscenti, the rosters marked fine and gross differences in wealth, pedigree, rank and title, and access to the shogun. But here, again, variation occurred across a fixed spectrum in a closed community of privilege. The Mirrors ultimately reified the daimyo elite.

The effect was reinforced, moreover, by a remarkable development in the Mirrors that fundamentally shaped their message. This change occurred early, about 1659, when publishers began adding to the daimyo catalogue a list of the chief officeholders in the shogunal bureaucracy. These were the men, some of daimyo rank but most from the lesser levels of Tokugawa retainers, who staffed the shogunal institution in Edo, other sensitive areas under direct shogunal administration, and properties across the country that produced shogunal revenue. Each entry in the bureaucratic list begins with the title of a particular office, the amount of the supplementary allowance (if any) accompanying appointment, the number of subordinate functionaries (*yoriki, dōshin*) in regular service, and sometimes the dates of scheduled meetings. Each entry continues with the names of incumbents and chief deputies, in each case with notes about their addresses and stipends. Entries frequently include crests and sometimes the names of an incumbent's father and predecessors in office. The bureaucratic lists conclude, finally, with lengthening rosters of commoners in direct service to the shogunate. The full inventory was prodigious: a list of 1683 includes the names of over 1,700 officials in 215 job categories. The number of subordinate functionaries, enumerated under each office entry but individually unnamed, is considerably larger.[35]

The two lists in the Mirrors—one of daimyo, one of officials— were sufficiently different in kind to describe, and focus attention on, two distinct orders of power. In the daimyo order, a power of multifaceted prestige but inchoate practical application attached to individual iconic figures. In the official order, a specifically administrative power, demarcated by a job title, attached to the office and devolved through appointment upon the officeholder.

As any mindful reader of the Mirrors would discover, moreover, officeholding tended to be yoked to pedigree but, in many cases, was neither hereditary nor permanent. Comparison of the names of incumbent officials with the names and terms of their predecessors (often catalogued at length) indicates that significant administrative posts did not pass automatically or even frequently from father to son. And inspection of the job histories of those incumbents (also catalogued at length) reveals that promotion required harrowing in a series of assignments of limited rather than lifetime tenure.[36] Indeed, the entry of appointment dates in the ros-

---

35. Untitled roster of Tenna 3, in *Dai bukan*, 1: 194–209.
36. See, e.g., the *Shōen bukan* (Shōtoku 3), in *Dai bukan*, 1: 465–92 *passim*.

ters draws attention to the principle of replaceability and the reality of routine movement in a system with complex career paths. Perhaps the clearest signal of competition, which was always implicit in an administration with some 2,000 consequential officers and some 22,500 housemen, came with the introduction of "office allowances." Pervasive by the eighteenth century, these boosts in income and status made lesser retainers eligible for posts above their birth station and hence decoupled appointment from hereditary rank.[37]

Plenty of jobs in the shogunate did pass, if not inevitably or exclusively, through families—particularly those at lower levels hidden from the rosters and those requiring the prolonged expert training (in music, medicine, or textual scholarship, say) often commenced in the household. The regime also created a number of titular offices, high in prestige if not impact, to dignify families with exceptional histories.[38] But such bloating effectively conceded the paramount importance of office. Sheer membership in the lord's retainer band—with the chivalric distinction of pedigree, vestiture, and status privilege—was insufficient. When the regime needed to distinguish a claimant to attention, it found him a job. And the honor of office depended on the principle of selectivity. The shogunate did not expand posts indefinitely to accommodate all candidates. It did not obscure with honorary sinecures the focus of most posts on specialized work and competitive recruitment. Never, in fact, did it even seek to ameliorate status anxiety by circulating some sort of inclusive retainer list, thick with heraldry and ancestry in the style of the daimyo lists, that might have rivaled the bureaucratic rosters.

The effect was to transpose a lordship into a government. The bureaucratic profiles in the Mirrors conveyed a message not only about professional recruitment to office but about the structure of rule itself. The regime apparently had clear work to do as well as

---

37. See the notation of office allowances in ibid. On the size and organization of the body of housemen, see Conrad Totman, *Politics in the Tokugawa Bakufu* (Cambridge, Mass.: Harvard University Press, 1967), pp. 131–52.

38. The chief honorary offices were those of the masters of shogunal ceremony (*sōshaban*), the masters of court ceremony (*kōke*), and the assemblymen (*yoriai*).

the ability both to translate work into jobs and to arrange jobs into a hierarchy of command. This arrangement, moreover, was so elaborate as to bear the mark of invention: neither natural nor inevitable, the structure was made up. It was also so specific as to require a specialized, carefully graded body of worker-officials. Some held lofty offices and received great stipends. Most attended to more modest but critical work (as police and prison guards, engineers, comptrollers, foresters, scholars, and doctors) for very small stipends. All, however, bore the distinction of appointments implicitly linked to preparation. Critically, several hundred were commoners—including, for example, neighborhood elders, heads of the gold and silver guilds, handlers of imported silks, sword connoisseurs, and painters. Official competence crossed boundaries of station. Finally, the scale and scope of their work cast the administration that employed them as a national establishment.

Many of the offices listed in the Mirrors pertained to the life of Edo and other shogunal castles—their ceremonies and protocols, upkeep and provisioning. Many, too, pertained to the life of the great cities that grew around those castles; for legions of deputies assumed responsibility for engineering, public works, fire control, policing, and prisons. Many other offices pertained to martial functions ranging from oversight of the Kantō and the Kansai to routine guard and police duty. Yet a substantial number of posts engaged the broadly civil mission of an administration that had grown from a lordly genesis into far-ranging rule.

This range was defined, in part, by specific geographical claims. The Mirrors identified shogunal magistrates responsible for major cities and sites across the country, including Kyoto, Fushimi, Osaka, Nara, Sakai, Sunpu, Ise, Nagasaki, Shimoda, Sado, and Nikkō. They also identified officers appointed to at least 26 provinces as intendants of Tokugawa properties. But the Mirrors more insistently associated the shogunate with a general public dominion by listing officers responsible for four encompassing arenas of public interest: religion, transport, coinage, and adjudication. Here was an institution in charge of the country's common resources and the activities of its common life.

The actual operation of the shogunate, as well as the vexed boundary between shogunal and daimyo jurisdictions, was not at issue in the Military Mirrors. They were representations of the polity that hewed close to normative standards. Indeed, Tokugawa deputies themselves undoubtedly supplied the lists of offices to publishers as another edifying image of the regime's power and integrity. But the general messages about governance contained in the lists—particularly when circulated to general audiences of consumers—went beyond edification. Insofar as the lists defined public administration in terms of particular functions, they broached the notions of responsibility and accountability in rule. Insofar as the lists described an invented system, they broached the plausibility of change in that system. Insofar as the lists associated employment with professional specialists, they broached the possibility of access to appointment through training and merit. And insofar as the lists laid out the broad dimensions of the shogunal enterprise, they returned to the idea, already expressed in official cartography, that this place called Honchō or Nihon might be a nation.

Concluding Observations

The implications about governance contained in the lists of offices were pursued chiefly in the academies and intellectual circles of both samurai and commoner scholars. So, too, the questions raised by maps—concerning the relationships between court and shogunate, center and locale, culture and territory—were explored by students of National Learning and Dutch (or Western) Learning as well as thinkers engaged by the foreign crises of the nineteenth century. Even as conflict increasingly roiled the sphere of scholarship, and of agrarian politics, the information library remained a seemingly safe place where familiar tropes and normative standards organized a predictable world.

But it was only seemingly safe. Underlying the texts was a quiet radicalism as important in the nineteenth century as in the seventeenth. They affirmed the knowability through investigation of social phenomena. And they implicitly told readers that they were entitled to share (even expected to master) what was known. This approach removed knowledge from status-bound audiences of insiders to an undifferentiated realm of the public. It was a common property. Messages about a certain leveling of society were more specific in instructional texts that variously taught readers the arts of gentlemen and women (in everything from poetry to love) and the skills of proficient workers (in callings from brewing to agriculture). Performance, and often enough profit, was the measure of the person. In their cumulatively vast assembly of information, moreover, the texts portrayed a society bigger than the polity. Their treatment of the complex domain of the market economy or of ritual life and play spilled profusely beyond the frames of rule to suggest that particular relations of power fit within broader social constructions that could outlive them.

Radical in orientation, the texts were challenging in message as well. The very suppleness in interpretation that made the maps and Mirrors so durable also made them equivocal. National cartography appeared to blend but could just as easily put in tension the disparate claims of imperial and shogunal power, regional and central institutions, people and rulers. The Military Mirrors amplified the honor but ossified the significance of the daimyo; they plotted the grand reach of the shogunal bureaucracy even as they linked governance to responsibility and professional performance.

These messages remained latent. They nonetheless complicated an information library that circulated far beyond the academy to induct into social knowledge and ready for social scrutiny a public of ordinary readers. They took information for granted. If it was conventional, it was not innocent.

CHAPTER TWO

Local Autonomy in Early Meiji Japan: Competing Conceptions

Kyu Hyun Kim

Local autonomy (*chihō bunken* or *chihō jichi*) was one of the most important political ideas in early Meiji Japan, and also one of the most controversial and difficult to define. The new imperial government and its critics were cognizant of the value of local autonomy, or, in a more institutionally oriented context, local self-government, in completing Japan's transition into a modern nation-state. In English-language scholarship, the study of local autonomy or local self-government in Meiji Japan has tended to focus on specific regions;[1] in contrast, the present chapter is con-

---

I would like to thank Gail Lee Bernstein, Andrew Gordon, and Kate Nakai for shepherding the present chapter through the revision process. Special thanks are due to Kate Nakai for a series of detailed comments on both structure and argumentation. I also gratefully acknowledge many helpful comments from Timothy George, Harold Bolitho, Sophie Volpp, Karen Shimakawa, and Ming Cheng Lo.

1. James Baxter, *The Meiji Unification Through the Lens of Ishikawa Prefecture* (Cambridge, Mass.: Harvard University, Council on East Asian Studies, 1994); Neil Waters, *Japan's Local Pragmatists: The Transition from Bakumatsu to Meiji in the Kawasaki Region* (Cambridge, Mass.: Harvard University, Council on East Asian Studies, 1983); Marion W. Steele, "From Custom to Right: The Politicization of the Village in Early Meiji Japan," *Modern Asian Studies* 23, no. 4 (1989): 729–48; Andrew Fraser, "Local Administration: The Example of Awa-Tokushima," in *Japan in Transition: From Tokugawa to Meiji*, ed. Marius B. Jansen and Gilbert Rozman (Princeton: Princeton University Press, 1986), pp. 91–110. Kurt Steiner, *Local*

cerned with the *idea* of local autonomy. It seeks to delineate, in rather bold strokes, several key conceptions of local autonomy articulated within the public discourse on the Japanese political system that flourished during the 1870s and 1880s.

As I hope to show, the varying conceptions of local autonomy expressed by the constituents of the "national public sphere" of early to mid-Meiji Japan serve to illuminate their diverse understandings of the ideal relationship between state and society in the context of a modern nation-state.[2] The discourse on local autonomy was never simply a controversy over the shape and form of the political system, although that in itself was an important issue. Rather, it was undergirded by theoretical views and ideological beliefs concerning the boundaries of the political and the nature of "society."

This chapter presents a series of readings of texts from Meiji Japan, the majority of them overlooked in English-language scholarship, including essays and letters of Fukuzawa Yukichi (1835–90) and Inoue Kowashi (1843–95), as well as writings in newspapers and news magazines sympathetic to the Popular Rights Movement. I begin by presenting a brief institutional history of the forms of local self-government in early Meiji Japan from the Meiji Restoration in 1868 to the establishment of the National Diet in 1890 in order to delineate the political and intellectual context in which thinkers such as Fukuzawa and Inoue formulated their ideas about local autonomy.

Establishment of the Small and Large District System, 1868–77

Villages and towns were allowed a degree of self-government during the Tokugawa period. Even though there was considerable regional variation, functionaries appointed from among local farmers and merchants served in a variety of capacities: record keeping, the

---

Government in Japan (Stanford: Stanford University Press, 1965), is a useful survey of the local government system throughout Japan's modern history.

2. For a detailed analysis of the national public sphere and its relationship with the discourse on parliamentarian representation in early Meiji Japan, see my *Age of Visions and Arguments: Parliamentarianism and the National Public Sphere in Early Meiji Japan* (Cambridge, Mass.: Harvard University Asia Center, forthcoming).

collection of land taxes, the propagation of ordinances issued by samurai bureaucracies, and other administrative tasks. Over the course of the Tokugawa period, the posts of village and town headmen became *de facto* the lowest-level offices of the domainal (*han*) and shogunal bureaucracies, although differences in status continued to remain. In most cases, these officials were not paid salaries or stipends.[3] The village and town headmen acted and saw themselves primarily as local leaders, not as agents of the Tokugawa shogunate or the domainal government. In practice, the administrative apparatuses of the ruling samurai and the village communities were not integrated into a single hierarchy. For its part, the samurai bureaucracy left the village and town communities relatively undisturbed, despite the injunctions and ordinances issued from the castle towns seeking to regulate and control the social life of the commoners.[4]

After the Meiji Restoration, the new imperial government felt compelled to conduct a census to prepare for nation-building programs such as land tax reform. Its first step was to divide existing domains into districts (*ku*), generally composed of several preexisting villages and townships. This measure was enacted in early 1871, just before the abolition of the domains and the establishment of prefectures. In most cases, the incumbent village and town headmen were appointed census chiefs (*kochō*) by the new government. In October of that same year, the districts were further classified into large and small units, and district chiefs (*kuchō*) were made responsible for the administration of these units. District and census chiefs were, among other tasks, made responsible for the dissemination of government directives, collection of taxes, promotion of school attendance, military conscription, and reception

---

3. Andrew Fraser ("Local Administration," pp. 116–17) notes what is obviously an exception to this general situation in the Awa-Tokushima region: the *ōdoshiyori* and *yotō shōya*, whose jurisdictions were much wider than their equivalents in villages and towns, were apparently treated as samurai, and their salaries were paid from the domain treasury.

4. Cf. Ishikawa Hisao, *Kindai Nihon no meibōka to jichi* (Notables and self-government of modern Japan) (Tokyo: Bokutakusha, 1987), pp. 39–40.

of applications and petitions.[5] The salaries of these officials were
paid from civic expenditures (*minpi*), which were collected within
the locality separately from national taxes.[6] From a formal perspective, these petty functionaries were government officials, with
rankings and salaries commensurate with their seniority and responsibilities and determined and formally codified by the Finance
Ministry. Nevertheless, from the central government's standpoint,
the extension of the state bureaucracy into local communities
through these new posts was only a qualified success. In order to
pursue its programs of modernization in the countryside, the Meiji
government still had to rely by and large on village and town
headmen who had served during the Tokugawa period. Land tax
reform, in particular, had to be mediated and assisted by village
headmen familiar with their area and capable of accurately assessing land values based on productivity.[7]

As a compromise solution to the problem of implementing
policies at the local level, the Meiji state also allowed local communities to mobilize themselves. In the short term, this meant institutional representation in the form of village and town assemblies. Limited representation was deemed necessary to ensure the
cooperation of the community in public projects such as land tax
reform. In some regions, villages and towns began to elect their officials. In Miyagi prefecture, for example, elections were conducted
by secret ballot in order to guarantee impartiality.[8] By 1874, local
assemblies more or less independent of the government bureaucracies had been created in many regions, often under the initiative
and supervision of "progressive" local governors. One of the earliest experiments with local assemblies was conducted in 1872 by the
governor of Hyōgo prefecture, Kanda Takahira, who convened

---

5. Ōshima Mitsuko, "Chihō seiji" (Local politics and government), in *Nihon
kindai hō taisei no keisei* (The formation of the modern Japanese legal system),
ed. Fukushima Masao (Tokyo: Nihon hyōronsha, 1981), 1: 158–59.

6. According to the 1873 Ordinances on Land Tax Reform, civic expenditures
were set at 1.0 percent of land value, later revised to 0.5 percent in 1877.

7. Kim Yong-dŏk, *Myŏngch'i yusin ŭi t'oji seje kaeh'yŏk* (The land tax reform
during the Meiji Restoration) (Seoul: Ilchokak, 1989), pp. 95–96.

8. Kikegawa Hiroshi, *Jichi gojūnenshi: seido-hen* (Fifty years of self-government:
institutions) (Tokyo: Bunsei shoin, 1977), pp. 30–35, 38–39.

township and village assemblies through public elections. Similar developments took place in Tottori, Chiba, Ibaraki, and Oda (later absorbed into Hiroshima) prefectures.[9] In Osaka prefecture, Governor Watanabe Noboru permitted the establishment of a popularly elected assembly in November 1873, with the power to propose new bills. The first members were chosen from among government-appointed census and district chiefs; revisions to the regulations in 1878 permitted those who owned more than ¥100 worth of real estate, that is, middle- to upper-middle-level self-cultivators or landlords, to qualify as either a candidate or a voter.[10]

In fact, the need for the general public to participate in affairs of state, especially in the form of local self-government, had been acknowledged within the imperial government since its inception. As Marius Jansen points out, "The Meiji government, in its eagerness for local support, tried to channel local enthusiasm for participation in local government and taxation. . . . From an early point, representation was seen as a necessary part of centralization."[11] Government leaders, however, wanted to keep the process of extending participation gradual, initiated by the center, and strictly under their control. In the late 1860s and early 1870s, they experimented with such institutions as the Public Deliberation Council (Kōgisho), Chamber for the Collection of Opinions (Shūgiin), Left Chamber (Sain), and Senate (Genrōin) but refused to entrust real legislative power to these bodies. Instead state leaders briefly entertained the notion of gradually expanding the Assembly of Local Governors (Chihōkan kaigi) into a legislative organ. Kido Takayoshi, appointed as chair of the assembly, had been sympathetic to the notion of local autonomy. In a letter of opinion

---

9. Ōishi Kaichirō, "Chihō jichi" (Local self-government), in *Iwanami kōza Nihon rekishi*, vol. 16, *Kindai 3* (Iwanami lectures on Japanese history: modern period 3) (Tokyo: Iwanami shoten, 1962), pp. 241–42; Ushiki Yukio, "Chihō minkai to chihō jichi yōkyū" (Local popular assemblies and the demands for local self-government), *Chihōshi kenkyū*, 34, no. 5 (1984): 64.

10. Kitazawa Toyoji, *Kindai chihō minshūshi kenkyū* (A study of the popular history of localities in the modern period) (Tokyo: Hōritsu bunkasha, 1985), pp. 84–98.

11. Marius Jansen, "Introduction to Part One: Administration," in *Japan in Transition: From Tokugawa to Meiji*, pp. 34–35.

submitted in September 1876, for instance, he claimed that excessive centralization of the state had depleted the material and human resources of the countryside; the Japanese nation, he wrote, was like a human body whose limbs were withering from lack of blood circulation. Kido also conceded the desirability of parliamentarian representation but evinced strong distrust of the Popular Rights Movement and its mobilization of public opinion. He still believed that at this juncture township and village assemblies were free from the disruptive influences of the Popular Rights Movement and that these assemblies could gradually be expanded into district and prefectural assemblies and ultimately into a national assembly.[12] However, in the course of managing the Assembly of Local Governors, Kido increasingly found himself disturbed by the governors' behavior.

During one of the assembly's sessions, Kido presented a bill drafted by the central government. The bill stipulated that district and census chiefs were to be chosen from among village headmen, landlords, and other local notables, and they were in turn to participate in the prefectural-level congresses presided over by the state-appointed governors. This bill sought to streamline the local political system into a vertical chain of command reaching down from the central government. However, Kido's bill was quickly pushed aside by a group of governors, who insisted on prioritizing the issue of the public election of local assemblymen. Kanda Takahira of Hyōgo, Nakajima Nobuyuki of Kanagawa, Sekiguchi Ryūkichi of Yamagata, and others argued strongly in favor of public elections. Some of them drew on the theory of division of powers and argued that the local assemblies at all levels, including the Assembly of Local Governors, constituted the legislative branch of the government, should eventually be expanded into a national

---

12. Kido Takayoshi, "Chihōkan saiyō to chōsonkai kaisetsu ni tsuki ikensho" (An opinion letter regarding the appointment of local governors and the establishment of township and village assemblies) (1876/5), in *Nihon kindai shisō taikei*, vol. 3, *Kanryōsei keisatsu* (An outline of modern Japanese thought: bureaucracy, police), ed. Yui Masamichi and Obinata Sumio (Tokyo: Iwanami shoten, 1990), pp. 108–11.

representative body, and should be independent of the administrative branch.[13] Even though the governors supporting elections were in the minority (39 supported the government's bill as opposed to 22 who favored local elections), Kido privately expressed his distress at the situation: "[There] are men who seek fame through their insistent advocacy of publicly selected assemblies when they have not even opened assemblies made up of district and census chiefs in their own jurisdiction. These men are at odds with His Majesty's purpose, and contrary to what they expect, they will bring unhappiness to the masses. Alas!"[14]

In the end, the Assembly of Local Governors, which was never designed to serve as a genuine legislature, only ratified government bills, to the disappointment of rural notables—wealthy farmers and discontented former samurai—looking for an opportunity to participate in the national decision-making. From Kido's viewpoint, the disturbing turn of events in the Assembly of Local Governors was yet another sign that the incendiary rhetoric and theories of the Popular Rights Movement had made significant inroads into the public mind; this made him move away from a possible compromise with Itagaki Taisuke and other proponents of the movement on the question of local autonomy.

Local Administration Under the Three New Laws, 1878–81

A new system of local administration was formally announced on July 22, 1878, in a set of three regulations, collectively known as the Three New Laws, or *Sanshinpō*. These were the Regulations Concerning the Reorganization of Counties, Districts, Towns, and Villages (*Gunku chōson henseihō*); Regulations Concerning the Prefectural Assemblies (*Fukenkai kisoku*); and Regulations Concerning

---

13. "Chihōkan kaigi nisshi" (Daily reports of the assembly of local governors) (1875/7/8), in *Meiji bunka zenshū*, vol. 1, *Kensei-hen* (The complete collection on Meiji culture: constitutional politics), ed. Meiji bunka kenkyūkai, new ed. (Tokyo: Nihon hyōronsha, 1969), pp. 312–21.

14. *The Diary of Kido Takayoshi*, entry for 1875/7/9, trans. Sidney Devere Brown and Akiko Hirota (Tokyo: University of Tokyo Press, 1986), vol. 3.

Local Taxes (*Chihōzei kisoku*).[15] The first law modified the existing large and small district system by introducing two new administrative units, counties (*gun*) and cities (*shi*), thus restructuring the framework into a three-tier system. Counties and cities occupied a middle position between prefectural/metropolitan offices and village/township offices. Although villages and townships were still not directly controlled by the central administration, county chiefs could exercise supervisory power over village and township assemblies, suspend their sessions, and veto their resolutions. The county chief was in practical terms a government official, although he was supposed to be a resident of the county he supervised.[16] By inserting this new level of administration into the local government system, the central government sought to accommodate the continued presence of the traditional "village communities" while simultaneously extending its sinews of power into them by incorporating their elite strata into centrally controlled bureaucratic structures.

As it turned out, the post of county chief did not provide an effective buffer against the agitations of the Popular Rights Movement. Within two years of establishing the county system, the state had to transfer the domiciles of some county chiefs from their original birthplaces, an act that suggests recruitment from other prefectures. Local notables submitted petitions calling for either public election of county chiefs or the establishment of county assemblies to serve as a check and balance on the chief's office.[17] For instance, the Fukushima prefectural assembly sent a petition to the

---

15. For explanations of the Three New Laws, see Ōshima Mitsuko, *Meiji kokka to chiiki shakai* (The Meiji nation-state and local society) (Tokyo: Iwanami shoten, 1994), pp. 106–37; and Ōshima Tarō, *Nihon chihō gyōzaiseishi josetsu* (A preliminary study of the administrative and financial history of Japan's localities) (Tokyo: Miraisha, 1968), pp. 16–109. For a short description of the laws in English, see Steiner, *Local Government in Japan*, pp. 30–32; see also Baxter, *The Meiji Unification*, pp. 160–200.

16. Yamanaka Einosuke, *Kindai Nihon no chihō seido to meibōka* (Notables and the local institutions of modern Japan) (Tokyo: Kōbundō, 1990), pp. 60–64; Ōshima Mitsuko, *Meiji kokka to chiiki shakai*, pp. 111–12.

17. Yamanaka Einosuke, *Kindai Nihon no chihō seido to meibōka*, pp. 64–72, 77–79.

Home Ministry claiming that the bureaucratic status of the county chiefs violated "the proper distinction between the officialdom and the people" and left the people inordinately suspicious of the local officials. The petition also asserted that it was unfair to pay the salaries of county chiefs out of local taxes when the taxpayers had no say in their appointment. The proposed solution was for the county constituency to elect its chief directly, subject to ratification by the prefectural governor.[18]

The Regulations Concerning the Prefectural Assemblies made it possible for respected local figures to participate in the decision-making processes of subnational governments. Prefectural assemblies were given the power to deliberate on the annual budget submitted by prefectural offices. As we have seen, popular assemblies at the village and township level already existed in many regions, but this was the first time deliberative institutions at the prefectural level received recognition from the central government. Not surprisingly, the new prefectural assembly was far from the ideal of a legislative institution demanded by Popular Rights activists. The prefectural governor monopolized the right to draft bills, and all assembly resolutions were subject to the governor's final approval. He also could suspend or disband an assembly session and call for new elections, and implement by executive order a policy rejected by the assembly. On the other hand, the assemblymen could draft petitions on issues relating to particular local interests and submit them to the Home Ministry. In the event, assemblymen frequently exercised this option to voice their opinions on larger political issues, including criticism of the very local representative system they participated in.

The regulations, in addition, had a far-reaching effect on the contours of local civic and political activism by stipulating strict qualifications for voters and candidates for seats in the prefectural assemblies: these categories eventually were used to distinguish the "public subject" (*kōmin*) from the "resident" (*jūmin*). A voter had

---

18. "Gunchō kōsen no gi ni tsuki kengen" (1879/7/24), in Shōji Kichinosuke, *Nihon seisha seitō hattatsushi* (A history of the development of political associations and parties in Japan) (Tokyo: Ochanomizu shobō, 1959), p. 269.

to be an adult male over twenty years of age, a registered inhabitant of the prefecture, and capable of paying an annual land tax of
¥5 or more. A candidate had to be over 25 years of age, a registered
inhabitant of the prefecture, in residence in the prefecture for at
least three years, and capable of paying a land tax of ¥10 or more.
In 1880, 1,513,308 men (4.27 percent of the entire population) qualified to vote under these regulations, and 867,192 men (2.45 percent)
qualified to run as candidates.[19] These qualifications were apparently intended to incorporate the most affluent stratum of the local
population into the state's administrative apparatuses and thus dis-
courage them from participating in the Popular Rights Movement,
but without giving them any real power to intervene in national
affairs.

The third leg supporting the triumvirate of the new local laws,
the Regulations Concerning Local Taxes, combined the prefectural
taxes and levies for civic expenditures (minpi) into one comprehensive system of local taxes (chihōzei). Collected from each household,
local taxes were entirely separate from land taxes and capped at 20
percent of the latter. They covered expenditures for policing; construction and repair of harbor facilities, roads, riverbanks, and
bridges; public exhibition of government ordinances and other miscellaneous public tasks; subsidies for public and elementary schools;
salaries and travel expenses for district and county officials; funds
for hospitals, nurseries, and epidemic prevention; and loans to private enterprises. The change was in part designed to rationalize the
taxation system—the dual system of prefectural taxes and civic expenditures that it replaced had not been a model of efficiency.

The Three New Laws were typical of the legislation that the
early Meiji state enacted and illustrate its carrot-and-stick approach
to dealing with the increasingly contentious civil society. The
Three New Laws, which did acknowledge the arbitrary and in-
flexible character of the small and large district system, sought to
address the discontents of local elites by softening administrative
rigidity and addressing economic inefficiency. The immediate consequence of the Three New Laws, however, was further politicization of the local communities. The prefectural assemblies them-

---

19. Baxter, The Meiji Unification, p. 183.

selves became fertile ground for political activism by local notables looking for ways to intervene in national decision-making. This was, of course, an important step in the development of the Popular Rights Movement.

Toward the City, Township, and Village System, 1881–90

In 1881, an imperial edict promising the establishment of the National Diet and promulgation of the constitution within a decade was issued. In this year, the state leaders expelled State Councilor Ōkuma Shigenobu, who was suspected of colluding with civilian critics against the state bureaucracy, and consolidated their ranks against the Popular Rights Movement. Led by Itō Hirobumi, they came together on a series of decisions that determined the basic contours of the Japanese political system in the prewar period—adopting the Prussian model for the Imperial Constitution; establishing a cabinet system of government, officially implemented in 1885; and creating the peerage, partly so that members of the state-approved elite could act as a countervailing force against elected politicians.

As Itō started his researches on constitutions, Home Minister Yamagata Aritomo began working on a long-term plan to create a system of local government. In a memorial to the emperor in May 1882, Yamagata, calling Popular Rights activists "dogs who pretend to be tigers" and "Jacobins," elucidated the need to rein in "the members of the political parties and associations . . . who routinely break laws and regulations, resist the government, disrupt social order, destroy morality, and yet call themselves free and autonomous (*jichi*), thinking that [this] allows them to lie outside the framework of the law." Yamagata's definition of "autonomy," whether applied to individuals or to institutions, rigorously excluded political engagement as a part of civic life. Autonomous bodies of local administration should remain apolitical, swayed neither by local interests nor by political theories of rights and representation.[20]

---

20. "Jihei o ronji seikō o furui okosen to suru hōhō o ronzu" (Discussing current problems and the ways to achieve success) (1882/5), in *Meiji hyakunenshi sōsho*,

The specific designs for local self-government developed under Yamagata were greatly influenced by the German legal scholar Alfred Mosse, whom Yamagata recruited as the foreign advisor to the Committee for Organization of Local Government in 1887. It was Mosse who introduced key features of the city, township, and village system, put into full practice, after minor revisions, in 1889 and generally recognized as the first systematic implementation of local self-government in modern Japanese history. Mosse argued that the local community or municipality, for which he used the German term *Gemeinde*, should be defined as the basic unit of a local self-government system. In Japan, villages and townships corresponded to the *Gemeinde*. Reflecting on the Prussian example, Mosse believed that local communities should possess internal economic strength and a sufficiently large pool of human resources. Villages and townships without such resources ought to be combined into larger bodies. The positions of town and census chiefs should remain nonsalaried posts, to be staffed by members of the local community. However, the right to be elected to these posts should belong strictly to landlords, owners of substantial real estate, and other well-to-do members of the local society.[21]

Under the new city, township, and village system, officially promulgated in April 1888, public subjects (*kōmin*) in the areas outside cities were defined as male Japanese, 25 years or older, who had resided in the locality for two or more years and had paid the national tax of ¥2 or more per annum. These public subjects were qualified to vote for town and village assemblymen. Moreover, the

vol. 16, *Yamagata Aritomo ikensho* (The Meiji centennial collection: the opinion papers of Yamagata Aritomo), ed. Ōyama Azusa (Tokyo: Hara shobō, 1966), pp. 110–11.

    21. Alfred Mosse, "Jichisei kōgi: shichōson sōron" (Lectures on local self-government: general remarks on the townships and villages) (1888/11/9), excerpted from *Jichisei kōgi* (Lectures on local self-government) (1890), in *Nihon kindai shisō taikei*, vol. 20, *Ie to mura* (Households and villages), ed. Unno Fukuju and Ōshima Mitsuko (Tokyo: Iwanami shoten, 1989), pp. 257–71. See Richard Louis Staubitz, "The Establishment of the System of Local Self-Government (1888–1890) in Meiji Japan: Yamagata Aritomo and the Meaning of *Jichi* [Self-Government]" (Ph.D. diss., Yale University, 1973), for Mosse's theory of local self-government and Rudolf von Gneist's influence on it.

law allowed those whose local tax payment exceeded two-thirds of the total to claim voting rights without having to meet the residence requirements. The official commentary on the laws explicitly stated that such qualifications were necessary to prevent the subprefectural deliberative bodies from being "overtaken by the poor, who constitute the majority [of local residents]." [22] The notion of local autonomy reflected in the city, township, and village system was succinctly expressed by Ōmori Shōichi, one of its drafters at the Home Ministry: "Local self-government is not about allowing the people to handle the tasks of government directly. Direct government cannot be practiced even in a small district. How could we expect it for the entire nation?" Any issue requiring application of a uniform policy throughout the nation, speedy implementation of a policy, or administrative expertise should fall entirely under the jurisdiction of the central government. Anything that concerned specific localities ought to be left to the institutions of local autonomy, which should allow "a certain level of indirect participation (*tashō kansetsu ni san'yo seshimuru*) by the people." [23]

The Popular Rights Movement and the Critique of Centralization

As we have seen, at every stage of the institutional reform of local government, the Meiji state had to grapple with the challenges presented by the Popular Rights Movement. The movement is commonly traced to a proposal calling for the establishment of a popu-

---

22. "Shichō sonsei" (Town and village system) (1881/4/17) in *Kindai Nihon chihō jichi rippō shiryō shūsei* (Collected materials on the laws on local self-governance in modern Japan), ed. Yamanaka Einosuke et al. (Tokyo: Kōbundō, 1994), 2: 381. Ōshima Mitsuko (*Meiji kokka to chiiki shakai*, pp. 196–215) notes that the independence of town and village assemblies was further restricted under the new system, which strengthened the bureaucratic supervision of the Home Ministry and prefectural governors over these local assemblies.

23. "Jichi rippō ni kanshi kōyo kakitome" (An unofficial letter on the establishment of the laws regarding self-government), in *Ōmori Shōichi monjo* (Ōmori Shōichi papers); quoted in Sasaki Ryūji, "Ōmori Shōichi no 'chihō jichi' ron" (Ōmori Shōichi's theory of "local self-government"), in *Kindai Nihon shakai to shisō* (Modern Japanese society and thought), ed. Gotō Yasushi (Tokyo: Yoshikawa kōbunkan, 1992), p. 90.

larly elected national assembly, submitted to the government in
January 1874. Most of the signatories were high-ranking officials
such as Itagaki Taisuke, who had resigned from the government following the controversy in 1873 over the expedition to Korea. The
proposal was published in the influential *Nisshin shinjishi* almost as
soon as it was submitted. The ensuing public controversy contributed greatly to the dissemination of parliamentarian ideas into local
areas and eventually to the consolidation of an organized opposition
against the government. This opposition made extensive use of both
old and new media and forums for public discourse, such as newspapers, petitions, and lecture meetings. Many Japanese historians
recognize this new development of political activism and discursive
effervescence as the beginning of the Popular Rights Movement.

By 1875, making the local assembly free of state control had become a hot political issue among the local notables. In that year,
Popular Rights activists from thirteen prefectures attended the Assembly of Local Governors and later submitted a proposal calling
for the public election of local assemblies.[24] Many of them already
belonged to political associations of one kind or another and seized
the opportunity provided by the 1875 assembly to initiate a campaign to open the existing subnational deliberative bodies to greater
popular participation. This project received much support from
news media catering to urban intellectuals and professionals. An
editorial in *Yokohama mainichi shinbun*, for instance, criticized the
counterargument advanced by opponents of the Popular Rights
Movement that the absence of a tradition of local elections made
public election of census and district chiefs an unrealistic proposi-
tion. "Even in the prefectures still mired in the state of chaos and
barbarism," the author wrote, "people would be able to understand
when they are told, 'Look, the district and census chiefs will be decided by who receives the largest numbers of your tallies (*irefuda*) or
name cards (*tefuda*); so there is absolutely nothing to fear. All you
have to do is just count the tallies after you throw them in.'"[25]

---

24. Ōishi Kaichirō, "Chihō jichi," p. 243.
25. "Ku-kochō kōsenron" (On public election of district and census chiefs),
Yokohama mainichi shinbun, 1875/7/12. See also "Chihō minkai no nisshi o yomu"
(Reading the daily records of local popular assemblies), *Yokohama mainichi shin-*

By the late 1870s, many local notables elected to prefectural assemblies were engaged in mobilizing themselves into a nationwide organization. In late 1879, for instance, Sakurai Shizuka, a prefectural assemblyman and former journalist from Chiba, printed 10,000 copies of a pamphlet entitled "Kokkai kaisetsu konsei gian" (Draft proposal for establishing a national assembly) and distributed them to prefectural assemblymen in various regions. The pamphlet asserted that the local assemblies instituted by the Three New Laws were inadequate vehicles for the people to exercise their rights of political participation, because their roles hardly extended beyond "attending to inquiries from above regarding local taxes." Therefore, local activists had no recourse other than to create an alliance and demand the establishment of a national assembly that would give the people true power to determine national policy. He suggested that local assemblymen throughout the nation send representatives to convene a meeting in Tokyo.[26] A document entitled "Chihō rengōkai sōritsu shuisho" (A prospectus for the foundation of the local alliance), most likely a product of the efforts of Sakurai and his colleagues to organize such an alliance, notes that campaigns of the mainstream Popular Rights Movement, represented by the Kōchi-based Patriotic Society (Aikokusha), had failed to attract nationwide support. Other efforts by prefectural associations to extend their influence beyond prefectural boundaries were limited by geography. Only with a nationwide alliance of the local notables, the document asserted, could one expect the cause of the Popular Rights Move-

---

bun, 1875/7/17; and Adachi Magoroku, "Minkairon" (On popular assemblies), *Yūbin hōchi shinbun*, 1875/8/3. Even the *Tōkyō nichi nichi shinbun*, which took a moderate position on the pace of democratization, published a series of editorials and letters between 1876 and 1877 advocating the establishment of local assemblies. In response to the criticism that the local population was too "uncivilized" to cope with self-government, they deployed the argument, adapted from the ideas expressed in John Stuart Mill's *Considerations on Representative Government*, that local popular assemblies could be a training ground for participatory politics; see Murata Kan, "Bunkenron" (On the division of power), *Tōkyō nichi nichi shinbun*, 1876/12/15; Kubota Kan'ichi, editorial, *Tōkyō nichi nichi shinbun*, 1877/1/20; and Andō Katsutaka, "Minkairon" (On popular assemblies), *Tōkyō nichi nichi shinbun*, 1877/2/17.

26. *Chōya shinbun*, 1879/7/24.

ment to make real headway. [27] Likewise, in November 1882, Hyōgo prefectural assemblymen Nakai Jōtarō and Kabe Seigorō led a meeting of 68 prefectural assemblymen from two cities and 24 prefectures. They agreed on nineteen items for a joint petition to be submitted to the central government; among the items were proposals that the prefectural assembly be granted the power to arbitrate jurisdictional conflicts among district and township/village assemblies; that the franchise be extended to those registered within a prefecture, without limitations based on property or taxation; that the prefectural assembly be allowed by law to initiate a wider range of local economic projects; and that a national federation of prefectures (*rengō fukenkai*) be legally recognized. [28]

The politicization of the prefectural assemblies and the accompanying critique of the forms of local government instituted by the Three New Laws received support in newspapers and journals sympathetic to the cause of the Popular Rights Movement. In particular, *Jiyū shinbun*, the organ of the Liberal Party (Jiyūtō), published trenchant criticisms of local government as it was practiced, arguing that prefectural assemblies should be seen as a step toward the establishment of a national assembly and a civic constitution. One editorial suggested that prefectural assemblies without a national assembly were like fields and paddies without the protection of riverbanks. They could not withstand the floodwaters of state power. If the government sincerely desired the "stability" of prefectural assemblies, it should accede to the demands of the Popular

----

27. "Chihō rengōkai sōritsu shuisho" (A prospectus for the foundation of the local alliance) (1880/2/20), in "Chihō rengōkai shiryō" (Papers on the local alliance) (1880), in Kenseishi hensankai shūshū monjo (Papers collected by the Editorial Committee for the History of Constitutional Politics), document collection in the Kensei shiryōshitsu, National Diet Library).

28. *Tōkyō Yokohama mainichi shinbun*, 1882/11/21; quoted in Kobayashi Takao, *Ōmori Shōichi to Yamagata Aritomo: jiyū minken taisaku to chihō jichi-kan no kenkyū* (Ōmori Shōichi and Yamagata Aritomo: a study of the countermeasures against the Popular Rights Movement and perspectives on local self-government) (Tokyo: Shuppan bunkasha, 1989), pp. 160–61. According to Kobayashi, this was not an isolated case; cf. reports in *Chōya shinbun*, 1882/11/4; and *Tōkyō nichi nichi shinbun*, 1882/11/25.

Rights activists, establish a national constitution according to their specifications, define the perimeters of administrative power, and determine the rules of conduct for prefectural assemblies, local administrations, and local judiciaries.[29] Another editorial pointed out that the responsibilities of local governors were so extensive and weighty that they could not be entrusted to the routine appointees of the central government. The government should consider, the author asserted, "abandoning the policy of centralization" and "adopting the policy of decentralization (*chihō bunken*)." Local governors, like "British *meyōru* [mayors] and American *gabanōru* [governors]," should be elected by the people.[30]

Even though the Popular Rights Movement led to the creation of Japan's first national political parties, the Liberal Party and the Constitutional Progressive Party (Rikken kaishintō), almost a decade before the establishment of the national assembly, the movement gradually declined, following the initiatives taken by the Meiji state in 1881. However, it briefly revived in the late 1880s, as activists began regrouping themselves in preparation for the convening of the first National Diet. Local activism in the late 1880s revolved around organizational networks of political parties rather than prefectural assemblies or political associations.

The Liberal Party, temporarily disbanded in 1884, drew support from numerous local branches, but it continued to reflect the ideas of the Kōchi faction, led by Itagaki Taisuke. Around 1887, former members of the Liberal Party started a national campaign of mass petitions calling for the withdrawal of Foreign Minister Inoue Kaoru's proposal for the revision of the unequal treaties, as well as land tax reduction and freedom of press and assembly. These three issues were often combined in the petitions.

Most of the petitions, however, while arguing that land tax reduction and the resulting rehabilitation of the agrarian economy were of utmost urgency, did not bother to tie this to a coherent critique of local government. Occasionally the petitions invoked

---

29. "Kokkai naki no kenkai" (Prefectural assemblies without a national assembly), *Jiyū shinbun*, 1882/11/1.

30. "Seifu wa yoroshiku chihō seiji ni chūmoku subeshi" (The government ought to pay attention to local government), *Jiyū shinbun*, 1882/9/7.

the rhetoric of "local autonomy." And yet, on close inspection, even these dealt largely with specifically local concerns such as disputes over the irrigation of rice paddies and the reduction of civic expenditures. For instance, a petition submitted by a census chief in Saitama prefecture in early 1888 espoused "reform of the local political system." The actual argument here turned out to be that nine local county offices be combined into five. This measure, the author asserted, would save approximately ¥10,200 in official expenditures. Ultimately, what the author was calling for was the enlargement of the jurisdiction of census chiefs like himself as a cost-saving measure and a more rational way to manage local affairs.[31] Indeed, among local leaders who were actively involved in party organizations, the main criticism of the city, township, and village system centered around the merger of small villages and townships into larger units. The grievances articulated to local governors by census chiefs and other representatives of local communities appear to be concerned almost exclusively with specific regional situations and not with theoretical or ideological critiques. The rhetoric of these leaders tended to focus on the need to protect traditional practices and inherited customs of the village communities, rather than on their rights to resist the arbitrary impositions of the state.[32]

In contrast, the Kōchi faction of the Liberal Party engaged the (perceived) defects of the city, township, and village system in a consistent, theoretical way. Ueki Emori (1857–92), perhaps the most important ideologue of the Liberal Party and a self-educated political theorist, provided a thorough critique of the system in an

---

31. "Jōchinsho" (kōso kōka no keigen, chihō seido no kaikaku, kochō yakuba kuiki no kakudai nado no gi) (A memorial to the government: regarding such items as the reduction of public taxation, reform of the local administration, and expansion of the jurisdiction of the census chief office) (1888/1/28), in *Meiji kenpakusho shūsei* (Collected Meiji-era petitions), ed. Obinata Sumio and Anzai Kunio (Tokyo: Chikuma shobō, 1999), 8: 764.

32. For a discussion of public complaints against the state-enforced merger of villages and townships in Saitama and Niigata prefectures, see Satō Masanori, "Meiji chihō jichi to 'mura'" (Meiji local autonomy and the "village"), in *Kindai Nihon no tōgō to teikō* (Integration and protest in modern Japan), ed. Kano Masanao and Yui Masaomi (Tokyo: Nihon Hyōronsha, 1982), 1: 215–46; and Ōshima Mitsuko, *Meiji kokka to chiiki shakai*, pp. 188–95, respectively.

1888 essay entitled "Shichōsonsei" (The city, township, and village system). Local autonomy per se did not attract Ueki's attention until he returned to his native prefecture of Kōchi in 1885. There he became directly involved in local government as a member of the Kōchi prefectural assembly and chief editor of the *Doyō shinbun*, a liberal newspaper still committed to the ideals of the Popular Rights Movement. "Shichōsonsei" was originally serialized in *Doyō shinbun* from May 2 to May 10, 1888.[33]

Ueki began his critique of the city, township, and village system by exploring the economic qualifications for voters and candidates for township and village assemblies and offices. Ueki saw the government's division of the local population into "public subjects" and "residents" as a flagrant violation of the principle of equality before the law. As he reminded readers, "A city, a town, or a village is not owned by a minority of well-to-do folks." Hence, decisions made in local governments should "always be determined by targeting the general population, that is, the majority of the people, as their constituents."[34] Ueki was particularly riled by the official explanation that one purpose of this policy was to prevent local government from being overrun by the economically impoverished numerical majority. He indignantly pointed out that in reality it was the impoverished majority who were deprived of a voice by the wealthy few. Second, the regulation stipulated that the position of town or census chief was only honorary, and yet anyone who resigned without a legitimate reason or without completing the term of three years was punishable by fine or by the loss of public rights. Why should this be the case, Ueki asked, when participation in local self-government was a *right* and not a duty? If assuming a responsible post in local government was defined as an obligation for the state, how was it different from, say, being conscripted into the army? Finally, Ueki raised the issue of why

---

33. For comprehensive biographies of Ueki, see Ienaga Saburō, *Ueki Emori kenkyū* (A study of Ueki Emori) (Tokyo: Iwanami shoten, 1960); and Yonehara Ken, *Ueki Emori* (Tokyo: Chūō kōron sha, 1992).

34. "Shichōsonsei" (Township and village administration) (1888), in *Ueki Emori shū* (Collected works of Ueki Emori), ed. Ienaga Saburō et al. (Tokyo: Iwanami shoten, 1990), 5: 236.

women were excluded from being "public subjects." Men and women should have equal rights of participation, and it was unconscionable that women could neither vote in local government elections nor be elected to a local office.[35]

We cannot help but notice that, in the arguments Ueki marshaled against the statist and elitist features of the city, township, and village system, he did not touch on the actual social life of local communities and its potential incompatibilities with the system. Instead, he deployed the language of equality before the law, of individual rights, and of the people's right to participate in political affairs. At the same time, it is true that Ueki's single-minded commitment to the notions of rights and equality enabled him to recognize the injustice in the lack of women's participation in local government, at a time when other male thinkers who held positions similar to his could not.

Fukuzawa Yukichi's Conception of Local Autonomy

Despite being a proponent of modernization, Fukuzawa Yukichi was highly critical of the Popular Rights Movement. This major intellectual of the Meiji period also developed a cohesive set of ideas about the theory and practice of local autonomy. In describing European city-states and municipal governments to Japanese readers in his earlier works, Fukuzawa emphasized the connection between the promotion of "local interests" and "class interests" on the one hand and the spirit of independence and freedom among European subjects on the other.[36]

---

35. Ibid., pp. 239–40. Ueki himself was from early on a staunch defender of equal rights for men and women, although he was not unique in leveling a feminist critique at the city, township, and village system. Similar criticisms were made by early feminist activists; see, e.g., Yamazaki Take, "Jichisei shikō ni tsuite kan ari" (Thoughts on the implementation of the local administration system) (1889/5/31, 6/1), in *Nihon josei undō shiryō shūsei*, vol. 1, *Shisō, seiji* (A collection of the documents on the Japanese women's movement: thought, politics), ed. Suzuki Yūko (Tokyo: Fuji shuppan, 1996), pp. 121–22. I thank Barbara Molony for alerting me to the feminist discourse on local government in Meiji Japan.

36. Fukuzawa Yukichi, "Bunmeiron no gairyaku" (An outline of the theory of civilization) (1875), in *Fukuzawa Yukichi zenshū* (The complete works of Fuku-

In a treatise published in 1877 entitled "Bunkenron" (On the division of power; written in 1876), Fukuzawa methodically analyzed the problem of local autonomy the modern Japanese nation faced in its early stages of self-development. One influential reading of "Bunkenron" considers Fukuzawa's argument for local self-government essentially instrumentalist. According to this view, Fukuzawa hoped to placate the local *shizoku* (ex-samurai) by employing them as local administrators and to co-opt their energy for the centralization of the state power.[37] Others highlight the progressive character of his argument and its potential challenge to the state.[38] However, the view that Fukuzawa advocated local self-government merely to subdue disgruntled local *shizoku* is reductionist. Neither can Fukuzawa's support for local autonomy in this essay be subsumed under his generally positive assessment of liberalism. A more balanced reading of the text, which considers both his polemical stance and his theoretical concerns, is needed.

Fukuzawa began the essay with a bold statement of what appears to be a version of the physical law of the conservation of energy. No force or object is completely obliterated in our universe, he wrote. Similarly, no force or object can spring forth out of nothing. All forces and all matter in the universe merely change form. Based on this universal premise, Fukuzawa argued that the mental and social energies of the *shizoku* would not dissipate; rather, they would find an outlet in another form, despite the fact

---

zawa Yukichi) (Tokyo: Iwanami shoten, 1959), 4: 155–56. The best and most comprehensive analysis of Fukuzawa's ideas on local autonomy is Ishikawa Hisao, *Nihonteki jichi no tankyū* (An investigation of Japanese-style local autonomy) (Nagoya: Nagoya daigaku shuppankai, 1995).

37. See, e.g., Tōyama Shigeki, *Fukuzawa Yukichi* (Tokyo: Tōkyō daigaku shuppankai, 1970); and Yamada Kōhei, "Meiji shonen no rikkenka to chihō bunken shisō" (The emergence of constitutional politics in the early Meiji years and the theory of the division of power into localities), *Nagoya daigaku hōsei ronshū* 1988: 121.

38. Iida Kanae, *Fukuzawa Yukichi* (Tokyo: Chūō kōron sha, 1984). Iida (p. 154) claims that Fukuzawa's argument in the treatise constituted "not only promotion of democracy but also criticism of absolutism" and was "seriously dangerous from the standpoint of the Meiji government." See also Miwa Kimitada, "Fukuzawa Yukichi's Essay on Division of Power," Institute of International Relations Research Paper, A-44 (Tokyo: Sophia University, 1983).

that the samurai had lost their status and economic privileges. Fukuzawa had little sympathy for the discontented *shizoku*'s opposition to the imperial government, which he regarded as the well-
spring of the civilizing reforms.[39] Fukuzawa unsparingly criticized
the violent, antigovernment activities of this group, including the
Satsuma Rebellion of 1877, led by the much-admired Saigō Taka-
mori. "The government has done the right thing since the Restoration," he wrote, "by annihilating the treasonous rebels."[40]

At the same time, Fukuzawa recognized that the Popular Rights
Movement, unlike the armed insurrections of the "treasonous"
samurai rebels, had the power to challenge the legitimacy of government policies by providing the disgruntled *shizoku* rhetorical
and theoretical justifications for their opposition. He pointed out
that most Popular Rights activists were local *shizoku* who had had
the good sense to renounce their old ways and commit themselves
to the progress of Japanese civilization. Yet they were united with
their reactionary counterparts in their dissatisfaction with the state.
Why had the Popular Rights activists come to harbor such resentment against the state? It is at this point that Fukuzawa called into
question the overextension of state power and the weakness of civil
society in Japan.

Fukuzawa confidently observed that the civilizing reforms implemented by the imperial government would successfully solidify
its hold over Japanese society in the coming years. However, a
state's dominance of society creates its own problems. The population of a strong and civilized nation should have cultivated their
public spirit and be independent from the state in their pursuit of
private interests and aspirations. An overly powerful state that
meddled in the private domain would sap the people's social energy (*kiryoku*) and spirit of autonomy. Unfortunately, according to

---

39. In "Bunkenron," Fukuzawa extended the meaning of the term *shizoku* to
include "medical doctors, scholars, or even townsmen and farmers who aspire toward expertise both martial and scholarly, and who are mindful of national affairs," even though he admitted that in his estimation 80–90 percent of this group
came from the samurai class (*Fukuzawa Yukichi zenshū*, 4: 264). Following Fukuzawa's qualification, the present chapter refrains from using the terms *shizoku* and
(ex-)samurai interchangeably.

40. Fukuzawa Yukichi, "Bunkenron," p. 254.

Fukuzawa, state intervention had left little room for contemporary Japanese, especially the *shizoku*, to engage freely in socioeconomic activities. Those who wished to succeed in commerce and industry, for instance, were likely to find themselves without capital, much of which had been monopolized by the state. Even if they were able to raise the capital they needed, the state had already seized the lead in most of the potentially lucrative enterprises. The same could be said of land development projects and the mining industry. In the area of education, it was difficult for private schools to obtain funding; even if they were to do so, they could not compete with public schools in terms of teachers' salaries. Similarly, books published by commercial firms could not compete with the cheaper publications issued or subsidized by the government. The founders of local assemblies, in the end, considered themselves lucky to obtain a post as a district chief and obediently followed the instructions of the local governor.[41] In order for a society to be productive and stable, Fukuzawa argued, it has to be free of state intervention. "Intervention into the private spheres of the people's lives," he wrote, "either to protect them or to prohibit or suppress them, ultimately results in harm rather than in good."[42] One of the harmful effects was their resentment of an overly powerful government, which in turn motivated them to engage in reckless political activism such as the Popular Rights Movement.

Fukuzawa, quoting Alexis de Tocqueville, distinguished the "administrative power" (*chiken*) and "political power" (*seiken*) of the government. He firmly rejected the view that the state's political power should be decentralized and a federalist system instituted in Japan. However, he cautioned that the state, for the reasons discussed above, should not impair the natural development of social forces by insisting on the expansion of its administrative powers. Even the national imposition of uniform standards was disadvanta-

---

41. Ibid., p. 257–59.

42. Ibid., pp. 270–71. Fukuzawa cited examples of industrial failures caused by excessive regulation and intervention by domain authorities from Ōkura Nagatsune's late Tokugawa classic *Kōeki kokusan kō* (Considerations on the improvement of national production), adding that Ōkura's view "corresponds well to Western economic theories" ("Bunkenron," p. 271).

geous. Customs differed from one region to another. Each village or town had to develop priorities commensurate with its own resources and capacity. The administration of local affairs, Fukuzawa concluded, should not and, in reality, could not be carried out directly by the central state:

Distributing the [political] power [of the central government] among local governors is tantamount to increasing the number of ministers in the government. It is as if, for one government, there were 30 to 50 ministers. This would not only result in a loss of balance within the government but also cause the deterioration of the spirit of the local population, for whom it would be hardly different from serving under domain lords. . . . Moreover, there are some who take a popularly elected assembly as the basis for local autonomy. However, it is one thing to establish an elected assembly in the capital of Japan and quite another to distribute power among localities. . . . The true contribution of a popularly elected assembly would be to prevent the central government from abusing its political power (*seiken*). This is why such an assembly does occupy an important position within the government. Those who promote the distribution of power should unfailingly distinguish between the two types of power [administrative and political] of the government, and argue for the devolution of administrative power to the localities.[43]

From Fukuzawa's standpoint of encouraging the growth and development of localities, the excessive authority of local governors resulted in a situation not unlike a despotic government's using its local offices to suffocate the population.

The duties of the local administration, in Fukuzawa's view, should include all efforts to promote the happiness and welfare of the local populace, such as policing and surveillance; construction of roads, bridges, and dikes; establishment of schools, temples, and public parks; supervision of hygiene; and management of local expenses. Delegating these tasks to the local *shizoku* would be one way of transforming their mental and social energies and channeling them in a productive direction. Let the local population, led by the *shizoku*, suggested Fukuzawa, actively administer their own lives, participate in national affairs, complement the activities of the state, and finally, for the first time in Japanese history, perceive them-

---

43. Fukuzawa Yukichi, "Bunkenron," pp. 266–67.

selves as members of the Japanese nation. "Public and private interests will then find their point of convergence."[44] For Fukuzawa, local autonomy was not merely an instrument for controlling the unruly masses but both an active strategy and a necessary condition for the development of an autonomous civil society. In "Bunkenron," Fukuzawa construed civil society not as being in opposition to the state but as complementing it. As he had consistently stated since his earliest works, for Japan to maintain its national independence, its people had to be independent.[45] To achieve this goal, there was no substitute for giving the people power over local administration and thus allowing them to participate in national affairs.[46]

Between 1878 and 1881, Fukuzawa authored a series of essays that closely followed and commented on current affairs.[47] He continued to criticize the Popular Rights Movement and distance himself from it, while still noting the ultimate desirability of establishing a national assembly in which the private interests of society and the public good pursued by the state could be reconciled through deliberation. However, with the expulsion of Ōkuma Shigenobu from the government in 1881 and the imperial government's declaration that the National Diet would be established in a decade, Fukuzawa increasingly turned his attention to analyses of potential problems within the national assembly. Although he was willing to defend Liberal Party activists against the authoritarianism of the central state in select cases such as the Fukushima Incident of 1882,[48] he came to see the Diet as a potential battleground among forces devoted to naked pursuit of power and expressed concern that the resulting struggles could overflow from the realm of politics into

---

44. Ibid., p. 278.

45. Fukuzawa Yukichi, *An Encouragement of Learning*, trans. David Dilworth and Umeyo Hirano (Tokyo: Sophia University Press, 1973), pp. 10–20.

46. Fukuzawa Yukichi, "Bunkenron," p. 290.

47. "Tsūzoku minken ron" (A common theory of popular rights) (1878) and "Tsūzoku kokken ron" (A common theory of state rights) (1878), in *Fukuzawa Yukichi zenshū*, vol. 4; "Minjō isshin" (Renewal of popular sentiments) (1879) and "Jiji shōgen" (Brief remarks on current affairs) (1881), in *Fukuzawa Yukichi zenshū*, vol. 5.

48. "Kokkai nankyoku no yurai" (The origins of the difficulties faced by the Diet) (1892/1/28–2/5), in *Fukuzawa Yukichi zenshū*, 6: 79–80.

other spheres of life. Fukuzawa correctly surmised that political parties organized as the result of the Popular Rights Movement, specifically the Liberal Party and Constitutional Progressive Party, would dominate the Diet.[49]

By the time the National Diet became a reality, Fukuzawa had re-evaluated the positive qualities of the traditional village and town communities. He emphasized local autonomy as a critical element that could provide the bedrock of stability against political struggles that would inevitably take place within the National Diet, and, if unchecked, would overflow into other areas of public life. In an essay entitled "Kokkai no zento" (The future of the National Diet; 1892) Fukuzawa argued that there had been a resilient tradition of local autonomy since the early modern period. Tokugawa society had suffered from great disparities in wealth and power among social classes, across regions, and between ruler and ruled, and these in turn had generated the *ressentiment* that ultimately toppled the system. And yet, ordinary Japanese, outside the realm of politics and administration, were able to conduct their lives peacefully. "The Tokugawa shogun and domain lords supposedly had despotic powers, and yet the samurai and commoners living under their rule hardly saw reason to complain about the benefits and harms of the policies implemented by these rulers."[50] Fukuzawa concluded that "Japanese people [in the pre-Meiji period], even though unable to exercise political power, had long practiced autonomy in the public affairs of local regions (*chihō kōkyō no jimu*) and successfully resisted intervention from the state."[51]

In another essay written shortly thereafter, Fukuzawa severely criticized the imperial government for its failure to allow local society to manage its own affairs and maintain its autonomy from the central state. When a high-ranking official from the central government visited a region, Fukuzawa pointed out, he was imme-

---

49. This section is much indebted to Professor Matsuzawa Hiroaki's analysis of Fukuzawa's political thought in this period; see, e.g., his *Nihon seiji shisō* (Japanese political thought) (Tokyo: Hōsō daigaku kyōiku shinkōkai, 1993), pp. 30–31, 41–45.

50. "Kokkai no zento" (The future of the National Diet) (1890/12/10–12/23), in *Fukuzawa Yukichi zenshū*, 6: 60–61.

51. Ibid., p. 65.

diately surrounded by sycophants and conspirators who sought to ingratiate themselves. Prefectural officials experienced the same treatment. These officials hardly ever came in contact with those who "live independently and steadily pursue their private enterprises," the people who, in Fukuzawa's view, constituted "the backbone of the Japanese nation."[52] Fukuzawa's main point in this essay, however, appears to be that the imperial government should stop opposing political parties with grandstanding gestures and authoritarian policies and work hand in hand with them. Fukuzawa suggested that the government and political parties had much to gain by sharing power in one form or another, perhaps in a "coalition cabinet"—a third possibility between the two extremes of the liberal parties' dominating the Diet and the imperial government's shutting them out of power altogether. Here, as in his earlier essays, Fukuzawa took the middle path between the imperial state and the opposition forces by envisioning local society as a bastion against both partisan political struggles and excessive control by the central state.

Inoue Kowashi's Conception of Local Autonomy

Inoue Kowashi devoted most of his adult life to designing, refining, and managing the ideological apparatus of the Meiji imperial state. His political position is at first glance diametrically opposed to that of Fukuzawa, in the sense that Inoue was a state ideologue whereas Fukuzawa doggedly remained a civilian intellectual all his life. Yet, surprisingly Inoue's and Fukuzawa's views of local autonomy overlap. Both thinkers consciously sought to rehabilitate the traditions of local autonomy that had existed in early modern Japan, in order to counteract both the Meiji state's excessive drive for centralization and what they viewed as the unfortunate politicization of local communities by the Popular Rights Movement.

Along with Nakae Chōmin, a major theorist of the Popular Rights camp, Inoue was among the first Japanese students sent to France, with the Iwakura Mission in 1872. Successively appointed as

---

52. "Kokkai nankyoku no yurai," pp. 85–86.

an official in the Justice Ministry, senior secretary in the State
Council (Dajōkan), and secretary of the Privy Council, Inoue had a
hand in drafting numerous key legal documents of the Meiji period
on such topics as the constitution, education, citizenship, treaty revision, and, of course, local self-government. On March 11, 1878,
Inoue, then a member of the Legislative Bureau of the State Council, and Matsuda Michiyuki, senior secretary in the Home Ministry,
drafted a proposal for a new system of local government. This proposal served as one of the key sources for the Three New Laws.

Underlying Inoue's draft proposal are the assumptions that state
and society, or officialdom (*kan*) and people (*min*), belonged to discrete spheres and that the distinction between them would become
more and more significant as "civilization" advanced. The proposal
acknowledged that the large and small district system imposed arti-
ficial divisions on traditional village and township communities,
and that this had led to general confusion about the responsibilities
of the state and society on such issues as public revenues and expenditures. It rejected the direct adoption of "Western" models as a solution to these problems and instead suggested that partial autonomy and deliberative power be granted to villages and townships.
The administrative system it envisioned was three-tiered, consisting
of prefectures and metropolitan areas, counties and cities, and villages and townships, with each level possessing some form of public
assembly. At the village and township level, administrative divisions
should reflect conditions dictated by an "autonomous society of
residents" (*jūmin dokuritsu shakai*), whereas at the prefectural level
the local government would have greater control over local society
and be given a larger bureaucracy. By carefully balancing the legislative power of the prefectural assemblies and the executive power of
the prefectural governors, the government "can eliminate the problems resulting from widespread support for Popular Rights theories
and the notion of a popularly elected assembly."[53] In other words,

---

53. "Chihō no taisei nado kaisei no gi mōshiage" (A memorandum on the revision of local governments and other items) (1878/3/11), in *Ōkubo Toshimichi monjo*
(Ōkubo Toshimichi papers), ed. Ōkubo Toshikazu et al. (Tokyo: Nihon shiseki
kyōkai, 1929), 10: 109.

Inoue and Matsuda recognized the need to grant a degree of local autonomy and political participation to the localities, partly to prevent them from embracing the Popular Rights Movement.

Throughout the 1870s and 1880s, Inoue continued to criticize the local government system, with the aim of improving the system's capacity to promote and develop local society and fend off the influence of the Popular Rights Movement. In a letter of opinion written in 1877, for instance, Inoue took issue with the inordinately heavy burden placed on the local populace by civic expenditures. He defined these as "local expenses to be spent for the interest of the people, dictated by the needs of the people, and directly paid by the people, the amount of which is determined through a process of public deliberation (*kōgi*)." Under the district system, he pointed out, the civic expenditures paid for what were essentially government projects, such as the construction of prefectural offices and prisons, public exhibition of government ordinances and decrees, and salaries of district chiefs. Inoue proposed that all these items as well as the costs of the land survey, conscription, and forest management be paid by the state treasury using national tax revenues.[54] This would, he reasoned, allow the central government to manage local finances more efficiently, while softening local discontent against what was perceived as unfair economic exploitation. However, in reality, in 1877 the imperial government was in no position to help the localities by subsidizing local projects, because of the expense of suppressing the Satsuma Rebellion. In fact, between 1878 and 1888, state subsidies in areas such as education and construction decreased. Most public outlays still had to be funded by the local populace.[55] Despite Inoue's efforts, following the promulgation of the Three New Laws, prefectural assemblies became increasingly politicized and the Popular Rights Movement even stronger.

In 1881, Inoue was appointed senior secretary of the State Council and devoted himself to the task of drafting what eventually

---

54. Inoue Kowashi, "Minpi ni kansuru iken" (An opinion on civic expenditures) (1877), in *Kindai Nihon chihō jichi rippō shiryō shūsei*, 1: 326–27.

55. Ōshima Mitsuko, *Meiji kokka to chiiki shakai*, pp. 109–10.

became the Imperial Constitution. However, although he believed that Japan should adopt the Prussian model for its constitution, an idea endorsed by Itō Hirobumi and other leaders of the imperial government following the expulsion of Ōkuma, Inoue was apparently not a wholesale proponent of the German theory of local self-government. Between the early 1870s and 1880s, he had developed a cluster of ideas and preferences, if not a coherent theory, about the proper boundaries of state and society and how to structure the framework of state control and surveillance without violating the integrity of society. His main concern was to allow society to be autonomous and flourish without letting it become "corrupted" by involvement in politics, yet keep it within reach of the state. This is discernible, for example, in his 1882 critique of the Regulations Concerning the Prefectural Assemblies. European examples indicated, according to Inoue, that the prefectural assembly was the primary engine for private industries in the localities, especially construction and land development firms. However, in Japan, prefectural assemblies did not have the power to deliberate on industrial policies and business matters; all they could do was to determine the budget for local expenses. Thus the state, Inoue pointed out, was not helping local society develop. Of course, he did not neglect to add strict injunctions against the prefectural assemblies becoming involved in national affairs and attempting to build coalitions across prefectural borders.[56]

Inoue's views on the goal and substance of local autonomy is perhaps best expressed in his "Chihō seiji kairyō iken an" (Draft proposal for the reformation of local governance; March 1886), based on observations in Nara prefecture. He prefaced the proposal with a positive appraisal of the imperial government's modernization efforts. In today's Japan, he claimed, there was hardly a small town without a park, a hospital, or a fairground. Neither was there a village without a primary school with white walls and blue

---

56. "Fukenkai chihōzei kaisei iken" (An opinion letter on the revision of prefectural assemblies and local taxes) (1882), in *Inoue Kowashi-den: shiryō-hen* (A biography of Inoue Kowashi: documents), ed. Inoue Kowashi denki hensan iinkai (Tokyo: Kokugakuin daigaku toshokan, 1966), 1: 323–30.

shingles. Not only had the state successfully extended the education system without relying on coercion in the past fifteen years, but it had also created a police force, stern against criminal elements yet devoted to aiding the needy. It was truly commendable, for instance, that some 45,000 residents had been rescued by the local police during the great Osaka flood of 1885. Still, many villages and towns that he had observed during his travels in Nara prefecture were suffering from the consequences of the deflationary policies instituted by the new finance minister, Matsukata Masayoshi. Some villagers were even starving to death. The state had once again placed the financial health of the nation before the well-being of the local population. Along with the revision of administrative regulations to reduce the tax burden and public expenses, he strongly urged that village representatives (*mura sōdai*) be given the authority to determine and implement all matters concerning self-government.[57] By "village representatives," Inoue meant the notables who had not been incorporated into local government bureaucracies as salaried officers. The use of the traditional term *sōdai* was a deliberate choice on the part of Inoue, who was a firm believer in the need to preserve as much as possible of the "natural" state of local society in Japan.

Inoue's criticism also turned to the management of local assemblies. Some prefectural assemblymen in Shiga, for instance, had voted to extend the length of their sessions so as to milk *per diem* and travel expenses out of the prefectural treasury, a scandal that had attracted the attention of a local newspaper. A consolidated village assembly he had attended at a Nara county office, he recalled bitterly, resembled a schoolchildren's game, meeting for two-and-half hours and then taking a ninety-minute lunch break! Compare this to a farmers' meeting held in a village, Inoue wrote. The farmers convened, still clad in their work clothes, and discussed their mutual concerns for six hours until seven o'clock. When the meeting adjourned, they expressed regret that, in order to avoid losing work time, they could meet only on rainy days. Now, Inoue asked,

---

57. "Chihō seiji kairyō iken an" (Draft proposal for the reformation of local governance) (1886), in *Inoue Kowashi-den: shiryō-hen*, 1: 474–75, 482–83.

which "assembly" truly represented the spirit of local self-government? The answer should be obvious to anyone who cared for the welfare of the local populace.[58]

Inoue's letter addressing the 1888 Yamagata bill on local government is often cited to justify the characterization of his views on local autonomy as "conservative" or "reactionary," since he attacked the bill for opening the gate to a "republic in disguise" in Japan, which would result in the "violation of the national body (*kokutai*) and the constitution."[59] In the context of the present chapter, however, what stands out as the real bone of contention is the relationship between the prefectural council (*fuken sanjikai*) and the prefectural governor envisioned in the Yamagata bill. Yamagata's revised County and Prefecture Law, made public in May 1890, allowed "propertied and knowledgeable" local notables, who were not "prone to arguing national politics based on fanciful theories (*kakūron*)," to participate in prefectural assemblies and councils and to take charge of local affairs. These "mature and reliable" (*rōsei chakujitsu*) notables would, Yamagata hoped, then be elected to the National Diet instead of the good-for-nothing, empty-theory-spouting Popular Rights activists.[60] Inoue argued that Yamagata's policy could be interpreted as subordinating the prefectural governor to the prefectural councils and assemblies. This could lead to acrimonious politicization of the prefectural government, as the Three New laws several years before had unwittingly done. For Inoue, "self-government" was appropriate only when it allowed the townships and villages to flourish and develop as basic units of local society. Empowering them beyond this level unintentionally helped the cause of Popular Rights activists. Despite his championing of local autonomy at the village and township levels, Inoue clearly opposed the politicization of local

---

58. Ibid., pp. 484–85.

59. Staubitz, "The Establishment of the System of Local Government," pp. 210–23.

60. "Shisei chōsonsei gunsei fukensei ni kansuru Genrōin kaigi enzetsu" (A speech given at a Senate conference regarding the city, township, and village system, county system, and prefectural system) (1888/11/20), in *Yamagata Aritomo ikensho*, p. 191.

communities, including what we today would recognize as "democratizing" steps.[61]

Like Fukuzawa, Inoue believed that practices and customs developed under the much-maligned "feudal system" of the Tokugawa period could be revived and rendered useful for modern Japan. He argued that prior to the Meiji Restoration village communities had already laid the foundations of modern local self-government. In many areas of Japan, he pointed out in an opinion letter, village headmen, often elected by ballot, had managed public lands and forests and punished those who violated the village rules, quite independently of the domain magistrates.[62] Inoue's ideal for a self-governing local community is illustrated by his somewhat embellished description of French municipal government, which he had observed in the early 1870s.

The mayor of a town is elected to office. He is commonly a mature and sincere individual and is loyal to the townspeople before he is loyal to the central government. The mayor's office uses a room in the town school. His secretary works in the school as a teacher. Boys and girls of the town attend the school diligently, learning writing and arithmetic. The townspeople look up to their mayor as children look up to their parent. . . . Does this not demonstrate what splendid government is all about, and from whence the fountain of civilization flows?[63]

Concluding Thoughts

This sketch of conceptions of local autonomy found in Japanese political discourse in the 1870s and 1880s reveals meaningful differences and surprising commonalties. A wide political spectrum of thinkers from Inoue Kowashi to Ueki Emori agreed that overcentralization of state power was undesirable. However, their proposed solutions for countering overcentralization diverged significantly. One important reason for this divergence was their

---

61. "Chihō jichi iken" (An opinion on local self-government) (1888/10), in *Inoue Kowashi-den: shiryō-hen*, 2: 28–31.

62. Ibid., p. 47.

63. "Kanri kaikaku iken an" (A draft opinion on reforming the bureaucracy) (1874/4), in *Inoue Kowashi-den: shiryō-hen*, 1: 17–18.

different conceptions of the state-society relationship or, to be more precise, different conceptions of *civil society*. This intellectual and discursive linkage between conceptions of local autonomy and conceptions of the state-society relationship was not a product of the peculiar "late modernizer" status of Meiji Japan. We find a similar situation illustrated in Sudhir Hazareesingh's study of the public debates on decentralization in France during the 1860s and 1870s. Hazareesingh shows, among other things, that left-wing Bonapartists, Legitimists, and Liberals leaning toward constitutional democracy came to see excessive centralization as one of the negative legacies of the French Revolution. These critics of centralization were concerned that the unchecked surveillance and control by the central state over local communities would result in the loss of civic responsibility, the deterioration of the *esprit de corps*, the dominance of the politically ambitious and ideologically unyielding over the truly meritorious section of the local populace, and, consequently, the decline of French society and culture as such. As Hippolyte Taine lamented, "A society is like a garden: it can be laid out to produce peaches and oranges, or else carrots and cabbages. Ours is entirely laid out for carrots and cabbages."[64] Analogous, if not exactly corresponding, critiques of the imperial government's centralization drive can be observed in the public discourse on local autonomy in Japan of the 1870s and 1880s.

Popular Rights discourse in the 1870s and 1880s, of which Ueki Emori was an important representative figure, looked on local autonomy as a right, commensurate with the duties of the Japanese people as members of a modern nation. Local autonomy was also seen as a necessary step in the democratization of Japan's political system; participation in local political institutions would facilitate participation in the prospective national assembly. Politicization of the prefectural assemblies was viewed as a desirable phenomenon, because it would allow the Japanese people to expand their political power and seize control of the political process leading to the establishment of a constitutional government and a national as-

---

64. Hippolyte Taine, *Carnets de voyage*; quoted in Sudhir Hazareesingh, *From Subject to Citizen: The Second Empire and the Emergence of Modern French Democracy* (Princeton: Princeton University Press, 1998), p. 171.

sembly. This view of local autonomy, broadly accepted in the Popular Rights discourse and strongly advocated in Ueki Emori's critique of contemporary local government, acknowledged the existence of a level of social life unencumbered by the state. However, society as understood in this discourse was so permeated by the language of politics that it may be appropriate to call it "political" rather than "civil" society. In this view, autonomous civic associations, including Popular Rights societies as well as local assemblies, functioned primarily as units for expressing political power and securing the rights of individuals. As Charles Taylor explains, for those who take such a perspective, civic associations are politically meaningful because they teach citizens "the taste and habit of self-rule," and in order for them to exist at all levels of the polity, government "should be decentralized, so that self-government can be practiced also at the local and not just the national level."[65]

In contrast, Fukuzawa Yukichi saw local society primarily as a space for independent socioeconomic activity, free from state intervention, that would counterbalance the political power of the state. The classical Anglo-American liberal conception of civil society, consisting of "the market" and independent, free citizens engaged in production, exchange, and consumption of goods in that market, best exemplifies this idea.[66] Inoue Kowashi also viewed civil society in this manner, as a place in which the local population could engage in rather extensive autonomous activity as long as it did not threaten the legal and political power of the state. Fukuzawa and Inoue, despite their different standings vis-à-vis the Meiji state—one being a tireless advocate of private entrepreneurship who never sought a government post, and the other a consummate legal bureaucrat and state ideologue *par excellence*—found substantial common ground in their conceptions of local autonomy. Although their conceptions of local autonomy tended to characterize the state as a potential partner or an ally of civil society rather than an opponent, they also firmly opposed the capitulation of society to state hegemony. Both emphasized the in-

---

65. Charles Taylor, "Invoking Civil Society," in idem, *Philosophical Arguments* (Cambridge, Mass.: Harvard University Press, 1995), pp. 222–23.

66. Ibid., pp. 215–16.

tegrity of the traditional (village and town) communities, praising
their contribution to public order and the successful implementation of modernizing reforms in local areas. And in their defense
of the freedom of local society, especially its socioeconomic
spheres, from government intervention, they sometimes went the
Popular Rights activists one better in the stringency of their
rhetoric and the rigor of their analyses.

Did Inoue's and Fukuzawa's conceptions of local autonomy provide the imperial government with the ideological tools to keep local society under its surveillance and control? We would have to
conclude that this hypothesis is too one-sided. Inoue's criticism of
the city, township, and village system, for instance, demonstrates
that he placed a higher priority on the protection of the integrity of
traditional local communities, and hence the civil society constituted of them, than on subversion of the Popular Rights Movement
and opposition parties. Local notables may have gained a new political awareness from the activities of the Popular Rights Movement, and the movement may have provided them with the incentives and means to organize and train themselves as political actors.
It seems evident, however, that the visions of local autonomy advanced by figures such as Inoue and Fukuzawa offered them other
strategies for preserving their leadership positions in local communities, especially in the areas of economic and social life, while allowing them to work with the state to use its resources for the benefit of their communities. The decline of the Popular Rights
Movement did not mean that local notables were abandoning independence. They could assert it in other ways. Further investigation
will determine whether these alternative conceptions of local
autonomy led in the long term to a form of capitulation to the state.

CHAPTER THREE

Tanaka Shōzō's Vision of an Alternative Constitutional Modernity for Japan

Timothy S. George

Tanaka Shōzō (1841–1913) is well known for his struggle on behalf of victims of pollution from the Ashio copper mine, not for his constitutional thought.[1] Most writing on Tanaka consequently focuses on him as a popular rights activist and the grandfather of grassroots environmentalism.[2] But Tanaka Shōzō was also an important thinker, one who envisioned an alternative constitutional modernity for Japan.

Tanaka never wrote a draft constitution or even a book or an essay on constitutionalism.[3] His constitutional ideas must be

---

1. I am grateful to Matsuzawa Hiroaki for introducing me to this topic and to Carol Gluck, Akira Iriye, Peter Nosco, and the editors of this volume for helpful comments.

2. In English, see Kenneth Strong, *Ox Against the Storm: A Biography of Tanaka Shōzō: Japan's Conservationist Pioneer* (Vancouver: University of British Columbia Press, 1977). There are a number of biographies of Tanaka in Japanese. Yui Masaomi, *Tanaka Shōzō* (Tokyo: Iwanami shoten, 1984) is concise and thoughtful. Komatsu Hiroshi, *Tanaka Shōzō no kindai* (Tanaka Shōzō's modernity) (Tokyo: Gendai kikakushitsu, 2001), includes useful listings of recent research on Tanaka.

3. Perhaps that is why Matsuzawa Hiroaki was until recently the only person who had written in any depth on Tanaka's constitutional thought; see his "Tanaka Shōzō no seiji shisō" (Tanaka Shōzō's political thought), in idem, *Nihon seiji*

pieced together from his speeches and writings (and for these we are fortunate to have his collected works, in 20 volumes) and from his life itself, because he expressed his views in actions as much as in words. In his thought and acts, especially after he was elected to the first Diet in 1890 and fought for the victims of pollution and flooding from the Ashio copper mine, he sketched a vision of a vigorous and democratic constitutional society in which the government, the emperor, and the constitution itself were subject to the "laws of heaven." Seen in this light, his later years—when he lived with villagers resisting forced relocation, surveyed the river systems of the Kantō area, and wrote mystically about the difficulties of entering heaven—were by no means a retreat from constitutional questions but an attempt to put his ideas into practice.

In this chapter I seek to represent Tanaka's vision through a consideration of (1) the "household constitution" he wrote for his family around 1874; (2) an editorial he wrote for the *Tochigi shinbun* in 1879 explaining the need for a parliament; (3) the interpretations of the constitution he expressed while serving in the Diet from 1890 to 1901;[4] (4) his 1901 attempt, after he resigned from the Diet, to petition the emperor on behalf of the Ashio victims; and (5) his 1904 move to Yanaka, a village slated to be destroyed by the government's Ashio-related flood control projects, and his investigations of Kantō area rivers until his death in 1913.[5]

These five key moments suggest two conclusions. First, the constitutional system Tanaka envisioned for Japan was designed to protect the vigor and independence of a constitutional civil society by requiring "harmonious cooperation" from *all* parties, including

---

shisō (Japanese political thought), rev. ed. (Tokyo: Hōsō daigaku kyōiku shinkō-kai, 1993), pp. 147–61. Komatsu, *Tanaka Shōzō no kindai*, may herald new interest in this topic; see esp. pp. 244–57 (on Tanaka's interpretation of the Meiji constitution), pp. 526–58 (on Tanaka's later rejection of the Meiji constitutional system and his visions of a broader system), and pp. 658–81 (on the significance in Japanese intellectual history of Tanaka's views of the state).

4. Matsuzawa Hiroaki identifies these Diet years as the first of two "peaks" in Tanaka's constitutional thought; see Matsuzawa, "Tanaka Shōzō no seiji shisō."

5. This last segment of his life includes the second creative "peak" in Tanaka's thought identified by Matsuzawa.

the government.[6] Second, Tanaka made this constitutional system seem less foreign by describing and justifying it in terms of traditional as much as modern vocabulary and values.

The "Tanaka Family Constitution"

Tanaka was from a relatively well-to-do farming family in the village of Konaka in Tochigi prefecture, north of Tokyo (see Fig. 3.1). He was tutored in the classics by a masterless samurai (*rōnin*) until the age of fourteen. Most of the rest of his education came from experience, reading, and traveling lecturers. Shōzō succeeded his father as village head (*nanushi*) at the age of seventeen. He was arrested in 1868 and imprisoned for nearly a year for protesting misgovernment by domain officials. In 1870 he took a job as a prefectural official in what is now Iwate. Later that year he was wrongly accused of murdering one of his superiors and imprisoned for over three years without ever being tried. During this prison stay, he began a new stage in his education, reading books such as Samuel Smiles's *Self-Help* and Rousseau's *Social Contract*.

This reading, at an early age (he was 32 years old when he left prison in 1874), is one reason I do not believe Tanaka's values derived solely from Japan's pre-Meiji, non-Western past, as some have suggested.[7] The question of the sources of Tanaka's ideas is

---

6. At the Association for Asian Studies panel in which I presented an earlier version of this chapter, Professor Mitani Hiroshi of the University of Tokyo raised important objections to the use of the term "civil society." He argued that a term so geographically and chronologically foreign to Meiji Japan implies too many similarities between the political thought of Meiji Japanese and present-day Westerners. I recognize the dangers of imposing our own mindset on the past. Although Tanaka certainly did not use the term "civil society," he *did* think in terms of a Hegelian distinction between state and society. However, one of my main arguments is that Tanaka's concept of state-society relations, while similar enough to justify the use of the term "civil society," *was* in fact different in important ways from the common understanding of civil society today. I therefore use the term "constitutional civil society."

7. Kenneth Strong writes that Tanaka's "lifelong campaign on behalf of the peasants against political oppression and industrial pollution is a striking demonstration of an active, defiant humanism that owed nothing to Western influences" ("Tanaka Shōzō," *Kōdansha Encyclopedia of Japan* [Tokyo: Kōdansha, 1983], 7: 338).

Fig. 3.1 Tanaka Shōzō (source: Ui Jun, *Nihon no mizu o kangaeru* [Tokyo: Nihon hōsō shuppan kyōkai, 1994], p. 35).

not a trivial one. If we argue that his thought derives only from the indigenous past, then we may imply that it was backward-looking; we risk painting him as a nativist or a Luddite; a crackpot, as his opponents described him, whose ideas were unsuited for Japan beyond the village or beyond early Meiji. It is important to understand that Tanaka's ideas were not premodern or antimodern. They were a compelling vision of an *alternative* modernity for Japan.

Reflecting the thinking he had done in prison, Tanaka wrote a four-point "family constitution" (*kasei no kenpō*):

Article. Debts shall be posted in the eating area and shall be kept in mind by all members of the family.

Article. Current possessions shall be used for the next three years, and the purchase of new items shall not be undertaken lightly.

Article. All members of the family shall rest on Sundays.

Article. Should new situations arise requiring the expenditure of money, this must be approved by a meeting of the entire family.[8]

He later explained that the last article meant "husband and wife may not violate each other's property and other rights."[9]

Obviously one of Tanaka's main goals in writing this "constitution" was to enforce frugality. While he was in prison, wrote Tanaka, "[I] read a life of Wellington, and his fear of debt deeply [impressed me]."[10] Upon his release, he attempted to pay off his debts by selling his possessions, but most of his creditors had simply forgiven the loans. Perhaps the family constitution was intended partly to keep expenses down so as to free up as much money as possible for the astute land speculation that soon secured Tanaka's financial future and provided some of the funds he used for his first election campaigns.

But two incidents shortly after he promulgated the constitution suggest another element of his thinking. His wife made him a coat and apron out of new cotton cloth without getting family approval; he later remarked: "This was a violation of Article 4 of the Tanaka family constitution, and I punished my wife by sending her back to her own family" for three days.[11] But on another day, he discovered the limits of constitutionalism when applied to the family. Tanaka "returned home to find that the *tatami* [floor mats] had been recovered. When I angrily demanded to know who had broken the law, I was told it was my father's doing. With this my stubbornness was temporarily overcome, as it seemed my father

---

8. For the "family constitution," see Tanaka Shōzō zenshū hensankai, ed., *Tanaka Shōzō zenshū* (Collected works of Tanaka Shōzō), 20 vols. (Tokyo: Iwanami shoten, 1977–80) (hereafter *TSZ*), 1: 88. This translation is my own; for a slightly different translation, see Strong, *Ox Against the Storm*, p. 31.

9. *TSZ* 1: 304.

10. *TSZ* 1: 87.

11. *TSZ* 1: 88.

was sacred and unpunishable. I had to hold my tongue and give up, and the constitution was suspended."[12]

The expression "my father was sacred and unpunishable" (*chichi wa shinsei ni shite batsu subekarazu*) that Tanaka used in this recounting of the incident in his 1895 autobiography is an intentional play on Article 3 of the Meiji Constitution, which reads: "The emperor is sacred and inviolable" (*tennō wa shinsei ni shite okasubekarazu*).[13] Tanaka meant that just as the family constitution was meaningless if his father could choose to ignore it, the nation's constitution could not be viable if the emperor was outside and above all law. What he had tried to do for his family, and what he came to desire for Japan, was to replace patriarchy with a system allowing for what one might call, without stretching the term too far, a form of civil society. This did not mean eliminating hierarchy, if that notion meant special respect and even privileges for the father or emperor, but it did mean there had to be rules that even they must obey and that would keep them from becoming so strong as to make a functioning civil society impossible.

In this way, Tanaka's family constitution led him far beyond the "household laws" of warrior families in pre-Meiji Japan, which, like Tanaka's rules, stressed frugality but would never have undermined the family head's authority by requiring major decisions to be made by meetings of the entire family. But at the same time, Tanaka's 1895 recounting shows the contradictions in his thought regarding the emperor, and therefore the limits of his constitutionalism. He could not bring himself to *require* the emperor to be subject to the constitution; Tanaka's system depended on the emperor's *voluntarily* choosing to be part of rather than above the system.

---

12. *TSZ* 1: 88–89. The story is from Tanaka's autobiography, *Tanaka Shōzō mukashibanashi* (Tanaka Shōzō's reminiscences), serialized in the *Yomiuri shinbun* from Sept. 1 to Nov. 24, 1895. Rather than writing it himself, Tanaka apparently dictated his story to a reporter. See Hayashi Shigeru, "Kaidai" (Explanatory notes), *TSZ* 1: 557, 560.

13. Strong's translation has Tanaka recalling: "'Father' was sacrosanct. I couldn't punish *him*!" and therefore misses this point (see Strong, *Ox Against the Storm*, p. 32). But Tanaka was obviously recalling and interpreting these events of 20 years earlier in the context of his interpretation of the Meiji Constitution while serving in the Diet in the 1890s.

The People as Masters, the Government as Clerks

Apart from writing the family constitution, Tanaka's life from the late 1870s until 1891 was not unusual for a village notable involved in the Popular Rights Movement. He moved from the family and village to the regional stage with his election to the local assembly in 1878. Tanaka petitioned for more powers for local government and helped found the *Tochigi shinbun*, one of Japan's earliest regional newspapers and a consistent advocate of popular rights. He served as editor until February 1880, and in a two-part editorial published on September 1 and September 15, 1879, entitled "Establishing a National Assembly Is an Urgent Necessity," he explained his views on the participation of the people in the national government.[14] (This was five years after the Risshisha [Self-Help Society], the political society founded by Itagaki Taisuke in Tosa, submitted a memorial demanding a parliament and two months before a national convention of the Aikokusha [Patriotic Society], the national political organization suggested by the Risshisha, issued a call for a petition campaign for a parliament.) Tanaka's editorial likened the government leaders, who, he said, argued that the "ignorant, lethargic" people were not ready for the franchise, with "the head clerks (*bantō*) of a wealthy merchant who, on the pretext that 'our master is a child,' refuse to let him take part in operating the business." In Tanaka's metaphor, then, the people were the owners of the nation, and therefore they were the masters of the government officials, who were their employees.

Tanaka's work with the newspaper, and the ¥3,000 he had earned through land speculation, helped him win election to the Tochigi prefectural assembly in 1880. He also continued to be active both above and below the prefectural level. In August 1880 he helped found a local political organization, the Aso ketsugōkai (Aso United Association, soon renamed the Chūsetsusha [Loyalty Society), which called for a national constitution to "support the right to liberty."[15] Both the Aso ketsugōkai and the Chūsetsusha drew up "covenants" (*seiyaku* or *kiyaku*) organized into sections

---

14. *TSZ* 1: 339–43; Yui, *Tanaka Shōzō*, pp. 47–50.
15. "Aso ketsugōkai nisshi" (Aso ketsugōkai diary), Aug. 13, 1880, *TSZ* 1: 354.

and articles like constitutions.[16] In November 1880, representing the Chūsetsusha, Tanaka attended the convention of the Kokkai kisei dōmei (League for the Establishment of a Parliament) in Tokyo and was one of the delegates who delivered petitions from throughout the nation to the Genrōin (a high-level government advisory body from 1875 to 1890). He also participated in the group preparing for the founding of the Jiyūtō (Liberal Party). But he was never comfortable with either the Jiyūtō or the Kaishintō (Progressive Party), which was founded in 1881 and which he eventually joined, because he had hoped instead for a single broad alliance of people from all classes, regions, and factions favoring a constitution that would guarantee popular rights. Back in Tochigi, Tanaka read all he could on European constitutional thought and worked with the Chūsetsusha to sponsor political debates and visiting lecturers.

But it was Tanaka's stubborn fight against the equally bullheaded Mishima Michitsune, appointed governor of Tochigi in 1883, that brought him the most attention in the 1880s. Mishima, who was nicknamed the "public works governor," seemed to want to develop the prefectures north of Tokyo overnight through forced labor and heavy taxation. He had already been the focus of controversy as governor of Fukushima.[17] Tanaka played a leading role in opposing him and in getting him removed by the Home Ministry in 1885. Soon after this, Tanaka persuaded Itō Hirobumi (who served from 1885 to 1888 as Japan's first prime minister) to grant more budgetary powers to the prefectural assemblies and was elected speaker of the Tochigi assembly.

The Diet Years: "Harmonious Cooperation"

As the assembly speaker, Tanaka was invited to the promulgation ceremony for the Meiji Constitution in 1889. He welcomed the constitution wholeheartedly and was grateful to the emperor for

---

16. *TSZ* 1: 382–85, 411–12.

17. For more on Mishima, especially as governor of Fukushima, see Roger W. Bowen, *Rebellion and Democracy in Meiji Japan: A Study of Commoners in the Popular Rights Movement* (Berkeley: University of California Press, 1980).

giving it to the people. But he had decidedly mixed feelings about those who were governing and had written the constitution in the emperor's name. To begin with, he and other prefectural assembly speakers protested to Yamagata Aritomo (home minister from 1885 to 1888 and 1889 to 1890, and prime minister from 1889 to 1891) their status at the ceremony. Tanaka felt strongly that they ought to *participate* as representatives of the people, rather than merely being "permitted to observe." He was mollified when the Home Ministry agreed to list the prefectural assembly speakers as being among "those in attendance." He was concerned, however, about the dislike of party cabinets expressed in a speech on February 15 by Itō Hirobumi, who had been in charge of drafting the constitution. That same night Tanaka wrote in a letter to Ōkuma Shigenobu (founder of the Kaishintō, foreign minister from 1888 to 1889, and a privy councilor from 1889 to 1891): "The majority of the audience seemed to agree [with Itō]. I shall not say here whether this [view] is right or wrong."[18] The point for Tanaka was not that parties should compete and the victor should control the government; as noted earlier, he was never an avid party member. His concern was that representatives of the people, not self-selected oligarchs, should govern.

However, in his decade as a Diet member—he was elected to the first Diet in 1890 and resigned in 1901—Tanaka made his own views loud and clear (see Fig. 3.2). Two of the major disputes in early Diet sessions concerned no-confidence votes and budgetary powers.[19] The premise behind Tanaka's interpretation of these issues, and of the constitution in general, was the idea that no constitutional system could work without what he called "harmonious cooperation" (*wachū kyōdō*). The term was taken from an imperial rescript the Itō cabinet requested in 1893, a rescript intended to break the stalemate caused by the House of Representatives' vociferous opposition to the government. But Tanaka's definition and application of the term were very much his own. "The people of a

---

18. Tanaka to Ōkuma Shigenobu, Feb. 15, 1889, *TSZ* 14: 151.

19. On his activities in this period, see Matsuzawa, "Tanaka Shōzō no seiji shisō," pp. 154–56; see also Yui, *Tanaka Shōzō*, pp. 105–7.

Fig. 3.2 Tanaka Shōzō exposing corruption, editorial
cartoon by Nakamura Fusetsu, from the newspaper
Shō Nihon, May 26, 1894 (source: Matsuzawa Hiroaki,
"Tanaka Shōzō no seiji shisō," in idem, *Nihon seiji
shisō*, rev. ed. [Tokyo: Hōsō daigaku kyōiku shinkōkai, 1993], p. 150).

constitutional nation must act with harmonious cooperation," he
told a Tokyo audience in November 1893. "The harmonious cooperation of human beings is like that which occurs in the cosmos. . . .
In the cosmos, in the universe, there is a constitution in the natural
order. . . . Human beings, too, have a constitution in them at
birth."[20] This idea of an inborn constitution is reminiscent of the
Mencian idea (and Tanaka had memorized the *Mencius* as a boy) that
all people are endowed with an innate capacity for goodness.

None of this would seem at first glance to differ from the conservative interpretations of "harmonious cooperation" intended by
the Itō cabinet. But Tanaka's application of this concept to the
constitutional questions of the day shows that his definition was
diametrically opposed to theirs. To them, "harmonious cooperation" required the parties to follow the government, since it spoke

---

20. "Wakyō no taii: Kanda Kikikan ni okeru enzetsu hikki" (Harmonious cooperation: notes from a speech at the Kanda Kikikan), Nov. 5, 1893, *TSZ* 2: 100–101.

for the emperor. But because for Tanaka the people, or their representatives, were masters of the government, "harmonious cooperation" meant that the government must accept the will of the Diet.

Because the "constitution of the universe," the natural law behind the Meiji Constitution, demanded such "harmonious cooperation" from the government, Tanaka's position in the debates over Article 55, which concerned ministers' responsibilities, was that cabinet ministers must be responsible not to the emperor alone but also to the Diet and through it to the people. Therefore the Cabinet, he believed, had to resign if the Diet passed a motion of no confidence. He applied the same logic to Article 64, which said that "expenditure and revenue . . . require the consent of the Imperial Diet," and Article 67, which said that legally necessary expenditures "shall be neither rejected nor reduced by the Imperial Diet, without the concurrence of the Government." Interpreting these articles in the light of the duty of "harmonious cooperation," Tanaka turned them on their head: whether the government agreed or disagreed with the budget passed by the Diet was irrelevant; if the Diet wished to spend more or less than the government considered necessary, the government was obligated to accept it. The laws of nature, he argued—the laws to which the constitution must conform and according to which it must be interpreted—required it. Tanaka's cosmic constitution, then, required the government and emperor to do more than cooperate. They had to give in; to agree to what the people's representatives in the Diet decided.[21]

Tanaka therefore envisioned a British-style system (but one with a written constitution) in which parliament was dominant. He made this clear and explained his interpretation in more conventional vocabulary in notes in his diary in 1894, in a passage he titled "The Difference Between Constitutional and Unconstitutional":

Of course it can be said that "constitutional" means in accord with the provisions of the Imperial Constitution, and "unconstitutional" means the opposite; this is the meaning in a narrow sense. "Constitutional" in its broader sense may be said to mean in accord with the entire spirit of the constitution, regardless of what is or is not stipulated in the constitution, and "unconstitutional" means the opposite. . . . [Tanaka then explains

---

21. For Tanaka's views on these issues, see "Wakyō no taii."

that the words used in English are "constitutional" and "unconstitutional"; he writes them in *katakana*.] In countries with unwritten constitutions such as England, unconstitutional actions are always [determined according to] this broader meaning. In countries with written constitutions, both the narrow and broad definitions are used.[22]

There is absolutely no question that Tanaka, through his reading and his attendance at lectures sponsored by Popular Rights groups, was well aware of Western constitutional concepts and vocabulary. But when he was writing and speaking for others, he translated these concepts into terms less foreign to a broad Japanese audience.

Tanaka's cosmic constitution—or natural law—required the co-operation of *all* parties, including the government and even the emperor. In contrast to later in his life, during this period of his thinking about the constitution, Tanaka was still optimistic that the government would come to understand and abide by this responsibility. In his 1893 speech, he said that until 1890 the government had been "an absolutist government, an oppressive government"; now it was "no more than a third-grade elementary-school student" when it came to "acting constitutionally," something in which it still "lacked experience." Reversing the oligarchs' criticism of the people and parties as not yet ready for political power and responsibility, Tanaka said that the "popular parties have over ten years [of experience] and have graduated and gone on to college." It was the *government* that was only "a new-born child." We must "treat it as we would a young child, and the government must diligently train itself in constitutional behavior."[23]

He explained that the "spirit of the constitution" referred not to the intentions of its drafters but to the "constitution of the universe," which was a higher law. But for Tanaka, the constitution of the universe—he uses the terms *uchū* (cosmos, universe), *tenchikan* (heaven and earth, universe), and *tennen shizen* (nature)—was by no means an abstract concept. Nature and its laws were very real. His autobiography begins with the words: "I am a farmer from Shimotsuke" (a former province, now part of Tochigi prefecture).[24] All

---

22. April 28, 1894, *TSZ* 9: 388–89.
23. "Wakyō no taii," p. 108.
24. *TSZ* 1: 3.

his life, he identified most strongly with the village community and the farming lifestyle, and this was the primary source of his metaphors. This identification was strengthened, not weakened, during his years in the Diet, because the focus of his political life from 1891 on was the ecological and social destruction of his district and surrounding areas by the Ashio copper mine in what F. G. Notehelfer calls "Japan's first pollution incident."[25]

The Ashio mine was bought in 1877 by the entrepreneur Furukawa Ichibei (see Fig. 3.3). It had been mined since the seventeenth century, but by late Tokugawa times little more could be extracted using old-fashioned methods. Furukawa expanded and modernized rapidly, with financial support from Shibusawa Eiichi (the leading entrepreneur of the Meiji period), and new lodes were discovered. Output had increased to 164 times the 1877 level by 1891, when Ashio accounted for 40 percent of Japan's copper production.[26] The acidic runoff killed the Watarase and Tone rivers. Virtually all life disappeared from the rivers, and thousands of fishers were put out of work. The floods that had formerly nourished the soil now poisoned it and sickened and impoverished those who worked the fields. These floods were made more frequent and more severe by the deforestation of the mountains, due to air pollution from the mining and smelting equipment and to the cutting of trees for construction and fuel. By 1893, 12,698 hectares of once forested area in the mountains surrounding the mine were without trees, 1,097 hectares had no vegetation at all, and 298 hectares were bare rock from which all topsoil had disappeared. Tanaka reported to the Diet that twelve villages affected by the poisoning averaged 2.80 births and 4.12 deaths per 100 persons in 1898, as compared to national

---

25. F. G. Notehelfer, "Japan's First Pollution Incident," *Journal of Japanese Studies* 1, no. 2 (Spring 1975): 351–83.

26. Shōji Kichirō and Sugai Masurō, "Ashio dōzan kōdoku jiken: kōgai no genten" (The Ashio mine copper pollution incident), in *Gijutsu to sangyō kōgai* (Technology and industrial pollution) ed. Ui Jun (Tokyo: Kokusai Rengō Daigaku, 1985), pp. 17–24; for an English translation of this article, see "The Ashio Copper Mine Pollution Case: The Origins of Environmental Destruction," in *Industrial Pollution in Japan*, ed. Ui Jun (Tokyo: United Nations University Press, 1992), pp. 18–63.

Fig. 3.3 The Ashio copper mine complex (source: Amamiya Yoshihito, *Tanaka Shōzō no hito to shōgai* [Tokyo: Meikeidō], 1971, n.p.).

averages for 1896 of 3.21 births and 2.60 deaths.[27] The responses by victims, government, and the mining company deserve a book-length study for the light they shed on the late Meiji political economy. But the focus here is on how they helped shape Tanaka Shōzō's thought.

Tanaka first raised the Ashio issue in the Diet when he questioned the government in December 1891 about its policies toward the mine and its victims in his home district.[28] Here again he offered his own interpretation of the Meiji Constitution. This time he focused on Article 27: "The right of property of every Japanese shall remain inviolate. Measures necessary to be taken for the public benefit shall be provided for by law." Rather than allowing the government to *take* property by eminent domain, Tanaka saw this article as requiring the government to *protect* the property of its people from destruction by the corporation. He demanded that the government, under both Article 27 and the Mining Law, revoke

27. Ibid., p. 29. The twelve villages had a total population of 6,182 in 1898.
28. *TSZ* 7: 41–42.

Fig. 3.4 Tanaka Shōzō in the Diet, holding a poisoned plant (source: Kenneth Strong, *Ox Against the Storm: A Biography of Tanaka Shōzō: Japan's Conservationist Pioneer* [Vancouver: University of British Columbia Press, 1977], p. 40).

Furukawa's mining concession. He also insisted that it must provide relief for the victims and ensure that the pollution was halted. After much delay, the government finally replied. It said the damage was not sufficiently severe to revoke Furukawa's concession. Nor would it provide relief; this was a matter for the prefecture. Finally, it was satisfied that new equipment to be installed by Furukawa would end the problems. [29]

Tanaka raised the Ashio issue again and again throughout the rest of his Diet career but never received a satisfactory government reply (see Fig. 3.4). His optimism that the government would eventually learn to "behave constitutionally" soon faded. He finally gave up on parliamentary politics as the solution to the problem and resigned from the Diet in October 1901. One of his last exchanges with the government shows why. On February 17, 1900, four days after the Kawamata Incident (a violent confrontation between 3,000 people marching toward Tokyo to protest the

29. *TSZ* 7: 500.

pollution and the 400 policemen who stopped them), Tanaka addressed a question to Prime Minister Yamagata Aritomo: "To kill the people is to kill the nation. To treat the law with contempt is to treat the nation with contempt. This means the destruction of the nation. No country can survive the arbitrary destruction of property, the killing of the people, and the violation of the laws. What [will the government do] about this?" Yamagata's written response: "Since the question is impertinent, no reply will be made."[30]

Petitioning the Emperor: Using the Modern Public Sphere to Demand Confucian Benevolence

As Tanaka lost hope in the Diet, he increasingly turned his focus elsewhere. He had already been active for several years in organizing and advising victims in their protests and their demands for compensation and an end to the pollution.[31] He continued to gather support in the public sphere for Ashio victims from women's groups, from university students (including Kawakami Hajime, the future Marxist economist), from the *Yomiuri* and *Yorozu chōhō* newspapers, and from figures such as the Christian Uchimura Kanzō, the socialist and labor organizer Katayama Sen, and journalists Miyake Setsurei and Tokutomi Sohō.

Having given up on parliamentary politics, Tanaka made a dramatic attempt to present a petition regarding the Ashio pollution directly to the emperor on December 10, 1901.[32] The text had been written the night before by the socialist journalist Kōtoku Shūsui, whose formal prose Tanaka trusted to be less likely than his own to offend the emperor.[33] Tanaka intended to present the petition

---

30. *TSZ* 8: 257–58, 461. For slightly different translations, see Strong, *Ox Against the Storm*, pp. 119, 121.

31. Interestingly, although the antipollution citizens' groups of the late 1960s and early 1970s often considered themselves to be following in the footsteps of the Ashio protesters, none of these more recent groups had as an advocate a politician as well known and stubborn as Tanaka Shōzō.

32. For the petition, see *TSZ* 3: 5–7.

33. Kōtoku later became an anarchist and was executed in 1911 for his part in the 1910 "high treason incident," a plot to assassinate the emperor; see F. G. Note-

to the emperor as he left the Diet, where he was announcing the opening of a new session. While waiting, Tanaka carefully corrected the text in several places, crossing out Kōtoku's characters, adding his own changes, and stamping the corrections with his seal. The petition explained the suffering of "Your Majesty's subjects" and begged for the emperor's "benevolence." As the emperor's carriage passed, Tanaka ran from the crowd with his petition but stumbled and fell while trying to avoid a mounted policeman, who also fell. He was immediately taken into custody and questioned for an entire night (see Fig. 3.5). He had expected to be sentenced to death but was instead released without charge. Although it was widely reported that he had been freed on grounds of insanity, no official explanation was given.

Why did Tanaka take such a rash step? His action is most often compared to that of Sakura Sōgorō, the seventeenth-century village headman said to have appealed directly to the shogun on behalf of his district for relief from oppressive taxation by the local daimyo. The relief was granted, but Sakura and his family were executed, an act that ensured his status as *gimin*, or martyr. Sakura had virtually been apotheosized, and his name had been invoked by farmers rebelling in Chichibu in 1884.[34] Tanaka does fit the Sakura Sōgorō mold in several ways. He identified with and acted on behalf of the villagers of his home area, and he had in fact been a village headman. He first appealed to the government leaders and then went over their heads in his petition to the emperor, just as Sakura had petitioned his daimyo before appealing to the shogun. Most important, Tanaka, like the Tokugawa peasant rebels and petitioners described by Irwin Scheiner, believed that the rulers were

---

helfer, *Kōtoku Shūsui: Portrait of a Japanese Radical* (Cambridge, Eng.: Cambridge University Press, 1971).

34. See Herbert P. Bix, *Peasant Protest in Japan, 1590–1884* (New Haven: Yale University Press, 1986), pp. xxxiii, xxxv; and several works by Anne Walthall: "Japanese *Gimin*: Peasant Martyrs in Popular Memory," *American Historical Review* 91, no. 5 (1986): 1076–102; *Peasant Uprisings in Japan: A Critical Anthology of Peasant Histories* (Chicago: University of Chicago Press, 1991); and *Social Protest and Popular Culture in Eighteenth-Century Japan* (Tucson: University of Arizona Press, 1986), esp. chap. 8, "Tales of Protest."

Fig. 3.5 Tanaka Shōzō attempts to petition the Meiji emperor, December 10, 1901 (source: Yui Masaomi, *Tanaka Shōzō* [Tokyo: Iwanami, 1984], p. 131).

required by a "covenant" to be "benevolent" (*jin*).[35] But although Tanaka used the same Confucian term in his petition, for him benevolence—though it might have the same results—was dictated by a different covenant, a modern constitution and the natural law, or "constitution of the universe," that governed it. Behind Tanaka's petition was his belief that, while "harmonious cooperation" from the government was unlikely, the emperor might extend such cooperation if he knew the extent of the people's suffering.

Another reason for the petition was more modern: if Tanaka could not change government policy from the floor of the Diet, he hoped to do so from the outside, from the public sphere. As Kyu Hyun Kim has demonstrated, Japan had had a functioning public sphere for two decades by the time of Tanaka's petition, thanks to the Popular Rights Movement and the creation of modern newspa-

---

35. Irwin Scheiner, "Benevolent Lords and Honorable Peasants: Rebellion and Peasant Consciousness in Tokugawa Japan," in *Japanese Thought in the Tokugawa Period, 1600–1868*, ed. Tetsuo Najita and Irwin Scheiner (Chicago: University of Chicago Press, 1978), pp. 39–62.

pers, political discussion groups, and political parties.[36] Tanaka had been a part of all of these. Newspapers had played an important role in bringing Ashio to national attention even before Tanaka's petition. Foremost among these was the *Yokohama mainichi*, edited by Shimada Saburō, which carried a number of reports by Kinoshita Naoe after the Kawamata Incident in February 1900. Special editions of newspapers appeared in Tokyo to report Tanaka's petition attempt within hours of his arrest, and newspapers throughout the country reported the story by the next day. The government's decision to release Tanaka served to focus much of the resulting media discussion on the question of Tanaka's sanity, but the publicity nevertheless put the Ashio problem in the forefront of the news. From November 1901 through March of the following year, some seventy lecture meetings were held in support of the pollution victims.[37] Women's, students', Christian, and Buddhist groups stepped up their activities. At least part of this increased tempo was due to Tanaka. As he did in interpreting the constitution, Tanaka in his attempt to petition the emperor used traditional forms, but with a meaning and purpose that mixed tradition and modernity in a tense combination that illustrated the limits of a Mencian democracy. In desperation, he turned to the emperor but simultaneously appealed through the public sphere to a constitutional civil society.

The intensified, nationwide attention in the wake of Tanaka's petition attempt did force the government to take action. In March 1902 it created (for the second time) a Mine Pollution Investigation Committee to study the Ashio problem. Tanaka probably expected little to come of this, and with good reason. But in fact the

---

36. Kyu Hyun Kim, "The State, Civil Society, and Public Discourse in Early Meiji Japan: Parliamentarianism in Ascendancy, 1868–1884" (Ph.D. thesis, Harvard University, 1996). See also James L. Huffman, *Creating a Public: People and Press in Meiji Japan* (Honolulu: University of Hawai'i Press, 1997).

37. Yui, *Tanaka Shōzō*, p. 172. Fukawa Satoru (*Tanaka Shōzō to tennō jikiso jiken* [Tanaka Shōzō and the imperial petition incident] [Utsunomiya: Zuisōsha, 2001]) makes a convincing case for understanding Tanaka's petition attempt as more than an individual act. It was, he says, a group effort dependent on concentric circles of supporters including Kōtoku Shūsui and the journalists Kinoshita Naoe, Kuga Katsunan, and Ishikawa Hanzan, a network that mobilized rapidly to publicize the petition attempt after Tanaka's arrest.

committee's recommendations helped push him into a new phase of his life and constitutional thought.

Back to the Village: Building a Constitutional Society from the Bottom Up

In January 1903, the government's Mine Pollution Investigation Committee issued its recommendations. It saw the problem as one of flood control rather than pollution control. Rather than remove the source of the pollutants, its plan was designed to keep them out of the fields. But unlike earlier plans, which had required Furukawa to build containment facilities at the Ashio complex, the new plan called for a giant catchment basin 80 kilometers downriver from Ashio that would replace the village of Yanaka with a lake. In addition to turning attention away from the company, this effective divide-and-conquer strategy enticed other villages to leave the movement and focused the power of the government on one village.

In the summer of 1904, Tanaka moved to Yanaka in an attempt to help hold this village that was now the geographical and political center of the Ashio struggle. Yanaka had an even broader symbolism for Tanaka. In his last years, after fighting for Yanaka, his faith in Japan's rulers and in the parliament and constitution they had created waned. Their views and actions had never matured in the ways he had hoped. They had not learned "constitutional behavior." They had not come to put the interests of the common people, their villages, and agriculture ahead of industry and the military. Their destruction of a village could not *save* the nation; it would *destroy* the nation. Conversely, saving the *village* became for Tanaka the only way to save the *nation*.

Yanaka remained Tanaka's home base until his death nine years later. For the rest of his life, he had almost no possessions and moved frequently from the home of one village family to another. Like the village head he had once been, he was defending the villagers against harsh rulers. But now he was arguing that the constitution entitled them to their living and to their property; that the constitution must be defended, and the government made to respect it. In 1904 he still hoped this could happen, but his experiences over the next few years shook this faith.

Fig. 3.6 Villagers and shack in Yanaka village after 1907 demolition of buildings (source: Amamiya Yoshihito, *Tanaka Shōzō no hito to shōgai* [Tokyo: Meikeidō, 1971], n.p.).

Government officials informed the villagers that their land was to be taken by eminent domain and that they would be compensated and resettled. Tanaka urged them to stay. He visited the governor of Tochigi to plead their case but was rebuffed in several attempts to see government officials in Tokyo. (Hara Takashi, the new home minister, had been a vice president of Furukawa since its reorganization in 1905, two years after Furukawa Ichibei's death.) Gradually, more and more families in the relatively poor village gave in and moved out. Their homes were destroyed by the prefecture as soon as they left Yanaka. In 1906 the village was legally abolished, and its elementary school was torn down. In the summer of 1907, the homes of the remaining families were demolished, and soon thereafter floods swept away the shacks built in their place. Only sixteen families stayed and built new huts (see Fig. 3.6).

The floods recurred several times, and those of 1910 were particularly severe, reaching as far downriver as Tokyo. The government's flood control projects, although not yet completed, were clearly of only limited effectiveness. Tanaka had no doubt that this was due to a lack of understanding and respect for rivers, for the mountains in which they originated, and for nature in general. He devoted as much as possible of the remainder of his life to the study of the rivers of the Kantō area. As always for Tanaka, nature—rivers in this case—served as metaphor for the nation and its foundations in village life. But in his study of rivers, he was doing more than demonstrating the need for the government to understand nature and the villagers of Japan. Having come to Yanaka to attempt to defend and rebuild the polity from the bottom up, starting with the village, he was now moving on to the next level. He organized villagers up and down the Watarase and Tone rivers to cooperate on flood control and irrigation projects.

After he left the Diet in 1901, Tanaka was greatly influenced by Christianity, socialism, and pacifism. He read the Bible while spending several weeks in prison in 1902 as punishment for contempt of court during the trial of those arrested in the Kawamata Incident. Biblical metaphors subsequently appeared frequently in his speech and writing. Shortly before his death, for example, he wrote in his diary: "Christ said it is more difficult for a wealthy man to enter heaven than for a camel to pass through the eye of a needle." Two lines later, he wrote: "Human rights belong to heaven. Human beings must protect them."[38] Tanaka also spoke on behalf of world disarmament, even during the Russo-Japanese War of 1904–5, and wanted to use the savings for international educational exchanges (see Fig. 3.7).

More than Christianity or socialism, however, it was the experience of living again with the common people and the lessons he drew from it that shaped Tanaka's late constitutional thought. He wrote in 1909: "The rights and duties of subjects are sacred. They must be sacred and inviolable."[39] The next month he noted the same article, "[The emperor is] 'sacred because the people are also sacred.'"[40] Here Tanaka may have been drawing on the *Mencius* he

---

38. Diary entry for June 7, 1913, *TSZ* 13: 508.
39. Notebook entry for Mar. 7, 1909, *TSZ* 11: 170.
40. Notebook entry for Apr. 11, 1909, *TSZ* 11: 187.

Fig. 3.7 Tanaka Shōzō in his later years (source: Kenneth Strong, *Ox Against the Storm: A Biography of Tanaka Shōzō: Japan's Conservationist Pioneer* [Vancouver: University of British Columbia Press, 1977], n.p.).

had studied as a boy: "The people rank highest in a state, the spirits of the Land and Grain come next, and the sovereign is of least account. Therefore to win the people is the way to become emperor."[41] But even as Tanaka demanded that the government follow the constitution, he began to feel that the constitution itself

---

41. Ch'u Chai and Winberg Chai, eds. and trans., *The Sacred Books of Confucius and Other Confucian Classics* (New York: Bantam, 1965), p. 134.

would have to be replaced: "We must completely do away with the constitution and all of our laws and education and put in place a broad constitution based on the ways of the gods in heaven."[42]

Tanaka Shōzō died in September 1913, not far from his home village of Konaka, while traveling on one of his river surveys. His worldly possessions consisted of the clothes he wore, plus "a haversack, a list of persons interested in the care of rivers, a New Testament, a copy of the Japanese Constitution bound in one cover with an edition of Matthew's gospel, three notebooks and a few stones."[43] Within four years after Tanaka's death, the last stragglers had left Yanaka.

Tanaka's Constitutional Thought: Its Essence and Implications

CONSTITUTIONAL CIVIL SOCIETY

Tanaka Shōzō's interpretations of the Meiji Constitution are among the most distinctive. He insisted that it offered a great deal of scope for interpretation, debate, and dissent. He saw the Japanese polity as constructed from the bottom up, with the people and the villages as its foundation. His own career mirrors this trajectory, as he went from village head to member, successively, of the local assembly, prefectural assembly, and Diet; similarly, he wrote a "family constitution" before prescribing and interpreting a constitutional order for the nation. And in his final years he retreated to the village as his last hope for realizing the sort of system he envisioned.

What he wanted was not patriarchy or unchecked imperial sovereignty but a viable, constitutional, civil society. Tanaka's concepts fit the basic Hegelian definition of "civil society" as a sphere separate from the state. More specifically, what he envisioned was less the Tocquevillean idea of a network of civic groups making democracy possible (described most recently by Robert Putnam in his book *Bowling Alone*) than the sort of civil society discussed in

---

42. Diary entry for Jan. 1912, *TSZ* 13: 55–56.
43. Strong, *Ox Against the Storm*, p. 212.

the context of Eastern Europe and Latin America in recent decades, in which civil society is what challenges, and builds replacements for, autocratic governments. [44]

For Tanaka the continued existence of the emperor need not threaten the rights of the people. In the first stage of his constitutional thought, he believed the emperor and the state were not so strong as to choke off civil society, because all understood that they were bound to obey the laws of the "constitution of the cosmos," the natural law that underlay the constitution and enjoined all, including the emperor, to practice "harmonious cooperation." In fact, as he defined it, this "harmonious cooperation" did not mean equal compromise by all. When push came to shove, the government had to give in to the wishes of the people's representatives. The people, not the emperor or his ministers, were the owners of the nation. This is where Tanaka's ideas departed most radically from the Meiji ideology of an organic society centered around, and under, a sovereign emperor.

Andrew Gordon and Kyu Hyun Kim have shown how the Japanese experience can help us refine concepts derived from the West, such as democracy, fascism, and the public sphere.[45] Their work shows that we need to qualify and define these terms for a particular time and place. Tanaka's case is rather different, since the constitutional system he envisioned was never realized. But his constitutional civil society, like the "national public sphere" described by Kim and the "imperial democracy" studied by Gordon, blends elements that may seem incompatible today. Tanaka's system would retain and respect the emperor—but the emperor and his government would respect the rights of their citizens/subjects

---

44. Robert D. Putnam, *Bowling Alone: The Collapse and Revival of American Community* (New York: Simon & Schuster, 2000). Putnam first put forward these ideas in his article "Bowling Alone: America's Declining Social Capital," *Journal of Democracy* 6, no. 1 (Jan. 1995): 65–78. My distinction here between two types of civil society is drawn from Michael W. Foley and Bob Edwards, "The Paradox of Civil Society," *Journal of Democracy* 7, no. 3 (July 1996): 39–40.

45. Andrew Gordon, *Labor and Imperial Democracy in Prewar Japan* (Berkeley: University of California Press, 1991); Kim, "The State, Civil Society, and Public Discourse in Early Meiji Japan."

and obey the "laws of heaven."[46] Although Tanaka never found a way to guarantee that they would do so, his was a remarkable vision for Meiji Japan.

TRANSLATING TRADITION AND MODERNITY:
A JANUS FOR MODERN JAPAN

A study of Tanaka can help us reconsider the relevance of pre-Meiji thought and traditions to Japan's modern project. The oligarchs who created the Meiji imperial system, although they claimed to be returning to Japan's purest traditions, largely invented those traditions. Fukuzawa Yukichi, and later Maruyama Masao, insisted that a modern consciousness required the rejection of Confucian concepts.

Tanaka saw things differently. He was certainly at odds with the top-down, centralizing, Asia-escaping (ideologically, at least) trajectory of imperial Japan, and he certainly failed to see his vision realized. But he did offer a unique *justification* for a people-centered constitutional order. Unlike the Meiji Constitution, the system he envisioned was not legitimized by the emperor himself. Neither was it informed and justified primarily by Western constitutional and natural law theory, as were most of the draft constitutions written by groups outside the government. Tanaka's contribution was to defend his constitutional system in terms of a higher form of law, the "laws of the universe," and to describe these laws in vocabulary and metaphors meaningful even to Japanese who had no exposure to foreign constitutional thought. He drew on the Confucian ideas that people were born good and that the government was responsible for the people's well-being and on the Neo-Confucian concept that there was a correspondence, or even identity, of the natural order with human government and society and that this could be discovered through the "investigation of things."

For Tanaka these concepts were *not* incompatible with a modern constitutional order. Among his contemporaries, perhaps only Nakae Chōmin drew on Neo-Confucianism in a similar way. But

---

46. There are obvious similarities here to the *minponshugi* of Yoshino Sakuzō.

Tanaka's blending of tradition and modernity resonates with recent arguments that Confucianism need not lead Asian societies only to a Singapore-style antidemocratic modernity.[47] And in many ways Tanaka fits into a broad pattern of political activism by "traditionalist" reformers and revolutionaries in imperial Japan. The Marxist Kawakami Hajime, who was inspired by Tanaka as a university student, also experimented with modern wine in Confucian bottles, and with Christianity.[48]

Tanaka Shōzō was a Janus figure. Like the two-faced Roman god of doorways and gates, Tanaka in his constitutional thought looked both ahead and behind. He was ahead of his time in several ways, as the environmental activists of the 1960s realized. But he looked back as much as ahead. Even in advocating "modern" ideas of constitutionalism and environmentalism, and even when deeply influenced by Western enlightenment thought, socialism, and Christianity, he expressed and justified his ideas in moral and linguistic contexts familiar to those with the sort of education and outlook considered orthodox in the Tokugawa period. Tanaka's political ideas resonated with Japan's past, but they were very much informed by Western thought as well. His wide reading in European thought and his diary entries make this clear. He did not misunderstand these Western concepts but rephrased and resituated them in the physical and intellectual context of Japan. Indeed,

---

47. Tu Weiming, for example, argues that Confucianism can provide the sort of public intellectuals needed by a healthy civil society. His ideas are neatly summarized in his "Tradition of Engagement: The Public Intellectual as a Confucian Idea," *Harvard Asia Pacific Review* 1, no. 2 (Summer 1997): 87–88. Recent works dealing with related issues include Wm. Theodore de Bary and Tu Weiming, eds., *Confucianism and Human Rights* (New York: Columbia University Press, 1998); and David L. Hall and Roger T. Ames, *The Democracy of the Dead: Dewey, Confucius, and the Hope for Democracy in China* (Chicago: Open Court, 1999).

48. Gail Lee Bernstein, *Japanese Marxist: A Portrait of Kawakami Hajime, 1879–1946* (Cambridge, Mass.: Harvard University Press, 1976); for Tanaka's influence on Kawakami, see pp. 21, 26, 31–32. Casting the net even more broadly, one might note parallels between Tanaka and the "protoindustrial elite" (*gōnō*) who lobbied the government on behalf of traditional rural industry and agriculture; see Edward E. Pratt, *Japan's Protoindustrial Elite: The Economic Foundations of the Gōnō* (Cambridge, Mass.: Harvard University Asia Center, 1999).

Tanaka's genius lay in his ability to draw on both traditions and translate each into the language of the other, to continue to grow intellectually throughout his life, and to find support for modern, foreign ideas—as well as a vocabulary in which to express them—in the Japanese past.

CHAPTER FOUR

A Land of Milk and Honey: Rural
Revitalization in the 1930s

Kerry Smith

Rural communities throughout Japan were the focus of unprecedented relief and reform efforts in the 1930s. The crises of the Great Depression, as severe in Japan as in other industrialized states, were the proximate causes of these new policies and programs. Many farm families began the 1930s in dire straits, mired in debt and barely making ends meet. The collapse of rice and silk-cocoon prices in 1930, the return of newly unemployed sons and daughters from idle factories, and a host of other depression-related economic calamities convinced policymakers and rural reformers that rural communities had been pushed to the brink.

For three years, from 1932 to 1934, the state channeled unprecedented sums of money to the countryside. These funds supported low-interest loans to local credit unions and other financial institutions and, more important, paid for public works projects. Some of the spending from those projects went to farm families as wages and thus helped shield the government from charges that it had abandoned farmers. But little apart from the scale of these projects was innovative—public works had been the state's first line of defense against unemployment and economic crisis on many prior occasions. The new and transformative qualities of state and private responses to the Great Depression belong instead to developments unique to the 1930s. For nine years, from 1932 to 1941, thousands of towns and villages participated in an ambitious and sweeping response to the rural crisis. The Farm, Mountain, and Fishing Village Economic Revitalization Campaign (*Nōsangyoson keizai kōsei undō*) offered more than just relief—it held out the promise of fundamental improvements in rural life.[1]

By the time the revitalization campaign ended in 1941, four out of five rural communities in Japan had been active in it, engaging in, among other activities, sophisticated economic planning, debt-management programs, reforms in daily life, and new approaches to local leadership in an attempt to reshape the countryside. Even though not all the villages participated with enthusiasm, and not all attempts at reform succeeded, depression-era relief and revitalization efforts offer a useful window on important changes in the relationships between the state and communities, policymakers and citizens, town and country.

They do so in at least two ways. First, crafting relief and reform policies for the countryside involved not just bureaucrats and politicians working in Tokyo but a diverse array of farmers' organizations, spokespersons for landlords and other local notables, and everyday farmers, all demanding a say in how the countryside was to be rescued. The importance of "outsiders" in the debates about relief and reform—the revitalization campaign in particular bears their imprint—suggests that farmers' groups and other rural activists were skilled in using the power of the state to help implement their vision of an ideal society. Such intersections of public power and private initiative are increasingly a focus of recent scholarship on modern Japan, as is a recognition of the diverse origins of those initiatives. Factory workers and women's groups are among those who have struggled to define new roles for themselves and gain access to various forms of power.[2] The desperate attempts by rural reformers and farmers' spokesmen to respond to the crises of the

---

1. The material in this chapter draws on Kerry Smith, *A Time of Crisis: Japan, the Great Depression, and Rural Revitalization* (Cambridge, Mass.: Harvard University Asia Center, 2001).

2. Sheldon Garon, "Rethinking Modernization and Modernity in Japanese History: A Focus on State-Society Relations," *Journal of Asian Studies* 53, no. 2 (May 1994): 346–66.

early 1930s speaks to the engagement of "average" citizens with the
state, politicians, and social reform more generally. They also hint
at some of the ways in which these early practices of policymaking
and social reform have been carried forward into postwar, contemporary Japan.[3]

Second, depression-era reform efforts illuminate another aspect
of modern Japan's history—namely, popular conceptions of how
society ought to function, and the possible role of the state in
community and private lives. Even before the depression, rural
Japanese claimed to feel threatened by the challenges of urbanization and modernity, threats made tangible in shifting patterns of
employment and in the means of accumulating wealth. By the end
of the 1920s, light industry had surpassed agriculture as the single
most important component of the economy. Farming would fall
further and further behind in the next decade, as heavy industry
and the large corporation emerged as the dominant expressions of
economic power and national strength. This gap between city and
country was reflected in many ways, some of them more obvious
than others. City dwellers had, in general, better access to education, health care, and other resources; factory wages tended to rise
more quickly and more predictably than farm incomes. Taxes on
farmland were perceived to be much more onerous than those on
businesses or other urban enterprises, a view that led to the unsur-
prising conclusion that farmers bore the brunt of the costs of development but realized few of the benefits. The Ginza's bright
lights brought little joy to farmers' hearts.

Revitalization spoke to these concerns by suggesting that better
economic and management practices could transform the family
farm into something more like a modern, maybe even lucrative enterprise. Both bureaucrats and rural reformers insisted that the
qualities associated with such enterprises—a measure of predictability, the promise of improvements over time, and so on—were necessary for the countryside's survival. The economic practices rec-

---

3. See, e.g., Timothy S. George, *Minamata: Pollution and the Struggle for Democracy in Postwar Japan* (Cambridge, Mass.: Harvard University Asia Center,
2001); and Sheldon Garon, *Molding Japanese Minds: The State in Everyday Life*
(Princeton: Princeton University Press, 1997).

ommended by reformers were far from revolutionary, but careful bookkeeping, crop diversification, and a more rational handling of local resources at least had the potential to improve standards of living for farmers and their families and thus to close some of the gaps between city and country.

The challenges of the era were also evident in the rise of new modes of expression and protest. Tenant and labor unrest, coupled with an urban culture that often appeared to embody decadence, could be seen as sure signs that the nation was traveling in uncharted waters. One development associated with revitalization was thus a powerful increase in popular interest in the reform of education, civic life, and rural culture more generally. As has been well documented, these reformist impulses were widespread in the Meiji and Taishō eras; the revitalization campaign suggests that similar concerns were very much a part of rural life in the 1930s as well.[4] The campaign itself provided a national framework for addressing these questions, as well as a stage on which local variations on those themes could be played out.

Crafting Reform

By spring 1932, strong demands for a substantive response to the crises in the countryside were coming from many directions. Politicians and bureaucrats had up to that point offered little concrete assistance to rural families hit hard by the depression, despite repeated pleas from mainstream farmers' groups. The political and social environment that developed in 1932, however, made some sort of response almost inevitable. One new factor was the return to power of the Seiyūkai in the form of a cabinet led by Inukai Tsuyoshi and featuring Takahashi Korekiyo as finance minister. The Seiyūkai had in the past been willing to spend to solve economic crises, and there were indications that the same approach might be in the offing from this new government. Inukai's assassi-

---

4. See Sharon Minichiello, *Japan's Competing Modernities: Issues in Culture and Democracy, 1900–1930* (Honolulu: University of Hawai'i Press, 1998); and Bernard S. Silberman and Harry D. Harootunian, *Japan in Crisis: Essays on Taishō Democracy*, Michigan Classics in Japanese Studies, no. 20 (Ann Arbor: University of Michigan, Center for Japanese Studies, 1999).

nation on May 15 by military officers allied with radical agrarianists ended both the Seiyūkai cabinet and the practice of party rule. Saitō Makoto's national unity cabinet retained Takahashi as finance minister, however, and eventually followed Seiyūkai policies of fueling recovery through government spending.

The May 15 Incident focused attention on the depression in agriculture and conditions in rural Japan, but neither the farmers nor the young officers involved in the incident effectively shaped the debates about how to rescue the villages.[5] Other actors played that role, foremost among them a motley collection of agrarianist activists who had not been directly involved in May's violence. Their ideas ranged widely, but they shared the beliefs that the values and traditions of rural communities were preferable to those of modern, urban society and that agriculture, not industry, should be the foundation of economic life. Brought together by longtime organizer Nagano Akira and inspired by the teachings of Gondō Seikyō, one of a handful of influential agrarianist theorists, the heads of several small agrarianist organizations put aside their differences temporarily to form the Local Autonomy Farmers' Conference (Jichi nōmin kyōgikai).[6] Based in Nagano and active in the surrounding prefectures, the conference ran one of the most successful petition campaigns the country had seen to that point, gathering more than 100,000 signatures and inspiring other rural activists and organizations to mount similar campaigns and to join more direct lobbying efforts in party offices and ministerial meeting rooms. These petitions were presented to the Diet in early June, shortly before the legislative session was to end. Although the Lower House took no action on the specific contents of the petitions, it convened a special emergency session devoted to the crisis in the

---

5. For insights into the goals and methods of the agrarianists led by Tachibana Kōzaburō, see Stephen Vlastos, "Agrarianism Without Tradition: The Radical Critique of Prewar Japanese Modernity," in *Mirror of Modernity: Invented Traditions of Modern Japan*, ed. idem (Berkeley: University of California, 1998), pp. 79–94.

6. Ann Waswo, "The Transformation of Rural Society, 1900–1950," in *The Twentieth Century*, ed. Peter Duus (Cambridge, Eng.: Cambridge University Press, 1988), p. 597; Thomas R. H. Havens, *Farm and Nation in Modern Japan: Agrarian Nationalism, 1870–1940* (Princeton: Princeton University Press, 1974), pp. 241–42.

countryside. That session, sometimes referred to as the Rural Relief Diet, began in August 1932.

Deciding that summer what to do about the villages was no simple matter; the list of problems plaguing rural Japan was long and the issues complex. The simplest and most direct policy response was the tried and true approach of spending more on public works. Although clearly a stopgap measure, public works spending had the advantage of putting money into farmers' hands quickly. The state eventually announced plans to spend approximately ¥800 million on public works programs beginning in 1932 and for the next two years and to help defray the cost of local participation in the projects. In addition, planners hoped to pump another ¥800 million into the countryside through debt-refinancing loans and other forms of "relief" credit. The three-year total came to roughly ¥1.6 billion in cash and loans, a substantial amount indicative of the new seriousness with which the government viewed the village problem.[7]

The agrarianist petitioners did their part to reshape depression-era rural life by demanding that the state impose a moratorium on the repayment of farmers' debts. This proposal was understandably popular among farm families. Rural indebtedness was seldom a part of discussions about the countryside until the early 1930s. The release of a series of surveys by the state and private farm organizations in 1932 substantiated the petitioners' claims that debt was indeed a serious problem. Ministry of Agriculture and Forestry agents dispatched in June to some of the hardest-hit prefectures revealed the following month that farm debt nation-

----

7. For an analysis that equates the contributions of relief spending in the early 1930s to that of new spending on the military, see Miwa Ryōichi, "Takahashi zaiseiki no keizai seisaku" (The economic policies of the Takahashi era), in *Senji Nihon keizai* (The wartime Japanese economy), ed. Tōkyō daigaku shakai kagaku kenkyūjo (Tokyo: Tōkyō daigaku shuppankai, 1979), pp. 138–39. For the state's assessment, see Nihon ginkō, Chōsakyoku, "Jikyoku zaisei no bōchō ga jigyōkai ni nobashitaru eikyō" (The effects of the growth in emergency spending on the business world), in *Nihon kin'yūshi shiryō: Shōwa hen* (Materials on Japan's financial history: Shōwa era), ed. idem (Tokyo: Ōkurashō insatsukyoku, 1973 [Sept. 1934]), pp. 1–12.

ally was estimated to be ¥4.7 billion, or an average of ¥837 per farm household.[8] As high as that figure seemed, other local surveys generated even more troubling results. Officials in Fukushima reported that their calculations placed the average household debt in the prefecture at almost ¥1,600; in neighboring Niigata the figure was more than ¥2,300.[9] As critics of the government's inaction were quick to point out, at those levels rural debt was for some families the equivalent of two or three years of income from farming, and even the ministry's own conservative estimates of the size of rural debt were easily twice the value of farm production that year.[10]

The agrarianists' efforts to draw attention to the rural crisis paid off, although not exactly as they had hoped. Debt relief became an important part of the Diet's agenda and eventually took the form of expanded low-interest loans from the government and legislation to create village-level debt-management unions. These unions were designed to help debtors negotiate repayment and perhaps limited debt forgiveness with creditors; membership in the union brought with it access to cheap loans not available to nonmembers and provided other forms of support during the negotiation process. The unions were also supposed to foster community solidarity by bringing debtors and creditors together in a spirit of cooperative problem solving, as opposed to the more litigious atmosphere that might otherwise prevail when the two sides

---

8. Nōrin daijin kanbō, Sōmuka, ed., *Nōrin gyōsei shi* (A history of the administration of agriculture and forestry) (Tokyo: Nōrin kyōkai, 1957), 2: 195–97. See also Nishida Yoshiaki, *Kindai Nihon nōmin undōshi kenkyū* (Farmers' social activism in modern Japan) (Tokyo: Tōkyō daigaku shuppankai, 1997), pp. 75–92; and *Tōkyō nichi nichi shinbun*, June 4, 1932; and *Tōkyō asahi shinbun*, June 5, 1932.

9. Teruoka Shūzō, *Nihon nōgyō mondai no tenkai* (The development of problems in Japanese agriculture) (Tokyo: Tōkyō daigaku shuppankai, 1984), 2: 80.

10. See ibid., pp. 79–80, for the comparisons to the value of farm production and farm income. GNP in 1932 (at current prices) was ¥13.7 billion (Kazushi Ohkawa, Nobukiyo Takamatsu, and Yuzo Yamamoto, *National Income*, vol. 1, *Estimates of Long-Term Economic Statistics of Japan Since 1868*, ed. Kazushi Ohkawa, Miyohei Shinohara, and Mataji Umemura [Tokyo: Tōyō keizai shinpōsha, 1974], p. 200).

met.[11] The thorny question of a debt moratorium was neatly side-stepped; borrowers were not really off the hook, and creditors were assured of eventual repayment of at least some of what was owed.

Public works and debt-management policies together were significant steps forward for the beleaguered countryside, but rural reformers felt that the crisis demanded a more ambitious response. As spokespersons for the Imperial Agricultural Association (Teikoku nōkai) and other mainstream farmers' organizations complained that summer, it was no longer enough to treat the symptoms. The time had come, they insisted, to attack the root causes of rural distress and impoverishment. The depression had clearly exacerbated existing problems and added new ones as well, and the arguments by farmers and their spokesmen that the countryside was in danger of both an economic and a social collapse were more convincing in 1932 than they would have been only a few years before.

The Economic Revitalization Campaign took shape against this background of agrarianist petitions and mainstream lobbying for rural relief. Bureaucrats in the Ministry of Agriculture and Forestry, many of them veterans of the failed efforts to win Diet approval for improved legal protection for tenants, oversaw the genesis of the campaign in June and July 1932. Most of what would eventually become the campaign's cornerstone policies of community-level economic planning and social reform, however, originated outside the ministry, in existing locally run programs. This saved time, since there was clearly an urgent need for a program and no time to create one from scratch, and the bureaucrats had the advantage of being able to pick from among projects that had already been tested in the field.[12] Their job was simplified by the Imperial Agricultural Association, which promoted one project in

---

11. For similar examples of state-mandated mediation and conciliation, see John Owen Haley, *Authority Without Power: Law and the Japanese Paradox* (Oxford: Oxford University Press, 1991).

12. Kusumoto Masahiro, *Nōsangyoson keizai kōsei undō to Kodaira Gon'ichi* (The farm, mountain, and fishing village Economic Revitalization Campaign and Kodaira Gon'ichi) (Tokyo: Fuji shuppan, 1983), p. 15.

particular as a viable model for the nation. The Hyōgo Prefecture Agricultural Association had for several years been experimenting with local reform, efforts built around household- and community-level planning and community-wide revamping of economic institutions. The association reported excellent results and ran its own lobbying campaign that summer by sending descriptive literature and other propaganda to the prime minister, cabinet members, and other potentially influential leaders. The Imperial Agricultural Association promoted a similar set of ideas to its members in conferences that summer.[13] In borrowing from the Hyōgo model, Ministry of Agriculture and Forestry bureaucrats not only were assured of ongoing support from outside the government but also were adapting an approach already familiar to many farmers.

Economic Revitalization rested on a framework of official and semiofficial support for what was essentially a local effort at reform. Once a village had applied for and received designation as a participant in the campaign, it began the process of revitalization by conducting detailed surveys of a wide range of economic and social indicators at the household and community levels, which produced a reasonably complete picture of the village's economic health. These surveys were then supplemented by equally detailed five-year plans, again drawn up at both the household and the village level, in which families and the village set goals for their farms, determined budgets, and indicated changes they hoped to make in other areas of community life. One goal of the planning process was for farmers to wrest more production from the land and, where possible, to expand their crop mix and their income-generating activities in other ways as well. Coupled with debt-management strategies and rejuvenated civic organizations, villages had the opportunity, they were told, to cast off the practices of the past and regain a measure of prosperity.

The Ministry of Agriculture and Forestry administered the campaign from Tokyo (an undertaking that required almost no

---

13. Communities elsewhere were experimenting as well; see *Fukushima-ken nō-kai hō*, no. 125 (Sept. 1931): 28–29, and no. 126 (Oct. 1931): 24–25; and Nōrin daijin kanbō, Sōmuka, *Nōrin gyōsei shi*, pp. 289, 292–93, for examples in Fukushima prefecture.

new staff), but it relied heavily on groups such as the Imperial Agriculture Association, the national leadership of the Industrial Cooperatives, and other civic groups for additional support. The ministry's role was to produce and promote guidelines for household-
and community-level economic planning, crop diversification, the
reform of daily life (*seikatsu kaizen*), and a host of other changes
within the basic infrastructure of the village. Some of what the
ministry did was provide legislative backing; not only did it make
sure that debt relief survived Diet challenges, but it also oversaw
changes in the regulations governing, for example, membership in
industrial cooperatives. Local cooperatives were in theory supposed to bring together all the farmers in a community, but in
practice they seldom did. Fees were often too high, and in many
villages the cooperative simply provided too few incentives to join.
By changing the regulations so as to allow farming associations
(*nōji jikkō kumiai*), to which almost everyone belonged, to join the
local industrial cooperative, the ministry expanded by many times
the number of families that it could reach through the cooperatives.[14] For the most part, however, the ministry's direct involvement in what was happening locally was minimal. There were no
mandatory quotas to be met, and prefectural committees vetted local plans and personnel; this left the bureaucrats back in Tokyo
free to sketch out the broader goals of the campaign. Initiative was
almost entirely in the hands of the communities themselves.

In many ways, this makes the spread of the Economic Revitalization Campaign all the more interesting. Local response to the

---

14. Farming associations brought together farmers from the same hamlet to
coordinate local practices and work. The new law made it relatively simple for
any farming association to become a legal organization and to join the industrial
cooperative in that form. See Nōrinshō, "Dai 63 kai teikoku gikai o chūshin to
shite okonawaretaru Nōrinshō kankei nōsangyoson fukyō kyōkyū shisetsu yōroku" (Records of Ministry of Agriculture and Forestry materials relating to provisions for rural relief in the 63rd session of the Imperial Diet), Nov. 1932, in *Nōsangyoson keizai kōsei undōshi shiryō shūsei* (Collected materials from the farm,
mountain, and fishing villages Economic Revitalization Campaign; hereafter cited
as *NSS*), first series (Tokyo: Kashiwa shobō, 1985), 2: 128–29. For a leading bureaucrat's thinking on the important role of the farming associations, see Kusumoto,
Nōsangyoson keizai kōsei undō to Kodaira Gon'ichi, pp. 40–42n48.

campaign quickly reached and then surpassed Ministry of Agriculture and Forestry expectations. Almost 1,500 communities were designated campaign participants in 1932, and a total of 1,769 joined the following year. Just over half of all communities that participated in the campaign began doing so between 1932 and 1934, but by 1941, the campaign's last year, almost 80 percent of rural communities had been designated an Economic Revitalization town or village.[15] Although it is important not to read too much into designation alone—there were certainly many cases of pro forma participation—part of the campaign's attraction lay in its endorsement of a rhetoric and practice of reform that appealed to a wide range of the rural population. The following section explores some ways in which revitalization reached the countryside.

Imagining the Revitalized Village

Official channels for the dissemination of information about the new campaign connected the Economic Revitalization Section of the Ministry of Agriculture and Forestry, through prefectural administrations, to every town and village in the country. Mayors and other local officials were sure to receive many reminders of the revitalization campaign's goals and processes. National and many local newspapers did their part by describing the campaign, and references to it were frequent in radio broadcasts of speeches by Prime Minister Saitō, Finance Minister Takahashi, and others in the summer and fall of 1932.

Less expected and much more interesting are some of the other ways revitalization surfaced in popular discourse about rural Japan. The official campaign, for example, spawned a small boom in semi-official publications on rural reform and revitalization. The monthly journal *Nōson kōsei jihō* (Village revitalization newsletter) was first issued in 1935 and was followed a year later by *Nōson kōsei dokuhon* (Village revitalization reader). Both were publications of the Nōson kōsei kyōkai (Village revitalization association), a group whose members included Ministry of Agriculture policymakers,

15. Nōrinshō, Nōseikyoku, "Nōson keizai kōsei shisetsu no keika gaiyō" (Outline of rural economic revitalization efforts), Apr. 1943, *NSS* 1, no. 7: 286–87.

scholars of rural economics, and other elites with an interest in rural life. Well-known rural activists were among those trying to ride the wave of public interest by offering lectures, extended seminars, and traveling workshops on topics related to revitalization and rural reform to farmers and local leaders, often with the endorsement of ministry officials. Although much of their content was devoted to the nuts and bolts of economic recovery, these publications and gatherings reflected the campaign's broader goals of affirming the inherent value and attractiveness of rural life. They spoke of communities transformed not only by better farming practices but also by an active engagement with rural culture and a commitment to the countryside's future. The campaign, coupled with the professional support that developed around it, quickly moved beyond restoring the countryside to where it had been before the depression struck. The agenda that emerged by the mid-1930s was considerably more ambitious and imagined villages that had been revitalized on many fronts.

Other media promoted similar visions of what the countryside might become. Popular magazines like *Fujin no tomo* and *Kingu* regularly included segments on rural life and the outlook of farming, as did other mainstream journals.[16] The best window on widely held views of rural revitalization, however, is almost certainly *Ie no hikari* (Light of the home), the official magazine of the *sangyō kumiai* (industrial cooperative) movement. *Ie no hikari* was distributed directly to cooperative members. In a moment of useful synergy, the revitalization campaign swelled the ranks of local cooperatives and thus ensured that even more households had access to the magazine. By the mid-1930s, *Ie no hikari* enjoyed a circulation of close to a million, or roughly one copy for every three rural families.[17] In the 1930s, the magazine's editorial policies moved away from an emphasis on purely didactic content and embraced a

---

16. See, e.g., "Zadankai: kōsei jidai" (Roundtable discussion: the age of revitalization), *Fujin no tomo* 28, no. 3 (1934): 42–68.

17. Itagaki Kuniko, *Shōwa senzen, senchūki no nōson seikatsu* (Rural life in the Shōwa era, before and during the war) (Tokyo: Mitsumine shobō, 1992), pp. 54–56; Adachi Ikitsune, "Jiriki kōsei undōka no *Ie no hikari*" (*Ie no hikari* during the self-revitalization campaign) *(Kikan) Gendai shi* 2 (May 1973): 106.

format intended to appeal to average readers, children, and others with interests outside the industrial cooperative movement. The editors managed to blend this more mainstream format with content that nevertheless met the needs of a rural readership.

Revitalization quickly became a prominent component of the magazine's vocabulary and mission in the 1930s. Roundtable discussions and how-to articles provided one type of advice; narratives like Nukada Roppuku and Takagi Seiga's "The Brothers of the Three-*tan* Field—An Economic Revitalization Drama" ("Sandanbatake no kyōdai—keizai kōsei geki") gave another set of examples about what to reform, and why.[18] One work that received considerable attention at the time and was remembered long after the depression was Christian social activist and former labor organizer Kagawa Toyohiko's novel *The Land of Milk and Honey*. The first installment of the novel appeared in the January 1934 issue of *Ie no hikari,* the twentieth and final segment in December 1935.[19] The novel is not explicitly about revitalization and seldom makes direct references to the revitalization campaign. What it does do—and here the resonances with the campaign are quite clear—is describe a long and difficult effort by a handful of committed individuals to overcome the particular challenges of the depression and the longstanding burdens of selfishness and adherence to tradition.

Kagawa's skill lies not so much in the plot, which is convoluted and far-fetched, but in his ability at moments to portray both the problems associated with rural life and potential solutions to them convincingly. The serialized novel follows 24-year-old Tanaka Tōsuke on his long quest to discover those solutions. Tanaka, the devoted son of an impoverished farming family, was driven to leave his small village in Fukushima's Aizu district by a desire to lessen the burden on his parents and siblings and by a belief that one day

---

18. Nukada Roppuku and Takagi Seiga, "Sandanbatake no kyōdai—keizai kōsei geki," *Ie no hikari* 12, no. 3 (March 1936): 66–80.

19. Kaizō published *The Land of Milk and Honey* in book form that year. My reading of the book is from Kagawa Toyohiko, *Chichi to mitsu no nagaruru sato,* in *Kagawa Toyohiko zenshū* (Complete works of Kagawa Toyohiko), ed. Kagawa Toyohiko zenshū kankōkai (Tokyo: Kiritsuto shinbunsha, 1982 [1935]). For an English translation, see Toyohiko Kagawa, *The Land of Milk and Honey,* trans. Marion Romer Draper (London: Hodder & Stoughton, 1937).

he would return with the skills necessary to rescue them and the village. After he leaves home in 1931, Tanaka's travels take him to encounters with mountain hermits, an apprenticeship in a Nagano consumer's union, and a stint as a cooperative worker in Tokyo. At each juncture, he acquires new insights into the countryside's problems and new skills that will help him improve conditions in Fukushima.

When after considerable hardship Tanaka manages to return home, he has new obstacles to overcome. Local elites (both a land-lord's son and a Diet politician figure prominently as villains) anxious to protect their interests oppose his plans to rebuild the village cooperative and, for a few anxious episodes, succeed in first turning the community against him and then having him jailed on false charges of financial impropriety. With the help of a sympathetic lawyer, the wrongdoers are eventually exposed. Freed from jail, Tanaka once again takes up the cause of reform. This time, how-ever, he decides that rather than lead the village to reform, he will make everyone an equal participant in the process by drawing on the expertise and passions of each member of the community. The response of the villagers is overwhelmingly positive, and in short order they are able to build a health-care facility for local women recovering from stints as textile-factory workers and to buy large tracts of land on which to begin cooperative farming. By the time Tanaka is done, and the novel concludes, the village is far better off than it was. His own family has regained a measure of financial stability, and Tanaka's introduction of goats (for milk) and bees (for honey) are just the first of many new measures designed to di-versify the local economy. In the end, Tanaka has clearly accom-plished what he set out to do and is poised to share his methods and their promise of a better tomorrow with the rest of the nation.

The Land of Milk and Honey illuminates the harsh realities of ru-ral life in the 1930s, even if Kagawa had to rely on fiction to make the narrative work. Tanaka's family circumstances, although tragic, were no worse than those reported in press accounts of life in the northeast. The other calamities confronting his village and his friends—disease, political corruption, police brutality, the sale of young women into prostitution—are treated as elements of an everyday landscape. By grounding those elements of the novel in a recognizable reality, Kagawa managed to make Tanaka's agenda equally plausible.[20] Nothing Tanaka does, whether it is getting farmers to raise goats or negotiating the purchase of land from a local landlord, requires massive outlays of money or highly specialized technical knowledge. The qualities that Kagawa identified as important to a successful reconstruction of the community, and the nation, are instead precisely those embraced by the revitalization campaign. Like the campaign, *The Land of Milk and Honey* envisioned a rural Japan made economically secure and culturally vibrant through careful planning, sound leadership, and a willingness to work together. The end result of the process, in other words, was to alter the circumstances of rural life in fundamental ways. No simple return to a predepression status quo was permissible; Kagawa thus mirrored revitalization's promises not only to help communities to recover but also to point the way toward a much better future. And, despite the obstacles Tanaka Tōsuke had to overcome in order to accomplish his goals, the novel also provides a compelling argument for the real-life viability of revitalization's central tenets.

Kagawa's novel was just one of the channels through which revitalization was introduced to rural Japanese. By the mid-1930s, it was possible to reach into villages and into the lives of farm families in ways that would not have been attempted even a decade before. Magazines like *Ie no hikari* and other popular journals had acquired an extensive rural readership, an expansion that went hand in hand with the growth of other forms of mass media.[21] The resurgence of the industrial cooperatives marks another watershed; whether it was in the form of the cooperatives, young men's asso-

---

20. Kagawa was careful to get the facts right, and prices and other details mentioned in the text were accurate or at least believable (Adachi Ikitsune, "*Ie no hikari* no rekishi: aru nōhon shugi to sono baitai" [A history of *Ie no hikari*: agrarianism and its medium], *Shisō no kagaku* 18 [June 1960]: 74–75).

21. Radio's penetration of the countryside grew significantly in the 1930s; see Gregory J. Kasza, *The State and the Mass Media in Japan, 1918–1945* (Berkeley: University of California Press, 1988), pp. 88, 94–97; and Iwasaki Akira, "Atarashii media no tenkai" (The development of new media), *Shisō*, no. 624 (June 1976): 240, 244.

ciations, or women's groups, or even the agrarianist societies
that helped spark the drive to rural reform, farmers were increasingly well organized in the 1920s and 1930s. Perhaps more important, the postdepression era marks a transformation not only in the
means of reaching into rural communities but also in the reasons
to do so. The Economic Revitalization Campaign implicated the
entire community in reform. Not only could everyone be involved
in reconstructing the village, but bureaucrats, activists, and, increasingly, rural Japanese themselves believed that they should be.
The next section explores one real-life example of revitalization's
impact.

Revitalization in Practice

Kagawa's fictitious account of rural revitalization was set in the
real village of Ōshio, tucked into the lower approaches of the
mountains at the eastern edge of the Aizu basin. Quite by coinci-
dence, one of the better-documented examples of actual rural revitalization took place a few kilometers from Ōshio, in the village of
Sekishiba. A farming community of a few thousand residents in
the 1930s, Sekishiba's initial responses to the depression were un-
remarkable. Already suffering from years of fluctuations in the agricultural economy, the village's civic organizations and households were even more seriously compromised by the unexpected
severity of the crises of the early 1930s. There was little villagers
could do other than watch rice and silk prices plummet and hope
that the market recovered sooner rather than later. Such was the
pattern in communities throughout Japan, as private misfortunes
inevitably had public implications. Tax defaults threatened schoolteachers' salaries, unpaid union dues weakened cooperative en-
deavors, and overdue loans put both borrower and creditor at risk.
To make matters worse, bad weather in much of northeastern Japan in the summer and early fall of 1934 led to massive crop damage and a widespread famine later that year. Only after the worst
months of the famine were past them were Sekishiba's residents
able to turn in earnest to the revitalization campaign.

The impetus for revitalization came from two local leaders. The
mayor, a relatively young former school principal, worked closely

with a prominent merchant from the neighboring town of Kita-kata to rally villagers around the campaign and then to sustain the reformist drive in Sekishiba. The two left their mark on the campaign and were highly visible components in its success. Both men achieved a measure of local and regional fame as a result of their accomplishments, and the village was singled out by the prefecture and by the local media as an example of what revitalization could accomplish.[22]

The village's successful revitalization, coupled with the presence of two such committed proponents of reform, hints at how hard it is to speak in general terms about revitalization's impact on rural life. Location, the personality of village leaders, and any number of other factors affected the campaign's course and outcomes. By 1941 more than 9,000 villages were involved in the revitalization campaign.[23] Not every one was as energetically led as Sekishiba, few would win awards for their prowess at revitalization, and fewer still preserved documents on the workings of the campaign. Circumstances unique to Sekishiba shaped its implementation of the revitalization campaign and continue to shape the recollection of its experiences. Sekishiba clearly cannot stand for the entire countryside.

As a window on some aspects of the revitalization process and its implications for rural life, however, the experience of Sekishiba is revealing. Its patterns of landholding and productivity were on a par with regional and national averages—farmers in Sekishiba grew the same crops as rice cultivators throughout Japan, using more or less the same techniques and with roughly the same results. Although there were a few men of means in the village and in surrounding communities, no single landlord or group of landlords dominated village politics or community life. The basic structures of civic life and administration were the same in Sekishiba as in

---

22. *Fukushima minpō*, Feb. 11, 1937. In 1938 the national government bestowed an even higher honor on Sekishiba, by choosing it as one of two communities in Fukushima to receive an award on the fiftieth anniversary of the promulgation of the system of local self-government.

23. Nōrinshō, Nōseikyoku, "Nōson keizai kōsei shisetsu no keika gaiyō," p. 285.

any community of like size. And, as was true in most rural communities, public conflicts between landlords and tenants were rare. Home to neither tenant unions nor political activity outside the mainstream, Sekishiba looked a lot like its neighbors.

It helps, too, that the Ministry of Agriculture and Forestry established common templates for planning and implementing revitalization. There is a uniformity in the campaign that crosses village boundaries—the basic structures of the recovery plan established in Sekishiba in 1934 are almost identical to those of the village next door and closely resemble those from a community hundreds of kilometers distant. The categories used in planning revitalization did not vary much. All the farmers and communities active in the campaign shared an interest in reforming the production and marketing of crops, in controlling family finances, and in improving rural life more generally. Sekishiba's pursuit of these interests, described in more detail below, has more in common with processes under way elsewhere in Japan than the community's unique qualities might lead one to conclude. The rest of this section draws on Sekishiba's experiences within the shared framework of revitalization, both to illuminate how the depression reshaped rural life in one community and to shed light on common patterns of experience.

PRODUCTION

For the average Sekishiba farmer, the most concrete aspect of revitalization was surely the development of plans for economic recovery. Drawn up within the household and then collated at the hamlet and village levels, these plans were remarkable in their attention to detail. In over 120 different categories, respondents recorded their income, expenses, crops, family size, landholdings, and land use in 1933 and then set goals for the same again for each of the next five years.[24] The broader implications of this sort of discipline are interesting, but at their simplest the plans encouraged

---

24. Sekishibamura yakuba (hereafter SMY), "Komatsu buraku kakuto keizai chōsa bo" (Komatsu hamlet household economic surveys), Oct. 1934, held by Kitakata shiritsu toshokan, Shi-shi hensan shitsu (hereafter KST).

families to exploit new sources of income, diversify crops, and cut expenses. The Watanabe Taichi family offers one example of how this aspect of revitalization worked.

In 1933 this seven-member household from Komatsu, one of the hamlets making up Sekishiba, owned 1.6 *chō* of paddy land and just under 0.7 *chō* of upland fields.[25] The Watanabes owned all the land they farmed. Although it was more common for local farmers to both own and rent at least some land, the Watanabes were in most respects ordinary. Their landholdings placed them in the middle ranks of the hamlet's landed farmers and just under the median in terms of tax obligations. Almost all the household's income came from farming, and most of that (around 86 percent in 1933) was generated by the sale of rice. The Watanabes also produced a variety of other crops, including wheat, barley, soybeans, persimmons, silkworms, and rabbits. Together, these added incrementally to the amount of cash the family had available to maintain itself, meet farm expenses, and pay taxes.

Those expenses were not trivial. When the Watanabes surveyed their family finances in 1933, quite possibly for the first time, they discovered that spending had outpaced income by more than ¥263, or by roughly 43 percent, that year. (Here, too, they were in good company—most of the families in the hamlet were in the red.) As a rough gauge of financial stability, the imbalance between income and expenses would clearly have to be addressed.

Through the planning process itself and indirectly via lectures and other forms of outreach, the revitalization campaign encouraged families to examine their finances and to devise realistic proposals for improvement. In the Watanabes' case, those proposals focused on a series of incremental changes in spending on the family and the farm. These adjustments proceeded on several parallel tracks. Watanabe Taichi committed the family to drawing significantly more on their own hard work than they had in the past so as to cut total labor costs in half by the second year of the revitalization plan and in half again by the third. Similarly, Watanabe proposed an equally sharp cut in the amount of money spent on fertil-

---

25. A *chō* is roughly equivalent to a hectare; there are ten *tan* in a *chō*.

izer. Roughly 40 percent of the spending on farm inputs went to fertilizer in 1933. The family's revitalization plan cut outlays in that category in half after three years, or down to about 12 percent of spending on farming. A move toward increased self-sufficiency, a key theme of the revitalization campaign, was evident as well in the plan's description of the steps the family would take to produce more homemade fertilizer, seeds, and so on.

At the same time that the family was proposing to work harder with fewer outside resources, they were also contemplating a future in which they spent less on their own comfort and needs. Over the five years of the first revitalization plan, Watanabe sketched out a scenario in which spending on food, education, and entertainment would decline by about half. Most of the reduction took the form of sharp cuts in medical expenses, with incidental reductions in purchases of alcohol, sugar, tea, and a few other items. Perhaps even more tellingly, in none of the 22 categories of household expenses included in the revitalization plan did Watanabe make any allowances for possible increases in spending. The intent was clearly to constrict spending where possible, or at least keep it from growing.

There was more to the plan than simply cutting back. The family was equally committed to finding new sources of income and to teasing a few extra yen out of familiar crops. What they proposed was a not uncommon reconfiguration, one in which rice would eventually make up a smaller share of the family's total income from farming (and would shrink in absolute terms as well). This reduction was to be balanced by a shift of resources to other cash crops. The Watanabes planned on more than tripling their income from barley, soybeans, persimmons, and silkworm cocoons. They were even more ambitious about greens (which at the end of the five-year plan were expected to contribute almost six times as much as in 1933), chickens and eggs (new products for them), rabbits (to generate ten times as much income after the first revitalization planning cycle), and lumber (another new venture).

As a result, Watanabe Taichi imagined a future in which his family was considerably more productive and more resourceful and, better yet, no longer spending more than they brought in. In the first two years of the plan, total income would decline below 1933 levels, as the family regrouped and moved into new projects. After three years, however, it would rise above the 1933 baseline, and at the end of five years total income was expected to be more than 50 percent higher. Put another way, the household would increase its annual income per family member from around ¥87 to more than ¥131. In that final year of the plan, Watanabe predicted that his household would take in 44 percent more than it spent, neatly reversing the deficits of 1933. The Watanabes were less radical than many in the hamlet in their pursuit of revitalization, but their goals were nevertheless ambitious. The embracing by such an average farm household of revitalization's basic tenets of crop diversification, increased production when possible, and careful, rational planning is suggestive both of the campaign's particular attractions and of the broader appeal of sweeping changes in rural life.

When the village as a whole paused in 1939 to measure its progress after five years of planning and reform, the results were disappointing at first glance. Farmers had hoped to achieve higher levels of production in more than 50 different types of crops and crafts but had met those goals in only a dozen, falling far short of the projected increases in many areas.[26] Clearly the plans drawn up earlier in the decade had been much too optimistic and had seriously misjudged local farmers' abilities to do so much in so short a time. Village officials were nonetheless quick to point out that their accomplishments were still impressive. Diversification of the sort the Watanabe family pursued was evident village-wide in the form of sharp increases in the value of cash crops other than rice and sericulture. Persimmons, plums, and rabbits were among the many products that were much more important to local farmers at the end of the period than they had been at its start.

It is also significant that these forays into new products took place alongside equally serious efforts to improve productivity in staple crops. Yields per hectare of rice, which had risen slowly in

---

26. No record remains of how well individual families in Sekishiba did at reaching the goals they set for themselves over the course of the campaign. Compiled from SMY, "Keizai kōsei keikaku jikkō hōkoku" (Reports on the implementation of economic revitalization plans), 1936–41, KST.

the years before the revitalization plan was put into effect, shot up
after 1935. The increase between 1935 and 1936 alone was 8 percent
and was followed by similarly impressive yields over the next several years. Given that the village as a whole had cut back on purchases of commercial fertilizer, such improvements are all the
more remarkable.[27] They suggest that other components of the
campaign, such as providing better access to technical instruction
and knowledge of national "best practices" to all farmers, as well as
the introduction of community-owned and -operated farm machinery, were having the desired effects.

A final indicator of revitalization's impact on the local farm
economy is that by 1939 the value of the goods produced by a typical
Sekishiba household was roughly three times what it had been in
1931. By far the biggest leaps in income and productivity came after
1935. Even adjusted for the wartime inflation that swept the nation
late in the decade, the gains to farmers and to the community were
real. Earlier concerns about debt, despair, and unpaid taxes, which
for many years had dominated official pronouncements about the
state of the village, were replaced by more upbeat assessments of the
strong performance of Sekishiba's farmers and the goods they produced. Local leaders and outside observers were quick to connect
these tentative indications of prosperity and economic stability to
the workings of the Economic Revitalization Campaign and the village's adherence to its tenets.

COMMUNITY CONSTRUCTION

In contrast to the campaign's broad economic agenda, which covered almost every aspect of the business of farming, its scope in
other areas of rural life was carefully delineated. Revitalization left

---

27. See Kitakata-shi shi hensan iinkai, ed., *Kitakata-shi shi* (History of Kitakata
city) (Kitakata City: Kita Nihon insatsu, 1991), 8: 670–71; and SMY, "Zōsan keikaku juritsu jikkō ni kansuru chōsa" (Surveys on the development and implementation of plans to boost production), 1940–41, KST. See SMY, report following a
directive from the head of the Fukushima-ken keizaibu to designated villages entitled "Nōsangyoson keizai kōsei keikaku jikkō chōsa no ken" (Regarding surveys
of the implementation of farm, mountain, and fishing village economic revitalization plans), Oct. 18, 1937, in "Keizai kōsei" (1938), KST.

some of the countryside's most visible problems untouched. Neither relief nor the Economic Revitalization Campaign offered explicit solutions to tenancy, for example. What the depression-era reforms offered instead was a vision of the village in which class and tenancy were largely irrelevant. Farmers were encouraged to think about how best to manage their land and how to wrest the most profit from it, but there were almost no provisions for helping landless farmers acquire land of their own. [28] The campaign glossed over the implications of tenancy for economic prosperity. Other sorts of difference were similarly overlooked, if not denied, as a way of thinking about rural society. Instead, the campaign explicitly pursued the creation of a rural community in which conflict and difference were absent. One of the qualifications for participation in the Economic Revitalization Campaign was testimony to the effect that the applying community was free from land disputes, political conflict, or other forms of social unrest. Sekishiba met those criteria, but clearly many communities either resolved existing tensions in order to participate or simply denied that any existed. The number of tenancy disputes peaked nationally in 1935, and it was not until 1943 that the figures fell back to roughly where they had been before the depression began. Against this rising tide of tenancy disturbances, the insistence on social harmony as both necessary and possible was an important component of the reformist vision.

Since only communities already free from overt conflict could participate in the campaign, the next step was to further strengthen the forces of stability and order. Rural revitalization sought the construction of community around several axes. On a practical level, revitalization ensured that residents saw more of one another and of the representatives of community-wide organizations. The constituent hamlets of Sekishiba began holding monthly meetings in the autumn of 1934, an old idea but a new experience for most

---

28. Emigration to Manchuria, which the state encouraged and included as a component of the revitalization campaign, did hold out the promise of land for the landless; see Louise Young, *Japan's Total Empire: Manchuria and the Culture of Wartime Imperialism* (Berkeley: University of California Press, 1998), chap. 7; and K. Smith, *A Time of Crisis*, chap. 10.

villagers, and continued to do so for the life of the campaign.[29] The mayor was a regular speaker at these functions, sometimes holding forth on technical aspects of local administration related to revitalization, at other times giving pep talks designed more to inspire than instruct. Speeches by officials from the industrial cooperative and agricultural association were almost always on the agenda as well. The meetings were a simple and effective way to keep the entire community informed about the campaign's progress and the state of the village more generally. The importance of the meetings to the revitalization process, as part of the ongoing effort to maintain a common focus and to encourage widespread participation in the campaign, is hard to miss. The industrial cooperative's newsletter and eventually the village's newspaper, both of which began publication as a component of the revitalization campaign, accomplished similar goals.[30]

Revitalization's reach was deliberately broad. Every farm household was a potential and presumably welcome participant. In this, it differs in important ways from most earlier reform efforts in the countryside. The Local Improvement Movement of the early twentieth century, for example, had cast a much narrower net, focusing on landed local notables and established elites. In the 1930s and with the advent of revitalization, Ministry of Agriculture and Forestry officials took a decidedly different tack in identifying likely and future torchbearers for reform. Although landlords and other local powerbrokers continued to wield considerable influence in local life, the campaign clearly provided a stepping-stone for the emer-

---

29. See SMY, Mayor Satō Sakichi to governor of Fukushima, "Shichōson shinkō iinkai oyo(bi) buraku jōkai nado ni kansuru chōsa kaihō no ken" (Regarding the survey report of city, town, and village encouragement committees and hamlet assemblies), Feb. 7, 1937, in "Keizai kōsei" (1937), KST. John Embree's classic study of rural life in the 1930s pointed out that women attended the mandatory lectures that began when Suye village began participating in the campaign but did so reluctantly: they "listen passively, never raising any questions, and then go home and soon forget about it" (John F. Embree, *Suye Mura: A Japanese Village* [Chicago: University of Chicago Press, 1939], p. 168).

30. All comments referring to the contents of the hamlet assemblies are based on the four-volume *Buraku jōkai nisshi* (Minutes of the hamlet assembly). See also SMY, Satō to governor of Fukushima, "Shichōson shinkō iinkai oyo(bi) buraku jōkai nado ni kansuru chōsa kaihō no ken," Feb. 7, 1937, in "Keizai kōsei" (1937), KST.

gence of a new cohort of leaders. The Economic Revitalization Committee and other new civic structures, for example, recruited members with a wide variety of skills and statuses within the village. The campaign similarly encouraged the identification of promising young local reformers for additional training and nurturing. Village "mainstays," as the Ministry of Agriculture and Forestry label suggests, were expected to anchor the community and provide both technical know-how and a broader vision of rural improvement.[31] Methods and venues varied from place to place, but in Sekishiba the village administration sent several local farmers to seminars and workshops run by a national rural reform society. The local upper-school principal and a technical expert employed by the village agricultural association were sent for specialized training at one of Fukushima's designated "farmers' training halls."[32]

Sekishiba's experiences with mainstays and with the involvement of a younger, technically proficient cohort of leaders in the reform process was not at all uncommon.[33] The problems of the 1920s and the depression itself had challenged the legitimacy of a leadership

---

31. See Kenneth B. Pyle, "The Technology of Japanese Nationalism: The Local Improvement Movement, 1900–1918," *Journal of Asian Studies* 33, no. 4 (Nov. 1973): 51–65. For the Nōrinshō's proposal, see Nōrinshō, Keizai kōseibu, "Dai nikai nōson keizai kōsei chūō iinkai yōroku" (Summary of the second session of the rural economic revitalization central committee), *NSS* 1, no. 2: 288.

32. SMY, "Keizai kōsei keikaku juritsu jikkō jōkyō ni kansuru chōsa (seisan keikaku o nozoku)" (Survey of the development and implementation of economic revitalization plans [excluding production planning]), 1940, KST. The final extended lectures were offered in 1939. See also SMY, "Aizu sanson dōjō ichiran" (Catalog of the Aizu mountain village training hall), Jan. 1939, in "Keizai kōsei" (1938), KST.

33. Mori Takemaro, "Nihon fashizumu no keisei to nōson keizai kōsei undō" (The formation of Japanese fascism and the rural revitalization campaign), *Rekishigaku kenkyū*, special issue (1971): 135–52; idem, "Nōson no kiki no shinkō" (The development of the rural crisis), in *Kōza Nihon rekishi* (Lectures on Japanese history), ed. Rekishigaku kenkyūkai (Tokyo: Tōkyō daigaku shuppankai, 1985), pp. 135–6; Nishida Yoshiaki, *Shōwa kyōkōka no nōson shakai undō: yōsanchi ni okeru tenkai to kiketsu* (Rural social movements during the Shōwa depression: their development and conclusion in a sericulture region), Tōkyō daigaku shakai kagaku kenkyūjo kenkyū hōkoku, 27 (Tokyo: Ochanomizu shobō, 1978); for a more recent analysis, see Ōkado Masakatsu, *Kindai Nihon to nōson shakai: nōmin sekai no hen'yō to kokka* (Rural society in modern Japan: the state and the transformation of the world of the farmer) (Tokyo: Nihon keizai hyōronsha, 1994).

premised on wealth and age. The decade following World War I witnessed the emergence of an articulate, committed, and well-trained generation of young farmers, products of a successful national education system, conscription, and other formative experiences not shared by their elders.[34] Part of what the Ministry of Agriculture and Forestry was after in its mainstays program was to tap into this generation and mold them in ways that would assure the continued stability of the countryside.[35] The revitalization campaign offered both the opportunity for new leaders to shape the village's future and compelling reasons for them to do so. The result was an (admittedly slow) redefinition of who was qualified to lead and why. One of revitalization's more subtle effects, then, was a gradual broadening of the demographics of local leadership. The Pacific War and the postsurrender reforms would accelerate this process and provide additional opportunities for some veterans of revitalization to play a role in shaping the future of their community.

REFORM AT HOME

Watanabe Taichi's revitalization plan was detailed enough to spell out how much money the family intended to spend on sugar, salt, tea, and 22 other common household items, as well as another 25 farm and business expenses, every year for five years. However realistic such plans might be and whatever the likelihood of any given family being able to pursue them successfully, that the revitalization campaign even attempted to achieve this level of involvement with individual households is worth noting. Modern states had long used education, conscription, and any number of other institutional and ideological tools to shape the citizenry, and Japan was certainly no exception to this pattern. The revitalization campaign and related efforts to recover from the depression, however, point to the early stages of a new level of explicit involvement in private life.

---

34. Waswo, "The Transformation of Rural Society, 1900–1950," pp. 554–56; see also Ōkado Masakatsu, Review of *Nishiyama Kōichi nikki*, ed. Nishida Yoshiaki and Kubo Yasuo, *Rekishigaku kenkyū*, no. 662 (Sept. 1994): 50.

35. Ōkado Masakatsu, *Kindai Nihon to nōson shakai*, pp. 310–18.

Revitalization planning and household budgeting were two aspects of this involvement, and it was through these practices that families were most closely connected to the economic recovery of the community and the nation. As suggested above, all the households of a village participated in the process of revitalization; not just the landed or well-off but tenants and poorer families were important contributors to the nation's return to economic stability. Their participation at the start and at every juncture along the way is a sign that the state assigned a degree of agency to these often marginalized citizens. Although this makes it much harder to lump average citizens together as passive and without initiative, there were clearly costs associated with such redefinitions. At some level, declaring that even average citizens possessed the wherewithal to plan and to participate in the campaign effectively shifted much of the burden for recovery onto their shoulders. In other words, the campaign helped establish as reasonable the idea that recovery from economic downturns and continued economic prosperity are contingent not on what the state and businesses may or may not do but on how well average citizens adhere to the practices of revitalization. If the campaign gave farmers the power to improve their lot, it was also just as explicit in making them responsible for doing what was best for the village and the nation.

The revitalization campaign extended beyond economic affairs into other areas as well. This is especially evident at the household level, where even the mundane practices of everyday life were subject to increased scrutiny. In Sekishiba interest in reforming "traditional" ways in favor of more rational and frugal behavior was evident early in the campaign. Late in September 1935, the mayor notified the heads of the village's hamlets that henceforth, as part of the revitalization campaign, they were expected to help implement a new set of guidelines for daily life, guidelines he titled "The Sekishiba Village Compact on Economic Retrenchment and Moral Reform."[36] In 38 separate items, the agreement paints a picture of what daily life ought to be like and, in so doing, suggests that vil-

---

36. See SMY, "Sekishiba mura keizai kinshuku oyo(bi) kyōfū kiyaku," which appears as part of "Keizai kōsei keikaku jisshi ni kansuru ken" (On putting economic revitalization plans into practice), Sept. 9, 1935, KST.

lagers had a long way to go before they could begin to approximate such an austere ideal. In order to contain spending, for example, the agreement spelled out in considerable detail the size and duration of such ceremonies as weddings, funerals, and entry into military service, who ought to be invited, and under what circumstances it was appropriate to exchange gifts. The language employed in outlining the preferred practices makes it clear that existing habits were extravagant and wasteful. Similarly, prohibitions of overly lengthy social visits or visits of any kind in which alcohol might be served point to concerns not just about frivolous spending and squandered resources but about lost opportunities and wasted time. Hamlet officials were instructed to mount watches and announce the hours at the appropriate times to encourage residents to go to bed and get up early. One's waking hours, which under revitalization were assumed to be long and productively spent, were potentially as much a topic for planning and rationalization as household expenses.

These rules were not without effect. The village would later report a reduction in expenditures on ceremonial functions, a decrease in drinking, and a notable improvement in punctuality.[37] In some ways these successes are less interesting than the fact that the mayor and others thought it worthwhile to issue such guidelines and attempt to enforce them alongside more tangible instructions on economic revitalization. This pairing of material and "spiritual" revitalization was endorsed by Ministry of Agriculture and Forestry bureaucrats and others involved in the development of the revitalization campaign. "Spiritual" in this context referred not so

---

37. See Thomas C. Smith, "Peasant Time and Factory Time in Japan," in idem, *Native Sources of Japanese Industrialization, 1750–1920* (Berkeley: University of California Press, 1988), pp. 199–235, for a discussion of Tokugawa-era concerns about the management of time. SMY, "Seishin sakkō shisetsu jisshi seiseki" (Results of efforts to put into practice the improvement of spirit), no date, in "Keizai kōsei" (1938). SMY, report following a directive from the head of the Fukushima-ken keizaibu to designated villages entitled "Nōsangyoson keizai kōsei keikaku jikkō chōsa no ken" (Regarding surveys of the implementation of farm, mountain, and fishing village economic revitalization plans), Oct. 18, 1937, in "Keizai kōsei" (1938), KST. Similar comments appear in SMY, "Keizai kōsei keikaku juritsu jikkō jōkyō ni kansuru chōsa (seisan keikaku o nozoku)."

much to religious beliefs or practices as to an embrace of rationality and efficiency in everyday life, in part on the grounds that economic revitalization would be meaningless unless accompanied by an equally permanent adjustment in how people thought about farming and economic activity.[38]

Not all these concerns and ideas about how to address them were new. The "reform of daily life" predated revitalization by many years, and the concept if not a set of practices had been familiar to many citizens long before the depression. The revitalization campaign, in parallel with the rise of publications like *Ie no hikari*, became a powerful vehicle for the further integration of the reform of daily life into the experience of average citizens. The campaign gave structure to the reform program by incorporating it into the actions of local Economic Revitalization committees and village-wide revitalization plans, for example. Through hamlet meetings, newsletters, lectures, and any number of renewed institutional pathways, it provided access to just about every household in the community. At the same time, campaign rhetoric made clear why such reforms were so important. The point that the mayor of Sekishiba and other commentators made was that long-term economic recovery and stability were ultimately expressions of daily practices and shared values of frugality, efficiency, and rationality. Organizational reforms and detailed planning were only part of the equation. The prospects of the community were intimately connected to its ability to internalize these "reformed" practices and behaviors, and sooner rather than later.

Sekishiba was not unusual in pursuing goals like these. The intent of Sekishiba's "compact" appears, for example, in guidelines laid out in a 1934 *Ie no hikari* article describing measures families should take to reform the way they cooked, the clothes they wore, and the homes they lived in. These lists are similar to those in Sekishiba's "compact" in that they blend instructions focused on frugality ("Don't be extravagant!") with steps designed to improve ef-

---

38. The debate over "spiritual" versus economic revitalization was a common topic in *Ie no hikari*; see, e.g., "Seishin kōsei keizai kōsei—dochira ga saki ka" (Spiritual revitalization or economic revitalization—which one first?), *Ie no hikari* 10, no. 6 (June 1934): 52–58.

ficiency, or at least create the appearance of efficiency and rationality. Among the directives in this category are calls for families to set aside a room in which children do their schoolwork and for housewives to redesign their kitchens (both to improve hygiene and to allow for the quicker preparation of meals). The article also suggests that public health concerns make private bathing preferable to the communal variety.[39]

Translating these guidelines into actual behavior was almost certainly beyond the skill of even the most committed local leader. Even if Sekishiba's officials could claim success in inculcating punctuality and a few other markers of adherence to the spirit of reform, it seems unlikely that citizens there or anywhere else gave themselves over entirely to a reformist regime. Nevertheless, as did revitalization more generally, these campaigns help identify some commonly held ideas about the limits and direction of social transformation in the 1930s. The push to greater rationality and order in one's economic and personal life, for example, comes through clearly, as does a desire that rural citizens reconfigure key elements of their lives and their homes to reflect what were imagined to be common practices among middle-class urbanites. Setting aside a room so that children can study without distraction, for example, and modernizing the kitchen reflect ideals about family life that had to that point found their clearest articulation in the city.[40]

Nowhere are the contradictions in the reformist campaigns of this era clearer than in the programs involving women. Women were the targets of much of what revitalization sought to accomplish, either directly or indirectly. The responsibility for keeping the family's books and for other aspects of household management introduced by the campaign, to say nothing of the extra labor involved in substituting homemade clothes and foodstuffs for store bought, implicated women at all levels of the revitalization and re-

39. "Nōson seikatsu no tatenaoshi" (Rebuilding rural life), Ie no hikari 10, no. 10 (Oct. 1934): 122; see also "Nōka no seikatsu kaizen ni kansuru zadankai" (A roundtable discussion on the reform of everyday life in rural households), Ie no hikari 9, no. 7 (July 1933): 54–62.

40. Jordan Sand, "At Home in the Meiji Period: Inventing Japanese Domesticity," in Mirror of Modernity: Invented Traditions of Modern Japan, ed. Stephen Vlastos (Berkeley: University of California Press, 1998), pp. 191–207.

covery effort.[41] A careful reading of any village's revitalization plan
or even a typical *Ie no hikari* roundtable discussion leads to the conclusion that women were being asked to shoulder ever larger responsibilities for the well-being of the household and the community, responsibilities that were clearly defined as theirs alone.

It is easy to find examples of women who at least claimed to be
enthusiastic supporters of the campaign and who were proud to
have been thought important enough to be asked to contribute.[42]
At the same time, women publicly expressed discontent and disillu-
sionment about what revitalization was doing and what it had failed
to do. For these women, revitalization had at least raised the possibility that their lives might improve in tangible, useful ways. Apparently for many of them, revitalization and the reform of daily
life were attractive in part because they promised to generate not
just more money for the family but more time. A common com-
plaint, especially among young women writing to *Ie no hikari* or
participating in its forums, was that village elders, parents, and other
authorities wasted time that could be better spent and forced the
same behavior on everyone else. As a result, young women found
themselves unable to pursue their own interests, even though revitalization had seemingly offered to create such opportunities.

What emerges from these comments are glimpses of the expectations of at least some participants in the campaigns of the 1930s and
a sense of their frustration at how little had in fact changed. The
hoped-for improvements were for the most part incremental
changes in everyday practices within the community. Commonly
voiced desires included, for example, time to pursue leisure activi-

---

41. Kathleen S. Uno, "Women and Changes in the Household Division of Labor," in *Recreating Japanese Women, 1600–1945*, ed. Gail Lee Bernstein (Berkeley:
University of California Press, 1991), pp. 17–41; see also Mariko Tamanoi, *Under
the Shadow of Nationalism: Politics and Poetics of Rural Japanese Women* (Honolulu:
University of Hawai'i Press, 1998).

42. "Nōson fujin no koe o kiku zadankai" (Listening to the voices of rural
women: a roundtable discussion), *Ie no hikari* 8, no. 7 (July 1932): 104–14; "Nōson
seikatsu no fuhei to kibō o kiku" (Listening to the complaints and hopes of rural
life), *Ie no hikari* 12, no. 6 (June 1936): 72–78; "Machi ya mura o mamoru watakushidomo fujin no katsudō zadankai" (Actions we women can take to protect towns
and villages: a roundtable discussion), *Ie no hikari* 16, no. 7 (July 1940): 82–89.

ties, to engage in self-improvement, to simply do something other than work.[43] This is where concerns about the more efficient use of time come into play: many observers expressed the belief that one of the outcomes of revitalization and the introduction of more rational, modern behavior in the village should be the expansion of opportunities to learn and maybe even to play.[44] As one young woman from Aiichi prefecture complained, local elders who balked at giving women access to newspapers and magazines undercut whatever progress the village might have made in improving its economic situation. If careful planning and hard work led only to more of the same, what was the point?[45]

Conclusions

By the time *The Land of Milk and Honey* was republished in 1968, the countryside had changed in ways that few who had read the book in the 1930s would have thought possible. Tenancy and its attendant local inequalities were all but nonexistent, and the gaps between city and country in wealth and well-being, differences that had once seemed unbridgeable, had in many ways been rendered moot. Agriculture accounted for only a small fraction of the nation's economic activity and a dwindling share of its workforce; an ever-shrinking number of citizens described themselves as full-time

---

43. Men also made these points, arguing that women would be unwilling to become farmers' wives so long as opportunities for leisure were so few and far between; see, e.g., "Nōka no seikatsu kaizen ni kansuru zadankai," p. 60. Similar sentiments were expressed several years later in another *Ie no hikari* roundtable discussion. As one participant pointed out, a recent survey had asked 100 upper-school women about their preferences for husbands. Although many identified soldiers, government officials, and railroad workers as ideal mates, not one wanted to marry a farmer; see "Warera no fuhei fuman o hakidasu zadankai" (A roundtable for letting out our dissatisfaction and discontent), *Ie no hikari* 13, no. 9 (Sept. 1937): 60.

44. For examples, see Itagaki, *Shōwa senzen, senchūki no nōson seikatsu*; "Kōsei keikaku wa dore dake jitsugen shita ka" (To what extent have revitalization plans come to fruition?), *Ie no hikari* 11, no. 3 (March 1935): 60–69; "Keizai kōsei no ayumi to shōrai o kataru zadankai" (A roundtable to talk about economic revitalization's past and future), *Ie no hikari* 12, no. 3 (March 1936): 146–57; and "Nōson seikatsu no fuhei to kibō o kiku."

45. "Machi ya mura o mamoru watakushidomo fujin no katsudō zadankai"; see also "Nōson seikatsu no fuhei to kibō o kiku" for similar sentiments.

farmers. Mergers and amalgamations in the 1950s reduced the number of independent rural villages by roughly 80 percent.[46] Such was Sekishiba's fate—the village merged with six nearby villages and one neighboring town in 1954 to form the city of Kitakata. Although farming remains a part of the local economy, outside the area Kitakata is best known as a source of a unique noodle dish, "Kitakata ramen," and as a favorite tourist destination. These developments would have been hard to foresee in the mid-1930s. That Sekishiba thrives in part on marketing its old-fashioned noodles and the appeal of its rustic atmosphere speaks to the extent of rural Japan's transformation.

The connections between the countryside's postwar successes and the developments of the 1930s, revitalization in particular, are not direct. The campaign officially ended in 1941, which meant that neither the occupation officials nor Japanese policymakers ever had to decide what to do with it in the postsurrender world. Nor were the solutions proposed during the revitalization campaign those that ultimately addressed the persistent problems of tenancy, uncertain sources of income, and farm-factory disparities, which had plagued rural communities for so long. Both a sweeping land reform and a commitment from the government to subsidize agriculture (to ensure that farmers received an income equivalent to that of factory workers) were necessary to resolve those problems, and neither had been suggested as part of revitalization's response to the depression.

The legacies of the 1930s are complicated in other ways as well. The tensions between the goals of revitalization and its more limited impact in practice ultimately went unresolved. The start of the war in China in 1937 and the nation's subsequent mobilization made even a tentative pursuit of leisure and an improved quality of life more or less unthinkable, for example. Where it was once possible to connect concerns about productivity and efficiency to improvements in daily life, mobilization refocused the acceptable beneficiaries of harder and smarter work away from the individual

---

46. Between 1953 and 1956 alone, more than 6,000 villages were subject to merger and amalgamation; see Kurt Steiner, *Local Government in Japan* (Stanford: Stanford University Press, 1965), p. 192.

and the household and toward the military and the nation. In this effort, revitalization continued to play a role. The Economic Revitalization Campaign was not static and was revamped at the ministerial and local levels several times over the course of the 1930s. By the end of the decade, the campaign's focus was clearly on assisting mobilization, and specifically on increasing harvests while minimizing the use of scarce resources. It was but a small step from revitalization's insistence on productivity, diligence, and communal harmony to the more explicit rhetoric and regulations of the war era, which often harped on similar themes. Mobilization was almost certainly easier in the countryside because of the foundations laid by depression-era efforts at reform. The campaign's programs of community building and the changes they brought served the needs of mobilization almost as readily as they had those of revitalization.[47]

In Sekishiba as elsewhere, the planning and improved local coordination of farmers' groups associated with revitalization, to say nothing of community-building practices themselves, were easily shifted to the demands of a mobilized economy and society. The Economic Revitalization Committee's responsibilities, for example, were redefined and sharply narrowed during wartime. Its earlier goal of coordinating all aspects of local reform and improvement was abandoned in favor of focusing on increasing productivity and managing local resources.[48] The committee's membership changed

---

47. Early assessments of revitalization in the 1930s emphasized the connections between the campaign and the state's absolutist agenda. See, e.g., Ishida Takeshi, *Kindai Nihon seiji kōzō no kenkyū* (Research on the political structures of modern Japan) (Tokyo: Miraisha, 1956); and Inoue Harumaru, *Nihon shihonshugi no hatten to nōgyō oyobi nōsei* (Agriculture, agricultural administration, and the development of Japanese capitalism) (Tokyo: Chūō kōron sha, 1957). For more nuanced scholarship on the campaign's ideological and practical components, see, among others, Mori Yoshizō, "Shōwa shōki no nōson keizai kōsei undō ni tsuite: Yamagata-ken no baai" (On the rural Economic Revitalization Campaign in early Shōwa: the case of Yamagata prefecture), *Keizaigaku* 29, no. 1–2 (1968): 91–116; Mori Takemaro, *Senji Nihon nōson shakai no kenkyū* (Studies of rural society in wartime Japan) (Tokyo: Tōkyō daigaku shuppankai, 1999); and Ōkado Masakatsu, *Kindai Nihon to nōson shakai*.

48. SMY, "Keizai kōsei iinkai joseikin kōfu shinseisho" (Written applications for economic revitalization committee subsidies), Mar. 17, 1939, in "Keizai kōsei"

as well. The schoolteachers, the "honored farmers," and the others from a variety of backgrounds who had given the committee a somewhat diverse character were replaced by hamlet leaders, farm association officers, and others actually involved in farming.[49] Although these changes are another indication of a gradual transfer of power into the hands of younger, technically skilled but not necessarily land-rich farmers, they also clearly reinforced the campaign's exclusive focus on productivity and its role in the wartime mobilization.

The campaign's formal end in 1941 set the stage for new and expanded initiatives on fronts revitalization had ignored. Tenants, for example, began turning over their rice directly to the state instead of their landlord. Although landlords received a cash payment from the government in lieu of rent, they got much less than the tenants did. In addition, wartime revisions of an existing program to fund purchases of rented land finally made such transactions attractive to tenants. The financial and social advantages of being a landlord were thus sharply diminished by war's end, and the relative position of tenant farmers had improved considerably. Both these trends, one stripping landlords of power and wealth, the other elevating tenants and farmers more generally to positions of relative economic freedom, were expanded significantly by occupation authorities and continued by postoccupation Japanese administrations.

Depression-era efforts to recreate the countryside have had some resonance in the postwar rural landscape. Processes originating in the 1930s, among them a gradual transformation of local leadership, the modernization of farming practices, and even the strengthening of cooperative, community-wide organizations focused on farming, became important features of the democratized countryside. Much of the rhetoric and many of the practices associated with the re-

---

(1938), KST; see also the notice explaining the revisions in *Sekishiba sonpō*, no. 15 (Mar. 1939).

49. SMY, "Keizai kōsei iinkai joseikin kōfu shinseisho" (Written applications for economic revitalization committee subsidies), Jan. 17, 1941, in "Keizai kōsei" (1940), KST. These types of changes were apparently common throughout the country; for more examples, see Nishida Yoshiaki, *Shōwa kyōkōka no nōson shakai undō*, pp. 564–65.

form of daily life, farm planning, and rural revitalization have been recycled in one form or another, first in the 1950s and again in more recent efforts to preserve the countryside.[50] Their persistence is testimony to the ongoing negotiations between the state, local leaders, the modern (international) economy, agriculture, and an almost wholly urbanized nation.

These reminders of the extent of the transformation necessary to address agriculture's problems even in the prosperous postwar and of the tensions that continue to shape rural Japan serve other purposes as well. They inspire at once an appreciation for the effort that went into even imagining that "a land of milk and honey" might be constructed in the wake of the depression and a deep wariness of the promises embedded in such offers of salvation.

---

50. John Knight, "Rural Revitalization in Japan: Spirit of the Village and Taste of the Country," *Asian Survey* 34, no. 7 (1994): 634–46.

PART II

Adapting Technology: State Support and Private Institutions

CHAPTER FIVE

Chisui: *Creating a Sacred Domain in Early Modern and Modern Japan*

Patricia Sippel

In the late 1980s, the Nagara River became the focus of a bitter controversy when the Ministry of Construction implemented a long-discussed plan to build a dam 5.4 kilometers above the river's mouth at the town of Nagashima, located on Ise Bay in Mie prefecture. Nagashima occupies part of the Nōbi plain, which is crossed by three major rivers as they make their way to the ocean (see Fig. 5.1). The Nagara and the Ibi rivers rise in Gifu prefecture, follow roughly parallel courses, and then converge on the plain, entering Ise Bay as a single channel. The Kiso, which rises in Nagano prefecture, reaches the bay just east of the Ibi-Nagara confluence.

The dam at Nagashima was originally conceived as a flood-control measure after a massive typhoon that swept through the Ise Bay area in September 1959 burst dikes and caused more than 5,000 deaths. A quarter of a century later, the government's objectives in damming the Nagara had expanded to include the supply of water to industry and the control of saltwater intrusion upstream. Despite opposition from some local residents, anglers' associations, and internationally organized environmental groups,

This is a revised and expanded version of an earlier article. See Patricia Sippel, "Controlling the Nagara: Changing Approaches to Water Management in Japan," *Water Policy*, no. 2 (2000): 283–97. Used with the permission of IWA Publishing.

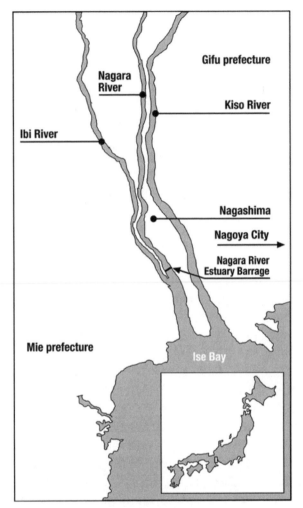

Fig. 5.1   The Kiso, Nagara, and Ibi rivers today.

construction of the Nagara River Estuary Barrage began in 1988
and was completed in 1995.

The damming of the Nagara was one of the most contested of
the *chisui* (literally, "controlling the water") projects that have been
a feature of national policymaking in modern and contemporary
Japan. Since the late nineteenth century, *chisui* has meant large-
scale, state-directed efforts designed to tame and utilize Japan's fast-
flowing rivers by reinforcing their banks, redirecting water flow,

and building dams.[1] For those who support such undertakings, *chisui* has united the people and the government in protecting lives and livelihoods from natural disasters. For critics, it has represented the ugly face of modern Japan, part of the larger enterprise of carelessly exploiting the natural environment for human gain and subordinating the needs of local communities to more powerful political and economic interests.[2] However one evaluates *chisui*, river projects have occupied a prominent place in public policy; only recently have there been signs that their status is diminishing. A March 31, 1999, editorial in the *Asahi shinbun* underscored its importance. Highlighting the unexpected reversal of a proposal to restructure Hokkaido's Chitose River, the editorial carried the title *"Chisui, Too, Is No Longer a Sacred Domain"* ("Chisui mo seiiki de nai").[3]

Chisui, however, was not the invention of modern Japan. Nor can it be characterized simply as the work of an overreaching and unconcerned state. Growing out of a long tradition of hydraulic engineering, it emerged as a "sacred domain" in the eighteenth century, when chronic flooding on an unprecedented scale prompted frequent petitions for help by villages along the Nagara and elsewhere to the highest levels of government. Although some critics pointed to the relentless clearing of land as the root cause of the repeated flooding, both farmers and government officials were committed to the economic benefits of intensive cultivation and to the survival of established rural communities. Moreover, although

---

1. For river-management policy in the twentieth century, see Kasen gyōsei kenkyūkai, ed., *Nihon no kasen* (Rivers of Japan) (Tokyo: Kensetsu kōhō kyōgikai, 1989), pp. 24–63, 90–180; and Christopher J. Gippel and Shubun Fukutome, "Rehabilitation of Japan's Waterways," in *Rehabilitation of Rivers: Principles and Implementation*, ed. Louise C. de Waal, Andrew R. G. Large, and P. Max Wade (Chichester, Eng.: John Wiley, 1998), pp. 301–17.

2. Whereas Kasen gyōsei kenkyūkai, ed., *Nihon no kasen*, reflects official policy, Ōkuma Takashi, *Kōzui to chisui no kasenshi: suigai no suiatsu kara juyō e* (A river history of floods and water control: from suppressing to accepting water damage) (Tokyo: Heibonsha, 1988), argues against the overreliance on dams for flood control. For specific arguments against the Nagara dam, see Reiko Amano and D. Brower, *Nagaragawa kara mita Nippon* (Japan seen from the Nagara River) (Tokyo: Iwanami shoten, 1993).

3. *Asahi shinbun*, Mar. 31, 1999, p. 5.

villages and districts were often divided over solutions to the flooding problem, they agreed on the need for government intervention. Finally, despite the costs, ruling elites could not afford to ignore chronic assaults on the livelihood of rural communities. Expensive, technologically challenging, and the source of ongoing friction, *chisui* was thus an important link in the relationship between state and local communities both before and during Japan's modern transformation.

This chapter examines the development of river engineering in early modern and modern Japan by focusing on two major projects conducted along the Nagara, Kiso, and Ibi rivers. The first was initiated in 1753. At the time, the three rivers were linked by a complex pattern of channels that crisscrossed the Nōbi plain and made it susceptible to catastrophic flooding. In response to local complaints, the Tokugawa bakufu ordered the Satsuma daimyo, based in distant southwestern Kyushu, to oversee and finance the construction of a wall to separate the Kiso and Ibi rivers in the southern part of the estuary and a dam further north to limit water flow from the Nagara to the Ibi. Local conflicts, mistrust of outsiders, and doubts about the environmental consequences combined to stymie the Satsuma project. Completed in 1755, it did little to protect against flooding, but it placed the idea of permanently separating the rivers at the center of discussions on flood control in the area.

The formation of the Meiji government in 1868 spurred local leaders and prefectural governors to press for a new flood-control effort in the Nōbi plain. Using the plans of a Dutch engineering consultant, in 1888 the Home Ministry initiated an ambitious project aimed at separating the Kiso, Ibi, and Nagara rivers at their points of confluence and cutting off the connecting streams. Funds came from national and prefectural taxes and from local and regional support associations. As in the eighteenth century, the work was long, expensive, and divisive. By 1912, however, the Kiso and Nagara conflux on the eastern side of Nagashima had been replaced by two separate rivers. To the west, the Nagara and Ibi had been divided as far as Nagashima, just a few kilometers from the ocean. Hailed as a major achievement in modern river management, the restructuring ended chronic flooding in the Nōbi plain and opened an era of regional economic expansion.

The Tokugawa and Meiji projects reflect an ongoing history of aggressive river engineering in the Nōbi plain from the eighteenth into the early twentieth centuries. Continuities can be seen in the common understanding of the causes of flooding and in the solutions sought. Although both were government-sponsored enterprises, they were undertaken at the insistence of local communities; in this, they reveal *chisui* as a continuing accommodation of state and private, national and regional, interests. But one can also detect changes, most strikingly a growing confidence in the power of technology to shape and control Japan's physical and human environment.

Chisui *in the Early Modern Era*

LAND DEVELOPMENT AND FLOODS
IN THE SEVENTEENTH CENTURY

As Mary Elizabeth Berry notes in her contribution to this volume, beginning in the late sixteenth century, political and military units were categorized primarily in terms of their estimated productive value expressed as units (*koku*) of rice. Not only did the *koku* system provide a standard by which daimyo and shogunal governments could assess taxes, calculate stipends and land grants, and pay for goods and services, it also contained incentives for them to boost revenues by expanding production. Supported by increases in the food supply, Japan's population more than doubled during the seventeenth century, from around 12 million to 27.7 million, a rate unmatched in the recorded history of premodern Japan.[4] At the same time, the *koku* system offered farmers the possibility of increasing household income by raising productivity above the level recorded in official registers. During the seventeenth century

---

4. Hayami Akira and Miyamoto Matao, "Gaisetsu 17–18 seiki" (Outline of the seventeenth and eighteenth centuries), in *Nihon keizai shi*, vol. 1, *Keizai shakai no seiritsu: 17–18 seiki* (Economic history of Japan: the establishment of an economic society in the 17th and 18th centuries), ed. idem (Tokyo: Iwanami shoten, 1988), pp. 42–44.

alone, official estimates of agricultural output rose from 18.5 million *koku* to 25.8 million *koku*; real agricultural output probably increased from 19.7 million to more than 30.6 million *koku*.[5]

Part of the increase in agricultural output can be attributed to longer work hours, better labor management, improved use of fertilizers, and the development of new seed strains. Another key factor was the aggressive transformation of untilled land into farmland and the conversion of dry fields into paddy. Spurred by the promise of long-term revenue gains, shogunal and daimyo governments offered incentives, such as temporary tax reductions, to developers of agricultural land. As late as 1722, the eighth Tokugawa shogun, Yoshimune (in office 1716–45), instructed local deputies, fief-holders, and farmers to seek out lands that could profitably be converted to agriculture.[6] The number of large-scale agricultural developments increased several times in the first half of the seventeenth century compared with the preceding fifty years; those figures came close to doubling again in the years 1651–1700 (see Table 5.1). During the seventeenth century, the area of cultivated land expanded from an estimated 2.1 to 2.8 million hectares.[7]

Agricultural development is the major explanation for the massive river engineering and irrigation schemes of the seventeenth century. Rulers, merchants, and well-to-do farmers changed and created river courses, dammed and dredged streams, and constructed ponds and dams in order to control the water supply for newly developed agricultural land. Table 5.1 notes 31 river-reconstruction projects in the period 1601–50, the high point of the early modern era. The construction of reservoirs and irrigation channels continued apace throughout the seventeenth century, reaching levels in the 1651–1700 period that were not matched until the closing decades of the early modern era.

By the turn of the eighteenth century, however, the effects of land development were being felt in the growing incidence of flood

---

5. Information in this and the next paragraph is taken from ibid., pp. 42–45.

6. Takayanagi Shinzō and Ishii Ryōsuke, eds., *Ofuregaki Kanpō shūsei* (A collection of laws from the Kanpō era) (Tokyo: Iwanami shoten, 1976), p. 65.

7. Hayami and Miyamoto, "Gaisetsu 17–18 seiki," p. 44.

Table 5.1
Large-Scale Engineering Projects in Japan, 1551–1850

Period	Paddy and dry-field developments	Irrigation channels	Reservoirs	River work
1551–1600	14	11	3	16
1601–1650	122	55	66	31
1651–1700	220	121	93	13
1701–1750	103	52	27	11
1751–1800	88	31	23	12
1801–1850	450	139	99	14

SOURCE: Hayami Akira and Miyamoto Matao, "Gaisetsu 17–18 seiki (Outline of the seventeenth and eighteenth centuries)," in *Nihon keizai shi*, vol. 1, *Keizai shakai no seiritsu: 17–18 seiki* (Economic history of Japan: the establishment of an economic society in the 17th and 18th centuries), ed. idem (Tokyo: Iwanami shoten, 1988), p. 45.

damage, particularly along major rivers.[8] Reclamation work on hillsides, along with logging, reduced the capacity of the soil to absorb water and increased the runoff after rain and snow melt. The growth of fields next to riverbanks and in flood plains narrowed streams and raised water levels. Although agricultural development continued in this period (see Table 5.1), bakufu attention shifted to the more pressing problem of flood control. Beginning at the end of the seventeenth century, it authorized large-scale public works almost annually along major rivers, notably the Tone and Arakawa in the Kantō region and the Kiso, Ibi, and Nagara in the Nōbi region of central Honshu.[9]

Named for the provinces of Mino (Nōshū) and Owari (Bishū) that it spans, the Nōbi plain exemplified some of the problems caused by aggressive development. It was marked for settlement from the late medieval era by its proximity to major political and military centers and by its expanse—some 1,800 square kilometers of flat land in a more characteristically mountainous country.

---

8. Conrad Totman, "Preindustrial River Conservancy: Causes and Consequences," *Monumenta Nipponica* 47, no. 1 (Spring 1992): 59–76.

9. Kasaya Kazuhiko, *Kinsei buke shakai no seiji kōzō* (The political structure of military society in the early modern period) (Tokyo: Yoshikawa kōbunkan, 1993), pp. 352–57.

Much of the fertile and well-watered lowlands were converted to agriculture during the sixteenth and seventeenth centuries. Not only were fields constructed along riverbanks, but polder islands known as *wajū* were also carved out within the mosaic of water channels that formed the three-river delta.[10] *Wajū* communities, comprising one or more villages, typically encircled themselves with dikes to protect against flooding. As many as 108 large and small *wajū* existed in a 40 by 44 kilometer area crisscrossed by the three rivers. Much of the reclaimed land lay at or below sea level.[11] Some five reinforced polders constituted the base of the Nagashima daimyo domain in Ise province, at the western edge of the plain (Fig. 5.2). The Nagashima polders took shape as a result of nineteen separate development projects undertaken in the seventeenth century, fifteen of them from the 1610s through the 1640s.[12]

Although battles against flooding had long been a way of life for the residents of the Nōbi plain, the increasing density of settlement made flood damage more likely and more destructive. Adding to the problem was a long-term shift of the geological plates along the Yōrō range on the western edge of the Nōbi plain that produced a downward tilt in the southwest and altered water flows.[13] A more immediate factor was logging, particularly in the upper reaches of the Kiso River, which changed drainage patterns, increased the volume of silt deposited downstream, and, of course, raised water levels. As the silt dumped at river bends was converted to agricultural land, water channels narrowed and overflow areas disappeared. What had once been fairly harmless spillovers turned into

---

10. Takamaki Minoru, "Bakuhan ryōshu no seiji seisaku to wajū" (Political policies of bakufu and *han* rulers and the polder), in *Bakuhansei kokka seiritsu katei no kenkyū* (Studies of the process of establishing the state system of bakufu and *han*), ed. Kitajima Masamoto (Tokyo: Yoshikawa kōbunkan, 1978), pp. 447–76; Itō Yasuo, *Chisui shisō no fūdo—kinsei kara gendai e* (The local environment of water control thinking from the early modern to the contemporary era) (Tokyo: Kokon shoin, 1994), pp. 242–311.

11. Gifu-ken, ed., *Gifu-ken shi: kinsei tsūshi hen* (History of Gifu prefecture: general history of the early modern period) (Gifu: Gifu-ken, 1968), 2: 128–37.

12. Itō Shigenobu, *Nagashima-chō shi* (History of Nagashima town) (Nagashima: Nagashima kyōiku iinkai, 1978), 1: 181.

13. Gifu-ken, ed., *Gifu-ken shi: kinsei tsūshi hen*, 2: 130.

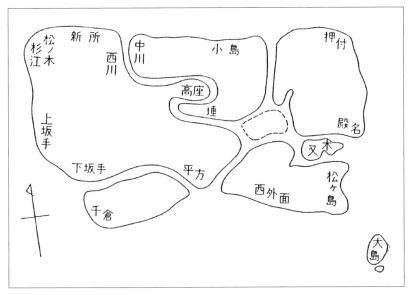

Fig. 5.2   Nagashima in the early seventeenth century (source: Itō Shigenobu, *Nagashima-chō shi* [Nagashima: Nagashima kyōiku iinkai, 1978], 1: 15).

floods that destroyed fields and houses, particularly in *wajū* communities, whose very existence was a significant factor in the increased clogging of the rivers.

Although a listing of water-related disasters in Mino province and Nagashima domain shows no significant increase through the seventeenth century (see Table 5.2), local perceptions were different. For example, in 1702 residents of 72 villages in three southern Mino polders claimed in a lawsuit filed with the bakufu court that recent development along the lower reaches of the Ibi River in the Kuwana domain of neighboring Ise province had caused repeated flooding.[14] Specifically, the villages complained that the narrowing of the river from 540 meters to 144 meters because of newly developed fields meant that high waters took five or six days, rather

14. Ibid., 2: 171–72; Gifu-ken, ed., *Gifu-ken shi: kinsei shiryō hen* (History of Gifu prefecture: early modern sources) (Gifu: Gifu-ken, 1969), 5: 200–208, 580–93. Itō Shin, *Hōreki chisui to Satsuma-han shi* (The Hōreki water control project and the retainers of Satsuma domain) (Tokyo: Tsuru shobō, 1943), pp. 43–50, lists floods in the Nōbi plain almost every year through the first half of the Edo period.

Table 5.2
Water-Related Disasters in
Mino Province and Nagashima Domain, 1601–1860

Period	Incidents in Mino province	Incidents in Nagashima domain
1601–1650	45	13
1651–1700	51	7
1701–1750	49	7
1751–1800	78	8
1801–1850	68	13
1851–1860	37	4

NOTE: Mino province figures are identified more narrowly as "flood damage."
SOURCES: Gifu-ken, ed., *Gifu-ken shi: kinsei tsūshi hen* (History of Gifu prefecture: general history of the early modern period) (Gifu: Gifu-ken, 1968), 2: 131; Itō Shigenobu, *Nagashima-chō shi* (History of Nagashima town) (Nagashima: Nagashima kyōiku iinkai, 1978), 1: 467–70.

than one day, to subside. The embankments that surrounded rice fields on all sides had weakened, collapsing under just a little pressure and allowing fields to flood. The bakufu court rejected the charges against the Kuwana development but ordered a cleanup of the lower Ibi. The focus was on removing obstacles—trees, rushes, stakes, even some houses—in order to get the water to flow as quickly as possible. In 1705, the bakufu conducted another, bigger dredging operation; during the next five years, it strengthened embankments and cleared ditches along the waterways of Mino.

THE TOKUGAWA BAKUFU

AND FLOOD CONTROL

It is not surprising that victims of repeated or catastrophic flooding appealed to the Tokugawa bakufu for help in repairing damage and warding off further disasters. At its peak in the middle of the eighteenth century, the Tokugawa domain extended across 46 of Japan's 67 provinces; in addition, the bakufu directly controlled key cities, ports, mines, roads, and waterways. Moreover, although the surveys and maps described by Berry portray a formal rather than a physical reality, the formality obscures a vigorous bakufu effort to control and reshape the physical environment of Japan. From its inception, the bakufu had its own corps of engineers and overseers who surveyed villages, built land- and water-transportation systems, and designed complex water systems for drinking and irrigation. Much of the agricultural expansion of the seventeenth century was conducted within the framework of a bakufu policy of vigorous development.

The Nōbi area was of special concern to the Tokugawa bakufu: Owari province to the east was Tokugawa branch family (*gosanke*) territory; in Mino province, which occupied the center of the plain, not quite one-quarter of the total assessed output came from villages that were part of the shogun's own domain. Mino was valuable for its strategic location, for its fertile soil, and for the access it offered to timber in the mountains of Hida and Nagano. From the early 1630s, bakufu deputies had coordinated a province-wide system aimed at getting labor or a cash equivalent for regular river maintenance from villages in all jurisdictions.[15] As flooding turned into a chronic and regional problem, Mino residents, again across administrative boundaries, appealed to the Tokugawa government for help.

Ironically, the emergence of flood control as a major policy issue coincided with the emergence of long-term fiscal stresses for the bakufu. The shogun's government drew its ordinary revenues from the annual agricultural taxes paid by villages in its own domain, which by 1700 accounted for some 15 percent of Japan's officially assessed agricultural output.[16] Initially, the bakufu had also drawn on extraordinary revenues: contributions of daimyo and merchants as well as gold and silver obtained in the final and most productive phase of a mining boom that began in the mid-sixteenth century and lasted for about a century. By the end of the seventeenth century, however, extraordinary revenues were drying up, and extraordinary expenses—such as the cost of rebuilding Edo after a fire in 1657—had brought the bakufu to an impasse. In 1704, bakufu officials announced that for the coming year "we

15. Gifu-ken, ed., *Gifu-ken shi: kinsei tsūshi hen*, 2: 147–60, 166–78.

16. On taxes and bakufu fiscal problems, see Patricia Sippel, "Financing the Long Peace: The Agricultural Tax in the Tokugawa Domain" (Ph.D. diss., Harvard University, 1994), chaps. 4 and 5.

cannot pay retainers' stipends [in full]; nor can we cover all other expenditures."[17]

Among the "other expenditures" were those associated with natural disasters, including flood control and, in 1707, the eruption of Mount Fuji. Pressed to deal with the frequent flooding along the Yamato River south of Osaka, the bakufu had ordered the daimyo of nearby Himeji in 1703 to provide funds for the rerouting of the river more directly to the ocean. The Yamato operation was an early example of what the bakufu termed "assisted public works" (*otetsudai fushin*), in which selected daimyo, singly or in groups, were required to provide funds and sometimes manage major projects, even if their own domains were not directly affected.[18] Between 1704 and 1714, the bakufu ordered daimyo to "assist" in at least nine major flood-control operations. Most of the rivers were close to the main corridor that connected the Kantō and Kinai regions, including the Nōbi plain.

Fiscal considerations produced a series of changes in the funding of river work.[19] On the one hand, the bakufu sought to reduce its involvement in projects carried out in daimyo-controlled territory. At the same time, it looked for public works funding outside its ordinary revenue sources. In 1720, Shogun Yoshimune drew on the model used for close to a century in Mino to determine that large-scale repair projects in areas touching on bakufu interests would be funded primarily by a provincial tax (*kuniyaku kin*) levied as necessary on commoners in affected districts. For just over a decade, provincial levies were to remain the prime financial support for river works in bakufu and daimyo territories in Honshu. In 1732, however, they were suspended, and daimyo assistance for large-

17. Takayanagi and Ishii, *Ofuregaki Kanpō shūsei*, p. 558.

18. Totman, "Preindustrial River Conservancy," p. 67. See the list in Kasaya, *Kinsei buke shakai*, pp. 351–52.

19. Information in this paragraph is drawn from Kasaya, *Kinsei buke shakai*, pp. 331–34, 351–58; Ōguchi Yūjirō, "Bakufu no zaisei" (The bakufu fisc), in *Nihon keizai shi*, vol. 2, *Kindai seichō no taidō* (Economic history of Japan: the emergence of modern growth), ed. Shinbo Hiroshi and Saitō Osamu (Tokyo: Iwanami shoten, 1989), pp. 153–55; Totman, "Preindustrial River Conservancy," pp. 65–71; Itō Shin, *Hōreki chisui*, pp. 51–56. The provincial tax levies mentioned below took pressure off the daimyo, who were required between 1722 and 1732 to pay a special annual contribution to the bakufu's ordinary accounts.

scale river work was revived. From this time on, the daimyo
drafted to help with these projects were often lords of large domains located far from the areas that needed help. For instance, after floods devastated the Kantō region in 1742, the bakufu mobilized the Ikeda, Mōri, Hosokawa, and eight other daimyo from far
western Japan to take special responsibility for the reconstruction.
And, from the late 1740s, when the bakufu again felt obliged to
take on the challenge of flood control in the Kiso, Nagara, and Ibi
delta, it turned to daimyo of distant domains: Nihonmatsu in the
Tōhoku region and Satsuma in southernmost Kyushu.

THE SATSUMA OPERATION

The flood-control project assigned to Satsuma domain in 1753–55 was
both a continuation of earlier attempts to remove impediments to
water flow in the Nōbi plain and an ambitious new attempt to restructure the delta itself.[20] In 1732, a 13-hectare (32.5 acre) rice-field
development known as Manju shinden was completed (after local
controversy but eventual bakufu consent) in the southern part of
Takasu *wajū* (see Fig. 5.3). Located right where the Ibi joined the
Nagara and just west of the Kuwana project that had caused problems three decades earlier, the development predictably slowed the
water flow in a key section of the delta. Reporting on the situation
in 1735, Mino deputy (*gundai*) Izawa Tamenaga, an expert in river
engineering, is said to have suggested to the bakufu that separating
the major rivers might solve the problem.[21]

Izawa died within months of his arrival in Mino, but local communities continued to press for a solution. In 1743, representatives
of 77 bakufu-administered villages traveled to Edo to appeal directly
for help. Then, in 1746, 40 villages of Takasu domain requested—in
what is the earliest surviving rationale for the plan—that the Kiso
and Ibi rivers be separated as they neared the ocean. The bakufu responded in 1747 with an order to the daimyo of Nihonmatsu to

---

20. Gifu-ken, ed., *Gifu-ken shi: kinsei tsūshi hen*, 2: 183–85.

21. Itō Shin, *Hōreki chisui*, pp. 59–60. No documentary evidence survives to
support this claim.

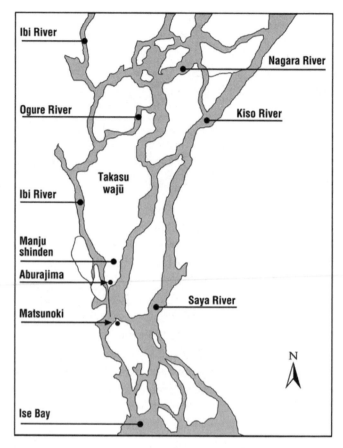

Fig. 5.3   The Kiso, Nagara, and Ibi rivers, 1753–55 (adapted from
a map included as a supplement to Gifu-ken, ed., *Gifu-ken shi:
kinsei shiryō hen* [Gifu: Gifu-ken, 1969], p. 5)

"assist" in a project that would include not just the customary
dredging and dike repairs but also the construction of a partial barrier between the Kiso and Ibi rivers. Work proceeded under the direction of Finance Commissioner Kan'o Haruhide. A set of pickets
was positioned to direct water from the Kiso into the Saya River on
the far eastern side of the delta. An earthen wall and more pickets
jutted into a stretch of water between Aburajima shinden and
Matsunoki; the location was just south of the Takasu *wajū* and the
last point at which the Kiso joined the Ibi before emptying into Ise

Bay. Both arrangements reflected the germ of the idea that the Satsuma domain officials attempted to realize in 1753.

The Satsuma operation arose directly from an investigation of flooding conducted by a bakufu official named Yoshida Kyūzaemon in summer 1753. The responses that Yoshida solicited from residents reinforced an emerging consensus that the only real solution was to separate the rivers.[22] At the end of the year, the bakufu ordered Satsuma domain to assist in a large operation that would clear debris and repair dikes after the recent flooding and advance the separation of the three rivers. The work would cover an area that extended 50 to 60 kilometers inland, including 193 villages in three provinces. According to the shogun's orders, "assisting" meant that Satsuma was responsible for procuring materials, hiring workers, overseeing operations, and paying for roughly 80 percent of the total cost. Satsuma overseers were to answer on site to shogunal officials, including Yoshida and the bakufu's Mino deputy. The goals for the project and basic policy were set in Edo, by senior councilors, working through the Finance Office.

The bakufu request took the Satsuma government by surprise.[23] Already in difficult fiscal straits, it could not supply the enormous resources—a projected 93,000 *ryō* in gold and 4,600 trees—necessary for the job. More than 947 samurai overseers traveled to the site, their leader stopping off in Osaka to borrow funds from merchants. From its beginning in spring 1754, the operation was

---

22. Gifu-ken, ed., *Gifu-ken shi: kinsei shiryō hen*, 5: 208–11.

23. Itō Shin, *Hōreki chisui*, pp. 84–125; Ikemizu Kiichi, *Hōreki chisui ketsurui Satsuma-han shi monogatari* (A blood and tears account of the Satsuma retainers and the Hōreki water control project) (Aira town, Kagoshima prefecture: The author, 1971), pp. 52–68; Yamada Teisaku, *Hōreki chisui Satsuma gishi jiseki gaiyō* (Outline of the facts of the Satsuma heroes and the Hōreki water control project) (Ikebe village, Gifu prefecture: Satsuma gishi kenshōkai, 1932), pp. 21–23. The Satsuma operation is fascinating for the hints that emerge about Satsuma-bakufu relations. According to Itō and other scholars sympathetic to the Satsuma cause, problems had arisen over marriage connections, worsening after Shogun Yoshimune's death in 1751. Some Satsuma retainers criticized the bakufu order as a ploy to impoverish the Shimazu family, but the domainal government saw no alternative to resentful compliance.

dogged with difficulties.[24] Heavy rain caused further damage and forced a modification of the work plan. Understandably, relations with bakufu representatives were strained. Moreover, although local residents presumably welcomed the work, the Satsuma overseers had difficulty hiring labor and getting their directions followed precisely. By summer, when the first phase of basic cleanup and repairs was declared finished, many of the Satsuma men had fallen ill; a few, demoralized, had killed themselves.

The second phase, begun in autumn 1754, aimed to separate the rivers of the delta at two locations: first, by extending the Kiso-Ibi divide between Aburajima and Matsunoki; and, second, by building a dam that would break the connection between the Ibi and Nagara rivers on the Ogure river north of Takasu (see Fig. 5.3). A distance of not quite 2.4 kilometers separated Aburajima from Matsunoki at the point where bakufu planners aimed to divide the Kiso and Ibi. The pickets constructed in 1747 measured barely 236 meters on the Aburajima side and 55 meters at Matsunoki, leaving some 2 kilometers of open river. Under Satsuma supervision, laborers hauled rocks, timber, and thatch to build the foundations of a wall from both sides. Work was slow and difficult. To hold back the force of the water, the Satsuma managers resorted to various devices, including sinking old boats filled with stones. Just over a month into the task and with less than 300 meters built across, they asked Yoshida whether a complete separation of the river was required.

Perhaps the sheer difficulty of the undertaking prompted Yoshida and others to reconsider. There may also have been other concerns, such as the threat of reduced shipping in the delta. Toward the end of the year, they advised the Satsuma managers against radical action: "If we make a complete divide now, it is difficult to calculate the problems we might encounter in the future. At this point, we think it best to leave an opening in the middle and watch the flow of water for a year or two. On that basis, we can decide

---

24. Details of the Satsuma operation are drawn from Gifu-ken, ed., *Gifu-ken shi: kinsei tsūshi hen*, 2: 183–96; Gifu-ken, ed., *Gifu-ken shi: kinsei shiryō hen*, 5: 211–529; and Itō Shin, *Hōreki chisui*, pp. 126–369.

whether to complete the divide."[25] After senior bakufu officials approved the more limited solution, the Satsuma overseers built a barricade about 3.6 meters high and a kilometer long on the Aburajima side and extending 273 meters on the Matsunoki side. They used 84,000 cubic meters of rock and 100,000 cubic meters of soil. Even when a 363-meter-long embankment was added on the Matsunoki side, about one-third of the river lay open in the middle. The work was finished in the third month of 1755, a bit ahead of schedule.

Similar hesitation marked the second prong of the effort to separate the three rivers: construction of a dam on the Ogure, a tributary of the Nagara that flowed into the Ibi. Because the bed of the Ogure was some 2.5 meters lower than that of the Nagara—the land sloped noticeably—water poured into the Ogure, causing flooding during heavy rain. In 1751 nearby villages had built a small dam at their own expense. Two years later, 88 villages had jointly petitioned Yoshida for a dam that would break the connection between the Nagara and the Ibi. Bakufu planners supported the idea, although they were uncertain whether a dam or a simple dividing wall would be better, and they worried about the unanticipated consequences that a divide at Aburajima might produce.

By the time preparatory work began in the eleventh month of 1754, villages along the Nagara were claiming that a second barricade—the work at Aburajima was nearing completion—would indeed be dangerous. In the first month of 1755, Satsuma managers began work on a modified plan: an entrapment basin, about 43 meters wide, located at the point where the Ogure joined the Nagara. (The original proposal called for a dam 62 meters wide.) Water pouring from the Nagara would be contained to a level of 1.3 meters; the overflow would make its way to the Ibi. Complex measures of river current were used to determine the depth of the dam, and the entire floor was lined with *jakago*, bamboo baskets filled with rocks. Some 26,000 cubic meters of rock and 180 cubic meters of soil were used. Heavy rains, even flooding, slowed progress but did not collapse the stone and wood supports.

Completion of the Ogure dam marked the end of the Satsuma river work. More than 30 Satsuma officials had died from injury or

25. Gifu-ken, ed., *Gifu-ken shi: kinsei tsūshi hen*, 2: 192.

illness, and as many as 52 had committed suicide in despair or protest. Moreover, the total cost to Satsuma was more than double the
original projection: the equivalent of 220,298 *ryō* in cash as well as
lumber, bamboo, stones, and rope.[26] (The bakufu's cash contribution was 9,895 *ryō*.) In the fifth month of 1755, eleven inspectors
sent from Edo reported satisfaction with the outcome. The leader
of the Satsuma team, Hirata Yukie, wrote his report to the domain
government on the following day. Then, taking responsibility for
the management problems, the billowing costs, and the sicknesses
and deaths caused by a year and a half of difficult work conducted
a thousand kilometers from home, Hirata turned in the direction
of Satsuma and killed himself.

Marked by avoidable human tragedy, the Satsuma project has
customarily been viewed as an extreme example of the inefficien-
cies, even bankruptcy, of bakufu fiscal and political management.
And it bought only short-lived protection from floods. As Table
5.2 shows, the incidence of flooding in Mino province and in Nagashima domain increased in the second half of the Edo period.
Floods around the Ogure dam also worsened.[27] In 1766, the shogun
ordered another daimyo to work on flood damage in the three-
river plain. As land use intensified and water problems continued,
a series of river works—after-the-fact and unambitious—followed at
shorter intervals into the nineteenth century.

The Meiji Restructuring

THE LOCAL CAMPAIGN
FOR CENTRAL SUPPORT

Despite the inadequacies of Tokugawa policy evident in the Satsuma operation of 1753–55, the idea of creating separate rivers survived into the Meiji era as the answer to the problem of chronic
flooding on the Nōbi plain. So, too, did local anticipation of help
from the highest level of government. Flood-weary farmers hoped
that the new Meiji government would shoulder the responsibility

---

26. Itō Shin, *Hōreki chisui*, pp. 361–69. Itō estimates (p. 363) that the money
paid by Satsuma amounted to more than two years of domainal rice revenues.

27. Itō Yasuo, *Chisui shisō no fūdo*, pp. 155–59.

for public works that the Tokugawa bakufu had shirked. Their expectation seemed to be justified when the Tokyo government moved promptly in 1868 to establish a "river envoy" to oversee "water utilization throughout the nation . . . and bring happiness to the people."[28] Excited at the new possibilities, local elites in the Nōbi region and governors of the newly created prefectures moved quickly to draw public attention to the problem of flooding. Their aim was to raise support at local, regional, and national levels for a major, permanent solution.

There was little disagreement about the proposed solution. Decrying the "makeshift" measures of the Tokugawa era, essays and petitions called for the complete separation of the Kiso, Nagara, and Ibi rivers. As the governors of Aichi and Mie prefectures warned in 1877, "If we try to resolve the problem now using stopgap measures, we will simply be wasting money."[29] But central government involvement was essential. Local and regional leaders argued that *chisui* was expensive and technically challenging; that finding solutions had in the past been complicated by conflicting local and regional interests; and that, therefore, the national government should exercise leadership by offering money and technical support and by mediating local conflicts to devise a comprehensive strategy of flood control.[30]

From the early 1870s, petitions for central government support typically included a further element: a request to raise the technological level of the work by drawing on foreign—specifically Dutch—expertise. As Michael Lewis has pointed out, rivers assumed importance early in Meiji government policy not because of the problem of flooding but because of the potential they seemed to hold for modern transportation.[31] Impressed by Dutch river transportation, Ōkubo Toshimichi, a leading member of the

---

28. Ibid., p. 160. The term "river envoy" is borrowed from Michael Lewis, who has analyzed national river management policy in Toyama prefecture in the Meiji era in *Becoming Apart: National Power and Local Politics in Toyama, 1868–1945* (Cambridge, Mass.: Harvard University Asia Center, 2000), pp. 73–117.

29. Gifu-ken, ed., *Gifu-ken chisui shi* (A history of water management in Gifu prefecture) (Gifu: Gifu-ken, 1953), 1: 196.

30. Ibid., pp. 194–202; Itō Yasuo, *Chisui shisō no fūdo*, pp. 159–62.

31. Lewis, *Becoming Apart*, p. 82.

government, decided to bring two engineers—C. J. van Doorn and
I. A. Lindo—to Japan to help realize his plan for a national water
transportation network.[32] After their arrival in early 1872, the foreigners were sent first to work on restructuring Osaka Bay. However, flooding inland along the Yodogawa River complicated the
project. At Doorn's request—and in the face of opposition by some
government members—a second group of five Dutch engineers arrived in 1873. In the 1870s, a total of ten foreign engineers, all of
them Dutch, traveled to Japan to advise on river management.[33]
After Ōkubo became head of the newly created Home Ministry in
1873, responsibility for river projects was moved to an Engineering
Bureau within that ministry. Convinced of the importance of water
transportation as a basis for industrialization, Ōkubo secured the
substantial annual budget of about ¥3 million and had the Dutch
work on major river systems: the Yodogawa and Tonegawa, and
then the Kiso and Shinano rivers. (Luckily for a policy that focused
on river transportation rather than flood protection, no major ca-
tastrophes caused by floods occurred in the first ten years of the
Meiji era.)

Even before the first Dutch engineers reached Japan, flood-
control advocates in the Nōbi plain had requested access to advanced Western expertise. In 1871 an official stationed in Nagoya
wrote to the central government of his desire to "use foreigners in
order to devise an engineering project that would be completely
different from those of the past."[34] Completion of the Osaka Bay
work pushed expectations higher, and in 1877 the governors of Mie
and Aichi prefectures wrote to the Home Ministry requesting
guidance on flood control from the foreign engineers employed
there. The Home Ministry responded by sending engineer Johan-
nis de Rijke (1842–1913) to survey the three-river delta with a view
to drawing up flood control plans. Rijke, who had come to Japan
in 1873 (and would stay until 1903), visited the area from February

32. Yamazaki Yūkō, "Naimushō no kasen seisaku" (River policy in the Home
Ministry), in Michi to kawa no kindai (Roads and rivers in the modern period),
ed. Takamura Naosuke (Tokyo: Yamakawa shuppankai, 1996), pp. 69–74.

33. Itō Yasuo, Chisui shisō no fūdo, p.101.

34. Gifu-ken, ed., Gifu-ken chisui shi, p. 202.

23 to March 6, 1878, and again for eight days in July that same year. During both trips he walked extensively, both in the delta and following river courses upstream. Armed with insights gathered from firsthand observation as well as his study of current European practice, Rijke wrote detailed reports after each trip.

Rijke's report of March 1878 confirmed that a basic cause of the flooding was the large volume of sand and soil that was constantly washing downstream, narrowing waterways and raising riverbeds.[35] That problem was exacerbated by the complexity of the network of channels that linked the three rivers and by the fact that riverbed levels and water heights varied considerably across the basin. What was the solution? Rijke noted past attempts to seal off tributaries and to use sluices to control water flow in specific areas. Such measures, he argued, addressed only part of the problem. In order to achieve a more comprehensive and enduring solution, Rijke concluded that the initial focus should be on upstream land management rather than on downstream engineering—in other words, on controlling the mountains (*chisan*) rather than on controlling the water (*chisui*).[36] Specifically, he recommended: (1) measures designed to reduce the movement of silt downstream, including a ban on lumbering, the planting of trees and ground covers, and the construction of upstream dams; and (2) the separation of the Kiso River (but not the division of the Nagara or Ibi) and the strengthening of dikes downstream to guard against sudden overflows. Rijke's supplementary reports emphasized the importance of upstream measures; he placed the responsibility for flood problems on the local people, "who will not give up the practice of devastating the mountains and the woods."[37]

Rijke's recommendations generated considerable local interest and some controversy. Although the principles of forest conservation were fairly well understood, his criticism of specific local practices (with the implication that floods had human as well as natural causes) created resentment. Moreover, Rijke's prioritizing of conservation ahead of river engineering refueled old conflicts about

---

35. For the Japanese translation of the original report, see ibid., pp. 205–19.
36. Itō Yasuo, *Chisui shisō no fūdo*, pp. 100–154.
37. Ibid., pp. 127–28.

fund allocations between upstream and downstream communities. In particular, his apparent de-emphasis on separating the three rivers prompted criticism from some Japanese engineers and from those local leaders whose principal objective in having Rijke view the area was to get the support of an outside expert for a major restructuring project.[38]

Local dissatisfaction with Rijke's recommendations was reflected in the formation of societies aimed specifically at promoting river engineering. The year 1878 witnessed the foundation of the Ōgaki Polder Flood Control Association (Ōgaki wajū chisui kai)—the earliest such group in Gifu prefecture.[39] Another center of active lobbying was Anpachi district (a few kilometers north of present-day Nagashima, in Mie prefecture), where Katano Ryūzō drew up a petition on behalf of 24 local notables, arguing that the cost of river restructuring would be repaid by the prosperity of the region and calling for work to begin immediately.[40] Katano's group reorganized itself in 1880 as the Cooperative Society for Flood Control (Chisui kyōdōsha). Its aim was to exert pressure on the central government to begin work in the three-river area; it also raised funds through membership fees.[41]

NATIONAL POLICY ON FLOOD CONTROL

In the late 1870s, the local campaign for restructuring the Nōbi rivers had to navigate not simply Rijke's conservationist approach but also the fiscal priorities of the central government. When Ōkubo Toshimichi was assassinated in 1878, much of the official enthusiasm for a Dutch-inspired river-transportation network died with him.[42] River utilization had already assumed a lower profile in 1880, when

---

38. For the entire statement, see Gifu-ken, ed., *Gifu-ken chisui shi*, pp. 221–23.

39. Gifu-ken, ed., *Gifu-ken shi: kindai tsūshi hen* (History of Gifu prefecture: general history of the modern era) (Gifu: Gifu-ken, 1972), 2: 1093–96; Itō Yasuo, *Chisui shisō no fūdo*, pp. 167–69.

40. Itō Yasuo, *Chisui shisō no fūdo*, pp. 167–68.

41. The Chisui kyōdōsha continued into the 1890s, transforming itself into the All-Japan Flood Control Alliance (Zenkoku chisui dōmeikai) in 1893. During 1890 and 1894, it produced a magazine with a circulation that reached 741 in 1891. Some 38 percent of the copies went to Nōbi area residents.

42. Yamazaki, "Naimushō no kasen seisaku," pp. 74–76.

Matsukata Masayoshi became head of the Home Ministry. Matsukata favored rail over water as the basis of a national transportation network; moreover, he doubted the applicability of Dutch river technology to Japan.[43] He dismissed all but two of the expensive foreign experts, leaving just the recently arrived A. L. T. Mulder and Rijke, whose environmental concerns had gained him a reputation for sensitivity to Japanese conditions.

Matsukata's ideas were reflected in fiscal and administrative policy. His 1880 revisions to the 1878 tax laws offered prefectures increased revenues by setting prefectural taxes at one-third rather than one-fifth of the land taxes paid to the central government.[44] At the same time, however, the revisions radically cut central grants to the prefectures for engineering projects, making both flood control and water transportation a provincial responsibility in principle. Administrative changes underscored the central government's diminished involvement: in 1881, administration of river management was transferred from the Home Ministry to the Ministry of Agriculture and Commerce (Nōshōmushō), newly established by Itō Hirobumi and Ōkuma Shigenobu to promote industrial development. Matsukata himself moved from the Home Ministry in October 1881 to take charge of the Finance Ministry; he was succeeded by Yamada Yoriyoshi. As heavy rains brought widespread flooding in the 1880s, prefectural officials looked to the Home Ministry for help, but Yamada's halfhearted efforts to wrest money from Finance Minister Matsukata proved mostly unsuccessful. Complaints of Yamada's incompetence abounded. In the twelfth month of 1883, he was dismissed as home minister and replaced by Yamagata Aritomo.

As head of the Home Ministry, Yamagata Aritomo made it his aim to regain control of river policy, increase the budget of the Engineering Bureau, and build a modern system of water transportation. In contrast to Matsukata, he argued that continued

---

43. Ibid., pp. 76–82.

44. Watanabe Naoko, "'Chihōzei' no sōshutsu—san shinpō taiseika no dobokuhi futan" (The emergence of local taxes: the burden of engineering costs in the Three New Laws system), in *Michi to kawa no kindai*, pp. 133–72; James C. Baxter, *The Meiji Unification Through the Lens of Ishikawa Prefecture* (Cambridge, Mass.: Harvard University, Council on East Asian Studies, 1994), pp. 186–93.

flooding made river work necessary and that central government funds had to be made available. Yamagata also claimed that, in flood control as well in transportation, Dutch technology was superior to Japanese. In May 1884 he detailed his views in a document entitled "Chisui no gi ni tsuki jōshin" (A statement on flood control).[45] Whereas Tokugawa-era flood control had primarily been a matter of building dikes, Dutch engineers, he maintained, had introduced new methods of river reconstruction and erosion control. In other words, in contrast to the "stopgap approaches of an earlier era," the foreigners were offering fundamental solutions: "Since their method incorporates recent advances, nothing can match it as a means of permanently improved water control."

Yamagata pointed out that the Home Ministry had begun work on major river systems, including the Kiso, but the tax revisions of 1880 that had taken funds away from the central bureaucracy had placed a significant financial burden on individual prefectures. Without money from Tokyo, ambitious river work could not be undertaken. Yamagata asked for ¥650,000 (¥50,000 for each of Japan's thirteen largest rivers) in order to "consolidate the basis of flood control." He also encouraged prefectural leaders to submit appeals for funds. Yamagata's was a powerful voice urging the return of river management to the Home Ministry and underscoring the importance of hydraulic engineering. Later in 1884, his ally Mishima Michitsune became head of the Engineering Bureau; Mishima requested ¥577,500 for river work in the 1885 regular budget, as well as ¥847,000 in a supplementary budget.

SEPARATING THE RIVERS

Yamagata's support helps explain the timing of the Kiso restructuring project.[46] In October 1884, the Home Ministry instructed Rijke to draw up a detailed plan for the reconstruction of the lower Kiso, Nagara, and Ibi rivers. By 1886, Rijke had produced a plan with the English title: "Kisogawa Polder: General Plan for Separating and

---

45. Analyzed in Yamazaki, "Naimushō no kasen seisaku," pp. 91–93. For the full text, see Kōbunroku (Government record), no. 2A-26-3699, Kokuritsu kōbunsho kan (National Archives of Japan).

46. See Lewis's comments in *Becoming Apart*, pp. 82–83.

Improving the Rivers, Facilitating the Discharge of Floods and Drainage of the Polders."[47] As the title suggests, Rijke envisaged a major project that would reduce the danger of flooding and improve drainage in the Kiso, Nagara, and Ibi delta. (A secondary aim was to improve water transportation.) The underlying idea was that if the rivers were separated, inflow from tributaries limited, and embankments raised to sea level on both banks, the water would flow faster, and silt would be washed away rather than simply accumulating. The aim of complete separation marked a contrast with the Satsuma project (which had worsened clogging by slowing the flow) and with Rijke's own 1878 proposal (which had not included the separation of the Nagara from the Ibi, even as a long-term measure).[48]

The specific details can be understood from Fig. 5.4. The Kiso was to be separated from the Nagara by cutting a new channel (through Tatsuta *wajū*) along the several-kilometer-long stretch where the two rivers flowed together; it would be separated from the Ibi by completion of the Aburajima divide. Cutting off the Saya tributary would allow the Kiso to reach the ocean as a single, relatively simple stream. The Ibi and Nagara would be separated by blocking off the three rivers (Ogure, Nakamura, and Nakasu) that linked them upstream and by cutting a new channel (through Takasu) where they converged downstream. Finally, water traffic would be enhanced by a lock gate built between the Nagara and Kiso rivers just north of Nagashima.

Reconstruction of the three-river basin according to Rijke's Kisogawa polder plan began in 1888 and took 24 years to complete. Unlike the Satsuma samurai in the 1750s, the managers of the Meiji undertaking did not face daunting technical difficulties. In fact, despite enormous interest in the "modern" aspects of the project, most of the physical work—cutting new river channels and build-

---

47. For details of the plan, see Gifu-ken, ed., *Gifu-ken chisui shi*, pp. 254–59; and Itō Shigenobu, *Nagashima-chō shi*, 2: 42–67.

48. Why Rijke changed his mind is not clear: he wrote once that separation of the Kiso alone might lower the water levels of the Ibi and Nagara and worsen drainage through the polders. Perhaps, too, he was succumbing to local pressure to do a complete job.

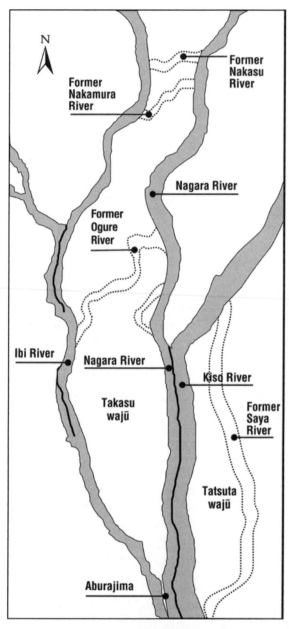

Fig. 5.4 Restructuring the Kiso, Nagara, and
Ibi rivers in the Meiji period (adapted from
Kiso 14 [Spring 1995]: 8).

ing earthen dikes—relied on familiar methods and materials. But there were other problems. One was the dislocation of polder communities, notably the roughly 1,800 households who lost land in Takasu, Tatsuta, and Nagashima. (Some 174 dispossessed households left Nagashima for Hokkaido, the United States, and elsewhere.)[49] An earthquake in 1891 and two major floods in 1896 slowed the work. And, finally, funding was difficult. Of the ¥4,198,554 total, the national government supplied roughly ¥3,128,118; the rest came from Mie, Aichi, and Gifu prefectural taxes and other sources, including contributions from local support groups.[50] (In 1897, public works expenses accounted for as much as 63.3 percent of Gifu prefectural spending.)[51]

Ironically, the restructuring of the Kiso, Nagara, and Ibi rivers also coincided with a decline of confidence in the possibilities of a Dutch-style river-transportation system. In 1885, long summer rains in western Japan burst dikes along the Yodogawa in what turned out to be record-breaking floods. The collapse of the Yodogawa dikes was also, in Yamazaki Aritsune's phrase, "the collapse of the Dutch myth."[52] Communities along the Yodogawa now requested high-water dikes, and even the Home Ministry turned its attention away from water transportation. Although Rijke's reputation remained high, he, too, suffered professional setbacks. By 1912, when the Kisogawa polder plan was finally realized, Rijke was no longer in Japan.

If the restructuring of the Kiso, Nagara, and Ibi rivers did not guarantee the privileged position of Dutch expertise in water transportation, it nevertheless did much to strengthen a different myth. Flooding was controlled, land values rose, and the Nōbi plain entered a phase of vigorous economic growth. The new arrangements, coming after some two hundred years of intense struggle against flooding, did much to consolidate the enterprise— and the near-invincible status of—*chisui* itself.

---

49. Itō Shigenobu, *Nagashima-chō shi*, 2: 83–105.

50. Ibid., 2: 58; Gifu-ken, ed., *Gifu-ken chisui shi*, pp. 260–65.

51. Nakano Kōshirō, *Gifu-ken no rekishi* (A history of Gifu prefecture) (Tokyo: Yamakawa shuppansha, 1972), p. 237. On the comparably high level of public works spending in Toyama prefecture, see Lewis, *Becoming Apart*, p. 88.

52. Yamazaki, "Naimushō no kasen seisaku," pp. 95–98.

Conclusion

The history of the Nagara, Ibi, and Kiso rivers points to several characteristics of river management and flood control in early modern and modern Japan. Most important, it is clear that, far from being a creation of modern Japan, *chisui* as a national undertaking dates at least to the state-building policies of the Tokugawa era. As Conrad Totman has pointed out, the explosive growth of early modern Japanese society rested on an unusually vigorous exploitation of the natural environment: on rocks, timber, and especially water.[53] So aggressive was the land clearing of the seventeenth century that by the turn of the eighteenth century, it had created a new energy equilibrium that required constant human intervention. In areas like the Nōbi plain, flooding was chronic. Given the convergence of interests between village communities dependent on farming and a government dependent on agricultural tax revenues, *chisui* emerged as the enterprise through which government and people worked to impose their will on rivers, a battle that, in Totman's words, they "dared not lose but seemed unable to win."[54] The contribution of the Meiji era lay neither in creating the problem nor in devising new ways to deal with it, but in providing the resources— funds, management, technology, and confidence—that allowed a measure of human success in the battle against flooding.

Two further points can be made. First, although flood control served the interests of both government and local communities, the impetus for action and ideas about the steps to be taken came largely from the communities. In the eighteenth century, when fiscal difficulties made bakufu policymakers reluctant to initiate systematic river management, flood-threatened villages in the Nōbi plain pushed for government help. The attempt to separate the rivers in 1753–55 was not so much a bakufu-imposed burden on a long-suffering population as a response to local pressure incorporating ideas canvassed from residents and commandeering the resources of an outside political rival. And although the project itself was a

---

53. Totman, "Preindustrial River Conservancy," pp. 59–76.
54. Ibid., p. 60.

massive failure, the idea of separation survived, to be advanced with even greater urgency in the opening years of the Meiji period. From the late 1870s, as Rijke preached the importance of sound land use over hydraulic engineering and Meiji government leaders hesitated to fund large-scale flood-control projects, local and regional associations continued their push for the separation of the Nagara, Ibi, and Kiso. In 1896, while the restructuring was in progress, local demands were reflected in the passage of a river law that placed flood control (rather than transportation) at the center of a national program of river management.[55]

Finally, the history of river management from the early modern through the modern era reveals a growing confidence—in and out of government—in the promise of technology and a willingness to engage in increasingly aggressive manipulation of the natural environment. Although the idea of separating the Kiso, Nagara, and Ibi rivers as a flood-control measure was incorporated into the plans for the 1753–55 project, Satsuma overseers had not accomplished it. Reflecting opinions expressed by bakufu overseers and village residents, they built a wall that extended two-thirds of the distance between the Kiso and Ibi, diminishing but not breaking the connections between the rivers. One of the reasons for this more timid approach was a reluctance to assume responsibility for extreme environmental reconstruction. However, no such timidity impeded plans for river restructuring a century or so later. Local and national leaders alike contrasted the makeshift approaches of the Tokugawa era with the permanent solutions offered by modern technology. When the separation was complete, they marveled at the extent to which they had been able to reform nature to serve human needs.

Heavily engineered river projects became a major policy priority of twentieth-century Japan. Following the passage of the 1896 river law, a new generation of Japanese engineers controlled the nation's rivers with pumps, lock gates, and dams. Japan's first concrete dam was built in 1900; by 1945 there were more than 87

---

55. Ōkuma, *Kōzui to chisui no kasenshi*, pp. 140–42; Kasen gyōsei kenkyūkai, ed., *Nihon no kasen*, pp. 24–39; Lewis, *Becoming Apart*, pp. 83–85.

concrete dams over 30 meters in height.[56] Rapid economic growth in the postwar era was accompanied by rising levels of urbanization and industrialization, especially in already densely settled lowlands. These trends exacerbated flood dangers, magnified the scale of disasters, and nurtured a consensus that aggressive water-control measures were essential. *Chisui* became enshrined as a core element in the social, political, and physical construction of Japan.

By the end of the twentieth century, however, there were signs that the era of *chisui* might be ending. The Nagara dam project was forced to completion against a background of local, national, and international protest. Since then, government planners have reviewed expensive, elaborate flood-control projects in the context of a severe fiscal crisis and a changing environmental consciousness. The River Planning Division of the Construction Ministry has undertaken a reassessment of traditional flood-control structures made of bamboo and stones.[57] The newest technology is being applied to build more natural-looking river environments. Evidence from the Nōbi plain and elsewhere suggests that *chisui*—in the form that it has had since the eighteenth century—may indeed be losing its status as a "sacred domain" in Japan.

---

56. Ōkuma, *Kōzui to chisui no kasenshi*, p. 181.
57. *Daily Yomiuri*, Aug. 26, 1999, p. 3.

CHAPTER SIX

Taming the Iron Horse: Western Locomotive Makers and Technology Transfer in Japan, 1870–1914

Steven J. Ericson

The railroad industry offers striking examples of the successful acquisition and mastery of advanced technology in modern Japan. In the area of line construction, for instance, the Japanese wrested independence from direct Western technical assistance within a decade or so after they started building railroads in 1870. Freedom from outside help took longer to achieve in the more sophisticated area of locomotive manufacturing, a fast-evolving, high-technology field in the late nineteenth and early twentieth centuries, but when the weaning process began in earnest after the turn of the century, Japan moved rapidly from almost complete dependence on standard locomotive imports to total self-sufficiency.[1] What is so aston-

1. I thank Professor Ellen Widmer of Wesleyan University for graciously lending me materials on her great-grandfather Willard Tyler. I am also grateful to Jonathan Landy and Alexander Hillel for their excellent research assistance under the Presidential Scholars Program at Dartmouth College, as well as to Professor Colin Divall and Michael Bailey of the University of York, U.K., and to Dr. Robert Schwantes for extremely helpful comments and suggestions. By permission of the publisher, I have adapted this chapter from Ericson, "Importing Locomotives," published by the University of Chicago Press in *Osiris*, vol. 13. © 1998 by the History of Science Society. All rights reserved. "Standard" locomo-

ishing about this transition is that it seemed to occur virtually overnight: until the very end of the Meiji period, Japanese railroads had obtained all but a fraction of their engines from Western makers; yet from 1913 on, the railroads acquired new generations of standard locomotives entirely from domestic producers. The speed of this change, however, was more apparent than real, for Japan had laid the foundations for self-sufficiency in locomotive manufacturing during the preceding four decades of import reliance and limited but experientially critical domestic production.

As in other areas of technology transfer, Japan went through successive, albeit overlapping, stages of importation and imitation on its way to independent production of locomotives. During the initial phase of importation, the Japanese did not just venture out into the world in search of the best technology the West had to offer; they also faced aggressive marketing at home by European and American producers who competed fiercely to win Japanese contracts for locomotives. Ironically, exemplifying a more general pattern, the very success of Western makers in penetrating the Japanese market and supplying the railroad industry with what it wanted helped pave the way for their eventual displacement by domestic manufacturers in one of the culminating cases of import substitution in pre–World War I Japan.

Britain's Priority and Staying Power in the Japanese Market

Throughout the Meiji period, Japanese railroads relied overwhelmingly on imports from the West for motive power. In fact, it was not until 1893 that the state railways' Kobe workshop produced the first locomotive made in Japan (see Fig. 6.1a). In the late 1890s and 1900s, the workshops of two of the largest private railway companies, San'yō and Nippon, followed the state railways' lead in manufacturing standard locomotives, as did at least three independent producers, the Train Manufacturing Company (Kisha seizō kaisha)

---

tives here refers not to *standard-gauge* engines but to locomotives built for Japan's main-line, narrow-gauge railroads, as opposed to its smaller-gauge, local light railways.

and the Kawasaki and Ishikawajima shipbuilding firms.[2] In 1906–7, the central government's nationalization of the major private railroads raised its share of Japan's total locomotive stock from 35 percent in 1905 to 95 percent in 1907.[3] Yet as late as July 1912 domestic products accounted for less than 7 percent of the nearly 2,400 engines owned by the government (see Table 6.1). Even in the last decade of the Meiji era, when domestic manufacturers increased their average combined output per annum to around twenty locomotives, Japanese railroads imported on average nearly four times that number of engines a year; and each of the principal Western suppliers—Britain's Dubs and Beyer Peacock and America's Baldwin and Schenectady—exported more locomotives to Japan than the Japanese themselves produced during the entire Meiji period.[4] By the end of that era, British imports, which had begun to lose ground to cheaper and technologically more appropriate American makes in the mid-1890s, had fallen behind locomotives imported from both the United States and Germany.

Throughout the 1870s, however, British manufacturers monopolized locomotive orders in Japan, and they maintained their dominance over late-entering American and German producers for at least another decade. Japan naturally turned to British technology at the very beginning of the Meiji period, when Britain was the acknowledged world leader in the railway field. Besides technical concerns, diplomatic and political considerations also influenced this choice: the British minister to Japan, Sir Harry Parkes, played a key role in persuading the Meiji government to undertake railroad construction and to secure from Britain the personnel and equipment needed to build and operate the first railroads. By ordering locomotives from British suppliers in the 1870s, these hired experts set the pattern for the state railways, which continued to

---

2. Sawai Minoru, "Senzenki Nihon tetsudō sharyō kōgyō no tenkai katei, 1890 nendai–1920 nendai" (Development of the prewar Japanese railway rolling-stock industry, 1890s–1920s), *Shakai kagaku kenkyū* 37, no. 3 (1985): 29–31, 48–49.

3. *Tetsudō kyoku nenpō* (Annual report of the Railway Bureau), 1907 (Tokyo: Tetsudō in, 1909), appendix, pp. 21, 45.

4. Sawai, "Senzenki Nihon tetsudō sharyō kōgyō," *passim*.

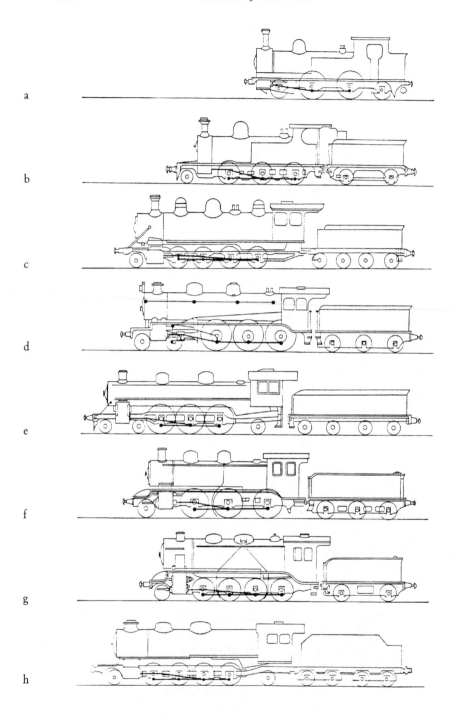

a

b

c

d

e

f

g

h

(*facing page*) Fig. 6.1 Selected locomotives in use in Japan, produced between 1889 and 1931 (source: Noda Masaho et al., eds., *Nihon no tetsudō: seiritsu to tenkai* [Japanese railroads: formation and development] [Tokyo: Nihon keizai hyōron-sha, 1986], pp. 84–85, 144, 242; drawings reprinted by permission of the publisher).

(*a*) Type 860. The first domestic-made locomotive, built at the state railways' Kobe workshop in 1893.

(*b*) Type 7600. Mogul (2-6-0) engine for use on high-gradient main lines manufactured by the British firm Nasmyth, Wilson for the Nippon Railway Company in 1889.

(*c*) Type 9200. Consolidation (2-8-0) engine for hauling coal in Hokkaido produced for the state railways by the American maker Baldwin in 1905.

(*d*) Type 8850. Superheater for express passenger service built by the German firm Borsig for the state railways in 1911, twelve copies of which Kawasaki Shipbuilding Company made in 1913.

(*e*) Type 8900. Superheater for express passenger service manufactured by the American Locomotive Company for the state railways in 1911–12.

(*f*) Type 8620. Express passenger locomotive of standard Japanese design built between 1914 and 1929, mostly by the Train Manufacturing Company.

(*g*) Type 9600. Freight engine of standard Japanese design produced during the years 1913–26, mainly by Kawasaki Shipbuilding.

(*h*) Type 9900. Freight engine of the Mikado (2-8-2) type manufactured by several Japanese firms from 1923 to 1931.

purchase British products long after the foreign employees had been replaced by native specialists they themselves had helped to train. The government railways passed on their bias in favor of British engines to the first and biggest private railroad, the Nippon Railway Company, which remained totally dependent on the state for both line construction and operation from its founding in 1881 until 1892 and, as late as 1905, held almost a third of all privately owned locomotives in Japan (see Fig. 6.1b for an example of a British engine imported by Nippon Railway).[5]

In Britain as elsewhere in the nineteenth and early twentieth centuries, the locomotive industry was marked by wildly fluctuating demand and continuous technological change. These characteristics made mass production of standardized engines impracticable in the West. As John Brown has demonstrated, far from being the products of high-volume, assembly-line manufacturing, locomo-

---

5. *Nihon tetsudō shi* (History of Japanese railroads) (Tokyo: Tetsudōshō, 1921), 1: 747; and *Tetsudō kyoku nenpō*, appendix, pp. 22, 45.

Table 6.1

Additions to Locomotive Stock Held by the
Japanese State Railways, 1870–1912, by Country of Manufacture

Years	British	U.S.	German	Swiss	Japanese	Total
1870–72	10	0	0	0	0	10
1873–77	26	0	0	0	0	26
1878–82	11	0	0	0	0	11
1883–87	48	2	0	0	0	50
1888–92	145	24	28	0	0	197
1893–97	244	256	27	3	11	541
1898–1902	200	242	15	8	19	484
1903–7	282	384	90	0	65	821
1908–12	17	87	66	0	67	237
TOTAL	983	995	226	11	162	2,377

NOTE: The figures for 1908–12 cover only a third of fiscal-year 1912, that is, through July 1912 rather than March 1913.
SOURCE: Sawai Minoru, "Senzenki Nihon tetsudō sharyō kōgyō no tenkai katei, 1890 nendai–1920 nendai" (Development of the prewar Japanese railway rolling-stock industry, 1890s–1920s), *Shakai kagaku kenkyū* 37, no. 3 (1985): 22.

tives were made-to-order items or customized versions of standard designs, built in relatively small batches to buyers' specifications.[6] Accordingly, successful locomotive works like the leading American manufacturer, Baldwin of Philadelphia, strove to maintain productive flexibility to cope with expanding product diversity and roller-coaster demand. For example, in 1890, its biggest sales year of the nineteenth century, Baldwin constructed 946 locomotives to 316 different designs; in 1894, with the onset of the prolonged American recession following the 1893 panic, the company filled orders for only 313 engines.[7]

The cyclical, feast-or-famine nature of the industry not only combined with the need for constant technical improvements to rule out the use of mass-production techniques by Western locomotive makers but also drove them to seek customers in a variety of markets, including foreign ones. In general, British builders were far more reliant on overseas business than were their American counterparts. By 1907, for instance, Beyer Peacock had exported nearly 70 percent of the 5,000 engines it had constructed to that date, and other producers such as Vulcan Foundry, supplier of Japan's first locomotive, was even more dependent on foreign markets, which the British found primarily in Europe, South America, and their vast colonial empire.[8] By contrast, U.S. builders sold less than 20 percent of their total output abroad during the 1890s.[9] The difference in export reliance stemmed mainly from the fact that British contractors faced stiff competition at home from railroad workshops, with several of the leading British railroads making almost all of their own motive power, whereas American

---

6. See John K. Brown, *The Baldwin Locomotive Works, 1831–1915* (Baltimore: Johns Hopkins University Press, 1995).

7. Ibid., pp. 85, 241. On custom and batch production in the locomotive industry, see also Philip Scranton, *Endless Novelty: Specialty Production and American Industrialization, 1865–1925* (Princeton: Princeton University Press, 1997), pp. 11–12, 99, 276–77; and John H. White, Jr., *A Short History of American Locomotive Builders in the Steam Era* (Washington, D.C.: Bass, 1982), p. 9.

8. James W. Lowe, *British Steam Locomotive Builders* (Cambridge, Eng.: Goose, 1975), pp. 61, 631.

9. White, *Short History*, pp. 17, 21.

contract builders had the domestic field essentially to themselves, since most U.S. railroads confined their own shops to repair work.[10] With such an enormous home market, American locomotive producers generally "showed only middling interest in going after foreign orders."[11]

A major problem with the home market, however, was its pronounced instability. During recessions, American builders' interest in exports picked up considerably; conversely, at times of strong domestic demand, their willingness and ability to meet foreign requirements diminished. Although not necessarily a priority for American locomotive makers, export production thus played a vital role in offsetting the effects of downturns in the U.S. market. During the 1890s, spurred by the extended domestic depression in the middle of that decade, American firms made a particularly determined effort to invade foreign locomotive markets, which British suppliers had largely dominated until then. Trade statistics testify to America's success in the resulting competition with Britain: between 1890 and 1900, the total value of locomotive exports from the United Kingdom fell from $9 million to $7.3 million, while that from the United States rose from $1.3 million to $5.6 million.[12]

The Japanese market was not immune to these trends. British hegemony there began to crumble in the 1890s, as data for the Japanese state railways indicate (see Table 6.1). American and German engine makers had made inroads during the 1880s and early 1890s on the three smaller of Japan's four main islands, with the United States supplying the first locomotives in Hokkaido, and Germany in Shikoku and Kyushu.[13] The challenge to Britain's monopoly in the largest market, that on the big island of Honshu, began in 1893 when the San'yō Railway Company

---

10. Ibid., p. 15; Lowe, British Steam Locomotive Builders, p. 7; and Brown, Baldwin Locomotive Works, pp. 30, 44–45.

11. White, Short History, p. 17.

12. Brown, Baldwin Locomotive Works, p. 47.

13. For details, see Steven T. Ericson, The Sound of the Whistle: Railroads and the State in Meiji Japan (Cambridge, Mass.: Harvard University, Council on East Asian Studies, 1996), pp. 32–34.

purchased powerful tender locomotives from Baldwin.[14] This American breakthrough signaled the start of fierce competition among British, U.S., and German manufacturers in Honshu; in the course of this competition, the Americans, and eventually the Germans as well, increasingly won out over their British rivals. Symbolic of the U.S. ascendance by the end of Meiji was that the engine on the funeral train bearing the body of the Meiji emperor in September 1912 was a recent import from the American Locomotive Company (see Fig. 6.1e).

Despite the surge by American and, ultimately, German producers, the British held on to a relatively large share of the Japanese locomotive market until late in the Meiji period. Between 1894 and 1904, for example, Beyer Peacock sold 138 engines to the Nippon Railway Company, 46 to the state railways, and 34 to other private railroads in Japan.[15] The staying power of British makers was partly due to their first-comer advantage, especially with the two biggest buyers, the government and Nippon Railway. Product familiarity and perhaps loyalty on the part of these two customers, combined with a desire to maintain at least a modicum of standardization and interchangeability in their motive power, helped sustain British locomotive sales in Japan well into the first decade of the twentieth century.

Contrary to what some Japanese historians have suggested, British locomotive technology did not fall behind that of the United States in the late Meiji period.[16] In fact, as San'yō Railway officials,

---

14. *Nihon kokuyū tetsudō hyakunenshi: tsūshi* (Centennial history of the Japanese National Railways: general survey) (Tokyo: Nihon kokuyū tetsudō, 1974), p. 127.

15. Takeshi Yuzawa, "The Transfer of Railway Technologies from Britain to Japan, with Special Reference to Locomotive Manufacture," in *International Technology Transfer: Europe, Japan and the USA, 1700–1914*, ed. David J. Jeremy (Aldershot, Eng., and Brookfield, Vt.: Elgar, 1991), pp. 201–2.

16. Harada Katsumasa maintains, for example, that in 1911 British producers were as yet unable to construct superheated engines; see his *Tetsudō no kataru Nihon no kindai* (Japan's modern history as told through railroads) (Tokyo: Sōshiete, 1977), pp. 182–83. Colin Divall (pers. comm., Dec. 30, 1997) points out, to the contrary, that by that time British manufacturers had fitted superheaters—usually of the German Schmidt design and therefore under license—"to any number of locomotives built for export."

who were among the strongest proponents of American makes, admitted in 1901, "the English engine has countervailing points of advantage."[17] These characteristics helped prolong Britain's export success in Japan. Among the points of advantage were greater durability and superior "workmanship." For instance, the boiler in American locomotives proved "more liable to leak than the English boiler, which is very tight and well fitted."[18] British engines in general required fewer repairs. They also consumed significantly less fuel: during a three-month period in 1901, San'yō Railway found that its British locomotives burned an average of 10 percent less coal than the railroad's preferred Baldwin imports and 22 percent less than recently introduced Schenectady products.[19] In 1902 the U.S. consul in Yokohama advised American manufacturers that, in addition to low cost and quick delivery, the Japanese "want engines economical in coal, well finished and durable,"[20] an apt description of the relative strengths of British locomotives.

Pulling Ahead of the British: The Comparative Advantages of American Engines

Several factors thus combined to slow the overall decline of British imports in the Japanese locomotive market, but those factors were not enough to offset the competitive edge that U.S. producers enjoyed abroad. In 1901 a British journal summed up two of the American advantages: "cheapness and dispatch."[21] Especially during periods of depressed domestic demand, American engines simply ran circles around their British counterparts in terms of price and speed of delivery. The experience of the San'yō Railway Company with both British and American locomotives, for example,

---

17. "American and English Locomotives," *Kobe Herald*, n.d., citing a report in the British journal *Engineering*, reprinted in *U.S. Consular Reports* 67, no. 254 (Nov. 1901): 405.

18. Ibid.

19. Willard C. Tyler, notebook, Oct. 23, 1901. Tyler kept this notebook during his trips to East Asia in 1901 and 1902.

20. U.S. Department of State, *Commercial Relations of the United States, 1902* (Washington, D.C.: Government Printing Office, 1903), p. 980.

21. "American and English Locomotives," p. 405.

prompted its officials to announce in late 1901: "We do not intend to order any more English engines just now. Our principal reasons are that we can not get them quickly enough, and that they cost one and a half times more than the American engine."[22] Whereas American locomotives sold for approximately $10,000 each and required seven to nine months for delivery, the comparable figures for British products were $15,000 and nine to twelve months. "And we always want quick delivery," the San'yō representatives reportedly added.[23] The official cheerleader of American business in Yokohama, U.S. Consul-General E. C. Bellows, underscored the prime importance of speed when he noted in his annual report for 1901: "Quick deliveries help sales materially. . . . It will therefore be well to remember that, other things being equal, the American [locomotive] maker is often given preference because of his ability to give quicker dates."[24] By the same token, "the question of time," as an English railway executive acknowledged in 1904, "is a great drawback to British firms, who are not able to contract for delivery as speedily as the Japanese wish."[25] In 1901, for instance, British manufacturers gained permission to bid on locomotives for the Hokkaido Railway, "but both the limit of time and price obtainable were insuperable obstacles to the order being given to the United Kingdom."[26]

Nevertheless, speed of delivery, although usually an American advantage, fluctuated with the state of the builders' primary markets both at home and abroad. During boom periods, when American contractors' order books filled up, delivery dates could stretch out to twelve months or even two years.[27] By the same token, at times of low demand British producers were capable of expediting their construction work; for instance, in 1894 Neilson, the

---

22. Ibid., p. 404.

23. Ibid.

24. U.S. Department of State, *Commercial Relations of the United States, 1902*, p. 980.

25. Alfred W. Arthurton, "The Railways of Japan," *Railway Magazine* 15, no. 90 (Dec. 1904): 501.

26. "American and English Locomotives," p. 405.

27. Brown, *Baldwin Locomotive Works*, pp. 49, 205.

largest British maker, completed an order for twelve engines from Nippon Railway in just 84 days.[28]

Over the long term, however, U.S. exporters clearly had the upper hand in terms of prices and delivery dates. The price competitiveness of American producers resulted partly from their use of cheaper materials and simpler workmanship, but the primary source of their superiority in both cost and delivery lay in their production methods and facilities. As noted above, locomotive builders were unable to achieve efficiencies by mass-producing standard designs; control over engine design had passed into the hands of customers well before the 1890s. Besides turning out countless made-to-order engines, the builders kept adding new custom designs to their "standard" product lines. By 1908 Baldwin's catalogue, for instance, listed 379 different types of locomotives, each of which the company could modify to suit a client's needs.[29] To manage this chaos of diversity, U.S. makers sought in the latter half of the nineteenth century to systematize, as opposed to standardize, engine construction. Philip Scranton points out that "system" became the buzzword in American flexible-manufacturing sectors like locomotive building.[30] As a British observer marveled of the Baldwin Works in 1899: "What struck me there . . . was the system they had throughout, both shops and offices. Talk about system, method, indexing—management generally, in fact—they have got it here down to a fine art."[31] Baldwin's systematizing efforts involved innovations that anticipated the flexible production techniques of, say, Japanese automakers in recent decades, such as a rudimentary just-in-time system for the delivery of parts by a large network of subcontractors.[32] Perhaps most important, although American builders failed to standardize their engines, they did implement an extensive standardization of components across a range of locomotive models. Baldwin led the way in this regard, attaining parts interchangeability and attendant savings in cost and produc-

---

28. Lowe, *British Steam Locomotive Builders*, p. 505.
29. Brown, *Baldwin Locomotive Works*, pp. 78, 230.
30. Scranton, *Endless Novelty*, p. 18.
31. H. Rolfe, "American Locomotives," *Engineering*, Mar. 31, 1899, p. 423.
32. Brown, *Baldwin Locomotive Works*, pp. 15–16.

tion time during the 1860s; within a decade and a half, its systematizing methods had spread throughout the American locomotive industry.[33] The published work on British engine makers does not yet allow a ready comparison on these matters, but one source suggests that British producers "often had very primitive managerial systems compared with American firms."[34]

The relative advantages of American builders in price and delivery time also stemmed from their larger scale of operations. The top U.S. makers were massive; their enormous size enabled them to accept numerous orders at one time and, in the process of filling them, to capture substantial economies through the use of standard, interchangeable parts. For instance, in 1892 the Schenectady Locomotive Works, with its extensive plant equipped with the latest traveling cranes "for the rapid handling of work," had a production capacity of 400 locomotives per year, a figure that increased to 450 once the company completed expansion plans then under way.[35] During the 1890s, Baldwin, the largest locomotive works in the world, twice recorded an annual output of over 900 engines; in fact, the rapid increase in its U.S. market share, which had grown to 40 percent by 1900, drove Schenectady and seven other independent works to consolidate as the American Locomotive Company (ALCo) in 1901.[36] Meanwhile, Baldwin continued to expand its capacity to the point where in 1905, a year in which it produced a total of 2,250 engines and employed nearly 15,000 workers, the company could fill an order for 77 locomotives placed by the Japanese government—the biggest purchase to that date by a foreign government in the United States—at the rate of a dozen engines per

---

33. Ibid., pp. 21, 170–83; Scranton, *Endless Novelty*, p. 99.

34. L. T. C. Rolt, *Landscape with Machines* (London: Longman, 1971), p. 103; cited in Brown, *Baldwin Locomotive Works*, p. 265n62.

35. "The Schenectady Locomotive Works," *Railroad Gazette*, July 15, 1892, p. 524.

36. Brown, *Baldwin Locomotive Works*, p. 241; John H. White, Jr., "Afterword: The Final Years of the Steam Locomotive in America," in Angus Sinclair, *Development of the Locomotive Engine* (1907; reprinted—Cambridge, Mass.: MIT Press, 1970), p. 679; Frank M. Swengel, *The American Steam Locomotive*, vol. 1, *The Evolution of the Steam Locomotive* (Davenport, Iowa: Midwest Rail Publications, 1967), p. 76.

month.[37] By contrast, at the turn of the twentieth century, the
yearly output of each of the top six British contract builders
ranged from 75 to 200 locomotives.[38] In an effort to meet increased
American competition, the three major contractors in Glasgow—
Neilson, Dubs, and Sharp Stewart—merged in 1903 to form the
North British Locomotive Company, the world's largest engine
builder outside the United States, with an annual production capacity of about 600 locomotives.[39] Because of the proximity of its
constituent plants, North British probably achieved greater economies of scale than did ALCo, which had factories scattered along
the eastern seaboard from Richmond, Virginia, to Montreal.
Nevertheless, each of ALCo's biggest works roughly equaled the
Scottish combine in total output per annum, and Baldwin's capacity dwarfed that of North British.

Another American advantage was more appropriate technology.
Simply put, American engines were better suited to the railway
lines found in most export markets in the late nineteenth and early
twentieth centuries. An article published in a trade journal in 1916
explained why:

The early railways of Great Britain and Europe were built in a most substantial manner, with comparatively light grades and easy curves, and
with tracks, bridges and other structures of a most permanent character.
The locomotives as a rule had rigid wheel-bases, and the frames were suspended directly on the springs without the intervention of equalizing gear.
In contrast, the early American railways were quickly built; and in order
to save expense, cuttings, embankments and tunnels were avoided wher-
ever possible; steep grades and sharp curves were frequent; and tracks
were laid with light rails and were poorly surfaced. The European type of
locomotive proved too rigid for service on such lines, and American in-
genuity accordingly devised, first the swivelling bogie and then the equal-

---

37. "Japan Has Ordered 102 of Our Locomotives," *New York Times*, Feb. 19,
1905, p. 20 (the 102 locomotives mentioned in this title include 25 to be manufactured by the Atlantic Equipment Company of New York, in addition to the 77
Baldwin engines). Baldwin's annual output peaked in 1906 at 2,666 engines, its
employment the following year at 18,499 workers (Brown, *Baldwin Locomotive
Works*, p. 241).

38. Michael Bailey, pers. comm. Jan. 5, 1998.

39. Lowe, *British Steam Locomotive Builders*, pp. 504–6.

izing beam.[40] With these devices, the locomotives successfully negotiated sharp curves and all wheels kept a bearing on the rail, even when passing over very uneven tracks.

The features which characterized American railway construction at that early day are often found in Colonial and newly-developed countries; hence the success which locomotives of American design have usually had in these localities.[41]

Cheap construction methods were certainly characteristic of Japanese railroads during the Meiji period; like their antebellum U.S. counterparts,[42] they, too, sought to minimize capital expenditures by, among other things, employing high gradients and avoiding tunnels. No wonder, then, that flexible American engines appealed to Japanese railway administrators, especially those of private lines, which tended to be poorly built and maintained compared to those of the state.

The U.S. locomotive makers were also willing to modify their designs for export to satisfy local requirements, a practice that came naturally to flexible producers like Baldwin. In one such modification for the Japanese market, American builders adapted the firebox to burn the soft coal that prevailed in Japan. In 1905, for instance, on a number of freight engines built for the Japanese state railways, Baldwin extended the firebox over the rear driving wheels, making the box substantially longer than that on locomotives produced for American railroads. This design change had the further benefit of "adding much to the adhesive force [that is, the traction] of these comparatively small but powerful engines," thereby partially offsetting the loss of weight and power necessi-

---

40. A bogie is a low, swiveled undercarriage at either end of a railroad car. An equalizing beam is a lever that distributes the weight of the locomotive frame equally on the driving axles.

41. "American Locomotives Recently Built for Export," *Railway Magazine* 39, no. 234 (Dec. 1916): 371.

42. On the sacrificing of "durability . . . for lower capital costs" on the early American lines, see Albert Fishlow, *American Railroads and the Transformation of the Ante-bellum Economy* (Cambridge, Mass.: Harvard University Press, 1965), p. 308.

tated by building for the narrow gauge the Japanese employed in their railway network (see Fig. 6.1c).[43]

The epitome of the American customized locomotive export was a similar freight engine that Baldwin initially manufactured in 1897 for the Nippon Railway Company. This locomotive was the world's first 2-8-2 (two leading wheels, eight driving wheels, and two trailing wheels). As with the 1905 engine, Baldwin designed it to burn low-grade coal such as that from the Jōban field Nippon Railway serviced. Accordingly, the 2-8-2 had an enlarged firebox— in fact the biggest of the Meiji period—which Baldwin placed entirely behind the driving wheels and over the rear truck.[44] This type of engine, among the first U.S. models Nippon Railway purchased, proved highly successful and became a standard American class; American manufacturers subsequently introduced variants of the 2-8-2, appropriately nicknamed the "Mikado," into the United States as well as other export markets (see Fig. 6.1h for a later Japanese version).[45]

As with speed of delivery, however, American willingness to meet foreign design requirements varied with the level of demand at home. When the domestic market slowed and U.S. builders needed work, they tended to be more accommodating of specifications that diverged from American design traditions; the reverse was generally true during periods of strong domestic demand. Brit-

---

43. "Consolidation Locomotive for the Imperial Government of Japan," *Railway and Locomotive Engineering*, Nov. 1905, pp. 493–94.

44. *History of the Baldwin Locomotive Works, 1831–1920* (Philadelphia: Baldwin-Lima-Hamilton, 1920), pp. 85–86; Tominaga Yūji, *Kōtsū ni okeru shihonshugi no hatten: Nihon kōtsūgyō no kindaika katei* (Development of capitalism in the transport field: the modernization process in the Japanese transportation industry) (Tokyo: Iwanami shoten, 1953), pp. 226–27.

45. For example, Baldwin and the American Locomotive Company later manufactured Mikado-type engines for the Erie Railroad, and Baldwin did the same for the Jamaica Government Railway. See "Erie Buys Mikado Engines," *New York Times*, July 18, 1912, p. 11; and "American Locomotives Recently Built for Export," p. 373. Swengel (*American Steam Locomotive*, pp. 86, 136) notes: "Nearly 10,000 Mikados were to go into [U.S.] main line service, and were to be so successful that they were among the last locomotives to feel the scrapper's touch"; in particular, the highly versatile lighter model of the "Mike" was "one of the most useful freight locomotive types ever developed."

ish producers were also adept at modifying their engine designs; yet, perhaps because they were accustomed to largely captive markets in the empire and other areas with British-controlled railroads, they seemed, on the whole, less flexible than their American rivals, often telling "their customers exactly what they proposed to supply, rather than consult their wishes."[46]

A variety of factors thus contributed to the overall increase in the U.S. share of the Japanese locomotive market at British expense, a trend that received a fillip in the waning years of the Meiji period. At that time the Japanese state railways, fresh from the nationalization of 1906–7, rushed to acquire a new generation of powerful locomotives for express passenger and freight service on the now-unified main-line network. Railway authorities went on a final overseas spending spree in 1911–12, ordering 136 of the most powerful and up-to-date engines obtainable; several of these machines then served as prototypes for domestic makers, as Japan moved toward complete self-sufficiency in standard locomotive production from 1913 on.[47] The bulk of the orders went to American companies, which by that time had mastered the latest innovations in locomotive technology, especially the German Schmidt-type superheater (see Figs. 6.1d and e) and the Mallet articulated engine for use on high-gradient lines.[48] ALCo, for example, won contracts for 36 of the 60 locomotives equipped with superheating technology that the Japanese purchased from abroad in 1911–12.[49]

------

46. *American Engineering Competition* (New York: Harper, 1901), p. 69, cited in Brown, *Baldwin Locomotive Works*, p. 265n62.

47. On the importing of this last batch of foreign-made locomotives in Meiji Japan and the production of exact replicas and modified versions by domestic manufacturers, see Harada, *Tetsudō no kataru*, pp. 177–84; and Hirofumi Yamamoto, ed., *Technological Innovation and the Development of Transportation in Japan* (Tokyo: United Nations University Press, 1993), pp. 88–89.

48. The Mallet was essentially two engines hinged together and carrying a single boiler, the result being a freight locomotive with double the tractive power of nonarticulated models (Swengel, *American Steam Locomotive*, p. 124).

49. The new technology involved "superheating" the steam generated in the boiler by circulating gases from the firebox through tubes that ran back through the boiler; this method yielded a significant increase in power and a 15 percent savings in coal consumption, to boot (Harada, *Tetsudō no kataru*, pp. 178–79; Swengel, *American Steam Locomotive*, p. 122; Divall, pers. comm.).

German makers supplied the remaining 24 superheaters and joined American firms in filling orders for 64 high-gradient engines. Bowing to pressure from the British government, the Japanese also placed an order with the North British Locomotive Company, but only for a dozen nonsuperheater engines—a clear indication of the decline in Britain's reputation as a locomotive producer by the end of Meiji.[50]

Representing U.S. Manufacturers in Japan: Willard Tyler and ALCo

Besides comparative advantages in manufacturing, another factor behind the American success in the Japanese locomotive market was direct sales representation. All the foreign makers depended on Japanese or Western trading companies to handle their bidding and marketing activities in Japan; with each call for tenders, the trading firms, led by Mitsui and Ōkura on the Japanese side and Jardine Matheson and Frazer among the Western participants, engaged in a fierce competition to secure orders for locomotive imports on behalf of their clients.[51] American manufacturers, however, went beyond relying on intermediaries and sent their own agents to Japan to market their products firsthand. In the mid-1890s, for example, Baldwin Locomotive Works had an employee by the name of William H. Crawford as its representative in Japan. A flamboyant man who called himself "Captain Jack," Crawford had managed by 1897 to sell about 200 Baldwin locomotives to Japanese state and private railways; he had done so, according to an American trade journal, by accomplishing "the no mean feat of learning the Japanese language" and being "successful in a position of an exceedingly trying nature and where he must be a diplomat as well as an engineer and

---

50. Harada, *Tetsudō no kataru*, pp. 181–82; Sawai, "Senzenki Nihon tetsudō sharyō kōgyō," p. 58.

51. Sawai, "Senzenki Nihon tetsudō sharyō kōgyō," p. 25. For instance, Ōkura, which placed the low bids for both Dubs and Rogers on the 1902 order by the state railways, was in competition with seven other trading companies representing British and German makers (Tyler, notebook, Nov. 19, 1902).

salesman."[52] In addition to supervising the construction of the inaugural Mikado engines for the Nippon Railway Company, Crawford helped convince San'yō Railway to switch from British to Baldwin locomotives.[53] The Baldwin make subsequently became "the typical engine" of San'yō as well as a model for locomotives built in the company's Hyōgo workshop.[54]

British and American consular officials were fully aware of the advantages such direct marketing gave to American business. In 1896, following Baldwin's coup with San'yō, a member of the British legation in Tokyo warned his countrymen: "American firms are careful to be represented in Japan, while only some of the most important British firms have agents there. . . . British manufacturers of railway material would find it advantageous to be properly represented in Japan, as large shipbuilding firms have been with success."[55] The purchasing pipeline established by British employees of the early Meiji government railways had previously obviated the need for sales agents, and British locomotive makers apparently ignored the legation member's advice. When ALCo managed to gain admission to the bidding on engines for the state railways in 1901 and proceeded to outcompete four British builders for the order, the U.S. consul in Yokohama proclaimed: "Credit must be given to the fact that the American manufacturer had a representative in Japan, a manifest advantage in every case."[56]

The agent to whom the consul referred was Willard C. Tyler (1856–1936), a Massachusetts businessman who traveled to East Asia

---

52. "Industrial Notes: Cars and Locomotives," *Railway Review* 37 (Mar. 6, 1897): 143; Robert S. Schwantes (pers. comm., May 14, 2001). I thank Dr. Schwantes for generously sharing materials on "Captain Jack" and for pointing out my conflation of William Crawford with another American railwayman in Meiji Japan—Joseph Crawford—in Steven J. Ericson, "Importing Locomotives in Meiji Japan: International Business and Technology Transfer in the Railroad Industry," *Osiris* 13 (1998): 144.

53. "American and English Locomotives," p. 403.

54. Wakuda Yasuo, *Shiryō Nihon no shitetsu* (Source materials on Japanese private railroads), 4th ed. (Tokyo: Tetsudō tosho kankōkai, 1984), p. 18.

55. "Hints for Americans: Advice to English Manufacturers That Is Worth Heeding Here," *New York Times*, May 10, 1896, p. 26.

56. U.S. Department of State, *Commercial Relations of the United States, 1902*, p. 980.

on behalf of ALCo and other U.S. railroad-equipment manufacturers (see Fig. 6.2). Tyler made four trips to Japan between 1898 and
1902, spending altogether about a year and a half there.[57] He was a
tireless promoter of American products, making the rounds of almost all the leading state and private railway officials during his
visits to Japan. Indeed, the notebook he kept of his 1901 and 1902
trips reads like a Who's Who of the contemporary Japanese railroad world. In repeated meetings with the director, locomotive superintendent, and chief engineer of the state railways and with the
top managers and engineers of the six biggest private railroads, including the Japanese-owned Seoul–Pusan Railway in Korea, Tyler
pushed everything from Janney couplers and Westinghouse air
brakes to Klinger water gauges and Consolidated Electric lights,
urging the Japanese to switch from British to American parts suppliers and leaving samples and catalogues in his wake.

Above all, however, Tyler sought to persuade the Japanese railroads to accept bids for engines manufactured by ALCo, especially
its Schenectady works. Tyler was above all eager to help his main
client break into the lucrative, British-dominated markets represented by the government and the Nippon Railway Company.
During his 1901 visit, he found the opening he hoped for when the
head of the state railways, Matsumoto Sōichirō, informed him in
October that the government would ask for tenders on 30 or 40
engines the following month and would allow ALCo to bid "if
they will build on British plans."[58] Matsumoto showed his awareness of the versatility of American producers when he told Tyler
in a follow-up meeting: "Why don't your people build purely British locomotives? You can do it quicker and cheaper and just as well
if you really set out to."[59]

Contrary to Matsumoto's suggestion, however, in this instance
the state railways decided to issue only the most general specifications, for, as the government's locomotive superintendent assured

---

57. "Japan and Its Transportation Facilities," *Official Proceedings of the New
York Railroad Club* 11, no. 4 (Feb. 21, 1901): 6; and Tyler, notebook.

58. Tyler, notebook, undated entry.

59. Ibid., Oct. 19, 1901. I have done some minor editing of Tyler's notes.

Fig. 6.2 Willard C. Tyler (1856–1936), agent for U.S. locomotive suppliers, with an unidentified Japanese contact in Kyoto in March 1900 (photograph courtesy of Ellen Widmer).

Tyler, the authorities were eager "to give the American Locomotive Company a great opportunity on these thirty or forty locomotives. They will specify but little."[60] The Japanese did limit U.S. tenders to the Schenectady works of the ALCo combine, but Matsumoto made it clear to Tyler that his administration was determined to break Britain's near-monopoly on locomotive orders, declaring in their second meeting: "I hope you can save us some money on the British bid. This is the first time the Imperial Railways has ever asked for competitive designs on the same lot of engines from both American and English bidders. Heretofore it has either been all one or all the other. . . . It is four years since the Imperial Railways has asked for bids on locomotives from America,

---

60. Ibid., Oct. 14, 1901.

and we hope you can please us."[61] The U.S. consul in Yokohama reported on the outcome of this contest: "The Government railway bureau for the main island had for some time previous advertised for tenders of British locomotives only, but during 1901, they admitted the Schenectady Locomotive Works into competition with four English manufacturers, and the result was that the American locomotives filled the order."[62]

State railway officials apparently considered this departure from normal practice to have had the desired effect of forcing British prices down; by the time Tyler returned to Japan the following year, they had reverted to the practice of issuing exact specifications along British lines for their next order of engines. The authorities did expand the list of approved bidders to include three other ALCo plants, the Rogers Locomotive Works of Paterson, New Jersey, and four German makers.[63] But this time, despite the vaunted flexibility of U.S. manufacturers, ALCo insisted in a telegram to Tyler: "We will not quote Government Railway Locomotive Engine according to English practice, will quote our own design if accepted."[64] After conferring with Japanese officials, Tyler cabled back: "We have done everything possible without success. . . . Specifications cannot be altered."[65] The Japanese had explained to the American agent that "the law would not permit any change in specifications after they were issued, and so no other design could be considered." For its part, ALCo refused to modify its own designs because, according to Tyler, its factories were "too busy to go into any work outside of our regular production of which we make great quantities and cheaply. Thus if we have to make just now extraordinary types they would cost so much that our bid would be too high and cost to us under present circumstances too great with the work we would lose of the regular kind."[66] Tyler clarified those "circumstances" when he pointed out

---

61. Ibid., Oct. 19, 1901.

62. U.S. Department of State, *Commercial Relations of the United States, 1902*, p. 980.

63. Tyler, notebook, Aug. 26, 1902.

64. Ibid., Oct. 1, 1902.

65. Ibid., Oct. 2, 1902.

66. Ibid.

to the American consul in Yokohama in mid-1902 that U.S. locomotive producers were not actively competing for orders in Japan
at the time because of "increased home demand":[67] it was simply
more profitable for American manufacturers to produce large
batches of standard models or customized versions of them for the
booming domestic market. In the end, ALCo declined to submit a
bid that year. Of the nine eventual bidders, Dubs of Glasgow and
the sole American entry, Rogers, tied for the lowest offer; not surprisingly the entire order went to the British firm.[68]

Much to Tyler's frustration, he had even less success in 1902
with the Nippon Railway Company, which did not allow any
U.S. manufacturer to bid on its next order for locomotives. In
spite of his request that Nippon officials include ALCo in the
competition, the railroad confined tenders on this order for 32 engines to British and German makers.[69] The chief obstacle to
American business at Nippon Railway, and Tyler's principal
nemesis in Japan, was the locomotive superintendent, Tanaka
Shōhei. Tanaka's partiality for British imports continually exas-
perated the American agent. What made the superintendent's bias
all the more galling was that his subordinates, in Tyler's words,
"have found a lot of bad work in Beyer Peacock engines"—up to
then the railroad's preferred make—and "favor American engines
but are overridden by that *fool of a* Tanaka."[70] As an official at the
railroad's Ōmiya workshop explained to Tyler, the reason Nippon
was excluding U.S. manufacturers from the bidding that year was
that the frames on several of its old Baldwin locomotives had broken because of Nippon's rough rail joints; even though the railroad's Schenectady engines were giving it no trouble, Tanaka had
drawn up the specifications for the new imports to require British-
style frames.[71] The American agent was not about to give up, however. No sooner did he learn that Nippon Railway would ask for

67. U.S. Department of State, *Commercial Relations of the United States, 1903*
(Washington, D.C., Government Printing Office, 1904), p. 432.

68. Tyler, notebook, Nov. 18–19, 1902.

69. Ibid., July 23 and Nov. 18, 1902.

70. Ibid., Oct. 1, 1902 (Tyler's emphasis).

71. Ibid., Aug. 27 and Oct. 1, 1902.

bids on an additional 25 engines in 1903 than Tyler resolved: "A strong effort will be made to get them to approve Schenectady Works." On the eve of his departure from Japan in November 1902, he called on Tanaka and Kanbe Kyoichi, Nippon's purchasing agent, to make a final appeal in person for Schenectady's inclusion on the approved list, concluding his diary entry on the hopeful note that "Kanbe is for us."[72]

In general, Tyler had a more favorable reception at the other major private railroads. He felt especially welcome at the second largest railway company, the Kyushu. Under its progressive president, Sengoku Mitsugu, Kyushu had been investing heavily in upgrading its plant and equipment since the late 1890s and had made American locomotives, especially those from Schenectady, its engines of choice.[73] The hard-nosed Sengoku, though, was not above using pressure tactics to force down ALCo's prices; as Tyler wrote in mid-September 1902, showing his determination to maintain his firm's dominant position in the railroad: "If we don't come down Kiushiu Railway will advertise public international tender for 12 locomotives. We should not let them get away to anyone else."[74] ALCo's response to this threat evidently pleased the Kyushu president, for a few days later Tyler recorded: "Sengoku will accept our price on 12 locomotives if his Directors will."[75] The American agent then noted with satisfaction in early October: "Kiushiu Railway has ordered 12 more moguls [2-6-0 all-purpose engines], same as previous 24. This makes 84 Schenectady locomotives for that road. And 167 Schenectadys in Japan."[76]

Tyler's dealings with other private Japanese railroads also suggest the intensity of the growing competition for market share between ALCo and its principal U.S. rival, Baldwin. For example, soon after the formation in 1901 of the Seoul–Pusan Railway, which would become the fourth largest Japanese railway company,

---

72. Ibid., Nov. 23 and 25, 1902.

73. Ericson, *Sound of the Whistle*, pp. 326–28; Wakuda, *Shiryō Nihon no shitetsu*, p. 18.

74. Tyler, notebook, Sept. 16, 1902.

75. Ibid., Sept. 20, 1902.

76. Ibid., Oct. 7, 1902.

its officials met with Tyler and indicated their desire to obtain as soon as possible four switch engines for construction work. The American agent wrote that he had "put in strong word against Baldwin engines on Seoul–Pusan railroad. Told them they better build their repair shop *first* before they bought any." He concluded with a sense of urgency: "If we don't do this, Baldwin will. If we do, we can have all their business etc."[77] Unfortunately for Tyler, the Seoul–Pusan Railway disregarded his warning and placed its initial order for locomotives with the Baldwin Locomotive Works. On his next visit to Japan, in 1902, Tyler redoubled his efforts, calling on the managing director of the railroad, Adachi Tarō, and two of the company's top engineers to press his client's case. ALCo's prospects for entering the Korean market remained uncertain, however, for, although the Seoul–Pusan engineers "would like Schenectadys," Tyler noted, "Adachi liked Baldwins."[78]

Tyler's firm seemed to have a brighter future in the two Japanese railway companies that had depended heavily on Baldwin engines during the 1890s, San'yō and the Hokkaido Colliery and Railway, both of which had already imported some Schenectady engines. The Schenectady makes, a few technical problems notwithstanding, appeared to be winning over the engineers at those two railroads. The locomotive superintendent of San'yō Railway told Tyler in 1901 that "the Schenectady locomotives are giving much satisfaction but burn much coal although that is decreasing."[79] Similarly, the next year the chief engineer of the Hokkaido Colliery and Railway assured the American agent that "[we] like Schenectadys very much, they are all better workmanship than Baldwins. . . . Nearly all of our 8 Schenectadys troubled [us] with leaking tubes but that is now overcome. The engines are better built than the Baldwins anyway."[80]

Tyler's activities in Japan involved more than promoting imports of America's high-tech manufactured goods; they also touched on other methods by which the Japanese sought to ac-

---

77. Ibid., Nov. 19, 1901.
78. Ibid., Aug. 1 and Nov. 20, 1902.
79. Ibid., Oct. 23, 1901.
80. Ibid., Nov. 19, 1902.

quire advanced technology from the West. In particular, the American agent concerned himself in a small way with Japanese efforts to learn the technology of locomotive production and thereby gain independence from foreign imports. The locomotive superintendents of both San'yō and Nippon railways, whose workshops were pioneers among private engine makers in Japan, asked Tyler for full details and blueprints of the latest locomotive shops and components in the United States. Tyler was solicitous in 1901 of the San'yō superintendent's entreaties for such information on the most up-to-date locomotive firebox and repair shop, but the next year he was less accommodating toward the request of Nippon Railway's Tanaka Shōhei for blueprints on the most current rotary steam plant, saying that he would send him only a photograph and an outline drawing.[81] Also in 1902 Tyler suggested a remarkable course of action to ALCo; had it been followed, it would have blunted Japan's drive for technological independence. With an international businessman's eye for the potential advantages of offshore production, he proposed that his firm buy out the Train Manufacturing Company of Osaka "and run it and build locomotives for all the Far East. Its capacity is now six locomotives a year and will be twelve."[82] Nothing came of this proposal, however, and the Train Manufacturing Company, having mastered the technology of locomotive construction in part by assembling and copying imported engines, increased its output to 40 a year by 1914 and, together with the even larger producer Kawasaki Shipbuilding and other later-entering domestic firms, supplied all of Japan's needs for standard locomotives from 1913 on.[83]

---

81. Ibid., Oct. 23, 1901, undated entry for 1901, and July 9, 1902.

82. Ibid., Sept. 13, 1902.

83. For more on the domestication of locomotive manufacturing in Meiji Japan, see, e.g., Sawai, "Senzenki Nihon tetsudō sharyō kōgyō," pp. 28–68; Noda Masaho et al., eds., *Nihon no tetsudō: seiritsu to tenkai* (Japanese railroads: formation and development) (Tokyo: Nihon keizai hyōronsha, 1986), pp. 143–46; Harada, *Tetsudō no kataru*, pp. 181–89; Eisuke Daito, "Railways and Scientific Management in Japan, 1907–30," *Business History* 31, no. 1 (Jan. 1989): 9–11, 20–26; and Ericson, "Importing Locomotives," pp. 149–52.

Achieving Self-Sufficiency

The first stage in Japan's acquisition of locomotive technology—importation—overlapped with the subsequent phase of imitation and trial manufacturing, as Sawai Minoru has shown in his pathbreaking study.[84] Much like their counterparts in the domestic mining industry, the workshops of Japanese railroads, which led the way in the home production of locomotives, "made the leap from mere repair or improvement of imported machinery to manufacturing"[85] via imitation in the last two decades of the Meiji era. Providing a solid foundation for this preliminary phase of manufacturing, however, was the high level of expertise that workshop engineers and laborers attained through the repair and rebuilding of imported engines. One of the most striking instances of locomotive reconstruction occurred in 1876 when the state railways' Kobe workshop converted two 0-6-0 freight engines purchased from the British firm Kitson into 4-4-0 passenger models equipped with enlarged driving wheels.[86] By 1905 the Kobe shop had expanded its labor force to over 1,500 employees, as had the Ōmiya workshop of the soon-to-be-nationalized Nippon Railway.[87] In the waning years of Meiji, these two works, together with the Hyōgo shop of the former San'yō Railway, became important centers for the diffusion of design and production technology to the two private contract builders, the Train Manufacturing and Kawasaki Shipbuilding companies. A number of engineers and laborers transferred to those firms after the state railway authorities ordered their shops in 1909 to cease building new locomotives and to concentrate on servicing existing ones.[88] This step was part

---

84. Sawai, "Senzenki Nihon tetsudō sharyō kōgyō." On the process of technology transfer in general and parallel examples from other Japanese industries such as mining, see Hayashi Takeshi, *The Japanese Experience in Technology: From Transfer to Self-Reliance* (Tokyo: United Nations University Press, 1990), esp. pp. 117–18.

85. Hayashi, *Japanese Experience in Technology*, p. 117.

86. Noda et al., *Nihon no tetsudō*, p. 86; O. S. Nock, *Railways in the Formative Years, 1851–1895* (New York: Macmillan, 1973), p. 138.

87. Sawai, "Senzenki Nihon tetsudō sharyō kōgyō," p. 38.

88. Ibid., pp. 28–29.

of the rationalization program pursued by the government railways following the nationalization of 1906–7 in which they turned their English-style general-purpose factories into more efficient single-purpose factories on the German model.[89]

The move toward workshop specialization also stemmed from an official desire to promote domestic manufacturing of locomotives by private contractors and led to an American-style division of labor between locomotive construction by independent builders and engine repair by railroad shops. Indeed, a battery of actions that the Japanese government took from the mid-1900s to the early 1910s sped the domestic locomotive-contracting industry into the final stage of technology transfer—full independence in design and production—immediately after the close of the Meiji period. First of all, the 1906–7 railway nationalization, by raising the government's share of the total rail network from around 30 percent to over 90 percent, created a vast, guaranteed market for Japanese locomotive makers once the national railway administration altered its policy on procurement of engines and rolling stock. That change came in a series of steps, which cumulatively spelled the end of standard locomotive imports into Japan. To begin with, in 1906 the authorities amended the regulations governing the state railways' acquisition of equipment and materials, making it possible for them to "use the free contract with capable suppliers" instead of the open bidding system that until that time had privileged Western locomotive builders.[90] Then, in 1909, the national railways, besides directing their own works to stop locomotive production, announced a policy of giving preference to Japanese contractors in ordering new engines and, in 1912, declared that from the following year they would purchase only domestic products. Also in 1912 the government designated four Japanese firms, including the two remaining locomotive makers, Train Manufacturing and Kawasaki Shipbuilding, as exclusive suppliers of engines and rolling stock to the state railways and promised each of them a set number of orders per year.[91] Reinforcing the new procurement policy was in-

---

89. Daito, "Railways and Scientific Management," pp. 9–10, 21.
90. Ibid., pp. 20–21.
91. Sawai, "Senzenki Nihon tetsudō sharyō kōgyō," pp. 28, 56–57.

creased tariff protection. In mid-1911, implementation of the final phase of treaty revision restored full customs sovereignty to the Japanese state. The authorities immediately raised the duty on imported engines from 5 percent ad valorem to 20 percent, effectively closing the price gap between imports and domestic makes and giving a further boost to Japanese locomotive producers.[92]

The achievement of total import substitution in this field also hinged on narrowing the technological gap between domestic and Western builders. Here, too, state intervention played a critical role. Following the railway nationalization, the government railroads enjoyed by far the largest concentration of technical skill in all of Japan, with a combined engineering force in 1910 of 514 university and higher-technical-school graduates. Those technicians who had worked on locomotives had attained a high level of expertise through their supervision of construction work at the various railroad workshops and their study of the latest design and production methods while dispatched as "work inspectors" to Western locomotive makers.[93] The national railways were thus able to nurture domestic private builders not only by creating a large and continuous demand but also by furnishing vital technological assistance and leadership.

The establishment of standard designs represented the main thrust of public technological support for the designated locomotive producers. The government railways, having inherited 177 different types of locomotives from the nationalized private railroads, placed a high priority on the standardization of new engines.[94] In 1909 state railway experts began working with the private makers to design three standard types of tender locomotives, one for light passenger work, one for freight, and one for express passenger service; together they completed these designs and moved them into production in 1913–14. In the meantime, to raise the technological level of the private contractors, the national railways sent their own engineers to oversee the manufacturing process, including the exact replication of locomotives imported by the government in 1911 (see

---

92. Ibid., pp. 60–61.
93. Ibid., p. 60; Daito, "Railways and Scientific Management," p. 11.
94. *Nihon kokuyū tetsudō*, pp. 195–96.

Fig. 6.1d),[95] and transferred experts outright to the designated firms.[96] As a result, the private builders rapidly accumulated know-how on the design and production of advanced engines such as superheaters and, by the early Taishō period, had managed to meet the exacting technological requirements of the railway authorities.

All the conditions for independent design and production, therefore, were in place at the start of Taishō. Thanks to the official program of tariff protection and, more important, to the favorable procurement policy of the national railways, the designated locomotive suppliers could proceed confidently with factory-expansion plans in the 1910s. As the railway authorities pushed them to reach Western technological levels and inundated them with orders for the new standard types of locomotives, Kawasaki Shipbuilding and Train Manufacturing took off into high-volume, efficient production after 1912. Because they could concentrate on a handful of standard models, the private builders were able to implement quickly and successfully an American-style system of manufacturing based on the interchangeability of parts, one that allowed them to reap the benefits of both economies of scale and "the learning curve effect."[97] Of the two most popular standard designs, basically compact versions of the German superheaters adapted to Japanese conditions, the private

---

95. The Train Manufacturing Company, having helped assemble the twelve nonsuperheaters purchased from Britain in 1911, made eighteen copies of them in 1912. The next year Kawasaki went one step further and, besides producing twelve exact copies of the Borsig superheaters, completed 39 superheated tank engines for high-gradient use that represented an improvement on another German model imported in 1912 (Harada, *Tetsudō no kataru*, pp. 183–84).

96. A prime example of state railway engineers who moved *amakudari* (descending from heaven) style to the private manufacturers was Ōta Yoshimatsu, who, after originating the standard design for light passenger locomotives, left government service in 1910 to become chief of the rolling-stock design department of Kawasaki Shipbuilding. Kawasaki went on to produce 88 light passenger engines based on an improved version of Ōta's initial design (Sawai, "Senzenki Nihon tetsudō sharyō kōgyō," p. 59; Daito, "Railways and Scientific Management," p. 22; Yuzawa, "Transfer of Railway Technologies," p. 211).

97. Daito, "Railways and Scientific Management," pp. 22–23, 25–26. On the suppliers' plant-expansion programs in the early 1910s, see Sawai, "Senzenki Nihon tetsudō sharyō kōgyō," pp. 63–65.

makers produced a total of 784 freight engines between 1913 and 1926 and 687 express passenger locomotives from 1914 to 1929 (see Figs. 6.1f and g).[98] The railway nationalization thus resulted in a virtual monopsony that enabled Japanese contract builders to overcome the usual constraints on locomotive manufacturing and engage in the bulk, if not mass, production of standardized engines, a situation unimaginable in the United States and Britain.[99] The continually expanding volume of railway traffic eventually necessitated upgrades in motive power, but the designs of 1913–14 were serviceable enough in the near term that the national railways did not require a new generation of standard models for another five to ten years.[100] In short, a confluence of positive factors, including a happy combination of largely German-inspired design and American-style manufacturing methods, propelled the domestic locomotive industry into the culminating phase of technology transfer ahead of virtually every other machine industry in Japan.

Nearly every one of those factors was the result of government action. Tessa Morris-Suzuki's assertion that from the early 1880s "the state's central role in the acquisition of foreign technology began to be supplanted . . . [by private entrepreneurial] schemes for importing and adapting western techniques"[101] clearly does not apply to railroads, nor does it fit the munitions industry, the other principal field in which the Meiji government held on to its enterprises even as it sold off most of its other factories and mines in the 1880s and 1890s.[102] In the locomotive industry in particular, the

---

98. Noda et al., *Nihon no tetsudō*, p. 143; Sawai, "Senzenki Nihon tetsudō sharyō kōgyō," p. 58. In the 1920s, Train Manufacturing and Kawasaki Shipbuilding were joined by several new domestic locomotive makers, including Hitachi and Mitsubishi Shipbuilding.

99. In Germany, however, the steady government purchase of private railroads beginning in 1879 may well have created a similar market for standard locomotives by the turn of the twentieth century.

100. Noda et al., *Nihon no tetsudō*, pp. 241–43.

101. Tessa Morris-Suzuki, *The Technological Transformation of Japan: From the Seventeenth to the Twenty-first Century* (Cambridge, Eng.: Cambridge University Press, 1994), p. 78.

102. On state munitions works, see Kozo Yamamura, "Success Illgotten? The Role of Meiji Militarism in Japan's Technological Progress," *Journal of Economic History* 37, no. 1 (Mar. 1977): 113–35.

state railways' Kobe workshop and the nationalized private railway works continued to be leading centers for importing and disseminating advanced technology well into the twentieth century, and several forms of state intervention were indispensable to the achievement of self-sufficiency in locomotive manufacturing.

Also critical to that achievement was the intensity of Western competition to penetrate the Japanese market. Western makers' zeal for exporting their latest models to Japan provided Japanese manufacturers with ready access to prototypes and the most advanced equipment and parts available. As Christopher Howe so aptly puts it, "Japan's technological receptivity was matched by the eagerness of the West to supply what Japan was seeking. Thus in the 1900s, as Japan's objectives and capabilities began to rise significantly, its businessmen could live à la carte on menus selected from the world's technological leaders." Howe goes on to cite the textile industry as having "benefited from the openness of the world economy and the willingness of British machinery manufacturers in particular to market their products worldwide."[103] Add American and German producers, and the statement applies equally well to the Japanese locomotive industry.

The relatively brief history of Western rivalry in the Japanese locomotive market tends to corroborate the larger story of British entrepreneurial failure and competitive decline. For the most part, British engine makers were not as enterprising as their American counterparts in pursuing sales in Japan or, more fundamentally, in seeking efficiencies in production. The general trend of British decline, however, fluctuated considerably in the short run owing to the volatile nature of the producers' domestic markets, with British sales in Japan temporarily rebounding as U.S. demand quickened after the turn of the century. Yet there seems no denying the overall pattern of British retreat in the face of U.S. and, to a lesser extent, German advances in the Japanese locomotive market.

As for the story of modern Japan's technological and industrial rise, the parallels between this case study and the Japanese drive to

---

103. Christopher Howe, *The Origins of Japanese Trade Supremacy: Development and Technology in Asia from 1540 to the Pacific War* (Chicago: University of Chicago Press, 1996), p. 328.

catch up technologically with advanced Western countries follow-ing World War II are rather striking. In the early postwar era, Japa-nese industry also capitalized on a free-trade environment and the willingness of Western businesses to sell or license their technology on liberal terms. In the prewar locomotive industry, however, the attainment of technological independence did not give rise to a boomerang effect, with Japanese manufacturers invading Western markets and outcompeting the erstwhile industry leaders—no "re-venge of the Mikado" took place. (As Fig. 6.1h illustrates, Japanese makers in fact introduced their own version of the Mikado engine for home consumption in the 1920s.) Japan exported locomotives in the prewar period exclusively to its colonies and other territorial possessions—the Train Manufacturing Company's first engine, which it built for the Taiwanese Government General in 1901, sank in a shipwreck en route to Taiwan.[104] After the Japanese began to make standard-gauge locomotives in Manchuria in 1914,[105] the po-tential for advancing into Western markets existed. But, like other branches of heavy engineering in prewar Japan, the locomotive in-dustry was unable to reach the price and quality levels that success-ful exporting to the West required.

Finally, some of the factors that enhanced the competitiveness of American locomotives in Meiji Japan exhibit a certain timeless-ness, seen against the backdrop of U.S. automobile and other manufacturers' attempts to break into the Japanese market today. Among those factors were a willingness to adapt exports to local conditions, epitomized by the development of the Mikado-type engine, and direct and persistent sales representation, best exempli-fied by ALCo's man in Japan, Willard Tyler. The final irony, however, is that the very success of Tyler and his rivals in market-ing their products furnished the Japanese with the latest technol-ogy and helped propel Japan to a position of self-sufficiency from which it could dispense with standard locomotive imports once and for all.

---

104. Harada, *Tetsudō no kataru*, p. 186.

105. H. J. Mullett-Merrick, "A New Epoch in Japanese Engineering: The First Standard Gauge Locomotive, Designed and Built at the South Manchurian Rail-way Workshops," *Railway Magazine* 36, no. 213 (Mar. 1915): 219–20.

PART III

Gender and Family

CHAPTER SEVEN

Women's Rights and
the Japanese State, 1880–1925
Barbara Molony

Recent scholarship on the relationship between women and the state in Japan has approached this question from a variety of perspectives. Among other subjects, scholars have looked at women as targets of government policies;[1] agents of specific parts of the state;[2] participants in organized or institutionalized politics or move-

---

1. For representative works in English, see Sharon H. Nolte and Sally Ann Hastings, "The Meiji State's Policy Toward Women, 1890–1910," in *Recreating Japanese Women, 1600–1945*, ed. Gail Lee Bernstein (Berkeley: University of California Press, 1991), pp. 151–74; Janet Hunter, "Factory Legislation and Employer Resistance: The Abolition of Night Work in the Cotton-Spinning Industry," in *Japanese Management in Historical Perspective*, ed. T. Yui and K. Nakagawa (Tokyo: University of Tokyo Press, 1989), pp. 243–72; Yoshiko Miyake, "Doubling Expectations: Motherhood and Women's Factory Work Under State Management in Japan in the 1930s and 1940s," in *Recreating Japanese Women*; and Sharon L. Sievers, *Flowers in Salt: The Beginnings of Feminist Consciousness in Modern Japan* (Stanford: Stanford University Press, 1983), pp. 267–95.

2. In English, see, e.g., Sumiko Otsubo, "Engendering Eugenics: Feminists and Marriage Restriction Legislation in the 1920s," in *Gendering Modern Japanese History*, ed. Barbara Molony and Kathleen Uno (Cambridge, Mass.: Harvard University Asia Center, forthcoming 2005); Barbara Molony and Kathleen Molony, *Ichikawa Fusae: A Political Biography* (Stanford: Stanford University Press, forthcoming); and Kathleen Uno, *Motherhood, Childhood, and Social Reform in Early Twentieth-Century Japan* (Honolulu: University of Hawai'i Press, 1999).

ments;[3] members of groups that interacted with state power;[4] and
objects of discourses about women and the state.[5] This chapter explores the relationship of women and the state by examining discourses on "women's rights" in the late nineteenth century (especially the 1880s and 1890s) and the interwar era (especially the 1910s
and 1920s). Rights were a frequent topic of discussion among Japanese intellectuals and political activists, including feminist advocates, throughout this period.[6] But the notion of rights underwent a
change as the structure of the state, and Japanese people's understanding of it, changed. Indeed, the discussion of rights in all their
forms constituted a key element in the building of the modern
Japanese nation.

Possession of rights assumes a degree of ownership of the state
and thus the ability to influence it. The struggle for women's rights,

---

3. See, e.g., Vera Mackie, *Creating Socialist Women in Japan: Gender, Labor,
and Activism, 1900-1937* (Cambridge, Eng.: Cambridge University Press, 1997);
Helen M. Hopper, *A New Woman of Japan: A Political Biography of Katō Shidzue*
(Boulder, Colo.: Westview Press, 1996); and Yukiko Matsukawa and Kaoru Tachi,
"Women's Suffrage and Gender Politics in Japan," in *Suffrage and Beyond: Interna-
tional Feminist Perspectives,* ed. Caroline Daley and Melanie Nolan (New York:
New York University Press, 1994), pp. 171-84.

4. See, e.g., Sheldon Garon, "The World's Oldest Debate? Prostitution and the
State in Imperial Japan, 1900-1945," *American Historical Review* 93, no. 3 (1993):
710-33; idem, "Women's Groups and the Japanese State: Contending Approaches
to Political Integration, 1890-1945," *Journal of Japanese Studies* 19, no. 1 (1993): 5-42;
and Noriyo Hayakawa, "Feminism and Nationalism in Japan, 1868-1945," *Journal
of Women's History* 7, no. 4 (1995): 108-20.

5. For some works in English, see, e.g., Barbara Molony, "The 1986 Equal Employment Opportunity Law and the Changing Discourse on Gender," *SIGNS* 20,
no. 2 (1995): 268-302; Kathleen Uno, "The Death of Good Wife, Wise Mother?" in
Postwar Japan as History, ed. Andrew Gordon (Berkeley: University of California
Press, 1993), pp. 293-322; and Laurel Rasplica Rodd, "Yosano Akiko and the Taishō Debate over the 'New Woman,'" in *Recreating Japanese Women,* pp. 175-98.

6. I also discuss some of the issues taken up in this chapter in Barbara Molony,
"Women's Rights, Feminism, and Suffragism in Japan, 1870-1925," *Pacific Historical
Review* 69, no. 4 (2000): 639-62. Although the term "feminism" (*feminizumu*) was
introduced in Japan in a 1910 article in *Hōgaku kyōkai zasshi* (Journal of the Association of Legal Studies), I use the term to refer to a broad range of discourses that, beginning in the early Meiji period, supported women's rights or the improvement of
women's condition or status. For more on the introduction of the term "feminism," see Sōgō joseishi kenkyūkai, ed., *Nihon josei no rekishi* (History of Japanese
women) (Tokyo: Kadokawa shoten, 1993), pp. 192-93.

overlooked by many historians in the past, has recently captured the imagination of historians as an instance of resistance against the state. The notion of resistance must, however, be understood in relation to its converse—resistance is always articulated in relationship to power.[7] Rights both embrace and resist power. A stress on resistance appears to offer points of view about women's relationship to the state vastly different from a stress on accommodation. Yet underlying the two emphases is an assumption that the state existed as an established entity that women might challenge or come to accept but could not change. Scholarship on women's rights tends to see the "state" as a separate and distinct entity with which women sought alliance to achieve shared goals, against which they struggled for justice, or in which they sought membership.[8] In fact, however, the contours of the modern Japanese state were not yet firmly established in the late nineteenth century. Accordingly, early discussions of "rights" in the 1880s and 1890s were based on a more imprecise definition of that term than they were in the 1920s and took place in a more fluid political situation. Indeed, nineteenth-century feminists hoped that their struggle for rights would help shape the very nature of the state.

As the central government apparatus grew stronger and its functions became more defined, the focus of women's rights discourse shifted. Beginning more as a demand for inclusion in the emerging state and civil society of late nineteenth-century Japan, feminist discourse at first centered on obtaining respect for women as human beings, an attitude that activists viewed as a prerequisite for women's participation in the public sphere. In the 1910s and 1920s, women's advocates intensified the call for political rights while advancing the notion of rights as state-enforced protections from institutionalized patriarchy (both state-supported patriarchy and the everyday version of domineering husbands) and safeguards against

---

7. Michel Foucault, *History of Sexuality*, vol. 1, *An Introduction* (New York: Vintage Books, 1980), p. 95.

8. For representative works in each of these categories, see, respectively, Garon, "Women's Groups and the Japanese State" (on alliances); Mackie, *Creating Socialist Women in Japan* (on the struggle for justice); and Molony and Molony, *Ichikawa Fusae* (on campaigns for membership in the state).

the economic exploitation of women and children. In the oppressive political climate of the two decades following the period discussed in this study, the suffragist cause collapsed, and discourse increasingly became confined to rights as state protection. The dual goals of full political rights and state aid and protection were not mutually exclusive in the eyes of most feminists, however. The relative emphasis on one or the other varied with changes in the political and social climate. Moreover, the meaning of inclusion itself was open to different interpretations, and feminists acknowledged various ways to achieve it. Both forms of rights discussions in the interwar era—resistance against exclusion from the political process and acceptance of the state's power to protect—assumed an existing state structure.

Rights Discourse in the 1880s and 1890s

In Japan, as elsewhere, "rights" had multiple meanings.[9] Talk of rights emerged in a variety of contexts and often blended aspects of Tokugawa antiauthoritarianism[10] and "Western" rights discourses.[11] Japanese conceptions of the state, nation, nationality, ethnicity, and gender were being constructed around the same time, and rights discourse was used selectively to resist the state's definition of one or

---

9. For a persuasive argument that "contemporary Western feminism may remain parochial in its insistence that its own *telos* of freedom and agency be at work in every record of women's lives," see Susan Mann, "The History of Chinese Women Before the Age of Orientalism," *Journal of Women's History* 8, no. 4 (Winter 1997): 174. In the case of Japanese discussions about rights, however, advocates were explicit about the quest for women's rights; the historian need not project her own feminist hopes of finding calls for agency.

10. George M. Wilson, *Patriots and Redeemers in Japan: Motives in the Meiji Restoration* (Chicago: University of Chicago Press, 1992) offers an insightful treatment of Tokugawa antiauthoritarianism. See also Matsumoto Sannosuke, "The Idea of Heaven: A Tokugawa Foundation for Natural Rights Theory," in *Japanese Thought in the Tokugawa Period, 1600–1868: Methods and Metaphors*, ed. Tetsuo Najita and Irvin Scheiner (Chicago: University of Chicago Press, 1978), pp. 181–99.

11. Mill's *On Liberty* was translated very early—in 1868. This translation was followed in the 1870s and early 1880s by translations of works by other Western political theorists. Rousseau's *Social Contract*, translated in 1882, was highly esteemed by Popular Rights advocates. See Masaaki Kosaka, ed., *Japanese Culture in the Meiji Era*, vol. 8, *Thought* (Tokyo: Tōyō bunko, 1958), pp. 115, 146.

another of these categories. Conversely, rights discourse could be employed to help define or support these categories or institutions. The Meiji-era neologisms for "rights" (*kenri*), "women's rights" (*joken*), "male-female equality" (*danjo byōdō*), and "male-female equal rights" (*danjo dōken*) were, at times, used interchangeably in regard to women, although their meanings were actually distinct.

With such notable exceptions as Popular Rights advocate Ueki Emori (1857–92), who held that people had a right and a duty to resist unresponsive government and that men and women were entitled to equal rights, most Meiji-era advocates of improving women's status did not call for feminist resistance to the state.[12] Until the rise of socialist feminism in the last decade of the Meiji period, proponents of women's rights called for *inclusion* in the state and civil society, not *revolution*—and even most socialists sought inclusion in the absence of a revolution.[13] I suggest there were two reasons for feminists' desire for inclusion: first, the fundamental nature of rights themselves; and second, their belief that rights should be the reward for education and self-cultivation.

Rights, fundamentally, have mutually contradictory qualities. One of the purposes of rights is protection from something—from harm caused by another public person or the state or from limitations on one's expression or movement, and so on. Rights often conflict—one's right to protection, for example, might limit another's freedom of expression. Although a definition of rights as protection from or resistance to encroachment was part of Meiji-era discourse, the view of rights as protection from the state was a minor thread in discussions of women's rights. Indeed, the notion

---

12. Ueki Emori, cited in Roger W. Bowen, *Rebellion and Democracy in Meiji Japan: A Study of Commoners in the Popular Rights Movement* (Berkeley: University of California Press, 1980), p. 205. Suzuki Yūko (*Nihon josei undō shiryō shūsei*, vol. 1, *Shisō, seiji: Josei kaihō shisō no tenkai to fujin sanseiken undō* [Collection of documents of the Japanese women's movement: thought, politics: the development of women's liberation thought and the women's political rights movement] [Tokyo: Fuji shuppan, 1996], p. 23) notes that other than Ueki, whose writings about women's rights were inspired by the demand for voting rights by Kusunose Kita, few of the leading male Popular Rights advocates discussed women's rights in their writings. Women like Fukuda Hideko and Kishida Toshiko (see below) were, therefore, particularly important. See also Sievers, *Flowers in Salt*, pp. 28–29.

13. See Mackie, *Creating Socialist Women*.

of protection was initially more closely connected to the idea of "liberation" (*kaihō*) than to rights. Liberation came to be associated with women's political rights only in 1907 when socialists began using the term. Earlier, *kaihō* had been used in discussing the liberation of prostituted women and girls from contractual bondage and, by the end of the nineteenth century, the liberation of wives, through divorce, from oppressive marriages.[14] The view of rights as protection was less important to Meiji-era thinkers than was the focus on inclusion in the state and equality in both the private domain of the family and the public domain of civil society.[15]

Although nineteenth-century Western theorists saw civil society as existing in the public sphere and, therefore, as standing in opposition to the family (the private),[16] women's rights advocates in turn-of-the-century Japan did not assume such an opposition.[17] They were of differing minds concerning the quality of Japanese family life. Some saw the family as a warm haven within a cold public world, whereas others believed the family itself oppressed women, but few viewed the family as separate from the public sphere. Indeed, many believed women deserved a public role not *despite* their family status but *because* of it. Thus, for instance, the mother who kept her family healthy received recognition during the first Sino-Japanese War (1894–95) for her public service to the

---

14. Sotozaki Mitsuhiro, *Nihon fujinronshi*, vol. 2, *Fujin kaihō ronsō* (History of discourse on Japanese women: the women's liberation debate) (Tokyo: Domesu, 1989), pp. 22–24.

15. See also Hayakawa, "Feminism and Nationalism in Japan," p. III.

16. Wendy Brown, *States of Injury: Power and Freedom in Late Modernity* (Princeton: Princeton University Press, 1995), p. 151. As theorist Carole Pateman (*The Sexual Contract* [Stanford: Stanford University Press, 1988], p. 11) and others have shown, the notion of "civil" has had shifting meanings in Western discourse. Before the creation of the social contract, "civil" was seen as the opposite of "natural"; thereafter, it was seen as the opposite of "private."

17. "Civil society" was not named in the late nineteenth century, but by the 1920s, rights of civic and civil participation were understood to be related to *kō-minken*. See, e.g., Molony and Molony, *Ichikawa Fusae*. The term "civil society" (*shimin shakai*) came to be used in Japan in the 1920s, but the Japanese translation's urban implications (*shimin*) made it unpopular with rural folk; see Kevin M. Doak, "What Is a Nation and Who Belongs? National Narratives and the Ethnic Imagination in Twentieth-Century Japan," *American Historical Review* 102, no. 2 (1997): 290.

nation.[18] The ideological opponents of women's rights advocates—gender conservatives who opposed any concept of inherent rights or even earned rights based on service in the public sphere—shared the belief that the family was the basis of the state.[19] But their idea of "family" was a patriarchy without rights for anyone except the family head, let alone equality among its members. Thus, any discussion of rights in the public sphere of state or civil society had to start with a close examination of the unequal relationships within the family as well as an understanding of who deserved those rights.

Although the earliest discussions of rights in the 1870s and 1880s often did not explicitly link rights and the male gender, Japanese discussants frequently employed the ideas of Jean-Jacques Rousseau, whose vision of the social contract was founded on the fraternal rights of all men.[20] Japanese advocates of rights in the 1870s viewed men's right to participate in politics through this Rousseauian lens. By 1890, following two decades of struggle, a small minority of men had been awarded the right to participate in the state and civil society, but all women were pointedly excluded.[21] After 1890, many male activists who had earlier demanded rights of fraternal inclusion joined parties and entered the government in some capac-

---

18. Iwamoto Yoshiharu, in *Taiyō*, "Katei" (Household) column, cited in Muta Kazue, "Images of the Family in Meiji Periodicals: The Paradox Underlying the Emergence of the 'Home,'" *U.S.-Japan Women's Journal*, English Supplement 7 (1994): 64.

19. See, e.g., Hozumi Yatsuka, quoted in Kosaka, *Japanese Culture in the Meiji Era*, pp. 381, 383. Conservatives and feminists saw "family" in a different light. For feminists, the family was made up of loving members whose sexually differentiated but complementary roles should be equally valued. Conservatives found that formulation of the family threatening and believed that it could undermine the foundation of the Japanese authoritarian state. That is, as the influential conservative legal scholar Hozumi Yatsuka wrote in 1896, "The obedience to . . . the headship of the family is, inferentially, what we confer on the Imperial House as the extant progenitor of the nation"; or, in 1898, "The family expanded becomes the country. . . . We cannot be indifferent to whether the family institution is maintained or abolished!"

20. For more on Rousseau's ideas, see, e.g., Pateman, *Sexual Contract*.

21. See, e.g. Sievers, *Flowers in Salt*, p. 52; and Yasukawa Junosuke and Yasukawa Etsuko, *Josei sabetsu no shakai shisōshi* (History of the social thought of discrimination against women) (Tokyo: Akaishi shobo, 1993), chap. 1.

ity.[22] By the turn of the twentieth century, many took the requirement of male gender for political participation for granted; the state itself was being constructed as a fraternity under a patriarchal emperor.[23]

Although holding various views about "women's rights," all nineteenth-century Japanese advocates for women started from the assumption that women did not enjoy such rights. To rectify this situation, some argued for a communitarian inclusiveness reminiscent of Rousseau.[24] Others, inspired by John Stuart Mill, stressed improved education as a way for women to gain the subjectivity (that is, full personhood with agency) that would make them eligible for rights. Others worked to eliminate patriarchal sexual privileges, such as those implied by patrilineality, polygamy, and prostitution, as a first step toward achieving women's full inclusion in society and the state.[25]

---

22. Suzuki, *Nihon josei undō shiryō shūsei*, p. 18.

23. On "fraternity," see, e.g., Donald Roden, *Schooldays in Imperial Japan: A Study in the Culture of a Student Elite* (Berkeley: University of California Press, 1980). Roden (pp. 139, 146) describes a fraternal communalism that violently resisted even the suggestion of a womanly presence in its hallowed halls. Male sex was a requirement for all government positions, including the emperorship. Many advocates of women's rights were surprised and disheartened when male gender was made a requirement for occupying the throne; although there had been only a minuscule number of empresses who had ruled in their own right in the ancient and early modern periods, female gender had not been an absolute bar to the throne. See Noheji Kiyoe, *Josei kaihō shisō no genryū: Iwamoto Yoshiharu to "Jogaku zasshi"* (The origins of women's liberation thought: Iwamoto Yoshiharu and *Jogaku zasshi*) (Tokyo: Azekura shobō, 1984), p. 14.

24. Although it seems ironic that advocates of women's rights would adopt notions of rights based on masculine privilege, Japanese women were not alone in extrapolating Rousseauian ideas to justify women's rights. As Carole Pateman points out throughout *The Sexual Contract*, Western feminist thought extended the notion of fraternity to women, despite that formulation's original limits.

25. For an effective problematization of patrilineality, see Kathleen Uno, "Questioning Patrilineality: On Western Studies of the Japanese *Ie*," *positions* 4, no. 3 (Winter 1996): 569–94. She argues convincingly that scholars have often distorted the historical roles of patrilineality. Meiji women's rights advocates also strongly contested what they saw as continuing patterns of women's subordination through patrilineality and its ties with the other "p's" of patriarchy, prostitution, and polygamy.

In its formulation and its legal applications, the concept of rights separates the individual from his or her community. People struggle for rights on behalf of an oppressed identity group (a class, a gender, an ethnicity), but when rights are granted, they are applied to individuals.[26] Japanese commentators on Meiji civil law rightly argued that this concept of individual rights conflicted with the notion, codified in the Civil Code of 1898, that women, especially married women, were under the jurisdiction of the patriarchal family head and thus had neither individual rights within the community of the family nor the independent right to enter contracts that would permit rights in the larger society.[27] The Civil Code, therefore, explicitly excluded the idea of rights held equally by individuals within the household.[28]

Nevertheless, Japanese seeking to improve the lot of women stressed rights as a means to elevate women's status. Mill and Rousseau and social contract theory were particularly important sources in the development of Japanese thinking about rights. Under the social contract, individuals voluntarily surrender some rights in return for the protection of civil law and inclusion in the fraternity of citizens.[29] Because women were assumed to be weak in strength and intellect, they were not entitled to self-ownership and were therefore not full persons or individuals. As a result, women could not even enter into the social contract. For Mill, women were thus not present in the public, or civil, sphere, and where they were— the home—was to be "private" or off-limits to the state and dominated by the home's own patriarch, who was himself part of the civil, egalitarian "fraternity." Advocates of women's rights (including Mill) reckoned education as one key to making women worthy

---

26. Brown, *States of Injury*, 98.

27. For an extended discussion of the Meiji Civil Code, see Ryōsuke Ishii, ed., *Japanese Culture in the Meiji Era*, vol. 9, *Japanese Legislation in the Meiji Era* (Tokyo: Tōyō bunko, 1958), pp. 601–92.

28. Ironically, critics of the first draft of the Civil Code complained that the code smacked of "European" ideas on civil rights. Of course, universal political rights for individuals irrespective of gender or other markers of exclusion did not then exist in any European country.

29. Pateman, *Sexual Contract*, *passim*; Yasukawa and Yasukawa, *Josei sabetsu no shakai shisōshi*, chap. 1.

of being "individuals" and thereby improving their status. Rousseau, male-centered though his writings often appear, did, in fact, suggest an important public role for women. Men could not be "brothers" unless they were ethical fathers and sons, and the mother was the key to nurturing the moral and ethical family. This idea resonated with women's rights thinking in turn-of-the-century Japan, which linked moral and intellectual cultivation with social respect.

Commentators have at times raised concerns about "state intrusion in the family," but patriarchal dominance may have felt just as confining to many women as state authoritarianism. (To be sure, the two were closely related, since one component of state authoritarianism was the codification of male dominance in family law.) Inclusion in the state, which must be preceded or accompanied by inclusion in the public sphere, has thus been a goal of many feminist political activists, whether Japanese or Western. The problems caused by patriarchy seemed so debilitating in Meiji Japan that marriage and sexuality became major concerns of the early advocates of women's rights. Here we can see the precursors of later feminists' emphases on "protection." However, Meiji-era feminists argued principally for respect for women and their personhood rather than for protection of them as weak.

In the 1880s and 1890s, discussions of women's rights, including rights in society and rights within the family, were closely related to discussions of women's education, particularly education beyond the elementary level. Cultivating a moral, ethical, responsible character capable of manifesting agency—by being an example to others or even a leader—was a goal of Confucian education as well as the recently introduced Western-style learning. Intellectual and moral cultivation produced persons worthy of respect and, therefore, worthy of having a recognized subjectivity or personhood—a prerequisite for entering the social contract. The centrality of education, with its deep connections to notions of respect and ethical leadership, in late nineteenth-century rights discourse suggests that rights were closely connected to the reformers' advocacy of respect for women's subjectivity. In Meiji Japan, even educators who believed women did not need *political* rights hoped to mold ethical wives and mothers to lead the family and society by example. These women would not be active in electoral politics, but they would participate in public activities such as poor relief or more controversial reforms such as the regulation of sexuality.[30]

From early in the Meiji period, women's education, especially as it affected morality in the family and, by extension, the nation, was a lively topic in Japanese journals. Contributors to *Meiroku zasshi* (Journal of the Meiji Six Society; founded 1873, circulation 3,000) joined this discussion early on.[31] Fukuzawa Yukichi (1835–90), perhaps the most famous early participant in the *fujin ronsō* (debate about women) and author of the influential *Nihon fujinron* (Discourse on Japanese womanhood; 1885), stressed monogamy as the basis of equality (*byōdō*).[32] Elsewhere, Fukuzawa linked "equality" closely to education.

Like Fukuzawa, female advocates of women's rights also linked education, monogamy, and respect. Kishida Toshiko (1861?–1901) and Fukuda Kageyama Hideko (1865–1927) took the feminist message to the public through political speeches. But they also imparted a more political edge to their advocacy by calling for women's inclusion in the state as well as the public sphere. The civic groups they and other advocates for women organized helped develop civil society in Meiji Japan by opening it to women. In numerous speeches between 1882 and 1884, Kishida Toshiko called for equal rights for men and women, denounced the equating of personhood with the male gender alone, decried the stultifying effects of repression of freedom of thought,[33] and, above all, called

---

30. See, e.g., the discussion of the Women's Reform Society in Sievers, *Flowers in Salt*, pp. 87–114.

31. Yamaguchi Miyoko, *Shiryō Meiji keimōki no fujin mondai ronsō no shūhen* (Data on the environment of the debate on the woman problem in the Meiji enlightenment period) (Tokyo: Domesu, 1989), p. 186.

32. Ibid., p. 199. For an extensive treatment of the philosophical basis for Fukuzawa's thought on equality and on education, see Yasukawa and Yasukawa, *Josei sabetsu no shakai shisōshi*, pp. 6–104.

33. Suzuki, *Nihon josei undō shiryō shūsei*, pp. 56–85, offers a wealth of information about Kishida and her public activities. The newspaper articles reprinted in Suzuki's collection show that Kishida had an extraordinarily busy schedule, rushing from city to city to speak out—with occasional censorship by the police—on women's rights.

on women to develop the mental strength (*seishin ryoku*) to be confident public persons.[34] Kishida tied the development of women's subjectivity—their existence as persons in society—both to national strength and to Popular Rights politics. Because "equality, independence, respect, and a monogamous relationship are the hallmarks of relationships between men and women in a civilized society," she stated, recognition of women's rights would elevate Japan in international esteem and thereby aid in its defense against a possible Western threat.[35] In a speech entitled "The Government Is the People's God; Man Is Woman's God" ("Seifu wa jinmin no ten otoko wa onna no ten"),[36] Kishida also denounced sexual inequality in terms familiar to her colleagues in the Popular Rights movement by equating male supremacy with the government's dominion over the people.

Kishida inspired women all over Japan.[37] Women's groups sprang up in cities and towns; many of them were formed to welcome speakers like Kishida. There were women's friendly societies (*joshi konshinkai*), women's freedom parties (*fujin jiyūtō*), women's rights associations (*jokenkai*), women's societies (*fujin kyōkai*), and at least one women's freedom hall (*joshi jiyūkan*).[38] Whether these groups continued to exist long after they sponsored Kishida and others is unclear. They helped set the stage, however, for the growth of larger feminist groups, such as the Japan Christian Women's Reform Society (Nihon Kirisutokyō fujin kyōfukai) and the Women's Morality Association (Fujin tokugikai) in the second half of the 1880s, and they created a readership for articles on women's rights in magazines and journals in the 1890s.[39] These

---

34. Kishida Toshiko, "Dōhō shimai ni tsugu" (To my brothers and sisters), reprinted in Suzuki, *Nihon josei undō shiryō shūsei*, pp. 74–85.

35. Kishida, "Dōhō," quoted and translated by Sievers, *Flowers in Salt*, p. 38. See also Hayakawa, "Feminism and Nationalism in Japan," for an excellent discussion of the relationship of feminism and nationalism.

36. Suzuki, *Nihon josei undō shiryō shūsei*, p. 57.

37. Ibid., p. 56.

38. See ibid., pp. 71–73, for articles describing the founding of several of these groups.

39. Hirota Masaki is not impressed with the Okayama Women's Friendly Society because its members were merely wives and daughters of men in the Popular Rights movement. He contrasts this group with those formed by women not re-

groups advocated monogamy and women's sexual dignity and fostered political discussion and collaborative feminist efforts to set up schools for girls and women.[40] In these groups *joseiron* (discourse on women) meant discussions about improving women's status by politicizing the private sphere by means of education and marital respect as well as the relationship of education and marital respect to women's public voice and self-cultivation.

Inspired by Kishida, educator Fukuda Hideko founded a community women's group that featured speakers on natural rights, equality, and freedom.[41] By 1890, Fukuda had petitioned the Diet to permit women to participate in politics.[42] The following year, Fukuda caught the attention of the mainstream media with her proposal to establish a newspaper for women run entirely by women.[43] Like Kishida, Fukuda linked women's rights and political involvement with strengthening the nation.[44]

The rhetoric of rights was further developed in new journals and magazines that appeared in the late nineteenth century. The most important of these new journals for women was *Jogaku zasshi* (Women's education journal), cofounded by Iwamoto Yoshiharu (1863–1942) in 1885 and edited by him for most of its eighteen-year run. At least eight women known in their day as advocates of rights, both women's rights and people's rights, wrote for *Jogaku zasshi*. The most famous of these were probably Kishida Toshiko, Shimizu Toyoko (1868–1933), and Wakamatsu Shizuko (1864–1896; she married Iwamoto in 1889).[45] These writers were influenced by

---

lated to male activists. See Hirota Masaki, "Kindai erīto josei no aidentitī to kokka" (Modern elite women's identity and the nation), in *Jendā no Nihonshi* (Gender history of Japan), vol. 1, ed. Wakita Haruko and S. B. Hanley (Tokyo: Tōkyō daigaku shuppankai, 1994), p. 203.

40. Suzuki, *Nihon josei undō shiryō shūsei*, p. 98.

41. Sievers, *Flowers in Salt*, p. 36; Mikiso Hane, *Reflections on the Way to the Gallows: Rebel Women in Prewar Japan* (Berkeley: University of California Press, 1988), p. 36.

42. Suzuki, *Nihon josei undō shiryō shūsei*, p. 127.

43. Ibid., p. 98.

44. Hirota, "Kindai erīto josei no aidentitī to kokka," p. 202.

45. Fujita Yoshimi, *Meiji jogakkō no sekai* (The world of the Meiji girls' higher schools) (Tokyo: Shōeisha, 1984), pp. 35, 79; Noheji, *Josei kaihō shisō no genryū*,

the readily accessible thought of the Popular Rights polemicists as well as lively commentary in other publications like the *Meiroku zasshi* of the previous decade and *Kokumin no tomo* (People's friend), a contemporary journal whose readership overlapped with that of *Jogaku zasshi*.[46]

Iwamoto Yoshiharu ardently supported the elevation of women's status. Although he rejected equal rights for men and women—*danjo dōken*—he argued for the fundamental equality of men and women—*danjo byōdō*.[47] He found the notion of *danson johi* (respect the male, despise the female) particularly odious.[48] Christianity, which permeated Iwamoto's thinking, emphasized the equal humanity of men and women in the eyes of God.[49] Though Iwamoto believed in gender equality before God, however, he found social stratification by gender perfectly natural, as did many contemporary social contract theorists in the West, whose grounding was also in Christianity; servants may be humans, but they do not have the same rights as their employers.[50]

From the mid-1880s to the early 1890s, Iwamoto advocated that the content of women's education should differ from men's. Although he used the "good wife, wise mother" discourse, however, he called for a "modern" type of wife and mother.[51] Education should create mothers who were intelligent and wives who were good persons, not merely mothers who were wise educators of their children and wives who served their husbands well. But be-

---

p. 24. The others were Tanabe Hanaho, Ogino Ginko, Yoshida Nobuko, Andō Tane, and Kojima Kiyo.

46. Noheji, *Josei kaihō shisō no genryū*, p. 68.

47. Ibid., p. 128.

48. Ibid., p. 133.

49. Aoyama Nao, *Meiji jogakkō no kenkyū* (Research on Meiji girls' higher schools) (Tokyo: Keiō tsūshin, 1983), p. 7.

50. Noheji, *Josei kaihō shisō no genryū*, p. 129.

51. Noheji (ibid., p. 155) notes that the four characters—*ryō, sai, ken*, and *bo*—were used throughout Iwamoto's famous collection of essays entitled *Waga tō no joshi kyōiku* (Women's education according to our side). This short collection, which first appeared as articles in *Jogaku zasshi* from 1890 to 1892, is cited in ibid., pp. 82–83, 131–32, 139–58. Iwamoto's use of "good wife, wise mother" (*ryōsai kenbo*), Noheji notes, differed from that of his contemporaries in his stress on Christianity as the basis for that type of education.

fore 1889, Iwamoto did not argue that the end of this type of education was to prepare women to enjoy equal political rights with
men.[52]

Iwamoto was bitterly disappointed in the 1889 Constitution and
the Imperial House Code (Kōshitsu tenpan) promulgated at the
same time, both of which stipulated that heirs to the imperial
throne must be male.[53] Shocked, Iwamoto adopted a new approach
to women's education and to women's rights. In a June 1889 article
entitled "100-Year Chronic Disease" ("Hyakunen no koshitsu"), he
presented a stinging criticism of sexism in education.[54] If Japanese
opposed women's higher schools, objected to women voting, rejected monogamy, insulted the morality of female students, and
failed to regard men and women as equally human, then Japan
would never cure the disease that had troubled it for a century.
The ruler would be separated from the people, the people from the
officials, the slave from the master, the rich from the poor. Advocacy of the education of women, of Christian moralism, of religious egalitarianism, and of women's civil rights are here brought
under one discursive umbrella. The article's rhetorical device of
equating the disease with standard symbols of Tokugawa authoritarianism like the separation of the ruler and the ruled or the people and the officials was a powerful one.

Jogaku zasshi subsequently published a number of criticisms of
the denial of women's right of inclusion in the state and civil society. An unsigned article called on women to take part in political
discussions in order to promote "political harmony among men
and women" (*seijijō danjo kyōwa*).[55] Shimizu Toyoko, writing in
August 1890, condemned the recent passage of legislation barring
women from political meetings. "If individual rights are to be protected, and the peace and order of society secured," she argued,
"laws should not be discriminatory, granting advantage to men

---

52. Ibid., p. 131.
53. Ibid., p. 14.
54. Iwamoto Yoshiharu, "Hyakunen no koshitsu," *Jogaku zasshi*, no. 167 (June
22, 1889), cited in Noheji, *Josei kaihō shisō no genryū*, p. 137.
55. Suzuki, *Nihon josei undō shiryō shūsei*, pp. 125–26.

only, and misfortune only to women."[56] In another article two months later, Shimizu proclaimed it irrational for "one part of humanity [to] arbitrarily control . . . the other part."[57]

Respect for women's personhood and recognition of women as subjects were central goals of rights advocates in the 1890s. Both goals were necessary preconditions for women's entry into the public sphere and civil society. Both had to precede equal rights. There were other approaches to improving the status of women as well. Some advocates focused on sexuality issues. In the 1870s, writers for journals such as *Meiroku zasshi* argued that polygamy compromised Japanese ethical values and impaired its image in the West. Feminists expanded on these ideas. The Tokyo (later Japan) Christian Women's Reform Society, founded by Yajima Kajiko (1833–1925) in 1886, stressed sexual reforms as a way of helping women develop as full, equal human beings.[58] Articles in *Shino-nome shinbun* (Daybreak newspaper) and *Tōkyō fujin kyōfūkai zasshi* (Journal of the Tokyo Women's Reform Society) from the late 1880s propounded the Reform Society's view that monogamy was moral, good for Japan, and respectful of nature's gender balance; monogamy would help move the country away from evil customs of the Confucian past.[59] An 1887 article by Iwamoto entitled "The Atmosphere of Adultery" ("Kan'in no kūki") also stressed control of male sexuality through the prohibition of polygamy, but the issue of *Jogaku zasshi* in which it was to appear was banned by the government.[60]

Women's advocates viewed polygamy as a denigration of women. *Tōkyō nichi nichi shinbun* (Tokyo daily news) reported that in November 1891 the Reform Society planned to petition the

---

56. Shimizu, quoted in Sievers, *Flowers in Salt*, pp. 52–53; Suzuki, *Nihon josei undō shiryō shūsei*, p. 127.

57. Shimizu, quoted in Sievers, *Flowers in Salt*, p. 101.

58. "Fujin kyōfūkai" (Women's Reform Society), in *Chōya shinbun*, Dec. 12, 1886, reprinted in Suzuki, *Nihon josei undō shiryō shūsei*, p. 85. See also Otsubo, "Engendering Eugenics."

59. See Suzuki, *Nihon josei undō shiryō shūsei*, pp. 86–94, for citations of several articles from these journals.

60. Aoyama, *Meiji jogakkō no kenkyū*, p. 4.

Diet for legislation banning polygamy.[61] Men's morality, linked to their sexuality, was the target of these legislative efforts as well as the subject of articles such as Shimizu Toyoko's "Discussing Japanese Males' Moral Character" ("Nihon danshi no hinkō o ronzu").[62] Discussions about controlling men's sexuality paralleled those concerning the control of some women's sexuality. Reform Society goals included the elimination of prostitution as well as concubinage.[63] The sex trade was seen as a women's rights issue because it humiliated legitimate wives by supporting their husbands' adultery. The Reform Society was often unsympathetic to women in the sex trades. Prostitution shamed Japan as a whole in foreigners' eyes, the *Tōkyō fujin kyōfūkai zasshi* noted, and may have contributed to anti-Japanese discrimination in the United States.[64] The journal called for shaming women into leaving sex work. The Reform Society's concern about prostitution appeared less related to saving fallen women—which was, in fact, a stated goal of the organization—than to supporting the human dignity and equal personhood of wives and improving Japan's foreign relations. This is a clear example of the intersection of (some) women's rights and nation-building.

Gaining respect as subjects was an important requirement for becoming eligible for rights. And morality was closely related to respect. This can be seen, for instance, in the journal *Joken* (Women's rights). Established in September 1891, *Joken* included articles by leading feminists such as Fukuda Hideko and reported extensively on the activities of branches of the Women's Morality Association throughout Japan.[65] The association called for freedom (*jiyū*), equality (*byōdō*), women's rights (*joken*), and morality (*toku-*

---

61. "Ippu ippu no seigan" (Petition for monogamy), *Tōkyō nichi nichi shinbun*, Nov. 26, 1891, reprinted in Suzuki, *Nihon josei undō shiryō shūsei*, p. 92.

62. Shimizu Toyoko, article in *Shinonome shinbun*, May 8–10, 1889, reprinted in Suzuki, *Nihon josei undō shiryō shūsei*, pp. 111–14.

63. Muta Kazue, "Senryaku to shite no onna" (Women as strategy), *Shisō* (Feb. 1992): 220–27; Sievers, *Flowers in Salt*, p. 95.

64. *Tōkyō fujin kyōfūkai zasshi*, Sept. 20, 1890, cited in Sievers, *Flowers in Salt*, p. 214n.

65. Suzuki, *Nihon josei undō shiryō shūsei*, pp. 132–42, cites several articles about Women's Morality Association branches in various locations.

gi),[66] and its goal was "the expansion of women's rights and the elimination of the evil of 'respect the male and despise the female.'"[67]

The activities of the Women's Reform Society, the Women's Morality Association, and other similar organizations suggest that their members believed women could change the state. Most significant, of course, was their view that the state would not be gendered "male"—which most feminists viewed as illogical—if women were included. Moreover, supporters of women's rights deeply resented masculine sexual privileges and believed that granting women political rights would help reduce patriarchal privileges that humiliated women and degraded Japan's international image. Women did not discuss all aspects of the Meiji state, but they did envision a state in which being female was not a barrier to participation. (Some of them, however, thought class and education should be taken into account.) Although later feminist thought called capitalism and its effects on families and women workers into question, these were not primary concerns of Meiji feminists. Attempting to push their agendas in the political arena, feminist groups had first to enlarge the boundaries of that arena. Even before the promulgation of the Law on Assembly and Political Association (*Shūkai oyobi seisha hō*) of 1890, which banned women from all political participation, including political speeches and assembly, the City Code and the Town and Village Code of 1888 had pointedly excluded women from participation.[68] Feminists' petitions to the Diet to eliminate these restrictions failed.[69] Feminist Shimizu Toyoko could only ask

---

66. At the same time, the Ministry of Education, in its compendium of regulations, stated that the goal of women's education was "womanly morality" (*jotoku*). Womanly morality required that the focus of girls' education be the fostering of "docility" (*wajun*) toward one's husband and "chastity" (*teisō*). This morality theme, which contrasted with the goals of the Women's Morality Association, was reiterated in another journal established in 1891, *Jokan* (Women's mirror); cited in Sōgō joseishi kenkyūkai, ed., *Nihon josei no rekishi*, p. 197.

67. Women's Morality Association goals, stated in "Fujin tokugikai kaisoku" (Women's Morality Association regulations), *Joken*, Sept. 29, 1891, reprinted in Suzuki, *Nihon josei undō shiryō shūsei*, pp. 141–42. The organization limited membership to women.

68. Suzuki, *Nihon josei undō shiryō shūsei*, p. 26.

69. Petitions and reactions, cited in ibid., pp. 126–31.

plaintively, in an article in *Jogaku zasshi*, "Why Are Women Not Permitted to Take Part in Political Meetings?" ("Naniyue ni joshi wa seidan shūkai ni sanchō suru to o yurusarezaru ka?").[70]

After failing at the end of the 1880s to gain a political voice for women, women's rights advocates intensified their focus on issues of sexuality, which after 1890 were redefined as "social" issues to avoid the ban on "political" activities by women. Shimizu and others connected the rights of citizen/subjects (*kokumin*) with social and moral issues.[71] Women needed to have the right of civic participation in order to educate their children as citizen/subjects and support their husbands in the exercise of their own citizenship. Thus, Shimizu posited that women's political rights arose from their relationship with those who had those rights (however limited). The Law on Assembly and Political Associations did not altogether silence advocacy of improving the situation of women; rather, by focusing on morality, the home, and economic conditions, women moved increasingly into civil society realms of advocacy. For late Meiji-era feminists, the state was still an entity in formation. Many hoped that women's involvement with the state through their quest for rights would alter it.

The political use of liberal notions of rights of participation and inclusion was not limited to "bourgeois" women in the late Meiji era. As Vera Mackie notes, socialist women led the earliest campaigns, from 1904 to 1909, to revise Article 5 (banning women's participation in political meetings and activities) of the 1900 Public Peace Police Law (*Chian keisatsuhō*), which superseded the 1890 Law on Assembly and Political Association.[72] Fukuda Hideko's socialist women's newspaper, *Sekai fujin* (Women of the world), labeled Article 5's inclusion of women in the same category as minors an insult.[73] The *Heimin shinbun* (Commoners' newspaper), blending class analysis, individual rights, and nationalism, reported

---

70. Entire article reprinted in ibid., pp. 127–29; excerpted translations in Sievers, *Flowers in Salt*, pp. 52–53.

71. "Citizenship" is a complicated term in this period. For insightful commentary on terms translated as "citizen," see Atsuko Hirai, "State and Ideology in Meiji Japan—A Review Article," *Journal of Asian Studies* 46, no. 1 (1987): 89–103.

72. Mackie, *Creating Socialist Women in Japan*, pp. 62–63.

73. Ibid., p. 63.

that these campaigns by socialist women to revise Article 5 were unsuccessful because the House of Peers, "an organization made up of members of the male class (*danshi kaikyū no ichi dantai*) . . . do[es] not see women as human individuals (*ikko no jinrui*) or as citizens of the nation (*ikko no kokumin*)."[74] This, the paper argued, had to be rectified.

Early Twentieth-Century Feminist Discourses and Actions

By World War I, a new type of Japanese subject was emerging. Literate, exposed to a variety of domestic and internationally inspired cultural and ideological influences, and helping construct ideologies and discourses through speech (men only, if the context was political) and writing (men and women alike), the post-Meiji subject reflected decades of institution-building in Japan. These institutions were diverse. They included, in the realm of culture, the expanding system of public and private schools, the exponential growth of the press and publishing, and the internationalization of the arts, such as film and theater. In a more political context, Japan emerged from World War I an industrial capitalist state, with the consequent demographic, social, and economic changes; an empire; and a constitutional monarchy, albeit one that was continuing to evolve. These institutional developments opened the door for wider discussion of many issues, including women's rights. Ironically, a narrowing of the approaches to the state accompanied the expansion of discussion. Viewing the state as a more established entity, women's rights advocates focused not only on inclusion but also on protection. By the 1910s, education had given women a more public voice, and industrialization had given many a public (although controversial and often dangerous) role in the workplace. In some ways, women had gained the public placement their mothers had desired. But unlike many nineteenth-century feminists, Taishō-era advocates for women no longer considered that public role as a sufficient and necessary condition for equal rights of citizenship for women.

---

74. "Fujin to kizoku" (Women and the aristocracy), *Nikkan heimin shinbun*, no. 62 (Mar. 30, 1907), quoted in ibid., p. 65.

Discussions of women's rights grew increasingly common in the Taishō era. This section addresses a narrow but important segment of women's rights discourse—that engaged in by leading proponents of full civil rights, including the vote. Most rights advocates (including some socialist feminists) in the 1910s and 1920s conceived of the state as a relatively fixed entity with which they sought alignment or from which they sought protection from social or economic oppression. This view of the state is evident in the early Taishō "motherhood protection debate" (*bosei hogo ronsō*) in the pages of magazines that circulated nationwide.[75] The shift from the 1890s views of women's rights is clear in the all but unanimous belief among the four principal discussants—Yosano Akiko (1878–1942), Hiratsuka Raichō (1886–1971), Yamada Waka (1879–1957), and Yamakawa Kikue (1890–1980)—that the state owed mothers "protection." Hiratsuka Raichō argued that women performed a service to the state by giving birth and, thus, deserved financial assistance. Socialist Yamakawa Kikue seemed to reject the arguments of the other three as bourgeois in stating that all members of society would be protected if the capitalist order were replaced by socialism; yet she, too, called for state support of maternity. Although Yamada Waka generally took an essentialist point of view of women's biological duties, she also called on both husbands and the state to support maternity. Only poet Yosano Akiko claimed that focusing on protection from the state was a reflection of "slave morality" (*dorei dōtoku*); yet, even she conceded the desirability of a system of insurance to compensate women for wages lost while recovering from childbirth. For all these feminists, then, the state had a role to play as protector of (gendered) rights of maternity. Feminists had come to accept the state as a fixed institution capable of protecting rights against societal or civil oppression as well as of

---

75. For treatments of this subject in English, see, e.g., Rodd, "Yosano Akiko," pp. 189–98; Mackie, *Creating Socialist Women in Japan*, pp. 86–91; and Barbara Molony, "Equality Versus Difference: The Japanese Debate over 'Motherhood Protection,'" in *Japanese Women Working*, ed. Janet Hunter (London: Routledge, 1993), pp. 122–48. For original documents, see Kouchi Nobuko, *Shiryō: bosei hogo ronsō* (Documents: motherhood protection debate) (Tokyo: Domesu, 1984).

denying rights to groups or individuals, who then must either resist the state or struggle for inclusion in it.[76]

Demanding both equal rights and state protection of "women's
personal physical and psychological integrity, through changes in
laws, regulations, and not least, in attitudes pertaining to sexuality
and family life," was common among the first wave of feminist
movements in Europe, the United States, and Asia.[77] Japanese advocates of women's rights were not unusual in making these demands simultaneously. What had become, perhaps, less common
in Europe or the United States in the late nineteenth century was
Japan's focus on equal rights based on equal educational attain-
ments and the relative insignificance of demands for protection of
women. Japanese rights advocates in the 1910s saw women as taking part in nation-building; this paralleled feminist movements in
nations under colonial rule.[78] As the Japanese state moved from being threatened by imperialism to being an imperialist threat itself
and as its institutions became established in the early twentieth
century, Japanese women increasingly made the same demands for
full political rights and for protection by the state that European
and American women were demanding.

The New Woman Association (Shin fujin kyōkai; hereafter
NWA), founded in 1919, was grounded in the dual beliefs that the
state consisted of individuals who had the right of membership and
that the state should protect classes of individuals against societal
exploitation. Hiratsuka Raichō, one of the group's three founding
mothers along with Ichikawa Fusae (1893–1981) and Oku Mumeo
(1895–1997), noted that to achieve the rights of protection and inclusion, women had to identify as a class. In a November 1919
speech to the All-Kansai Federation of Women's Organizations en-

76. Mackie (*Creating Socialist Women in Japan*, p. 92), finds this stance highly
problematic; she notes that these feminists "unwittingly reinforced the notion
that the normal relationship between the state and individual women is one of
'protector' and 'protected.' "

77. Ida Blom, "Feminism and Nationalism in the Early Twentieth Century: A
Cross-Cultural Perspective," *Journal of Women's History* 7, no. 4 (1995): 82–83.

78. See, e.g., Yung-Hee Kim, "Under the Mandate of Nationalism: Development of Feminist Enterprises in Modern Korea, 1860–1910," *Journal of Women's
History* 7, no. 4 (1995): 120–36.

titled "Toward the Unification of Women,"[79] Hiratsuka identified women as a class who should articulate common concerns and demand power. Women no longer needed to prove their wisdom and talent, as they had in the late nineteenth century. Hiratsuka's vision of rights included different but complementary roles and identities for men and women. In addition, she articulated two types of feminist rights in her comments—women's rights (*joken*) and mothers' rights (*boken*).

Following Hiratsuka's speech, Ichikawa Fusae joined her in drafting the NWA's two central demands. The first repeated a long-standing feminist demand to revise the Public Peace Police Law of 1900. The second, inspired by recent developments in domestic legislation in Europe and the United States, demanded state control of men's sexuality by limiting the right to marry of men diagnosed with sexually transmitted diseases, as well as assistance to wives who had been infected by their carrier husbands.[80] The NWA proposed reforms in the divorce laws so that women could reject husbands or fiancés infected with syphilis. The Civil Code of 1898 stipulated that a Japanese wife was subject to divorce and two years' imprisonment for committing adultery but did not allow her to file for divorce should she discover—and venereal disease was a strong indication—that her husband had engaged in extramarital sexual relations.[81] Thus, the NWA's demand directly challenged the patriarchal family system, which gave members other than the patriarch few rights.[82]

---

79. Hiratsuka Raichō, *Genshi josei wa taiyō de atta: Hiratsuka Raichō jiden 3* (In the beginning, woman was the sun: autobiography of Hiratsuka Raichō, 3) (Tokyo: Ōtsuki shoten, 1973), p. 41; Hiratsuka Raichō, *Watakushi no aruita michi* (The road I walked) (Tokyo: Shin hyōronsha, 1955), p. 195.

80. Hiratsuka, *Genshi josei*, p. 86. For a detailed analysis of Hiratsuka's focus on eugenics, see Otsubo, "Engendering Eugenics."

81. Rōdōshō, Fujin shōnen kyoku, ed., *Fujin no ayumi sanjūnen* (Thirty years of women's strides) (Tokyo: Rōdō hōrei kyōkai, 1975), pp. 28–29. Under the Civil Code, women enjoyed virtually no equal rights or privileges. Subject to strict supervision by the head of the "house" (*ie*), women were legally incompetent after marriage.

82. Ichikawa Fusae, *Ichikawa Fusae jiden* (Autobiography of Ichikawa Fusae) (Tokyo: Shinjuku shobō, 1974), p. 53. As Otsubo ("Engendering Eugenics") notes, Hiratsuka's advocacy of marriage restriction, influenced by the thinking of Ellen

The women's demands were framed in two petitions drafted by Hiratsuka, Ichikawa, Oku, and other activists at Hiratsuka's home on January 6, 1920. These petitions, presented to the Diet, were printed in the opening pages of almost every issue of *Josei dōmei* (Women's league), the NWA organ that began publication later that year. The petitions read:

1. We, the undersigned, seek repeal of the word "women" from Clause I and the words "women and" from Clause II [of Article 5 of the Public Peace Police Law].

2. We, the undersigned, support enactment of a law protecting women who marry men with venereal disease, according to the following provisions: (a) men who have contracted the disease are to be prevented from marrying; (b) a man wishing to marry must present the results of a doctor's physical exam to his intended spouse, ascertaining his freedom from disease; (c) this proof of health should accompany the marriage certificate and be incorporated into the family register; (d) a marriage may be annulled if it is discovered that the husband concealed the presence of venereal disease; (e) a wife whose husband becomes infected after marriage or who is infected by her husband may file for divorce; (f) a wife infected by her husband may collect monetary compensation for medical expenses and other damages even after divorce.[83]

Petition 1 demanded the identical rights of citizenship and inclusion in the state enjoyed by men (until 1925, tax qualifications continued to deny full rights of citizenship to some categories of men, particularly the poor, as well). Petition 2 called for women's protection by the state against potentially deadly aspects of the family system.

In response to opposition, the NWA focused on women's family roles, framed increasingly in terms of full civil rights. To those who maintained that granting women political rights would destroy the Japanese family by changing the wife's role, the NWA argued that revision of the Police Law would help women become better wives and wiser mothers; a politically aware mother was able to rear better children. This conflation of wifehood and

---

Key, was inspired as much by eugenics (albeit a gender-based variety of eugenics) as by women's rights thought.

83. Hiratsuka, *Genshi josei*, pp. 71–73.

motherhood sounded natural to contemporaries because the discourses on wifehood and motherhood were increasingly intertwined in the clichéd phrase "good wife, wise mother." Supporters of "motherhood" ranged from conservatives to feminists; the latter stressed that by valuing motherhood society would value women. But the official interpretation of "wifehood" was not liberatory. Wives were, at worst, under patriarchal control and, at best, responsible for family-supporting productivity.[84] Arguably, political rights for wise mothers, who had an important role in molding the future, were necessary; political rights for wives, who had no property to protect and who had productive responsibilities to the state and family, may have been harder to justify. In downplaying the wife by focusing on the mother, the NWA appears to have abandoned the nineteenth-century feminists' tack of linking women's rights—in an era when the state was still viewed as being under construction—with respect for wives and encouragement of their education as a basis for developing the subjectivity necessary for equality.

To those who contended that enactment of a law protecting married women's health would undermine the husband's dominance in the family, the NWA answered that a husband's venereal disease was even more debilitating to the family and especially its children.[85] This approach again shifted the discourse from wifehood to motherhood. Meiji-era feminists, who had identified

---

84. Nolte and Hastings, "The Meiji State's Policy Toward Women," p. 156.

85. Hiratsuka, *Genshi josei*, p. 82. This argument was not unique to Japan. In the United States, for example, venereal disease was viewed as destructive to the family, but it was also believed in the first decades of the twentieth century that a man's infection should be kept secret by his physician, lest he lose his dominance in the family; see Allan Brandt, *No Magic Bullet: A Social History of Venereal Disease in the United States Since 1850* (New York: Oxford University Press, 1985), pp. 18–19. As in Japan, U.S. feminists were infuriated with "men for infecting women and destroying the lives of children"; see Lois Rudnick, "The Male Identified Woman and Other Anxieties: The Life of Mabel Dodge Luhan," in *The Challenge of Feminist Biography*, ed. Sara Alpern et al., pp. 116–38 (Urbana: University of Illinois Press, 1992). Otsubo ("Engendering Eugenics") notes that Hiratsuka, in justifying the petition's focus on restricting only men's access to marriage, emphasized the importance of eugenics to the Japanese race and nation as well as to wives and children (the latter being the feminist emphasis).

women's rights with respect for women's full personhood in a society free of patriarchy, polygamy, and prostitution, had attacked extramarital male sexuality. By the 1910s, male sexuality was identified with patriarchy, which was supported in civil law. To change male sexual privilege, feminists had to cast their arguments in terms of other state-sponsored discourses, particularly the ideology of "good wife, wise mother."[86] The NWA exempted prospective brides from syphilis screening since activists considered only prostitutes, among women, as morally dissolute.[87]

But marital sexuality fell under the legal construction of patriarchy. Because the Public Peace Police Law restricted women's political activity, the NWA found that it had to give priority to revising the Police Law. Yet advocating a change in the law could itself be a violation of that law. The NWA's movement to gain full civil rights for women, which began with the attempt to revise Article 5 of the Police Law, was intimately bound to the gendered demand for protecting women's health. Civil rights and gender-based protections were not alternative views of women's rights; rather, they were two sides of the same coin.

The NWA submitted a petition to the Diet to revise Article 5 early in 1920. Because Prime Minister Hara Takashi (1856–1921) dissolved the Diet session on February 26, the NWA's petition did not come up for debate in the Diet until July 19, 1920. In presenting the proposal for amending the Public Peace Police Law, Representative Tabuchi Toyokichi argued that women needed protection not only because they were weak but also because the standards of civilization called for women's rights.[88]

There has recently been much talk concerning freedom of speech, but because this freedom is not respected in this country, there is, even in the Diet, little respect for freedom of speech. . . . I have, therefore, decided . . .

---

86. "Good wife, wise motherism" is treated by a number of scholars, most notably Kathleen Uno, whose numerous works on this topic cover the Meiji era through the present.

87. Hiratsuka Raichō, "Karyūbyō danshi kekkon seigenhō ni kansuru seigan undō" (The petition movement for the law limiting marriage by men with venereal disease), *Josei dōmei* 1 (Oct. 1920): 35.

88. Hiratsuka, *Genshi josei*, p. 117; Ichikawa, *Jiden*, p. 75.

to bring this problem to your attention . . . and to obtain your approval for changes in Japan's Police Law. . . . Specifically, [I support] elimination of the word "women" from Article 5 of the Public Peace Police Law. Gentlemen, one of the currents of our postwar world is socialism; a second current is feminism, [and these have] reached Japan. . . . I wonder if these momentous global changes will penetrate the Japanese Diet.

For Japan to be included among the postwar world's civilized democracies, Tabuchi emphasized, its leaders would have to expand the rights and freedoms of all subjects, including women.

Although I do not advocate giving women complete suffrage at this time . . . women are also human beings who have a right to free speech. . . . I believe we must exercise the basic premise of "democracy" which fosters concepts of equality and support for the weak. . . . I urge you not to derive pleasure from oppressing the weak, but to work for the thirty million [women] subjects of Japan.[89]

Shortly after Tabuchi's speech, however, the Diet was dissolved, and there was no opportunity for a vote.

A bill to revise Article 5 to permit women to attend political meetings and rallies, although not to join political parties, finally passed the House of Representatives in February 1921. It failed in the more conservative House of Peers, however, following its denunciation by Baron Fujimura Yoshiro, president of *Taishō nichi nichi shinbun*, who declared that "participation of women in political movements is extremely boring." Moreover, he continued,

it goes against natural laws in a physiological as well as psychological sense. It is not women's function to be active in political movements alongside men. The woman's place is in the home. Her role is a social and educational one. . . . Giving women the right to participate in political movements subverts the family system that is the basis of our social system. I think that the behavior of these new women—these groups of peculiar women trying to become politically active—is extremely shameful.

------

89. Tabuchi Toyokichi, "Fujin no seijiteki jiyū o shuchō Tabuchi-shi no enzetsu" (Mr. Tabuchi's speech advocating women's political freedom), *Josei dōmei* 3 (Dec. 1920): 8–9, 16. *Josei dōmei* published Tabuchi's speech in its entirety.

[The issue before us] concerns Japan's national polity. . . . I believe we should oppose [revision of the Police Law].[90]

Although NWA members were seeking political rights, they had to present their group as a social rather than a political organization, which women were prohibited from joining. Ichikawa Fusae, the best-known suffragist in the Taishō era, worked to dispel the idea that the NWA was interested only in "obtaining political rights for women."[91] She presented civil and political rights as a means to an end rather than as an end in themselves. The end advocated by the NWA was the improvement of women's lives through better health, elimination of poverty, better working conditions, and protection of motherhood; most of these goals required some form of state aid or protection. Hiratsuka wrote in the first issue of *Josei dōmei* that suffrage was not an end in itself but a means to inject feminine values into a masculine political system.[92] Feminists viewed the political system and state as institutionalized by the 1910s. Their campaign for civil rights, an attempt to become part of that state, was no more an attack on the state than was their working with the state to gain protections for women.

---

90. "Fujimura Yoshirō-shi no chikei kaikin hantairon hihan" (Criticism of Mr. Fujimura Yoshirō's opposition to amendment of the Public Peace Police Law), *Josei dōmei* 8 (May 1921): 5. Fujimura's stress on the greater importance of women's role in the household is similar to that espoused by the Home Ministry fifteen years earlier; as Nolte and Hastings ("The Meiji State's Policy Toward Women," p. 156) put it, "The state's claim on the home preempted women's claims on the state."

91. Ichikawa Fusae, "Sōritsu yori *Josei dōmei* hakkan made (2)" (From the founding till the publication of *Josei dōmei*, 2) *Josei dōmei* 2 (Nov. 1920): 46. It appears that Ichikawa's initial fears about the NWA's image, at least as far as the government was concerned, were unfounded. Although the NWA and other women's groups formed in later years gave high priority to acquiring political rights for women, their existence was not considered a violation of Article 5, Clause I, prohibiting women's participation in political associations; a political association was usually considered one composed of individuals capable of exercising political power, which women were unable to do without the vote. Women were more likely to have been closely supervised for violation of Clause II, which prohibited attendance at political rallies and meetings.

92. Hiratsuka Raichō, "Shakai kaizō ni taisuru fujin no shimei" (The mission of women in social reconstruction), *Josei dōmei* 1 (Oct. 1920): 10.

Motherhood protection, health issues, and labor protection were seen as social reform issues, and although they intersected with politics by being debated and funded by the cabinet and parliament, public officials viewed women's involvement with them as nonpolitical. In 1920, those outside feminist circles considered the struggle for political rights to be selfish when cast as an end rather than as a means; in contrast, feminist social reform activism was received more positively. Although women acted in many ways as if they were contributors to the state when they worked for health reform or labor issues, their "citizenship," since they lacked specific and articulated rights, was always inferior to men's. NWA leaders recognized this and consequently expanded their demands for complete inclusion in the state, including the vote. The December 1920 and January 1921 issues of *Josei dōmei* carried, along with the organization's earlier petitions for revision of the Police Law and regulation of men's access to marriage, a new demand calling for revision of the House of Representatives Election Law.[93] Under this law, in 1921, the right to vote was limited to males 25 or older who paid a minimum direct tax of ¥3 per year and who had been listed on the electoral rolls for one full year. This appeared to be a major shift in tactics to embrace a position that contemporaries viewed as distinctly more "political."

Revising the concept and application of women's rights to include suffrage required a more nuanced view of the diverse strands of women's rights. Some feminists stressed one type of rights activism over another, but only some socialist feminists—and then only for a brief period—considered suffrage inconsistent with protection. The top leaders of the NWA offer a good example of the differing emphases among supporters of women's suffrage. During the 1920s, Hiratsuka's ideology, according to Ichikawa, was based on the "principle of mothers' rights" (*bokenshugi*), a concept she distinguished from her own "principle of women's rights" (*jokenshugi*).[94] Although protection for mothers was important to Ichikawa,

---

93. This demand appears, along with the other two petitions, in the opening pages of several issues of the organization's bulletin; see, e.g., *Josei dōmei* 3 (Dec. 1920): 2.

94. Ichikawa, *Jiden*, p. 68.

women's political empowerment, she wrote in 1920, was best achieved through recognition of male-female equality.[95]

Aren't we [women] treated as completely feebleminded children? Why is it all right to know about science and literature and not all right to be familiar with politics and current events? Why is it acceptable to read and write but not to speak and listen? A man, no matter what his occupation or educational background, has political rights, but a woman, no matter how qualified, does not have the same rights. . . . If we do not understand the politics of the country we live in, we will not be able to understand conditions in our present society.[96]

For Ichikawa, cultivating oneself through education and thereby earning social respect was insufficient, particularly since that had failed to gain women the rights their Meiji-era sisters had assumed would be incorporated in the developing Meiji system.

The socialist feminist Yamakawa Kikue also believed it was the state's responsibility to protect women. But she differed from NWA leaders in envisioning a state without capitalism. Yamakawa helped organize Japan's first socialist women's association, the Red Wave Society (Sekirankai), in April 1921. The society's manifesto, written by Yamakawa, condemned capitalism for turning women into "slaves at home and oppress[ing] us as wage slaves outside the home. It turns many of our sisters into prostitutes."[97] She decried capitalism for engendering (in both senses of the word) imperialism, which deprived women of their male loved ones, and thereby defined the problems of capitalism in terms of women's losses rather than men's.[98]

---

95. This changed in the following decade, when Ichikawa became a principal supporter of the Mother-Child Protection Law of 1937 (Molony, "Equality Versus Difference," p. 131).

96. Ichikawa Fusae, "Chian keisatsuhō daigojō shūsei no undō (1)" (Movement to revise Article 5 of the Public Peace Police Law, 1), *Josei dōmei* 1 (Oct. 1920): 24.

97. Yamakawa Kikue's May Day manifesto, cited in Hane, *Reflections on the Way to the Gallows*, pp. 126–27.

98. This seems a rather weak critique of imperialism, given all we know today about the gender oppression that characterized Japanese imperialism in the 1930s and 1940s. But the comfort women would appear after Yamakawa wrote these criticisms of imperialism. And the socialist feminist theorizing about imperialism

In a 1921 article in *Taiyō* (The sun) entitled "The New Woman's Association and the Red Wave Society," Yamakawa opined:

There is absolutely no way in a capitalist society to alleviate the misery of female workers. We believe it is a sin to waste the strength of women workers in a . . . time-consuming Diet movement—that is, in any movement that digresses from the only road to salvation for women, the destruction of capitalism. However, bourgeois gentlewomen, because they cannot trust or imagine a society beyond capitalism, concentrate their energies on alleviating the misery of women workers in a superficial and ineffective way.[99]

Membership in an established state was not a priority for Yamakawa in 1921. Soon after Yamakawa's critical work appeared, however, Article 5, Clause II, of the Public Peace Police Law was amended.[100] Taking advantage of the newly won right to attend political rallies (women still were prohibited from joining political parties), women organized new groups to make additional demands. Women's groups of all sorts flourished in the early 1920s: consumer groups with various political agendas, socialist feminist groups, middle-class descendents of the NWA, the venerable Women's Reform Society and its suffragist arm, and so on. Socialist women began to give conditional support to full civil rights for women, even in a continuing capitalist state. Feminist reformism permeated Taishō liberal culture, but until mid-1923 it was not coordinated to focus on political rights for women as a class.

It was in response to a natural disaster that women across the spectrum organized for civil rights. Following the great Kantō earthquake of September 1, 1923, Kubushiro Ochimi (1882–1972) of the Women's Reform Society and other women devoted themselves to relief work and finding food, clothing, and shelter for thousands of the victims. Christian churchwomen and others developed a sense of solidarity through shared compassion and con-

---

widely available today would have seemed heretical in a 1920s context in which only class mattered.

99. Yamakawa Kikue, "Shin fujin kyōkai to Sekirankai," *Taiyō* 27 (July 1927): 135–37.

100. Yoshimi Kaneko, *Fujin sanseiken* (Women's suffrage) (Tokyo: Kajima shuppankai, 1971), p. 153.

cern while they distributed milk to children. Relief workers came
from all walks of life: housewives with little or no experience in
organized cooperative activities, members of alumnae groups and
women's auxiliary organizations, and socialists like Yamakawa Kikue.[101] By September 28, 1923, their spontaneous cooperative efforts were formalized when approximately a hundred leaders from
43 different organizations joined to form the Tokyo Federation of
Women's Organizations (Tōkyō rengō fujinkai).[102]

Even after the emergency distribution of food, clothing, and
shelter was no longer necessary, many members of the federation
continued to meet.[103] In late 1923 or early 1924, the organization
was divided into five sections: society, employment, labor, education, and government.[104] Within these sections, women discussed a
variety of issues that had long been concerns of rights and protection advocates, including motherhood protection, licensed prostitution, the problems of working women, and political rights for
women.

The federation's government section, focusing on issues of political rights, discussed means of using the state to earn inclusion.
In November 1924, the director of that section, Kubushiro Ochimi,
invited 60 to 70 women to a "women's suffrage movement workshop," and by December 13, 1924, the workshop had launched the
League for the Realization of Women's Suffrage (Fujin sanseiken
kakutoku kisei dōmei), the principal suffrage organization in the
nterwar years.[105] Political rights, declared the manifesto proclaim-

---

101. Yamakawa defended her actions in the March 1928 issue of *Rōnō* (Labor-
farmer); quoted in Ichikawa, *Jiden*, p. 147; and in Kaneko Shigeri, *Fujin mondai no
chishiki* (Information about women's issues) (Tokyo: Hibonkaku, 1934; reprinted—Tokyo: Nihon zusho sentā 1982), p. 218.

102. Ide Fumiko and Esashi Akiko, *Taishō demokurashī to josei* (Taishō democracy and women) (Tokyo: Gōdō shuppan, 1977), pp. 257–60; see also Shidzue Ishimoto, *Facing Two Ways: The Story of My Life* (Stanford: Stanford University Press,
1983; reissue of 1935 ed., with new introduction and afterword), p. 254.

103. Kaneko Shigeri, *Fujin mondai no chishiki*, p. 218.

104. Chino Yōichi, *Kindai Nihon fujin kyōikushi* (History of women's education in modern Japan) (Tokyo: Dōmesu, 1979), p. 242.

105. Kubushiro Ochimi, *Haishō hitosuji* (Focus on abolishing licensed prostitution) (Tokyo: Chūō kōron sha, 1973), p. 169; Izuma Satoko, "Fusen jisshi no
kekka o yososhite" (Imagining the results of implementing women's suffrage), in

ing the founding of the organization, were essential to improving the status of Japanese women:

1. It is our responsibility to destroy customs that have existed in this country for the past 2,600 years and to construct a new Japan that promotes the natural rights of men and women;

2. Because women have been attending public schools with men for half a century, since the beginning of the Meiji period, and our opportunities in higher education have continued to expand, it is unjust to exclude women from universal suffrage;

3. Political rights are necessary for the protection of the nearly four million working women in this country;

4. Women who work in the household must be recognized before the law to realize their full human potential;

5. Without political rights, we cannot achieve public recognition at either the national or the local level of government;

6. It is both necessary and possible to bring together women of different religions and occupations in a movement for women's suffrage.[106]

The suffragists' list is a succinct statement of what "rights" meant to middle-class feminists in the Taishō era. Article 1 contrasted the "natural rights of men and women" with venerable "customs" that must be destroyed. Japanese society had buried the rights of individual men and women under unnatural customs. In contrast to the Meiji-era belief that education would elevate the status of women, Article 2 rued the continuing denial of even educated women's rights, although it implicitly accepted the nineteenth-century feminists' linkage of education and rights. Article 3 tied together rights and protection for women. Article 4 called for recognition of all women's full humanity, and Article 5 connected rights and recognition in the public sphere, issues also central to nineteenth-century feminism. Article 6 focused on implementa-

---

Fujin mondai to fujin no yōkyū (The woman problem and women's demands), ed. Ichijima Kenkichi (Tokyo: Bunmei kyōkai, 1929), p. 121.

106. Cited in Kirisutokyō fujin kyōfukai, ed., *Nihon Kirisutokyō fujin kyōfukai hyakunenshi* (100-year history of the Japan Christian Women's Reform Society) (Domesu, 1986), pp. 526–27; see also Ichikawa, *Jiden*, p. 144; and Kubushiro, *Haishō*, pp. 170–71.

tion rather than on fundamental principles and recognized the need for a movement. Thus, this manifesto recalled some Meiji-era discourse on rights in terms of respectability, but it also explicitly demanded that the state include women. Article 1 went even further and suggested that including women on equal footing with men might not be enough, since both men and women had natural rights that had been inadequately honored in Japan. It suggested, in fact, that the state should not be a fixed entity; rather, it should be subject to continuing renovation to eliminate past customs.

To achieve the goals of the manifesto, the league demanded several types of civil rights. Echoing feminists the world over, Kubushiro noted that with civil rights came civic responsibilities. Both were aspects of being a public citizen (*kōmin*). Speaking to the women gathered to celebrate the founding of the league, Kubushiro connected rights and responsibilities: "We demand that the revisions in the House of Representatives Election Law to be presented before the upcoming Fiftieth Diet include the equality of women and men, so that we, as half the population of the nation, may fully carry out our responsibilities."[107] Even if women and men had different responsibilities, both were equally entitled to citizenship.

Energized by the manifesto, the new group petitioned the Diet for civil rights. Three weeks earlier, in late February 1925, the House of Representatives had passed a universal manhood suffrage bill that eliminated the remaining economic restrictions on male suffrage. Although many liberals welcomed the expansion of the electorate, feminist suffragists criticized the new legislation because, as Ichikawa wrote, "giving the vote only to men and excluding women is not universal suffrage."[108] Despite the Diet's recent limitation of suffrage rights by gender and its passage of the Peace Preservation Law, which was designed to curb leftist political expression, women's rights activists were optimistic about their own

---

107. Kubushiro, cited in Ichikawa, *Jiden*, p. 145.
108. Ichikawa, *Jiden*, p. 150.

chances for success.[109] In fact, they persuaded a small group of representatives to introduce several items for Diet discussion:

1. An amendment to the Public Peace Police Law of 1900 giving women the right to join political parties and associations;
2. A petition to encourage women's higher education;
3. A petition for women's suffrage in national elections;
4. A petition to make changes in the City Code (1888) and the Town and Village Code (1888), allowing women to vote and become candidates for office at the local level.[110]

Some 200 women filled the visitors' section in the balcony overlooking the Diet chambers to see these four items presented on March 10, a date designated by suffragists as Women's Diet Day (*Gikai fujin dē*).[111] The women's optimism contrasted with the cynicism of newspaper accounts. Describing those they dubbed—not accurately—"veterans of women's suffrage," the *Tōkyō asahi shinbun* reported on March 10, 1925 that "they talk big in their shrill voices."[112] The following day's *Asahi* carried a cartoon depicting four Diet members with ribbons in their hair to signify their sympathy toward women.

Despite vocal opposition, all the proposals were, in the end, approved by the House of Representatives. Three of the items were only petitions, and thus the favorable vote did not make them law, and the Police Law amendment was killed in the House of Peers, but the surprising reception of these proposals for expanding women's rights sustained the hopes of women's rights

---

109. The Peace Preservation Law, passed in 1925, was directed against groups and individuals who advocated a change in the "national polity" (*kokutai*) or who advocated the abolition of private property. Ambiguities in the law would later make it possible to increase the number of offenders and to increase government pressure on the women's movement; see Richard Mitchell, *Thought Control in Prewar Japan* (Ithaca, N.Y.: Cornell University Press, 1976), p. 63.

110. Ichikawa, *Jiden*, p. 150; Yoshimi, *Fujin sanseiken*, p. 155.

111. Kirisutokyō fujin kyōfūkai, *Nihon Kirisutokyō fujin kyōfūkai hyakunenshi*, p. 528.

112. *Tōkyō asahi shinbun* citations of March 10, 1925; quoted in Ichikawa, *Jiden*, p. 152.

advocates.[113] Seizing an opportunity offered by the richness of the Japanese written language, suffragists shortened the name of their group to Women's Suffrage League (Fusen kakutoku dōmei; hereafter WSL) in order to make a public appeal for *fusen*. *Fusen*, depending on the character used to write "fu," can mean either "universal suffrage" or "women's suffrage." For years *fusen* had been virtually synonymous with "male suffrage"; the WSL appropriated the more acceptable discourse on male rights by taking advantage of the homonym.[114] The women emphatically declared that *fusen*, or universal suffrage, was incomplete without *fusen*, or women's suffrage:

> The foundation for the construction of a new Japan has been laid and, as expected, the [male] suffrage bill was passed by the Fiftieth Diet session. However, along with men who are under 25 or who "receive public or private assistance," we women, who comprise half this country's population, have been left without political rights. . . . Therefore, women should put aside their emotional, religious, and ideological differences and cooperate as *women*. . . . We should concentrate our efforts on achieving the singular goal of political rights. We should work closely with the political parties but maintain a position of absolute neutrality [in partisan matters].[115]

By 1925, suffrage, the hallmark of citizenship, had emerged as a central feature of rights activism, fueling the rhetoric and actions not only of groups dedicated to winning the vote as a sine qua non of rights but also of groups with other primary goals.[116] Rights within the existing state system might be no more than a tempo-

---

113. For more on the activities of Diet supporters, see Murata Shizuko, "Daigishi Yamaguchi Masaji to fujin sanseiken undō" (Diet member Yamaguchi Masaji and the women's suffrage movement), *Rekishi hyōron* 517 (May 1993): 83–99.

114. Ichikawa, *Jiden*, p. 155. It is believed that in 1924 legal expert Hozumi Shigeto became the first person to apply the word *fusen* to women; see his "Fusen mondai" (The problem of women's suffrage), *Fusen* 1 (Mar. 1927): 10.

115. Ide Fumiko, "Nihon ni okeru fujin sanseiken undō" (The women's suffrage movement in Japan), *Rekishigaku kenkyū* (Nov. 1956): 18–19.

116. Works on feminists' actions and discourse in the remainder of the interwar period abound. See, e.g., Garon, "Women's Groups and the Japanese State"; Mackie, *Creating Socialist Women in Japan*; Molony and Molony, *Ichikawa Fusae*; and Hopper, *A New Woman of Japan*.

rary means of improving women's lives until a revolutionary state could be created—as socialist women argued in the early 1920s[117]— or they might be framed in terms of inclusion in the existing civil society.[118] In either case, they were articulated within existing structures of power. In this regard, the rights discourses of the 1910s and 1920s differed from those of the 1880s and 1890s. Earlier feminist thought assumed a state in the process of formation; by the 1910s, that state was taken as an established entity, and activism had to address itself to the state. By that time, the line between action and rhetoric had eroded, as advocacy came to have political motives and, at times, political outcomes.

Feminists increasingly formulated rights as protections in the 1930s, when concepts of rights based on the "individual" were potentially subversive. But there was a long tradition, dating to the 1910s, of equating rights with protection by a powerful state. Moreover, protection by and inclusion in the state were not viewed as incompatible. Inclusion in the state and/or civil society, many feminists believed in the 1930s, when overt suffragism was risky, could be achieved in multiple ways, such as participation in consumer movements and "election purification" movements,[119] advocacy of protections for laborers, welfare assistance to single mothers and their children, and engagement in other public-sphere activities producing gendered social-welfare reforms.

Rights remained a central feature of these various activities. Current feminist scholarship has viewed the tactical shifts of the 1930s as deeply problematic for rights advocacy in Japan. Hayakawa Noriyo, a leading scholar of women's rights movements, notes that the suffragists' involvement in election purification, "which was initiated by the government and designed to weaken

---

117. Molony, "Equality Versus Difference," pp. 129–30.

118. See, e.g., Fujime Yuki, "Zen Kansai fujin rengōkai no kōzō to tokushitsu" (Structure and characteristics of the All-Kansai Women's Federation), *Shiron* 71, no. 6 (1988): 71–100; and Garon, "Women's Groups and the Japanese State."

119. Election purification movements were political activities undertaken by women activists against politicians deemed corrupt as well as by conservative bureaucrats opposed to the power of the mainstream political parties. See Gordon Mark Berger, *Parties out of Power in Japan, 1932–1941* (Princeton: Princeton University Press, 1977).

the power of political parties, was a critical turning point for the suffrage movement."[120] Complicity with the government in the 1930s, she writes, differed significantly from the pursuits of activists in the 1910s and 1920s, when "feminism stood against the power of the state."[121] The WSL worked actively against fascism until 1932 and then shifted to cooperation with the increasingly militarist government. The suffragists' support for the government in the 1930s is a point of great disappointment for many contemporary feminist writers. Yet, if the pursuit of rights is construed as a quest for inclusion in the state, feminism could never truly stand against the power of the state; the possibility of feminist support for heinous state policies was always embedded in the liberatory rhetoric of full civil rights. In the end, the permutations of rights discourses against shifting social and political backgrounds, especially as the state became increasingly established in the early twentieth century, both accompanied and drove changes in the relationship of women to the state.

---

120. Hayakawa, "Feminism and Nationalism in Japan," p. 116.
121. Ibid., p. 113.

CHAPTER EIGHT

Men's Place in the Women's Kingdom: New Middle-Class Fatherhood in Taishō Japan

Harald Fuess

Fathers Without Fatherhood

In 1926 the philosopher Miyake Yūjirō argued that mothers had an overwhelming influence on their children, since they are "mostly at home." Fathers had less impact, since they usually "pursue work outside the home." In a sweeping statement, Miyake concluded, "If the father is good and the mother is bad, it is rare for the children to turn out good." As long as the mother was "good," however, "bad fathers" had less impact on the moral development of the children.[1] To Miyake, fathers played a minor role. The use of the innovative term "fatherhood" (*fusei*) in the title of the article, rarely employed in Taishō Japan, appears almost accidental, added to form a complementary pair with "motherhood." In contrast, the term "motherhood" (*bosei*), first introduced from the West to Japan in 1904, was more common. Widely disseminated during the feminist motherhood-protection debates of 1916–19, it had become

---

1. Miyake Yūjirō, "Bosei to fusei" (Motherhood and fatherhood), *Fujin no tomo* 20, no. 3 (Mar. 1926): 9–11. Miyake was more widely known as Miyake Setsurei.

a popular expression by the 1920s.[2] The word for "fatherhood," however, never gained much currency. This lack of a prevailing term or slogan to describe sets of beliefs or behavior expected of fathers suggests that the role of fathers may have generated little contention or public interest and that paternal attitudes or activities invited little comment. In contrast to the intellectual controversies over motherhood joined by women and men of all persuasions, there were few, if any, comparable debates on fatherhood calling for a new man or even any man at home.

This absence of a well-known discourse on fatherhood flies in the face of reality: not only did more Japanese men than ever before became fathers, but each one of them, on average, had more children. The population expanded from 44 million in 1900 to 56 million in 1920, and the 1920s recorded the highest official birthrate in Japan's modern history.[3] Growth in the average life span, too, made it increasingly likely that fathers would see their children reach adulthood. As the rates for divorce, out-of-wedlock birth, and adoption declined during the first three decades of the twentieth century, opportunities for men to raise their own biological children increased.

But even as demographic forces enabled more fathers to have a longer association with their children, other socioeconomic factors may have restricted paternal involvement. The possibility for daily interactions probably decreased overall, but this decline must have been most pronounced in the urban part of the population. Two factors drove what scholars have frequently called the "feminization of the home": the expansion of the educational system and modern wage work drew both school-age children and wage workers out of the family environment. By the end of the Meiji period, enrollment in elementary schools was nearly universal, and in 1907

---

2. First coined by Shimoda Jirō in the magazine *Joshi kyōiku* (Girls' education); see Ulrike Wöhr, *Frauen zwischen Rollenerwartungen und Selbstdeutung: Ehe, Mutterschaft und Liebe im Spiegel der japanischen Frauenzeitschrift "Shin shin fujin" von 1913 bis 1916* (Women between role expectations and self-awareness: marriage, motherhood, and love in the mirror of the Japanese women's magazine *New True Woman* from 1913 to 1916) (Wiesbaden: Harrassowitz Verlag, 1997), pp. 284, 326–28.

3. Irene B. Taeuber, *The Population of Japan* (Princeton: Princeton University Press, 1958), pp. 232–33.

the government further extended compulsory education to six years. At the higher end, a variety of new schools were established, especially in Tokyo. Similarly, wage earning, especially by men, became more common, and male labor participation rates surpassed those of women, who had been employed in greater numbers early in the industrialization process because of the development of the textile industry. Moreover, the flow of migration from countryside to city meant that fewer fathers could rely on their own childhood experiences in raising their children.

Despite the fact that most adult men were fathers, at least in biological terms, the dearth of public discussion in the 1910s and 1920s of the beliefs and behavior expected of fathers is surprising given the extensive contemporary debate on the role of women in the family and the heightened focus on children. By the Taishō period, specialized medical and educational journals on children, such as *Jidō kenkyū* (Child research), and *Shufu no tomo* (The housewife's companion), the most widely read women's mass magazine, devoted considerable attention to child rearing. In what one scholar calls the notion of "imperial motherhood" in Japan, the government's emphasis on women's domestic role increased along with the proliferation of new conceptions of childhood.[4] By the 1930s pronatalist propaganda had validated motherhood as an object of social policies.[5] This trend was symbolized in legislation such as the Mother-Child Protection Law enacted in 1937, which provided assistance to impoverished mothers and children in fatherless families.[6]

While women as mothers became ideologically ever more firmly rooted in the home and the family, men disappeared from it metaphorically. Scholars such as Arichi Tōru speak of an "absence" of fathers from children's education beginning in the Meiji period and

---

4. Kathleen S. Uno, *Passages to Modernity: Motherhood, Childhood, and Social Reform in Early Twentieth Century Japan* (Honolulu: University of Hawai'i Press, 1999), pp. 149–50.

5. Kathleen S. Uno, "The Death of 'Good Wife, Wise Mother'?" in *Postwar Japan as History*, ed. Andrew Gordon (Berkeley: University of California Press), pp. 294–99.

6. Sheldon Garon, "Women's Groups and the Japanese State: Contending Approaches to Political Integration, 1890–1945," *Journal of Japanese Studies* 19, no. 1 (Winter 1993): 37.

increasing during the Taishō period.[7] That the epithet "good husbands and wise fathers" never caught on in Japan, as some Taishō
intellectuals remarked with regret, also reflects the lack of popular
interest in the domestic activities of men as fathers.[8] At a time when
national ideologues began seeing the household as a basic social unit
in a family-state presided over by the emperor, men often appeared
in popular writing as the distant and detached sovereigns of the family. The last decade of the nineteenth century saw the birth of what
scholars commonly regard as two classic pieces of state-sponsored,
family-centered gender ideology, epitomized in the slogan "good
wife and wise mother": the 1898 Civil Code and the guidelines for
women's higher education issued by the Ministry of Education in
1899. Critics have referred to both as symbols of male patriarchy
and home-bound female domesticity and have held that the "penetration into all segments of Japanese society of [these] moral and legal norms of the ruling class inevitably reduced the power of
women in the family."[9] Schools, motion pictures, youth group programs, and popular magazines have been identified as the vehicles of
dissemination for this new gender orthodoxy to the population and
deep into the countryside.[10] Men linked ideologically to the family
as heads of household have often been seen exclusively in their role
of family patriarch, a view still found in recent scholarship.

The study of images of fatherhood in the 1910s and 1920s in Japan can contribute to our understanding of gender construction in
Japan. As research on the history of women in Japan has bloomed
in the past few decades, we have learned about women's roles in
social movements, politics, work, and culture.[11] Women now form
an integral part of the larger historical narrative. The history of
everyday and private lives, moreover, has become a focus of study,

---

7. Arichi Tōru, *Nihon no oyako nihyakunen* (200 years of parents and children
in Japan) (Tokyo: Shinchōsha, 1986).

8. Wöhr, *Frauen*, pp. 214, 336.

9. Robert J. Smith, "Making Village Women into 'Good Wives and Wise
Mothers' in Prewar Japan," *Journal of Family History* 8, no. 1 (Spring 1983): 73.

10. Ibid., p. 76.

11. Gail Lee Bernstein, ed., *Recreating Japanese Women, 1600–1945* (Berkeley:
University of California Press, 1991). See also the chapters by Barbara Molony and
Gail Lee Bernstein in this volume.

usually with an emphasis on women. Similar studies exploring the role of Japanese men in the home and the family are only beginning to emerge,[12] but their findings are not as yet integrated into English-language scholarship on men's experiences as fathers and the cultural construction of fatherhood in other societies.[13]

This chapter analyzes views of masculine domesticity, which historian Ralph LaRossa defines as men "doing domestic activities in a masculine way,"[14] in vehicles disseminating modern ideas of femininity and motherhood, namely, a women's magazine and advice books on home economics, education, and child rearing. Images of masculine domesticity accompanied the reinforcement of homebound femininity promoted by state agencies and influential intellectuals. These abstract notions of masculine domesticity contrasted with narratives by male intellectuals of their own attitudes toward their children and their interactions with them in the 1910s and 1920s. Such paternal narratives on masculine domesticity question easy generalizations about patriarchy in Taishō Japan.

Masculine Domesticity and Women's Magazines

After the turn of the twentieth century, discussions of the home, family, and domestic life shifted from general-interest magazines to more specialized publications.[15] In the late 1910s, magazines emerged for the growing number of educated and urban middle-

---

12. Harald Fuess, "A Golden Age of Fatherhood? Parent-Child Relations in Japanese Historiography," *Monumenta Nipponica* 52, no. 3 (Autumn 1997): 381–97. Gail Lee Bernstein, "Matsuura Isami: A Modern Patriarch in Rural Japan," in *The Human Tradition in Modern Japan*, ed. Anne Walthall (Wilmington, Del.: Scholarly Resources, 2002), pp. 137–53.

13. Robert L. Griswold, "Introduction to the Special Issue on Fatherhood," *Journal of Family History* 24, no. 3 (July 1999): 251–54.

14. Ralph LaRossa, *The Modernization of Fatherhood: A Social and Political History* (Chicago: University of Chicago Press, 1997), p. 32.

15. Kazue Muta, "Images of the Family in Meiji Periodicals: The Paradox Underlying the Emergence of the 'Home,'" *U.S.-Japan Women's Journal, English Supplement* 7 (1994): 61–64. See also Harald Fuess, "Home, School, and the Middle Class: Paternal Narratives of Child Rearing in *Shufu no tomo*, 1908–1926," in *Gender and Modernity: Rereading Japanese Women's Magazines*, ed. Barbara Hamill Sato and Ulrike Wöhr (Kyoto: International Research Center for Japanese Studies, 2000), pp. 69–83.

class women, who often worked in the modern economy. Practical advice on child rearing and household chores, as well as human-interest stories and confessional articles, made these magazines a popular forum for debate and exchange on issues of relevance to women's lives. To a large extent, this was a discourse on the role of women in family and home. Men found a place in these visions of feminine domesticity chiefly as husbands and only rarely as fathers.

Although family relationships, such as marriage and divorce, were standard fare in all women's magazines, *Fujin no tomo* (Woman's companion) published two special issues of reflections by intellectual men on themselves "as fathers," providing an unusual male perspective on masculine domesticity. Established in 1903 and renamed in January 1908, *Fujin no tomo* was one of the oldest magazines for female readers during the 1910s and 1920s. Contemporaries ranked *Fujin no tomo* with *Fujin kōron* (Women's review), female counterpart of *Chūō kōron*, among those magazines "superior in quality." Socialist Yamakawa Kikue categorized *Fujin no tomo* as "bourgeois-feminist"; others criticized it as "extremely moderate . . . but not practical."[16] Today, Western scholars of gender associate the magazine with Christian principles and scientific home management. Its editor, according to historian Sheldon Garon, propagated the virtues of the Western-style housewife "as the equal of her husband because she managed the domestic sphere."[17] Circulation figures for *Fujin no tomo* are not known, but considering its presumed upper-middle class appeal, they probably were at the lower end of the spectrum. In a 1931 survey, *Shufu no tomo* reported a circulation of 600,000, *Fujin kurabu* (Women's club) 350,000, *Fujin kōron* 200,000, and *Fujin sekai* (Women's world) 120,000.[18] Compared to *Shufu no tomo*, the market leader, *Fujin no tomo* seems to have had

---

16. Ulrike Wöhr, "Discourses on Media and Modernity: Criticism of Japanese Women's Magazines in the 1920s and Early 1930s," in *Gender and Modernity: Re-reading Japanese Women's Magazines*, p. 19.

17. Garon, "Women's Groups and the Japanese State," p. 26.

18. Saitō Michiko, *Hani Motoko—shōgai to shisō* (Hani Motoko: life and thought) (Tokyo: Domesu shuppan, 1988), p. 78; Barbara Hamill Sato, "The Emergence of Women's Mass Magazines and the Formation of a New Reading Culture in Early Twenties Japan," in *Gender and Modernity: Rereading Japanese Women's Magazines*, p. 50.

more affluent readers, to judge from the model household accounts for housewives printed in both magazines.[19] *Fujin no tomo* readers belonged, or aspired, to what scholars often call the "new middle class," which consisted prominently of the families of white-collar professionals, such as employees of government agencies and corporate or educational institutions. Estimated at 8.5 percent of the total Japanese population in 1920, in Tokyo the urban middle class of salaried workers amounted to 21.5 percent of the workforce.[20] In numerical terms this section of the population was still small, but it represented a growing vanguard for new lifestyles.

Unlike most of the other women's magazines, which were written by men for women, in Hani Motoko (1873–1957) *Fujin no tomo* had a female editor who was not only a prolific writer and contributor to other publications but also the founder of the Jiyū gakuen school. Born in 1873 into an Aomori samurai family, she studied in Tokyo at Meiji Girls' School, where she also worked for the girls' magazine *Jogaku zasshi* (Women's education journal) of Christian educator Iwamoto Yoshiharu (1863–1942). Unusual for a daughter from an elite family, she herself chose her first husband, whom she left after a brief marriage. Motoko later secured a position at the newspaper *Hōchi shinbun* and, in 1897, became Japan's first female reporter, with assignments covering women, education, and religion. In 1901 she married a colleague, who became her partner in journalistic and educational ventures.[21]

As turbulent and unconventional as her personal and professional life was, Hani Motoko often argued that home management was one of the most important tasks of women. She also contended that motherhood was compatible with working outside the home, unless there were several young children at home. In one instance, however, she advised an anguished female teacher worried that she was shortchanging her own child to give up her profession if she

---

19. Saitō, *Hani Motoko*, pp. 72, 118.

20. Margit Nagy, "Middle-Class Working Women During the Interwar Years," in *Recreating Japanese Women, 1600–1945*, ed. Gail Lee Bernstein (Berkeley: University of California Press, 1991), p. 201.

21. Chieko Irie Mulhern, "Japan's First Newspaperwoman: Hani Motoko," *Japan Interpreter* 12, no. 3/4 (Summer 1979): 310–29; Hani Motoko, "Stories of My Life," trans. Mulhern in *Japan Interpreter* 12, no. 3/4 (Summer 1979): 330–54.

could not reduce her work hours. Marriage, and romance, was a recurrent issue of interest in *Fujin no tomo*, and several feature series and numerous letters to the editors attest to the topic's continuing attraction.[22] Marital problems and divorce were also perennial issues for comments by readers and legal experts alike.[23] Hani advocated that individuals choose their own spouse in articles on the freedom to pursue love marriages and divorce.[24] This emphasis on the conjugal family went hand in hand with views on womanhood at odds with more conservative views. The state-sponsored slogan "good wife and wise mother" was not explicitly promoted. One of the rare references to it can be found in the article titled "I Hate Good Wives and Wise Mothers."[25] As the magazine expanded its readership base in the 1920s, *Fujin no tomo*'s editorial policy may have become less elitist and idealist.[26] Nevertheless, throughout the years the magazine seldom articulated doubts about the centrality of marriage and motherhood in the lives of women.

The focus on the husband-wife relationship and the preferences of a largely adult female readership may explain why men were portrayed mostly in their roles as future, current, or ex-husbands. Unlike writings on motherhood, articles explicitly about men as fathers or sons appeared only irregularly; in some years no article on either was published. Although this imbalance is typical for women's magazines of the period, with around twenty articles with "father" (*chichi*) in the title, the topic appears relatively more often in *Fujin no tomo* than elsewhere. By contrast, between 1917 and 1926, in *Shufu no tomo* only three articles are linked to fathers (*chichioya*), whereas 73 are on mothers (*hahaoya*).[27]

---

22. Large sections were "Fūfukan no mondai" (Marital problems), *Fujin no tomo* 11, no. 5 (May 1917): 7–43; and "Seikō shita fūfu no jirei" (Cases of successful spouses), *Fujin no tomo* 12, no. 10 (Nov. 1918): 34–61.

23. See the four-part series by Hozumi Shigetō, "Kon'in to rikon" (Marriage and divorce), *Fujin no tomo* 14, no. 1–4 (Jan.–Apr. 1920).

24. "Jiyū ren'ai to jiyū rikon" (Free love and free divorce), *Fujin no tomo* 6, no. 1 (Nov. 1922): 10–26.

25. Miyake Yūjirō, "Ryōsai kenbo girai" (I hate good wives and wise mothers), *Fujin no tomo* 9, no. 7 (July 1915): 10–14.

26. Saitō, *Hani Motoko*, pp. 95–100.

27. Ishikawa bunka jigyō zaidan, *Shufu no tomo, 1917–1926* (compact disk, n.d.).

Fujin no tomo authors commonly called parents by either one of two expressions: *oya* "parent," a gender-neutral term, and *fubo,* "father and mother." Particularly conspicuous is the interchangeable use of both words, often in the same article. There is no evidence to suggest that *fubo* emphasized fathers more than *oya.* Depending on context, these terms were sometimes used for both parents, only mothers, or only fathers. The authoritarian-sounding *fukei* (father and older brother) with its connotation of guardian or *ryō-shin* (both parents), which were used in prewar academic writing, appeared less frequently. Depending on the viewpoint and family relationship, the designation of fathers varied. Men usually used *chichi* to refer to themselves as fathers. Wives, to a surprising degree, called their husband *otto,* a rather egalitarian term, especially in comparison with the more hierarchical and formal alternative *kachō* "head of the household," but designations of husbands as *katei no shujin* "master of the family" also exist. In no instance did a wife refer to her spouse by his given name.

The March 1916 and March 1926 issues of *Fujin no tomo* included special sections on fatherhood, with about half a dozen articles each by well-known male intellectuals on the duties and activities of fathers. These men appear especially open to discussing children, their upbringing, and education from both a philosophical and a personal perspective. We do not know why the editor selected these particular men, but the authors must have been aware of the magazine's reputation for propagating more egalitarian family relationships, even if they did not adhere to such a model of behavior. Seen as a whole, the fatherhood specials present a collection of progressive middle-class men able to reflect on their role as fathers in the modern urban white-collar family. Many were interested in children not only as fathers but also as educators. Their common history of migration from the provinces to the capital probably influenced their choice of themes related to children growing up in an urban environment. Most were born between the mid-1860s and early 1880s, and modern education was a prerequisite for their professional accomplishments, encouraging them to value the education of their own children. The majority obtained their higher education at elite institutions in Tokyo, and several studied overseas in Germany, England, or the United States. Three of the men had served in the Lower House of the Imperial Diet by the late 1920s. In short, accomplished urban professionals discussed what it was like to be a father in Taishō Japan.

The following were contributors to the 1916 issue. Tagawa Daikichirō (1869–1947) was born in present-day Nagasaki prefecture, graduated from the Tokyo Technical School (Tōkyō senmon gakkō), became a journalist for the daily *Hōchi shinbun*, and in 1908 was elected to the Lower House of the Imperial Diet and later headed Meiji gakuin, a school founded by Protestant missionaries. Abe Isoo (1865–1949) was born in what is now Fukuoka prefecture and graduated from Dōshisha University in Kyoto. From 1891 to 1895 he studied in the United States, and in 1903 he became a professor at Waseda University. In 1928 he was elected to the Diet for the first time. Less famous, Hayakawa Tetsuji is known for translating a book on the fishing industry by the German agronomist Adolf Buchenberger in 1894. Sasaki Nobutsuna (1872–1963) was born in Mie prefecture and graduated from Tokyo Imperial University, where he lectured on Japanese literature after 1905. Okaasa Jirō (1868–1944) was born in Shizuoka prefecture and graduated from Tokyo Imperial University. He studied in Germany in 1891–94 and worked most of his life as a biologist at the Tokyo Higher Normal School (Tōkyō kōtō shihan gakkō). Uchigasaki Sakusaburō (1877–1947) was born in Miyagi prefecture and graduated from the English department of Tokyo Imperial University. Upon his return from one year at Oxford, he took a faculty position at Waseda University in 1911. He was a Diet member after 1924.[28]

---

28. The articles in *Fujin no tomo* 10, no. 3 (Mar. 1916) issue were: Tagawa Daikichirō, "Kodomo ni sumanai to omou koto bakari" (Filled with remorse toward my children), pp. 24–27; Abe Isoo, "Shakai no hito to shite tatsu tame no kyōiku" (Education for responsible membership in society), pp. 28–29; Hayakawa Tetsuji, "Katei de wa kodomo no mori" (Caretaker of children in the family), pp. 30–32; Sasaki Nobutsuna, "Wasureenu chichi no on'ai" (Unforgettable deep love of my father), pp. 33–34; Okaasa Jirō, "Nani mo shinai no ga kaette yoi ka mo shirenai" (It may rather be best to do nothing), pp. 35–36; and Uchigasaki Sakusaburō, "Shizen to shakai no chikara ni irai shite" (Relying on the power of nature and society), pp. 37–39.

Compared to the group writing in 1916, the authors on fatherhood in 1926 were less experienced internationally and attained fewer positions of public prominence, reflecting a broader shift in career experiences of graduates of higher educational institutions. In the second group only one man joined a university faculty permanently, no one studied overseas or became a Diet member, and writing for publication may have been an important source of income.[29] Miyake Yūjirō/Setsurei (1860–1945), who was born in Ishikawa prefecture, graduated in philosophy from Tokyo Imperial University and became a writer for major prewar cultural publications. Ogawa Mimei/Kensaku (1882–1961) was born in Niigata prefecture and studied at Waseda University. He became famous for his children's stories and joined the anarchist writers' group in the mid-1920s. Tsuchida Kyōson/Tsutomu (1891–1934) was born in Niigata prefecture and enrolled in philosophy at Kyoto Imperial University. Later he founded the cultural magazine *Bunka* (Culture). Chino Shōshō/Gitarō (1883–1946) from Nagano prefecture entered Tokyo Imperial University to study German literature. Beginning in 1920, Chino taught German literature at Keiō University. Tokuda Shūsei/Sueo (1871–1943) was born in Kanazawa; he dropped out of higher school when he was unable to pay the tuition after the death of his father. Tokuda later became associated with the literary movement known as naturalism. Akai Yonekichi (1887–1974) was born in Ishikawa prefecture and graduated from Hiroshima Higher Normal School (Hiroshima kōtō shihan gakkō). As a teacher, he became a leading member of the educational reform movement of the Taishō period, which was influenced by the ideas of Helen Parkhurst. In 1924 he founded Myōjō gakuen, a

---

29. The articles in the *Fujin no tomo* 20, no. 3 (Mar. 1926) issue were: Miyake Yūjirō, "Bosei to fusei" (see note 1 to this chapter), pp. 9–11; Ogawa Mimei, "Watashi wa kodomo no kōfuku o shiryo suru tame ni issai o shinrai suru gakkō kyōiku ni irantosu" (For the happiness of children I rely completely on trustworthy school education), pp. 12–14; Tsuchida Kyōson, "Chichi no kyōiku" (Father's education), pp. 15–20; Chino Shōshō, "Geijutsu kyōiku ni tsuite" (About art education), pp. 21–24; Tokuda Shūsei, "Chichi toshite" (As a father), pp. 25–26; and Akai Yonekichi, "Kodomo no kyōiku ni tsuite haha ni nozomu koto" (What is desired from a mother in educating children), pp. 27–31.

Tokyo school with a liberal educational outlook resembling that of Hani Motoko's Jiyū gakuen, established three years earlier.

Separate Spheres: Home as "Women's Kingdom"

In the first decades of the twentieth century, discourses on women were strongly influenced by the notion of separate spheres, with the political system and civic life gendered male and the home increasingly gendered female.[30] State agencies were active protagonists in this gendering enterprise. A former minister of education explained in 1907 that the "different characteristics of the sexes" required distinctions in secondary education, since "every one assumes that girls are going to marry, to become wives and mothers." The occupations of men and women were "naturally different," and "each must not forget his or her own proper sphere." Within this sexual division of labor, the task of women was to raise children. He glorified women as "worthy companions of the men of Meiji, noble mothers to bring up future generations of Japanese." Like other early twentieth-century state officials, he linked child rearing by women to nation building. "For the common interest of the house, and as a share of her duty to the State," the wife's role is to relieve her husband's anxieties at home by "managing household affairs, looking after the house expenses, and, above all, . . . bringing up the children in a fit and proper manner."[31] Female domesticity in the nation's service meant that, with proper education, women could safely be trusted with family management, so that men could concentrate even more on the state's goals of creating a wealthy country and strong army.

Although women were supposed to take care of home and children, men did not disappear altogether from accounts of appropriate forms of family life. Nevertheless, an image of separate spheres prevailed, such as in the depiction of spouses as a complementary pair. Common comparisons were with the political order. In 1903, the socialist Sakai Toshihiko (1870–1933), founder of *Katei zasshi*

---

30. See the Introduction to this volume and the chapter by Barbara Molony.

31. Kikuchi [Dairoku], "Female Education in Japan," *Transactions and Proceedings of the Japan Society, London* 7 (1905–7): 420–25, 429.

(Home magazine), wrote about the husband as "prime minister and foreign minister" and the wife as "finance minister and home minister," responsible for the household budget, education, and hygiene. In a 1917 book calling for a child-centered family, social democrat Abe Isoo distinguished conjugal roles in the home by drawing an analogy between men as "foreign ministers" and women as "home ministers."[32]

Parental roles in child rearing were often described as mirror images of ideal behavior and attributed to innate differences. One of the earliest examples of this theme is found in a 1894 book on home education by the influential journalist and publisher Tokutomi Sohō (1863–1957), who presented as a desired norm the notion of "a dignified father and a loving mother" (*igenfu jibo*).[33] Comparable associations of fathers with strict, stern, dignified, and distant attitudes and mothers with love, indulgence, and care continued to be popular in the first decades of the twentieth century.[34] Even when the ideals were reversed, a binary image was maintained, as if parental behavior was fixed under any circumstances. In 1919 Hatoyama Haruko (1861–1938), an important writer on female education and herself a school principal, advocated the reversal of the "old belief" of the "feudal age" of a strict father and loving mother. Instead, she favored "a loving father and a strict mother" (*jifu genbo*).[35] Her ideal was formed by the impression of parent-child inti-

---

32. Abe Isoo, *Kodomo hon'i no katei* (The child-centered home) (Tokyo: Jitsugyō no Nihonsha, 1917), pp. 111–12. See also David R. Ambaras, "Social Knowledge, Cultural Capital and the New Middle Class in Japan, 1895–1912," *Journal of Japanese Studies* 24, no. 1 (1998): 28–29.

33. Minyūsha, ed., *Katei kyōiku* (Home education) (Tokyo, 1894), pp. 8–9; reprinted in vol. 2 of *Katei kyōiku bunken sōsho* (Home education document series), ed. Ishikawa Matsutarō (Tokyo: Kuresu shuppan, 1990).

34. For the "dignified father, loving mother" (*igenfu jibo*) variation, see Tonegawa Yosaku, *Katei kyōikuhō* (1901), pp. 16, 25; reprinted in vol. 2 of *Katei kyōiku bunken sōsho*; and Takizawa Kikutarō and Ishida Katsutarō, *Kodomo to fubo* (Children and parents) (Tokyo: Kōbundō shoten, 1910), pp. 10–11. The authors of both books were educators working in Tokyo. For "strict father, loving mother" (*genpu jibo*), see Takeda Kanji, *Nihon no shitsuke* (Japanese upbringing) (Tokyo: Sankyō shoin, 1943).

35. Hatoyama Haruko, *Wagako no kyōiku* (My children's education) (Fujokaisha, 1919), p. 107.

macy that she found in the image of fatherhood presented by Cambridge University professor Charles Kingsley, whose children called him their "best friend." [36] Paternal love, she argued, was needed to counteract the absence of fathers from the home. Maternal strictness served as a corrective to what children knew to be the "unconditional and total love" of mothers, who spent most of their time in the home. [37] Hatoyama juxtaposed her new ideals to what she saw as ordinary parental inclinations. In that sense, both old and new slogans were based on the same assumptions of prevalent behavior, with the old endorsing it and the new ideal trying to mitigate or even overcome its worst effects.

The ideology of gender difference was little contested, but its implications for power relations in the family were. In Tokutomi's hierarchical vision of the family, the father set the guidelines for child rearing and education, and the mother cared for children in daily life. The mother pursued housework "according to his will," and one of her duties was to obey her husband "without thought for her own life and sufferings." [38] Western science, not Confucian ideals, was Tokutomi's source for idealizing these patriarchal structures. He drew, for instance, from the ideas of the influential German educator Johann Friedrich Herbart (1776–1841), who explained as a matter of course that family members submitted to the iron will of the dignified master of the house, the *Hausherr*. Despite their subordination, women, Tokutomi wrote, were significant in socializing their children. "According to the ideas of home education," the mother was the most crucial parent; this could be seen, for example, in talkative mothers producing talkative children. [39]

By contrast, other male authors accepted a sexual division of labor in spousal tasks without endorsing a gap in authority. Abe Isoo saw no "relationship of inferiority or superiority" as long as the wife performed her tasks at home as the mistress of the household (*shufu*) and not as a maid. The most important of these tasks

---

36. Charles Kingsley (1819–75), a priest in Eversley after 1844, was involved in Christian socialism and taught history at Cambridge University in 1860–69.

37. Hatoyama, *Waga ko*, p. 108.

38. Minyūsha, ed., *Katei kyōiku*, p. 13.

39. Ibid., p. 16.

was to educate the children.[40] In an earlier article, he had criticized the normal power imbalance in Japanese homes, where the father held rights over wife and children. In contrast, Abe asserted, "In my home there is equality between parents and children and between husband and wife." In terms frequently used by Taishō authors to signify spousal equality, Abe described himself as his wife's assistant (*joshu*) and her discussion partner (*sōdan aite*).[41] Male cooperation and conversation were construed as contributions to women's liberation because the husband who practiced these treated his wife as a partner in her domestic roles instead of as a domestic servant who obeyed male commands.

In its early years, *Fujin no tomo* endorsed these views of different, but almost equal, gender roles. In a 1908 article, the authoritative views of a president of Harvard University were drawn on to reiterate the prevalent view that men go outside the home to work and women manage the inside, but this division of labor was balanced by spousal cooperation in creating a happy family. The male contribution derived from the husband's experience in society, which he shared with his wife as a discussion partner. Knowledge and moral instruction from this outside perspective were also imparted to children so they could become members of "civilized society" and participants in an improved home life. Leading by example, fathers should share (*buntan*) in household labor by carrying firewood or fetching water, so that children would realize their responsibility toward the family. Similarly, husbandly sympathy, kindness, and respect toward one's wife were also not an end in itself but a means of encouraging children to value their mothers. Reading the newspaper and taking walks, too, should be turned into a family affair by including children. Last but not least, the husband's, wife's, and children's common enjoyment of pleasures was expected to generate further family happiness through togetherness.[42] As exotic as some of these ideas must have appeared

---

40. Abe Isoo, *Kodomo hon'i no katei*, pp. 111–12.

41. Abe Isoo, "Shakai no hito," pp. 28–29. Abe himself became leader of the Social Mass Party in the 1930s.

42. Hābādo daigaku sōchō Erioto (Harvard University President Eliot), "Katei ni okeru danshi no shokubun" (Men's duty at home), *Fujin no tomo* 1, no. 4 (Apr. 1908): 105–7. Charles William Eliot (1834–1926) was a leading proponent of

to Japanese readers, many elements of this ideal paternal behavior were later espoused by male middle-class intellectuals; Sundays were touted as a special day for fathers' activities, at a time when the traditional rest days for laborers in Japan were still the first and fifteenth days of the month.

A Japanese version of the happy family, also published in 1908, mentioned partnership but, instead of cooperation, stressed ideals of female autonomy. Although men represented the family to the outside as the head of the household (*kachō*), within the house, the husband (*otto*) should, if possible, let the wife work in freedom. The husband's respect for her responsibilities should be accompanied by self-restraint; the husband should not exceed his sphere (*ryōiki*) as his wife's assistant and discussion partner. Achieving a happy home meant putting an end to the kind of abusive behavior that saw men rule and wives obey "no differently from a maidservant." As domestic "superintendent," women should take charge of the family, for, after all, "the home was the woman's kingdom" (*fujin no ōkoku*).[43]

Paternal Leisure with Children and the "Joy of Home Life"

In the *Fujin no tomo* articles, the twelve authors described their activities as fathers almost without references to their wives. This seems a remarkable oversight, considering the strong duality in the abstract images of parenting roles. The male writers may have thought that mothers' tasks were so obvious and frequently discussed they needed no elaboration. One notable exception was Akai Yonekichi, who provided a four-page set of instructions on what he expected from mothers, repeating, as if it were seriously questioned, the view that "the mother has to be the center of the home."[44] In their narratives, most of the fathers chose to ignore this center, as if

---

educational reforms at the university and secondary-school level during his long tenure as president of Harvard University (1869–1909).

43. Roben Sei, "Tsuma no joshu toshite no otto" (The husband as wife's assistant), *Fujin no tomo* 1, no. 6 (June 1908): 171.

44. Akai, "Kodomo no kyōiku."

little coordination or interaction between mothers and fathers in terms of socializing and educating their children was required.

The second conspicuous absence is a detailed discussion by men on the importance of their role as economic providers. To be sure, several fathers, almost in passing, mention that they are constantly busy with work, usually as an excuse for not participating more in family life. But only Ogawa Mimei noted that he "had to support the life of one family." Fathers failed to stress that their main contributions to the family were financial support and security. This role may have been so familiar to them that they did not want to delve into it, or perhaps revealing their economic success in public may have been a taboo subject among intellectuals. Moreover, they may have linked the provider role to masculinity, not fatherhood. The 1898 Civil Code declared that the head of the house was to support the members of the house (Art. 747), but it also noted that "a child is subject to the parental power (*shinken*) of the father belonging to the same house" (Art. 877)."[45] Although this group of fathers did not emphasize their economic role, it loomed larger in the eyes of other contributors to *Fujin no tomo*; one article, for example, regretted that fathers did not matter, except as economic providers.[46]

References to the state in what are rather private depictions of fatherhood are also rare. In contrast to the frequent exhortations in other forums to male public service, such as the military, these fa-

---

45. Only when the father was dead or absent could the mother exercise parental power. In theory the head of the house and the father could be a different person, even if in the majority of the families this was not the case. Detailed, but still unexplored, population statistics exist on household headship according to gender and legal status. Although female heads of household almost disappeared among the Meiji peerage (*kazoku*), their percentages rose gradually for both samurai (*shizoku*) and commoners (*heimin*) and then remained constant during the first decades of the twentieth century. After 1900 around 90 percent of household heads were men; women assumed the position of headship mostly when eligible male successors were lacking or they lived in single-person households; see Hayami Akira, ed., *Kokusei chōsa izen Nihon jinkō tōkei shūsei* (A collection of Japanese population statistics prior to the national census), 22 vols. (Tokyo: Hara shobō, 1992–93).

46. Hatoyama Haruko, "Chichioya to kodomo no shitashimi" (Father and child intimacy), *Fujin no tomo* 3, no. 5 (June 1910): 185–86.

thers usually described paternal interaction with children as an end in itself rather than as an activity that served a higher national purpose. Abe Isoo was a noticeable exception, probably because of his desire to reform politics from the bottom to the top by changing family life. As noted above, this consisted of limiting the excesses of patriarchy in the family by respecting women as the mistress of the household, but it also included the preparation of children for adult life by teaching "actual problems of politics, economy, and society to boys and girls." In this sense, he presented fatherhood as a bridge between family and society for the benefit of both; this, incidentally, was also a common trope among the more abstract images of fathers in advice books.

By contrast to the neglect of "expected" themes, leisure and companionship were important topics intellectual men associated with their role as fathers in the 1910s. Evenings were a crucial time to enjoy family life. The scholar Hayakawa Tetsuji never came home late, "because the children were waiting without having eaten." "After dinner we all gather and play the piano, sing songs, and talk. In such a way we have friendly conversations, and I associate much with my children. . . . At eight I give them a bath and put them to bed."[47] Even fathers who professed to put little effort into child rearing participated in mealtime play. The biologist Okaasa Jirō conversed and played with his children after the evening meal, "because what I do for the children is not clearly decided. I just become a playmate (*asobi aite*) for the kids."[48] The journalist and politician Tagawa Daikichirō felt sorry for his children because of his frequent absences during meals. Although he assured his readers that he never entered teahouses or flirted with women, "unlike most of my friends," Tagawa still confessed to having fewer than two to three evening meals at home a week. Even those meals were rarely shared with his children, since his return was often so late that the children had already finished dinner, and in the mornings he slept through their breakfast. As a result, he pondered whether a person who behaved as he did really de-

---

47. Hayakawa, "Katei de wa kodomo no mori."

48. Okaasa, "Nani mo shinai." In another place he called himself a "discussion partner" (*sōdan aite*).

served to be called "father" (*chichi*); in the end, he expressed shame and promised to make a fresh start.[49] Even in the breach, *Fujin no tomo* fathers adhered to the ideal of father-child play around mealtime. If nothing else, their children could at least expect this much of them. Wives may also have hoped for this minimum fathering activity from their husbands.[50] In a long article, Hani Motoko rebuked fathers: "All too often fathers busy with work have no time to be together with their children, even once a day at the evening meal."[51] This reference to fathers' absence at dinner may have served to reinforce readers' expectations that fathers would be present at this main event of family togetherness.

Another form of paternal interaction with children was physical exercise. The scholar Uchigasaki Sakusaburō, who stressed the development of the child's healthy body in a natural environment, took walks with his children in the suburbs during summer evenings. His particular health consciousness also had a class bias. If parents did not live in the countryside, he said, they should strive for an elevated residence outside the city, with much sunshine, a large garden, and a playground for children. He consciously avoided the lower-class urban downtown on his excursions: "I have a policy not to take [the children] to the *shitamachi* at all." If not in the evening then at least on weekends, some fathers set aside time for the children. Okaasa Jirō took regular walks in the countryside with his children on Sundays after a train ride of up to one hour, a program that usually entailed modern snacks such as sandwiches at resting places.[52] Abe Isoo, a Christian, emphasized his particular duty toward the physical training of his seven children by walking with them on Sundays.[53] More than the evening meal, walks with

49. Tagawa, "Kodomo ni sumanai."

50. On Hatoyama's hopes for paternal presence at mealtimes, see her "Chichi-oya to kodomo," pp. 185–86.

51. Hani Motoko, "Oyako no ai no kansei" (Realization of love between parents and children), *Fujin no tomo* 12, no. 6 (June 1918): 5. Hani herself at times was so busy that she arrived home before sunset only once a week, according to her daughter Setsuko (cited in Saitō, *Hani Motoko*, p. 80).

52. Uchigasaki, "Shizen to shakai."

53. Although Abe did not speak about walking with his children in the 1916 *Fujin no tomo* issue, he referred to this activity in other publications, such as Abe Isoo, "Chichi toshite no kodomo kyōiku" (Educating children as a father), in

children seemed to depend on the particular preferences of the fathers. Abe Isoo, for example, was also an early promoter of baseball at Waseda University. It is questionable whether walking included the entire family in the same way as the common meal. At least none of these fathers mentioned their wife when talking about walks with their children. Mothers may have been excluded from these father and child exercises in togetherness; there is no evidence of their participation. Young children may also have been excluded because of their age, although Okaasa varied the distance according to whether he took the older or the younger children.

Paternal leisure also extended to sharing hobbies and preferences with children in the cultural fields of literature and exhibitions, painting and music, songs and poetry. More than other fathers, Uchigasaki Sakusaburō sought father-child intimacy in the common enjoyment of painting and music. His children developed interests in painting, he said, when painter friends visited and left examples of their works; one child even tried to imitate watercolor painting. Children acquired a taste for music when the family received a piano from relatives; "by their own will," they exerted themselves, sang and had fun "without learning the rules correctly."[54] Doctor of Literature Sasaki Nobutsuna, who was rather taciturn on the subject of his role in raising his children, indulged in memories of singing with his doting father and also enjoyed discussions of songs and poetry with other people's children.[55]

The emphasis on companionship in paternal narratives went together with a neglect of the favorite theme of advice books, paternal strictness. Only one father even mentioned it, and he did so in the context of finding a balance between the two extremes of close supervision of children and total noninvolvement. Until about high school children needed guidance, he said, and freedom and noninterference should not be confused. But even this author condoning paternal firmness rejected "excessive strictness" as counter-

---

vol. 7 of *Kodomo kenkyū kōza* (Lectures on child research), ed. Nihon ryōshin saikyōiku kyōkai (Tokyo: Senshinsha, 1929), pp. 338–40.

54. Uchigasaki, "Shizen to shakai."

55. Sasaki, "Wasureenu chichi."

productive. In teaching their children, fathers stressed persuasion and enthusiasm, not threat and punishment.

Deepening the affectionate bonding between father and child was even invoked in the pursuit of tedious housework tasks. Hayakawa Tetsuji, a single father since his wife had left him the year before "to recover from a disease," described the organization of daily routine work.[56] Calling himself the main caretaker of his children, he described his role in the morning routine as general supervisor. Getting up at 5:00 every morning, he assigned each family member over fifteen a task in the house. Most of the cleaning was done by 5:30 "since we live in a relatively simple house," and "at 6:00 we get out of the bath, and we all eat breakfast together; at 7:00 those who go to school leave, and I go, too." His unusually detailed description of housework by the father was presented under the subheading "Even the Morning Cleaning We Do Together." Although the concrete aim was to clean the house regularly, the more important issue was the creation of a feeling of family unity by working together under the father's direction.

Paternal leisure, an especially prominent theme of the pieces in the 1916 special issue, can be found in other articles in *Fujin no tomo* of the 1910s. Hatoyama Haruko urged more involvement of fathers with their children, especially in companionship and play. The intimacy between mothers and children, "natural throughout history," pushed fathers to the side, to the detriment, she regretted, of both fathers and children. Hatoyama encouraged mothers and children to make an effort to engage fathers as friends (*tomodachi*) of the children. Like other authors, she identified the daily evening bath as the best time and place for the display of fatherly affection and care. Many fathers already bathed children after their return from work, she observed. The deeper purpose of entrusting this routine ritual to fathers was to facilitate conversation, so that fathers and children listened to each other. Moreover, through diversions with sweet children, fathers tasted the great joy (*tanoshimi*) of home life.[57]

The self-perceptions of fathers in *Fujin no tomo* contrasts starkly with abstract notions of strict, distant, and uncaring fathers found

---

56. Hayakawa, "Katei de wa kodomo no mori."
57. Hatoyama, "Chichioya to kodomo," pp. 185–86.

in child-rearing manuals or as experienced by some children. The popularity of paternal play among these eminent urban intellectuals in the 1910s may have been encouraged by a personal sense of professional success and material satisfaction that enabled these men and their families to lead a stable lifestyle, which permitted leisure activities. A feeling of economic security was encouraged by a general rise in affluence during the period 1904–19, which saw strong industrial growth in Japan, fueled by the demands of World War I in Europe.[58] This sense of affluence also seems connected to notions of pride in their white-collar professional status. Fathers could afford to show that they took the time to play with small children in evenings and on Sundays and that they avoided taking children for walks in blue-collar, lower-class districts. The ideal of men as gentle fathers bore a marked middle-class bias.

Besides the sense of improvement in economic circumstances, contemporary ideas about daily family life as flourishing in a happy home based on mutual respect and emotional bonds probably influenced paternal narratives. As shown above, authors promoting the status of women as housewives often called for husbands to act as the "discussion partner" of their wives instead of their master. When fathers undertook to answer the question "What should fathers do?" they in turn described interactions with their children in terms of companionship as "play partners," not as teacher of morals or knowledge. Western-influenced ideas on the creation of a happy home promoted husbands and fathers as partners of wives and children, not as rulers of the household.

Paternal Anxieties over Schooling and Threats to Middle-Class Status

Despite fathers' explicit interest in their children, school education was not high on the agenda of paternal narratives in the 1910s; certainly none of the fathers writing in *Fujin no tomo* in this period saw supervision of children's studies as his main paternal duty. Some even showed indifference. Tagawa Daikichirō criticized

---

58. W. J. Macpherson, *The Economic Development of Japan, 1868–1941* (Cambridge, Eng.: Cambridge University Press, 1995), pp. 7–9.

other parents for their excessive educational ambition, which made them hire private teachers to tutor their children outside school. By contrast, he learned the name of his child's teacher only on the morning he had to go to the Fourth Middle School to consult on grades. Still he was sufficiently interested in his children's education that he bothered to meet the teacher; Sasaki Nobutsuna admitted that, to his regret, he never found much time to teach the many children he produced at an early age, who were essentially raised by schoolteachers.[59] In contrast, the contributors to the special section on fatherhood in 1926 worried more about their children's future, a concern that made schooling an overarching theme.

This shift in emphasis from leisure to schooling followed changes in the educational system. Education became more competitive as popular demand for higher education outpaced the growth in the number of schools, especially during the 1910s and 1920s. The ratio of applicants to the total number of seats in higher schools, for example, rose from 4.3 in 1910 to 10.5 in 1926.[60] Although access to higher education became more difficult, better schooling became more of a precondition for entry into the group of urban professionals through employment and marriage. As one member of this group defined the preconditions for middle-class marriage, "men should be above 25 years, wage-earners, and university graduates; women should be above 17 or 18 years, with a correct and healthy body, and a graduate of a women's school."[61] Together with the stiffening competition to gain admittance to a school, several years of drastic economic reversals and the Great Kantō Earthquake of 1923 left urban middle-class professional families feeling less secure by the mid-1920s. Moreover, by the early 1920s social problems had become associated with the cities, as public attention focused on the

---

59. Tagawa, "Kodomo ni sumanai"; Sasaki, "Wasureenu chichi."

60. *The New Encyclopaedia Britannica* (Chicago: University of Chicago, 1992), 18: 74.

61. Nagayo Yoshirō, "Hajimete chichi to natta tomo ni" (To a friend who just became a father), *Fujin no tomo* 14, no. 7 (July 1920): 178. Born in 1888 in Tokyo, he graduated from Tokyo Imperial University. Nagayo participated in the Shirakaba literary movement and continued to adhere to that group's humanistic philosophy after the emergence of the proletarian literature movement of the 1920s. He died in 1961.

destitution of the working poor and the increased participation of workers in labor unions.[62] As the middle class expanded, it may have felt more threatened from below.

Fathers' criticisms of selection through grades and examinations were often made in the context of what they perceived as an adult world of excessive competition intruding into children's innate purity. Tokuda Shūsei felt that children's purity (*junryō*) and charm (*aikyō*) prevented them from becoming successful adults. The academic selection process favored smart students, who became even smarter by enrolling in better schools. But there seemed no escape from this situation, when thinking "about the future of these young people sent into a world of severe existential competition."[63] Ogawa Mimei, the author of children's stories, anguished over his daughter's further school education. She was about to graduate from elementary school, and he wanted her to enroll in a private women's school. His school of choice, however, had many applicants and few available positions. As a result, students without special connections had little hope of getting accepted. Moreover, this popular school charged high tuition. Ogawa endorsed public elementary schools as a place where children of all classes could mingle "without knowledge of family circumstances" in common innocence (*junjō*).[64]

Tsuchida Kyōson was even more anxious than Ogawa about his children's educational prospects.[65] More than other intellectual fathers, he was obsessed with the necessity of a high level of schooling for his children. He compared his exceptional gifts with the mediocrity of his children in both intelligence and appearance. Tsuchida boasted that from the age of three or four he had constantly drawn pictures, and at age eleven he had been called a genius because of his works in the style of the grand artists. He bragged that he had never prepared or reviewed his lessons for school at home, always leaving his books at school. Still, he re-

---

62. Sheldon Garon, *Molding Japanese Minds: The State in Everyday Life* (Princeton: Princeton University Press, 1997), pp. 10–11.

63. Tokuda, "Chichi toshite."

64. Ogawa, "Watashi wa kodomo no kōfuku."

65. Tsuchida, "Chichi no kyōiku."

ceived perfect scores and took the top seat in class. By contrast, his children showed no special talents, and those attending elementary school ranked somewhere in the middle of their class, a fact that led him and his wife to worry about their children's chances for entering middle school. His children's dire prospects made him wonder whether they were defective or he and his wife were at fault as parents.

Tsuchida's ambitions for his children, he admitted, were in conflict with his educational principles. On the one hand, he thought children should develop their abilities at their own pace, and he "intended not to be disappointed" by his children or to provide them with special education, since that would compromise his belief in social fairness. Forcing children to receive an education beyond their abilities was not an example of true love. On the other hand, a university education seemed necessary, regardless of children's talents or inclinations, or their desire to become farmers or poets. He rationalized these contradictions by explaining that children should have an opportunity to manifest their talents, but it was difficult to predict when children would reach this stage: "At age five or ten, the child's future is impossible to foresee." Nevertheless, Tsuchida stressed that a child's development needed to come from the child him- or herself.

The fathers also debated trends in school education that had originated in the United States and Germany and spread to Japan. Tsuchida opposed the "so-called new education" for its excessive encouragement of schoolwork, as reflected, for example, in the foolish ambition of a school to have its students read as many books as possible in a year. To his relief, he discerned a backlash to this kind of education, which a certain Holmes had called "pay-for-results education." Tsuchida especially criticized the Dalton Plan, "at one time" popular in Japan, which stressed children's study according to yearly assignments. He labeled this approach "contract work," stemming from American-style "slave wages."[66] Again and

---

66. Helen Parkhurst first developed the learning methods of the Dalton Plan in 1903 in Massachusetts for one-class elementary schools. In 1920 it was adapted to four-class schools. The plan was translated into Japanese by educator Akai

again, he condemned the "new education" for cramming massive amounts of indigestible material into children and attempting to compartmentalize their brains by grading them according to each minute subject. In his endorsement of a philosophy of education named after the German educator Eduard Spranger, Tsuchida further demonstrated familiarity with international educational fashions.[67] He advocated a shift in education "from result to creativity" to improve civilization.

New trends in education also formed the framework for fathers' discussions of the training of children's artistic faculties. The German literature scholar Chino Shōshō, who thought about his children's education in the fine arts "every day," supported the movement for free drawing, which he saw as an improvement over more conventional mechanical methods. Chino wrote like an educator engaged in a philosophical argument with an audience of specialists when he discussed the finer points of institutional education in such fields as music and literature, distinguishing between fine arts and superficial arts and crafts. In the very last sentences, he finally got around to mentioning the home. Since understanding the fine arts contributed to a taste for life, he said, this should also be a "duty of the home"—and a crucial task of the housewife (shufu).[68] When Chino "thought as a father," he came up with a philosophy of education to be implemented by mothers.

Another reason for the prominence of education in the concerns of the fathers writing in 1926 may have been their more advanced age. Some were within the customary retirement age for household headship, such as the 66-year-old Miyake. The 57-year-old Tokuda Shūsei explained his status as a father of school-age children: "I am a father of six children, ranging in age from a boy who is receiving higher education to a small girl who has just entered elementary school." Tokuda stressed his children's individuality—they varied in "build and character" and in "essential quality"—but as a father he

---

Yonekichi, who incidentally contributed an article for the same volume in which the special section on fatherhood appeared; see Akai, "Kodomo no kyōiku."

67. German philosopher and educator Eduard Spranger (1882–1963) was influential in the German progressive movement of education, especially in the 1920s.

68. Chino, "Geijutsu kyōiku ni tsuite."

loved them equally.[69] At 35, the youngest writer of the group, Tsuchida Kyōson, informed the reader of the ages and gender of his three children: "I am certainly a father. My elder son is seven, the second son is five, my daughter is four." The context for Tsuchida's enumeration of his children was the problem he faced of defining fatherhood: he first resorted to his role as progenitor of children. He might not have lived up to his own parenting ideal otherwise, since, to his regret, his boys had to be raised in his wife's natal home for a while before they could live under his roof.[70]

Fathers on Gender Roles

The sexual division of labor between husbands and wives, linked by ideologues to the larger benefit of the nation, evoked little paternal encouragement or reflection among the *Fujin no tomo* writers. Most fathers failed to specify whether their attitudes and activities varied, or ought to have varied, by the gender or age of their children. This neglect runs counter to the assumption of a widespread belief in the importance of grooming male successors, especially first-born sons, to continue the family line. The male authors, as migrants to the metropolitan center, had broken with the professional traditions of their natal families. In some cases second or third sons without hope of succession, they had achieved their professional status more through a process of academic selection than inheritance. No writer addressed, positively or negatively, ideals of family continuity, as if this was not an issue of importance for modern fathers. Together with this neglect, the issue of gender socialization in different spheres invited surprisingly little interest. In fact, some fathers, such as Abe Isoo, encouraged his daughters as well as his sons to learn about the outside world to become informed citizens capable of an equal partnership between husband and wife for the purpose of rearing children together.

One of the few exceptions was an unidentified father who reflected on paternal influence on boys in 1909. He, as usual, acknowledged the primary importance of mothers for infants, but

---

69. Tokuda, "Chichi toshite."
70. Tsuchida, "Chichi no kyōiku," p. 15.

he saw an enlarged impact of fathers as children grew older, especially as role models for boys. Since children imitate the words and deeds of "the master of the house, that is, the father," men should be very careful about their behavior at home. The author was appalled at his eight-year-old son's arrogance toward his mother, but he realized that his son was merely imitating his own rough speech toward his wife. A father's bad example, he feared, could lead innocent children astray.

Children's admiration for their father, however, also gave fathers an opportunity to be effective as models and teachers. Fathers' self-improvement as a key to successful child rearing was also stressed in the author's rhetorical question, "More than educating our children, isn't it necessary to educate ourselves first?" References to a belief in piety, deep cultivation, and much effort as a means to turn children into good people made child rearing into a near religious mission. Morality and modern science informed the author's discussion when he extolled home education, which, "unlike school education," was about the parent's personality molding children. With a reference to "guilt" inherited from parents, this anonymous writer alluded to the Christian image of humanity in search of the lost paradise to be regained through moral education.[71]

The only father who concretely discussed socializing girls in their domestic gender roles was Hayakawa Tetsuji, who referred to his ideas as "Western style." As a single father, he was particularly sensitive to training his daughters. Before they married, he urged them to participate in housework to learn to become diligent and practical, especially with money. They could keep any amount left over from the monthly sum they were given for domestic expenses as their income. His views on savings and tracking money flows were in line with ideas on scientific household management often propagated by women's magazines such as *Fujin no tomo*. To him "Western style" precluded the possibility of his daughters' imitating "new women," whom he criticized as obsessed with outward appearances and ignoring the reality of life.

---

71. Anonymous, "Chichi toshite no yo no kansō" (A father's impression of the world), *Fujin no tomo* 2, no. 6 (July 1909): 255–57.

A rare narrative related to infants was published in the style of a letter in 1920 by the novelist Nagayo Yoshirō. The birth of a child triggered his reflections on a potential crisis in conjugal relations despite the "family" consciousness it generated. Although Nagayo ruminated about the past and present dangers of delivering a child and remembered his feelings of trepidation and expectation when attending the birth and holding his wife's hands to share the pain, relations between husband and wife were closer to his heart. Admitting that newlyweds loved each other, he sensed a growing boredom and unrest as time passed by, feelings that seemed especially pronounced in women but were mitigated by parenthood. The mere arrival of babies, he claimed, led to truly deep conjugal relations.[72]

To a very limited extent, *Fujin no tomo* fathers referred to father figures as role models. When they did so, they drew positive pictures in contrast to their own perceived shortcomings as fathers. Sasaki Nobutsuna filled half his article on fatherhood with nostalgic memories of his happy experiences with his own father. "Extremely spoiled" as a child of his father's "later years," he constantly followed his father around, even going on trips with him starting from age six or seven. "Singing songs together in the evening" and learning about birds, grasses, and trees, he received "the favor of child rearing and education" by his father. Besides a particular song his father used to sing, Sasaki appreciated most the sacrifice made by his father, who left his hometown in Ise to go to Tokyo for his son. By contrast, he self-critically depicted his attitude toward his own children as rather negligent and casual.[73] Another father wondered self-consciously what his children would think about him in 30 to 40 years, feeling that he had not lived up to his duty as a parent. When he had been a small child, his grandfather had made sure that he did not sleep until he had memorized his assignments. "In tears" he studied by himself and experienced great hardships, but in retrospect he was happy and grateful for his grandfather's "strict guidance."[74]

---

72. Nagayo, "Hajimete chichi to natta," pp. 173–82.
73. Sasaki, "Wasureenu chichi."
74. Tagawa, "Kodomo ni sumanai."

References to fathers by children, sons as well as daughters, also appear elsewhere in personal writings. One popular book alone includes 36 historical tales of parent-child relations among famous Japanese.[75] A recent English book critically explores the bonds between Japanese women writers and father figures "as a signifier of patriarchal authority."[76] Personal recollections show that the significance of fathers to children was not necessarily a function of physical presence around the home. The son of Yamamoto Isoroku, the Japanese admiral responsible for the attack on Pearl Harbor, graduated from Japan's most prestigious university. Nevertheless, when he failed the physical examination for the navy due to poor health, the son was extremely disappointed at not being able to follow in his father's footsteps. The son also readily absorbed paternal explanations of what it meant to grow into a man, noting that his father told him to pursue large goals in life and focus on study, exercise, and sleep. He reinforced the gender divide by admonishing, "The kitchen is not a place men should enter."[77]

Maternal Care

Unlike special publications devoted to fathers as caretakers of children, no analogous collection of essays "on being a mother" seems to exist, but women often wrote about their experiences as mothers. Birth control–activist Ishimoto Shizue revealed that she had begun to devour Western child-rearing literature when her child was born the previous year, and writer Hiratsuka Raichō pondered her eight years of maternal joys and sorrows.[78] Thematic features named

---

75. Mostly pairs with fathers are portrayed; see Sankei shinbun shuzaihan, ed., *Oya to ko no Nihonshi* (A Japanese history of parents and children) (Tokyo: Sankei shinbun, 2001).

76. Rebecca L. Copeland and Esperanza Ramirez-Christensen, *The Father-Daughter Plot: Japanese Literary Women and the Law of the Father* (Honolulu: University of Hawai'i Press, 2001), p. 7.

77. Yamamoto Yoshimasa, *Chichi Yamamoto Isoroku* (My father, Yamamoto Isoroku) (Tokyo: Kōbunsha, 2001), pp. 116–22.

78. Ishimoto Shizue, "Wakaki hahaoya no sankō" (Information for young mothers), *Fujin no tomo* 12, no. 6 (June 1918): 82–85; Hiratsuka Raichō, "Watashi no haha toshite no seikatsu" (My life as a mother), *Fujin no tomo* 18, no. 3 (June 1924): 23–26.

"motherhood" or "maternal love" contained mostly writings of a rather prescriptive variety revealed in such titles as "The Ultimate of Maternal Love."[79] Many articles linked motherhood to larger social, political, and national issues. One intellectual, for example, wrote an eulogy of mothers with the theme "great mothers bear great sons," stressing the importance of a wider recognition of mothers' contribution in a society "in which being a woman is not a happy condition." He noted that, according to a survey, "the majority of girls in the First Higher Girl's School want to be reborn as boys."[80]

Essays on mothers' actual child-rearing activities were often assembled under gender-blind headings, reflecting the assumption that the care of children was to fall in the maternal, or at least female, domain. Of the eighteen letters to the editor under the heading "experience with children," only one was submitted by a man.[81] This unusually long section of some forty pages featured contributors from the cities of Tokyo and Kobe as well as from various prefectures on the main islands of Honshu and Kyushu and from as far away as Korea. Authors were identified by their first name or a pseudonym such as "sad mother." Although they, or their husbands, were often employed in modern middle-class professions with salaried incomes, especially in teaching, they represented a far more diverse group, both in terms of place of residence and (husband's) occupation than the group of famous male urban intellectuals who ruminated about their role as fathers. Unlike the fathers, their concerns, even in this one section, went beyond the issues of play and education and included child-care arrangements, the cost of education, children's behavior and health, the difficulty of raising twins, and, last but not least, strongly emotional expressions of sadness at the death of children. Although the paternal contributions spoke for themselves, the magazine's editor commented on some of the letters, usually to explain why a particular mother deserved praise. In one case, for instance, the editor reas-

---

79. Miyake Yūjirō, "Boseiai no kyokuchi" (The ultimate of maternal love), *Fujin no tomo* 18, no. 3 (June 1924): 5–8.

80. Akai, "Kodomo no kyōiku."

81. *Fujin no tomo* 12, no. 9 (June 1918): 36–76.

sured a female teacher, torn between the demands of work and home, that she was full of maternal spirit, as could be seen in her devotion to both her students and her own offspring. The child of this reader, it was noted, was better provided for than many other children, who, although their mothers were housewives, still experienced neglect.

Men, as husbands, received somewhat more attention from "mothers" than they had granted to wives in their narratives. A husband's transfer was an important turning point in the life of a family, with which women had to cope, for better or worse. In one instance a small child's frail health improved dramatically due to the new sunny environment to which the family moved when the father was assigned to teach at a school on top of a remote mountain. In another case, the father's transfer meant the termination of a contract for a babysitter who had provided for twins almost since their birth. Men obtained respect as figures of authority and knowledge; the mother who waited for her husband to return before treating the insect bites of her children was only the most striking example of such a deferential attitude. The editor, herself a woman, criticized this contributor for her personal insecurity and pointed to the grave consequences the delay could have had for the injured children. Mothers, she implied, had to take charge of their children.

Mothers, more than fathers, referred to decisions about children and activities with them as undertaken jointly by the spouses. Whether this reflected literary convention, popular expectation, or their honest perception is difficult to tell, for there are almost no specifics on the actual or imagined role of men as fathers. Nevertheless, the image projected is one of child rearing as an inclusive parental enterprise of shared responsibilities marked by "we" and "our." Although other people, such as grandparents or babysitters, might contribute significantly to raising children, decision-making was firmly vested in the parents.

When mothers described specific domestic activities of their husbands in *Fujin no tomo*, they revealed their appreciation. Like the men, they recounted instances of fathers playing (*asobi*) with their children. Her husband's games with their daughter in their garden, one mother notes, were an important element in strengthening the health of the child. A husband's help with children could also be indirect because it freed the mother from other household tasks, as when he tended the vegetable garden or took care of the cat. Despite what to us may appear trivial contributions, these mothers neither complained about fathers' lack of involvement nor asked for more engagement.

Women expressed their experiences with children in rather more diverse ways than did the intellectual fathers who wrote for *Fujin no tomo*. Concerned less with child-rearing principles, they presented their interests as revolving more around solving the practical problems at hand in their everyday life. To them play and school education were not prominent reference points. This seems to indicate that a woman's role was defined more as the primary caregiver of children charged with ensuring that children actually survived into adulthood as physically robust human beings.

Men as Fathers, Not Patriarchs

The male authors contributing to magazine specials on fathers were expected to reveal a special interest in children when discussing parenting, if only by remonstrating with themselves for not always following their ideals in practice. While the attitudes of fathers ranged from those who professed that they did nothing to those who set up detailed guidelines on housework and education, they often presented their various fathering philosophies as being in the best interests of the child and valuable for fostering family togetherness.

The middle-class urban intellectual fathers in *Fujin no tomo* took ideas of separate spheres for granted but refrained from pushing the issue of paternal power. In fact, some articles propagated women's liberty from male interference in affairs of the household. The family was usually referred to in terms of the *katei* (home), and *ie* (household), with its connotations of lineage and patriarchy, was almost taboo. Although the writers generally imagined the home as under the management and control of wives and mothers, many also presented the home as a location of paternal recreation with children. Japanese renditions in the 1910s of the Western concept of a "happy home," one may argue, emphasized female domestic autonomy as the price of turning the home into a place of feminine work and masculine leisure.

Children's schooling was a prominent theme of fathers in the 1920s. The narrative was overshadowed by concern about their children's potential educational failure and anxiety over their children's success. Even in their frequent criticism of the educational system for its exclusive emphasis on intellectual abilities and for its excessive demands, the centrality of schooling and training in some paternal narratives is remarkable. This obsession with children's future as adults was informed by fathers' perception of the world as a highly competitive place and implicitly left little time and space to discuss their engagement with their children in terms of leisure activities or socializing.

Discussion of both schooling and leisure was remarkably free of injunctions on innate gender differences that determined different educational approaches for boys and girls by fathers. When one listens to fathers speaking in their own voice, just as women's history scholars have encouraged us to do for women, popular clichés of uncaring, stern patriarchs selfishly towering over their children become much less convincing as an accurate depiction of men's roles in child rearing. In the same way, the implications of increased paternal physical absence from home following the spread of wage work and urbanization need to be reconsidered. After all, the salaried status of urban middle-class professionals did not prevent the *Fujin no tomo* fathers from enjoying their leisure with their children or planning their education.

One important element in both fathers' and mothers' accounts is the lack of references to the state. Neither fathers nor mothers saw themselves as conceiving, raising, or educating children for the sake of the nation or the country. These middle-class families were not the nation writ small presided over by a distant and remote father in his role as emperor in miniature, as some prewar ideologues idealized. Neither fathers nor mothers perceived their interactions with their children in terms of fulfilling their domestic duties for the larger national benefit. Rather, parents described child rearing as a personal affair and themselves as people struggling with the changing demands of the outside world.

CHAPTER NINE

Social Networks Among the Daughters of a Japanese Family

Gail Lee Bernstein

"Kyōdai wa tanin no hajimari" (The sibling
is the beginning of the stranger).

English-language studies of the modern Japanese family have
tended to concentrate on the stem family, or *ie*, which allowed
only one adult child, usually the eldest son, to remain as heir of the
household.[1] Other children typically left the household, either to
marry or, in the case of sons, to become the adopted heirs of cou-

---

EPIGRAPH: This well-known Japanese saying is quoted in Chie Nakane, *Kinship
and Economic Organization in Rural Japan* (London: Athlone, 1967), p. 7. A variation is "Siblings are the closest strangers"; see Yamanaka Miyuki, "Shinzoku kankei" (Kin relations), in *Nihonjin no kazoku kankei* (Japanese family relations),
ed. Kamiko Takeji and Masuda Kōkichi (Tokyo: Yūhikaku, 1981), p. 228. *Tanin*
can also be rendered "outsiders" or "unrelated persons."

1. See, e.g., Francis L. K. Hsu, *Iemoto: The Heart of Japan* (New York: Schenk-
man, 1975). For a discussion of Western scholarship on the *ie*, see Kathleen Uno,
"Questioning Patrilineality: On Western Studies of the Japanese *Ie*," in *positions,
East Asia cultures critique*, no. 3 (Mar. 1996): 569–94. Akira Hayami argues that, before the Meiji Civil Code of 1898, inheritance was not uniform. The eldest son did
not always inherit: inheritance could be partible, and there were women-headed
households. See Hayami, "The Myth of Primogeniture and Impartible Inheritance
in Tokugawa Japan," *Family History* 8, no. 1 (Spring 1983): 3–29.

ples lacking male offspring.[2] Sometimes younger sons established branch families (*bunke*) nearby, and there are numerous studies of the interactions among these kin and fictive kin in village Japan.[3] However, we know little about married children who migrated to the cities.

Earlier ethnographic studies conveyed the impression that noninheriting offspring, once established in nuclear families (*kazoku*)[4] or in their in-laws' homes, severed ties with the *ie*, leaving the heir with both the family property and the sole responsibility for caring for his parents in their old age.[5] Rural dwellers who moved to the city in the early postwar period found requests for help from country relatives so troublesome that they were reluctant to return to their natal village, even for annual ancestral memorials. "If they do go back," Ezra Vogel reported, "they try to stay only a short time and to see only the most intimate friends."[6]

---

2. A son could also become the adopted son-in-law of another family, in which case he assumed his wife's surname, agreed to live with her family, and became its heir. Joy Hendry reports that unmarried adult siblings born in the household had the right to remain there, but there were "few of these" in the Kyushu village she studied; see her *Marriage in Changing Japan* (London: Croom Helm, 1981), p. 84. The exceptions were two single women over 30 who claimed to be ill or frail and one unmarried man who may have been "a little simple."

3. Social scientists in their family studies also have identified *dōzoku* (common kin), a corporate group "consisting of a hierarchy of households (*ie*) linked by kinship or fictive kinship ties"; see Richard K. Beardsley, John W. Hall, and Robert W. Ward, eds., *Village Japan* (Chicago: University of Chicago Press, 1959), p. 269.

4. *Kazoku*, according to Susan Orpett Long, implies nuclear family to the Japanese and is "probably the closest to the English 'family,' referring to people related by blood, marriage, or adoption who share household residence. . . . Sociologically, the emphasis on the conjugal bond in this definition stands in contrast to the main emphasis on lineality that characterizes the conception of *ie*." See Long, *Family Change and the Life Course in Japan* (Ithaca, N.Y.: China-Japan Program, Cornell University, 1987), p. 7. *Kaku kazoku* is a more precise rendering of "nuclear family."

5. The literature informs us that noninheriting, married children returned home only infrequently, for the funeral or memorial service of a parent or grandparent, at New Year's time, or for Obon in the summer, and, in the case of married daughters, to give birth.

6. Ezra Vogel, *Japan's New Middle Class* (Berkeley: University of California Press, 1963), pp. 134–35.

We have also assumed that ties among married siblings were tenuous, unless they remained in the countryside as branch families.[7] A hint of the importance of relatives, particularly the wife's relatives, as a source of advice and assistance appears in one study of contemporary urban Japanese housewives; the author briefly notes that over half of her interviewees preferred relatives to school friends as sources of advice.[8] Still, until recently the literature has minimized the importance of these extrahousehold kinship ties. "Urbanites," wrote one Japanese sociologist, "are especially inclined to belittle kinship relations."[9]

My research on one family, spanning the period from around World War I to the present, challenges some of these generalizations. I have uncovered a complex social network of relationships among urban, married brothers and sisters who grew up in a rural *ie*. I have also found that these married children maintained close ties not only with their siblings but with their natal home.[10]

These two findings lead me to suggest that, instead of focusing almost exclusively on either the rural *ie* or the urban *kazoku*, scholars of the modern Japanese "family" from the Meiji period to the present may want to look more closely at another kin group—the "kindred" (*shinseki* or *shinrui*)[11]—as it functioned in urban

----

7. Such branch families maintained carefully prescribed, special relationships that persisted for about three generations and included mutual aid and participation in rites of passage; see Hendry, *Marriage in Changing Japan*, p. 104.

8. Anne Imamura, *Urban Japanese Housewives* (Honolulu: University of Hawai'i Press, 1987), p. 102.

9. Takashi Koyama, "The Significance of Relatives at the Turning Point of the Family System in Japan," *Sociological Review Monograph* 10 (1966): 95.

10. I am grateful to the Northeast Asia Council of the Association for Asian Studies for a grant in 1993 that enabled me to do research in Japan for this paper, which is part of a book-length history of one Japanese family. The American Philosophical Society provided travel funds for research trips to Japan in 1993 and 1995, and the Social and Behavioral Sciences Division of the University of Arizona awarded me both a sabbatical leave and a funded research leave in 1995. I should also like to acknowledge Andrew Gordon, Kate Wildman Nakai, and Laura Hein, whose suggestions for revision, in one way or another and not always recognizable to them, were incorporated into this chapter.

11. Long, *Family Change and the Life Course in Japan*, p. 10, reports that this bilateral circle of relatives is known by a variety of terms, most commonly *shinrui*, *shinzoku*, or *shinseki*. Bilateral kinship reckoning, which may include the mother's rela-

Japan. These relatives, consisting mainly of married siblings and their husbands and children, formed a "modified extended family"—the term coined by American sociologist Eugene Litwak in his studies of Western family institutions.[12] Throughout their lifetimes, the relatives have helped one another in many important ways. Although urban Japanese sibling relationships were less specifically prescribed than conjugal and filial relationships, the study of their functioning adds a crucial dimension to our understanding of the dynamics of Japanese families in modern times.

The study of the *shinrui* speaks to a larger question as well. Networks of bilateral kindred were not unfamiliar in rural Japan. Living fairly close together and connected through a wife, sister, or mother as well as through male family members, relatives formed a "reciprocally cooperative, non-hierarchical group" whose members assisted one another by providing labor, help in crises, and money, and participated in ceremonial and social activities.[13] By observing

---

tives as well as the father's, and patrilineal descent groups, such as the *dōzoku*, are usually viewed by anthropologists as mutually exclusive in a given society. Yet, "there is no doubt that both principles have operated simultaneously in Japanese society" (ibid., p. 10). Sylvia Junko Yanagisako found that *issei* use the terms *shinseki* and *shinrui* interchangeably for what they said Americans call "relatives"; see Yanagisako, *Transforming the Past: Tradition and Kinship Among Japanese Americans* (Stanford: Stanford University Press, 1985), pp. 207–8. Hendry (*Marriage in Changing Japan*, p. 106) writes that bilateral kindred are called *shinseki* for about three generations, after which time they become *mukashi no shinseki* (distant relatives).

12. Eugene Litwak, "Extended Kin Relations in an Industrial Democratic Society," in *Social Structure and the Family: Generational Relations*, ed. E. Shana and Gordon F. Streib (Englewood Cliffs, N.J.: Prentice Hall, 1965), quoted in Nojiri (Meguro) Yoriko, "Family and Social Network in Modern Japan: A Study of an Urban Sample" (Ph.D. diss., Case Western Reserve University, 1974), p. 12. (The word "modified" is important here to distinguish the kindred from an actual extended family, which treats all children as heirs.) Hendry (*Marriage in Changing Japan*, p. 112n61) cites an example of one villager who refused to call a first cousin a *shinseki* because he had not been asked to help build the cousin's house. Without recognition of such ties of mutual obligation, he did not recognize a kinship relationship. Thus, kinship and mutual aid were almost synonymous in his mind.

13. Richard K. Beardsley, "Cultural Anthropology: Prehistoric and Contemporary Aspects," in *Twelve Doors to Japan*, ed. John Whitney Hall and Richard K. Beardsley (New York: McGraw-Hill, 1965), p. 78. See also Harumi Befu, "Patri-

how relatives, in effect, reproduced this particular kindred group in the large, impersonal city of Tokyo during a period of rapid changes in economic roles and lifestyles, we can gain a better understanding of Japanese strategies for handling the unsettling process of urbanization.

Finally, informal social networks among relatives also reveal an important dimension of women's family roles. Until recently, feminist scholarship has defined women's domestic work in terms of reproduction—their roles as mother and wife within the nuclear family. However, women in Japan and throughout the rest of the world also perform the crucial "kin work" that helps tie together many nuclear families related by kinship, especially the kindred on the wife's side.[14] If siblings did not become strangers, it is largely due to the work women did to create and preserve a network of kin.

The dominant role of women in the maintenance of family networks may help explain the neglect of such networks in scholarly literature, for women's work, in general, unless remunerated and done outside the home, tends to be invisible. Then, too, family networks, extending as they do beyond a single urban household or neighborhood and nurtured largely by women within the household, can easily get overlooked in studies focused on a single *ie* or on urban community relationships and structures.[15]

This chapter describes an active network of relatives over many decades. What I have learned about them from old photographs, interviews, participant-observation, and a family history written by the father of the twelfth generation has enabled me to identify the nature and frequency of their interactions over the past eighty

---

lineal Descent and Personal Kindred in Japan," *American Anthropologist* 65, no. 6 (1963): 1328–41.

14. Until the 1970s, women's kin work was invisible to scholars, who assumed that women-centered kin networks formed only in poor families and abroad, as part of a matrifocal pattern that exists in the absence of wage-earning men; see Micaela di Leonardo, *The Varieties of Ethnic Experience: Kinship, Class and Gender Among California Italian-Americans* (Ithaca, N.Y.: Cornell University Press, 1984), p. 206. Kin work encompasses a variety of activities, such as visits, letters, presents, telephone calls, and exchanges of money, services, and commodities (ibid., p. 194).

15. Two examples are Theodore C. Bestor, *Neighborhood Tokyo* (Stanford: Stanford University Press, 1989); and Jennifer Robertson, *Native and Newcomer: Making and Remaking a Japanese City* (Berkeley: University of California Press, 1991).

years. I am interested in how the network has been maintained, what kinds of activities are involved, and how and why women have come to play such a dominant role in administering it.

One might argue that we cannot confidently generalize on the basis of one family alone, especially since the one I have studied is atypical in several ways. First, the family is old, dating back to the late 1600s. Second, the family was wealthy: in its heyday in the late Meiji and Taishō periods, it was among the richest landowners in Fukushima prefecture. Third, the family belonged to the local elite: male family heads traditionally served as hereditary *shōya*— village heads. As a result of Occupation land reforms, the family lost almost all of its land, but most family members, especially the women of the twelfth generation, continued to be financially well off. Fourth, the generation I know best—the twelfth—was unusually large: there were seven brothers and eight sisters born between 1903 and 1930. In the 1960s, a family get-together with spouses, children, and one or two mothers-in-law might total as many as 35 or 40 people.[16] Fifth, members of this twelfth generation, ranging from 70 to 90 years of age when I interviewed them in the mid-1990s, were extremely well educated for their times; remarkably, all the daughters (except for one who died young) attended women's colleges. Finally, most of the siblings settled in or near Tokyo, an important factor facilitating their close ties.

Despite these distinctive features, the twelfth generation of women (whom I shall refer to as "the sisters") confronted circumstances not necessarily unique to their class.[17] It is true that, as young married women and again in late middle age, they enjoyed economic security. Although almost 50 percent of Japan's married women were gainfully employed in the 1930s, only the divorced

---

16. One such occasion was dinner at the Imperial Viking restaurant in Tokyo in 1964. Opened in the 1950s, the restaurant featured an all-you-can-eat dinner for a fixed price.

17. I am familiar mainly with six of the eight daughters of the twelfth generation, women whom I have known for forty years. I have lived with two of the eight and visited with four others. (Of the remaining two, one died at the age of eleven and the other died in her sixties, before I had a chance to meet her.) I also know their children and have met some of their grandchildren, as well as one sister-in-law. I have also met the present heir of the *ie*.

sister in this family worked for pay outside the home. Like every-one else during the long wartime and immediate postwar periods, however, the sisters endured illness, malnutrition, and disrupted family lives, and they worked hard within their homes to provide, without household help in most cases, the basic necessities of life for husbands, children, and in-laws. Although their husbands' income-earning potential enabled them to recover from the war faster than the less privileged, their educational and financial ad-vantages could not protect them from a full share of afflictions, in-cluding several cases of tuberculosis and children's deaths. Kin ties were crucial at such times.

The kin ties described here, far from being unique to one family or social class, resemble social networks identified by sociologist Koyama Takashi in his 1960s quantitative survey of approximately 300 families and by Nojiri Yoriko's 1970s survey of 129 metro-politan Tokyo families.[18] When Koyama asked respondents about their most reliable source of help in time of need, for example, the vast majority mentioned their relatives.[19] Matthews Hamabata's study of an upper-class family business likewise disclosed the impor-tance of the *shinseki,* whose "sudden appearance" at first surprised him: "People were supposed to marry out, to assume corporate po-sitions, to cut ties with their families of birth, yet *shinseki* seemed to be at the center of the way my informants organized their social lives beyond the immediate boundaries of their particular house-holds."[20] More recently, Scott Clark reported on similar lifelong re-lationships among six middle-aged sisters of an urban family of lim-ited resources, commenting that, in his experience, "Japanese people are well aware of the importance of natal family relationships."[21]

---

18. Koyama, "The Significance of Relatives at the Turning Point of the Family System," pp. 95–114; Nojiri, "Family and Social Network in Modern Japan," which was based on data collected by Cross-National Research Studies on the Family.

19. Koyama, "The Significance of Relatives at the Turning Point of the Family System," p. 96.

20. Matthews Masayuki Hamabata, *Crested Kimono: Power and Love in the Japanese Business Family* (Ithaca, N.Y.: Cornell University Press, 1990), p. 139.

21. Scott Clark, "My Other House: Lifelong Relationships Among Sisters of the Hayashi Family," in *Lives in Motion: Composing Circles of Self and Community*

My observations of one family reveal four ways in which the network of *shinseki* operated. (These correspond closely with Koyama's four categories, even though I devised my categories before reading Koyama's study.) In addition to rites of passage, such as funerals and weddings, the areas of cooperation were (1) marriage arrangement, (2) assistance in crises, (3) practical advice and information, and (4) companionship and social life. Not all the marriages were successful, and the aid and advice were not always solicited or even wanted and did not always turn out helpful to the recipient. Sometimes a well-meaning (or not so well-meaning) relative only made matters worse. The family was not without its share of failures, conflicts, and gossip. Nevertheless, the degree of interaction among family members, which sometimes included the exchange of considerable amounts of money, was vital to their wellbeing. I argue that the family network helps explain, in particular, how the sisters survived several perilous times in their lives.

The Operation of the Family Network

MARRIAGE ARRANGEMENT

We can imagine the money and effort involved in finding suitable mates for seven sons and seven daughters, a project that began in the 1920s and ended in 1956, with the remarriage of the youngest daughter. The seven daughters of the twelfth generation who, except for the oldest, were born one after the other between 1912 and 1924, met their husbands through marriages arranged with the help of family members

The search for appropriate spouses for so many girls was made more difficult because, despite their rural roots, all the girls had been sent to Tokyo around the age of ten (roughly the second and third decades of the twentieth century or the Taishō and early Shōwa periods) for further schooling. All had studied at prestigious private girls schools—Nihon joshi daigaku and Jiyū gakuen. No ordinary farmer's son could qualify as a husband for such well-

in Japan, ed. Susan O. Long (Ithaca, N.Y.: East Asia Program, Cornell University, 1999), pp. 41–58.

educated, citified girls. Indeed, the purpose of their Tokyo education was to prepare these farmer's daughters (albeit rich ones) to
serve as wives of college-educated men in the newly emerging,
salaried, urban middle-class. Whereas previous generations had been
married to fellow rural dwellers—the sons and daughters of other
village heads, for example, or to relatives, such as second cousins,
living nearby—this generation was on its way up and out of village
Japan, destined to marry strangers and to leave the countryside.

Their parents' education strategy proved successful: all the
daughters were married to college graduates in ceremonies that took
place in Tokyo, usually at a famous catering establishment in the
Ueno district of the city. Further befitting the upwardly mobile aspirations of the family, the daughters received from their parents
the bride's traditional trousseau of a sewing box, a chest of drawers
(*tansu*), and a mirror made of paulownia wood from Aizu Waka-
yama at a cost of approximately $6,000. [22] The eldest daughter's
husband, a member of a prominent family of native Tokyoites de-
scended from samurai lineage, confessed that he would not have
agreed to the match if she had not been a graduate of a prestigious
women's college.

The brothers proved helpful in finding marriage partners for
their sisters. This is the one area, in fact, where male kin played a
more important role than the women of the family. Having themselves studied at top men's universities like Tokyo Imperial and
Keiō, they had made friends with men later matched with their sisters. One woman's husband, for example, had rowed together with
her brother in a regatta club at Keiō. Another woman's husband,
although chosen through her father's contacts, knew her brother,
who had attended Tokyo Imperial University with him. Finding a
husband for the youngest daughter proved difficult because she
came of age at the end of World War II, when marriageable men
were scarce. Her marriage failed after only six years, and several
years afterward, she was remarried, this time to a Keiō University

---

22. The cost, ¥600,000, in Japanese currency, is estimated in 1993 dollar-*yen*
currency exchange rates. Brides also gave gifts to all members of their new husband's household, including the servants.

doctor whom she met through one of her older brothers, also a graduate of that university.

All the marriages, including the divorced sister's second one, were long-lasting, and several of the husbands had successful careers in the corporate world or as physicians. Nevertheless, there were many times in the sisters' married lives and after they were widowed when they relied on help from their natal home and their siblings to rescue them from crises.

ASSISTANCE IN CRISES

Family members came to one another's aid at critical times, providing cash, housing, medical attention, and other help. The Pacific War was one such time. By 1942, most of the brothers and husbands were serving in the military overseas. When Tokyo, where many of the siblings had settled, was bombed toward the end of the war, the sisters and sisters-in-law returned to the family home in the countryside. At one time, over 35 people, mainly women, children, and the elderly, were living there. Faithful servants of their parents and the sisters themselves grew food on the family's land.

After the war, family members continued to prove generous in opening their homes to one another. Three of the sisters and their husbands and children moved into new houses on the site of their parents' Tokyo property, where their father had originally built a large residence to house the children during their school years. One sister's two-story house, which had remained standing in the western suburbs of Tokyo, housed her divorced youngest sister, two of her brothers, and her husband's brother and sister-in-law. (Meanwhile, her husband remained in Russia as a prisoner of war until 1949.) When a sister who had survived the atom bombing of Hiroshima fell sick a few years later, the youngest sister traveled to Hiroshima to check on her condition and arranged for another sister's husband, a doctor, to get the ailing woman and her young daughter into the sanatorium where he worked. In the 1950s, this same sister and her daughter, newly returned from her husband's overseas post, stayed with another sister until they could resettle.

Help also came over the years from the siblings' natal home while the parents were still alive. Wartime conditions, of course, were extraordinary, but there were many other times when the parents came to the aid of their married children. For example, in the late 1930s, they arranged to send a village girl to one daughter's home in Manchuria to work as a servant. Later, they sent another maid to their newly remarried youngest daughter to help with household responsibilities. During her first marriage in the late 1940s, her parents had money and food delivered to her, since her husband, a medical student, was not earning an income.

After the death of their parents, the sisters relied even more on the network of relatives. Numerous examples illustrate the ready flow of resources, including money, among the married siblings. In times of serious illness and death, the sibling network was especially active. The socially expected, minimal obligation of relatives at such times is to visit hospitalized relatives and attend funerals. When their second oldest sister was hospitalized, each sibling contributed about $100 to her daughter as "condolence money." Three nephews also chipped in. When I arrived from the United States to pay a condolence call on her, the siblings contributed more money to my hostess, their youngest sister, to cover all her expenses and mine for the week that I was in Tokyo. Additional money was collected to tip the nurse. Money was exchanged so frequently for certain occasions that there was even a tacit understanding about appropriate amounts: in the mid-1990s, $100 for funerals and $300 per couple for weddings.

The siblings did more, however, than send money to their dying sister. Two of her brothers-in-law took it upon themselves to ask her daughter's boss to give her leave time to care for her mother. The youngest sister and her daughter went to the woman's house to clean it in preparation for the funeral, and she sent her handyman to the house of the deceased woman to remove the furniture from the living room in order to accommodate the mourners.

In addition to housing, loans, and outright gifts of cash, the sisters also provided medical, psychological, labor, and other support services. For example, they helped to care for one another's children and husbands in time of illness. When the second youngest sister's only child died suddenly, her widowed youngest sister temporarily moved in with the grieving parents to help them recover from the tragedy, and she took their brain-damaged grand-daughter on holidays to her country home. When the eldest sister's husband was dying, the two youngest sisters helped prepare his meals.

PRACTICAL ADVICE AND INFORMATION

The sisters routinely provided practical advice and assistance both to family members who asked for help and to those who did not. Advice covered such domestic matters as recipes, proper dress for social events, and appropriate gifts for specific occasions. When I first came to live with one sister in the 1960s, she consulted almost daily, or so it seemed, with another sister about what to feed me. When household members, myself included, had medical problems, she sought advice from a brother-in-law who was a doctor. After her death in 1993, her younger sister helped the deceased woman's middle-aged daughter choose new drapes and carpet for the house in preparation for the engagement ceremony of the niece's daughter. She also accompanied the engaged girl to the bridal shop for several fittings.

Advice occasionally graded into nagging, criticism, and moral exhortation. The sisters were critical of a niece who controlled her mother's activities and urged the older woman to be more assertive. In another example, one sister constantly urged another niece, an employed, middle-aged mother of three, to pay more attention to her physical appearance, bluntly recommending makeup to cover facial blemishes and clothing styles more flattering to her figure. The niece, in turn, advised this same aunt on how to handle a diffi-cult son-in-law.

The husbands of the women were also pressed into family ser-vice, mainly for medical help or career counseling. Thus, when one son announced that he wanted to become an audio engineer, the father, hoping the boy would become a salaried employee of a ma-jor company instead, took him to see his brother-in-law, who, be-cause he was well off and highly respected in his field, was chosen to "talk sense" to the young man. The brother-in-law, however, ruled that the boy should do what he wanted to do. Another uncle was asked to reason with a great-nephew who, because his parents were divorced and his grandfather dead, had no male relatives in his immediate household. The boy had dropped out of high school, and no amount of advice from his great-uncle could persuade him to return. His great-uncle pronounced the situation hopeless, because the boy's mother was not firm enough with him. (Nevertheless, the great-aunts took every opportunity to urge his mother, the older sister, and even me to remonstrate with him.) This same uncle helped the boy's sister choose a college in the United States after she graduated from the business school where he taught. In these ways, men of the family were delegated to handle the man's sphere—the "outside world" of business and career choices.

As some of these examples illustrate, family members, especially the sisters, always felt free to offer advice and to intervene in their own children's lives, no matter how old the children were. An errant husband's employer was even contacted by his widowed mother-in-law after his reckless handling of money proved harmful to her daughter. The company stepped in, forced the son-in-law, then almost 50 years old, to retire, and reallocated his company pension to his debtors and his wife, from whom he was estranged. Another sister contacted her son-in-law's parents when he pressured her for loans.

In all these ways, then, the extended family over the years operated a mutual assistance society, whose members not only directly helped one another but also served as intermediaries between relatives and employers, doctors, potential spouses, misbehaving spouses, and children. One area in which the family network did not operate, however, was employment. In contrast to Koyama's study, I found no evidence of relatives helping one another to find work. Even in the case of the woman divorced in her early forties, it was her mother's friend, not her mother's relatives, who helped her get a job.

Although the extended family network was obviously a positive benefit for the sisters, at times the advice passed back and forth among the women was unwise or hurtful. The sorts of interpersonal tensions found in most families also hounded this one. Thus, in the eyes of some of her nieces, one aunt was a busybody; to her other sisters, another woman was a chatterbox. A third had a reputation for being a little cheap. Sometimes relatives took steps to conceal their activities from the others for fear of meddling or criticism or simply because their problems were too embarrassing to share. Financial difficulties, discord between mother and daughter, and unfaithful husbands constituted the kinds of subject not easily discussed among all the siblings, although one sister might quietly borrow money from another sibling without telling any of the others or reveal confidences to only one trusted family member. Nevertheless, all the sisters remained lifelong friends and companions.

COMPANIONSHIP AND SOCIAL LIFE

Old family photographs spanning the eight decades between the 1920s and the 1990s bear testimony to the many occasions that brought the sisters together. Wedding pictures feature representatives of the *ie* and extended family, including the bride and groom's uncles, aunts, grandparents, and married siblings and their spouses. A sister's departure with her husband and child for an overseas job in Brazil in the 1950s was the occasion for a farewell gathering and a separate photograph of all the sisters and their children.

The women's father also remained in their lives. He came regularly to Tokyo in his later years after the war and stayed with one or another of his fourteen living offspring. In fact, he died in Tokyo of a stroke, and his body had to be sent back to his village for burial in the family cemetery. Other menfolk—brothers and husbands—appeared less frequently at family events, mainly attending weddings and funerals.

Throughout their married life, the sisters socialized with one another whenever they could, as long as doing so did not cause them to neglect their household responsibilities. A husband home for the day, ill, or retired constituted one such constraining circumstance: the women felt they had to "take care of" their husbands. In their later years, with their husbands deceased, the sisters frequently traveled together, with the oldest four going in one group, and the youngest two or three in another. Well into old age, the sisters continued to travel together overseas or to hot springs and on visits to their ancestral graves. The widow of a brother, who lived near the natal home, often joined them. All the sisters and their sister-in-law attended a kabuki performance together once a year.

In addition to vacations and other common outings, the sisters remained in telephone contact. The youngest sister, phoned by an older one every day, complained that she could not get through her daily chores because the telephone started ringing at 8 o'clock every morning. During the week I was in Tokyo to visit the hospitalized sister, who had treated me like a daughter when I had stayed with her in my student days, I received five phone calls from family members, was taken out to lunch and dinner by three other family members and their spouses and grand-children, had lunch at my hostess's house with four of her sisters and her married daughter, saw the hospitalized sister's daughter and three grandchildren, and met the fiancé of one of the grandchildren. All together, in the course of seven days, I was in touch with twenty relatives, including two nephews who phoned from other cities

Relatives of the siblings' spouses were only rarely included in the social network, although women living with their mothers-in-law might bring them along for a family outing, and during the wartime, the women's in-laws were sheltered with them in their natal village. Two fathers-in-law who died at the family's home during the war received proper burials in the family cemetery.

The married sisters not only stayed in close touch with one an-other into old age but continued to maintain ties to their natal vil-lage as well. They regularly returned to their home village to visit the family graves and to see a few familiar villagers, such as the lo-cal Buddhist priest and an old married couple who used to live in their home as servants.

The Significance of the Family Network

The family described here gives ample evidence of the social bonds among relatives in Japan. Indeed, my anecdotal evidence suggests even more frequent contact among family members than the re-sults of the survey research that Koyama and Nojiri did in the 1960s and 1970s, respectively.

The family network is significant for a number of reasons. First, it helps explain how women adapted to their new lives as urban dwellers in their husband's households. In essence, they recreated useful aspects of the kinship associations of village Japan and sustained these even in the absence of the kind of close, day-to-day physical contact and shared agricultural work and community concerns typical of village life. Much as with immigrants to the United States, kin ties played a more important role in their lives than did relationships with neighbors, friends, residentially based social networks, or government agencies. Indeed, in some cases kin ties meant more to them emotionally than their relationship with their own husbands.

Unlike many immigrants to America's shores, however, the sisters could return home again, at least temporarily, in times of need.[23] The social significance and function of wider kinship relations, therefore, bears close attention when we talk about the role of the "family" in modern Japanese history. The modified extended family helped ease the strain of urban migration in the course of industrialization and reduced the isolation of the urban nuclear family. So, too, did ongoing care from parents. "*Shinseki*," writes Hamabata, "are . . . a structural manifestation of this movement between *ie* and *uchi*, a linkage of households through the social and emotional ties that bind."[24]

Why did parents provide this long-term investment of resources in their married daughters? In terms of material repayment, they received little in return.[25] They genuinely cared about their daughters' wellbeing, however. Strong affective ties characterized their relationship to their children.[26] In addition, if the marriages failed,

---

23. One exception is the Mexican American immigration pattern: Mexican Americans tend to maintain ties with their families in Mexico and to cross the border frequently.

24. Hamabata, *Crested Kimono*, p. 141.

25. For his medical problems, the father consulted his fourth son and two sons-in-law who were all doctors; the mother, who contracted tuberculosis, was also cared for by her fourth-born son.

26. Anne Walthall portrays a similar affective bond between the daughter of a rural family and her parents in the Tokugawa period in "Fille de paysan, épouse de samouraï: les lettres de Yoshino Michi," in *Annales histoire sciences sociales* 54, no. 1 (Jan.–Feb. 1999): 55–86. Daughters in the family described by Scott Clark

they would have had to take their daughters back home, as they did temporarily in one case. Moreover, the marriage of a daughter to a man of higher social standing reflected well on the family's name and improved its social status in the local community. Illustrious connections bolstered their own influence and further separated them socially from their poorer, less cosmopolitan neighbors.[27] Furthermore, as power, wealth, and influence shifted away from the rural landholding class to the urban middle class in the course of Japan's race to modernity, the rural elite, through marriage as well as absentee landownership, established a foothold in the new world.

By the interwar period, spanning the early married years of the sisters' lives, it was already clear that agriculture was a declining occupation. Their father, in his own childhood, had been bitten by the bug of modernity, but he had been prevented from receiving a higher education and access to Tokyo's more modern culture because, as the eldest son, he had to assume his father's role as village head. To compensate for his own disappointment, he lived in Tokyo vicariously through his children, visiting them frequently and trying to promote various business ventures in the nation's capital. Like immigrant parents, he basked in his children's upward mobility, as defined, in the case of his daughters, by their marriage to husbands with professions or managerial-level jobs and their residence in the westernized world of Tokyo.

The study of the family network also illustrates the key role played by women in the household. Kin work was gendered among Japanese migrants to the cities: the job of maintaining the family network was primarily women's work. It is probably for this reason that urban families in Japan have more frequent contacts with the wife's relatives than with the husband's.[28]

("My Other House," p. 48) returned home for advice and consolation when they had marital problems.

27. The social status of relatives can help make a good match, and in turn, a good match can enhance the standing of the relatives. Families seeking a mate for one of their children provided the go-between with information on their relatives.

28. Koyama, "The Significance of Relatives at the Turning Point of the Family System," p. 109. Koyama also found that the "frequency of contact with the wife's

We can see similar sibling ties among Japanese immigrants to
the United States. A study of Japanese Americans in the Seattle
area found that among *nisei*, "sisters are in more frequent contact
than brothers."[29] They phone one another or their mother frequently. They rely on one another for emotional support and
practical help. *Nisei* kin networks, too, are "women centered." Sisters are the "kin keepers who facilitate communication, coordinate
gift exchanges and bring kin together."[30]

Nisei women are central to their family networks not simply
because food is important to family gatherings and women tend to
do the cooking. Rather, Sylvia Yanagisako argues, "women can
negotiate and cooperate with their sisters and mothers much better
than men can cooperate with brothers and fathers."[31] Thus, *nisei*
families reverse the usual Japanese expectation that daughters are
"lost" when they marry; they say that at marriage "a man is lost to
his family," because he is drawn into his wife's family.[32]

Most *nisei* men in Yanagisako's study claimed they have never
felt much in common with their brothers.[33] Because there is
only one heir in the Japanese family, the oldest son—the "heir
apparent"—becomes distanced from his younger brothers. The
successor is perceived by his other brothers as receiving preferen-
tial treatment from their parents. Perhaps these reasons explain the
uterine bias of the *nisei* family.

Although women in contemporary society worldwide appear to
be the creators and preservers of kinship networks, this has not
always been the case. It is true that, in earlier generations of Italian
Americans, the women apparently had an active role in kin work;
in Italy, they even had authority over marriages and occupational
choices for their children and nieces and nephews. They lent
money to relatives, lectured them on proper deportment and ap-

---

relatives (as opposed to the husband's) was greater in the urban sample than the
rural" (ibid., p. 74).

29. Yanagisako, *Transforming the Past*, pp. 215–17.

30. Ibid. The women's ties in this instance, like the sisters' network, tend to be
consanguineous: they are sisters rather than relatives by marriage.

31. Ibid.

32. Ibid.

33. Ibid., p. 230.

pearance, and in other ways demonstrated domestic power through their kin work.[34]

Among *issei* families in Yanagisako's study, however, it was the men who were more active as kin workers, and they created strong bonds with their brothers. Relations between sisters played a lesser role. This may be because in village Japan, brothers tended to be closer to one another than to their sisters: their sisters moved away from the village after marriage, whereas younger brothers were more likely to settle nearby. Even so, these relationships were fairly thin. By the second generation of Japanese Americans, kin work clearly became women's work.

In the case of the family described here, the father performed a great deal of kin work. He traveled frequently to visit his married children and their in-laws, arranged marriages, visited his wife's family members, and, in the family history he wrote, demonstrated a profound commitment to preserving the family's lineage and harmony. Only with the migration of his many children to the city did kin work become women's work. Why did women take over the task of preserving the family network?

The literal sisterhood of the family was crucial to women's survival and successful functioning in their new families because they were largely confined to their homes, whereas their menfolk were often physically absent, as the demands of the new nation-state occupied their energies in either the business or military world. The men were emotionally absent, too, for the family ethics minimized affective ties between them and their wives.

This separation from the man's world was an unfamiliar circumstance for the sisters, who had grown up in the countryside in a large family in which both parents as well as many brothers, grandparents, and male and female servants lived together and shared child-rearing tasks. Both their father and their grandfather, as village leaders, had conducted their business in the home. Their father had taken an active interest in all his children's upbringing and education, helping to bathe them, imparting discipline and a clear sense of moral values, and carefully choosing their schools in Tokyo, where he regularly visited them and their teachers to

---

34. Di Leonardo, *The Varieties of Ethnic Experience*, pp. 213–14.

monitor their progress. He was a visible presence in their lives. In the words of his eldest daughter, he was "an education papa."

In contrast, the husbands of the sisters played a far less signifi- cant role in their urban family life. Not only did the men's salaried work take them away from the home and into the new work places created by industrialization, but they were preoccupied with the demands of company and nation. With no hope of inheriting land from their parents, these salaried workers were freed of exten- sive filial obligations that typically accompanied the heir's rights of inheritance. At the same time, exclusion from inheritance made it all the more imperative to devote themselves to their place of em- ployment. "Kinship ties," Ezra Vogel points out, "did not interfere and, if anything, worked to reinforce the ties between the em- ployer and the employee."[35]

The sisters, who were not employed outside the home, became the main child rearers and household managers, upholding the "good wife, wise mother" (ryōsai kenbo) ideal articulated by Meiji leaders at the turn of the twentieth century and reinforced by the women's alma maters, which had emphasized domestic skills and rational homemaking. They lacked the domestic assistance not only of husbands but of the multiple caregivers typical of their own parents' rural family life. Even the three women who lived with mothers-in-law throughout their children's early years re- ceived little help from the older women, whose ailments required their care. Indeed, by the interwar period, when most of the sisters were starting their married lives, childcare specialists and Home Ministry officials (who themselves tended to be members of the urban middle class) had already adopted the view that mothers played the crucial role in child rearing.[36] This may explain why ar- ticles on parenting in the Taishō period, as described by Harald

---

35. Ezra F. Vogel, "Kinship Structure, Migration to the City, and Moderniza- tion," in Aspects of Social Change in Modern Japan, ed. Ronald P. Dore (Princeton: Princeton University Press, 1967), p. 99.

36. Kathleen S. Uno, Passages to Modernity: Motherhood, Childhood, and Social Reform in Early Twentieth Century Japan (Honolulu: University of Hawai'i Press, 1999), pp. 108, 113. In contrast, founders of day-care facilities for urban poor at the start of the twentieth century "did not assume that mothers alone would take charge of child-rearing (or even housework)" (ibid., p. 56).

Fuess, depicted the home as "a location of paternal recreation with children."

Dependent on their spouses for income but on themselves for everything else, the sisters came to rely on one another for mutual aid, advice, and companionship. They created a "separate sphere" of womanhood, within which they acquired a certain amount of influence and authority. As they became older, they became arbiters of manners and taste, authorities on fashion and cooking, and dispensers of money in the form of cash gifts and loans. Although largely confined to their homes in the early years of their marriage, they could and did draw on a wide network of family members, including brothers and brothers-in-law, for assistance and favors. Moreover, unlike the specific and nonnegotiable obligations encountered by women who lived in their husband's *ie*, they were free to decide how much or how little kin work to do among their own relatives. Depending on the individual woman's economic resources, free time, and life-cycle status, some of the sisters were more active and influential than others: kin work among the relatives was not defined with any degree of specificity, and women could usually choose how much or how little to do. Significantly, when asked whether she and her siblings consciously built kin ties, one sister replied that the ties were "natural," not consciously constructed.

Women in nineteenth-century New England also operated in their own female spheres on a voluntary basis, but their ties reached beyond the realm of relatives. The "bonds of womanhood" extended to organized church groups, which became one of the institutional contexts in which women could "connect purposefully to the community." Such church groups set "a pattern of reliance on female friendships for emotional expression and security."[37] There were also women's clubs, colleges, settlement houses, political organizations, and trade unions, and women's buildings were featured at the International Centennial Exposition in 1876 and the

---

37. Linda K. Kerber, "Separate Spheres, Female Worlds, Woman's Place: The Rhetoric of Women's History," *Journal of American History* 75, no. 1 (June 1988): 15. See also Nancy F. Cott, *The Bonds of Womanhood: "Woman's Sphere" in New England, 1780–1835* (New Haven: Yale University Press, 1977).

World's Columbian Exposition in 1892.[38] In other words, by the late nineteenth century, American women had established a public female sphere.[39]

Although the sisters studied here attended private women's colleges and maintained ties with school friends, their closest support came from one another. To this extent, their kin ties did not lead to feminist activity outside the home or set the stage for social or political activity, even though the older sisters came of age in the turbulent 1920s, when many Japanese women threw themselves into the suffrage movement or joined women's associations.[40] Had their lives not been disrupted by war and closely controlled first by their father and then, in at least two cases, by their mother-in-law, they might conceivably have joined feminist causes or at least worked outside the home. One sister, influenced by educator and journalist Hani Motoko, wanted to work for a women's magazine in the early 1930s, but her father quickly married her off. Other sisters were too young to become active during the heyday of the prewar women's movement, and by the late 1930s and early 1940s, they had either returned to their natal village or were swept into Japan's wartime activities. (Two relocated with their husbands to Manchuria.) The 1950s saw them still struggling to put their lives back together again, with three suffering from tuberculosis. Three of the sisters, in their widowed years, ended up caring for grandchildren whose mothers were employed outside the home.

But these circumstances alone do not explain the absence of political involvement in women's issues among these college-educated women. Although some of the sisters were unhappy with

---

38. Estelle Freedman, "Separatism as Strategy: Female Institution Building and American Feminism, 1870–1930," *Feminist Studies* 5 (Fall 1979): 512–29.

39. Sarah Deutsch's research has uncovered over 1,000 women's organizations in Boston in 1900, with each having from 400 to 1,000 members. All middle-class and elite women belonged to a club by the turn of the century. Working-class women had church groups and informal family networks but were less well institutionally organized. See Deutsch, *Women and the City: Gender, Space, and Power in Boston, 1870–1940* (Oxford: Oxford University Press, 2000).

40. See, e.g., Barbara Molony's chapter in this volume; and Miriam Silverberg, "The Moga as Militant," in *Recreating Japanese Women*, ed. Gail Lee Bernstein (Berkeley: University of California Press, 1991), pp. 239–66.

their husbands (and more typically with their mothers-in-law), their discontent did not rise to the level of open rebellion or even quiet questioning of their roles. They believed in the ethos of the good wife, and they criticized other women who did not carry out their wifely obligations with the same thoroughgoing zeal and efficiency. A female relative, for example, who was not at her dying husband's side night and day earned opprobrium. Another relative's marital problems were explained by her slovenly housekeeping.

The women of the twelfth generation viewed their roles as housewives as demanding, fulltime jobs—the work of "taking care of" their husbands as well as their children and in-laws, for which they were paid by their husband's salaries. They were appreciative of spouses who had worked hard and succeeded in supporting their families. Women whose marriages to husbands, despite their emotional remoteness, had generated bonds of gratitude or security or respect, if not close emotional ties, genuine affection, and physical intimacy, expressed in their later years a sense of pride in a job well done. Indeed, a husband's death constituted a kind of retirement for his wife, although her work continued beyond his death in her performance of the customary daily rituals in his memory.

The women did not see themselves as locked in a power struggle with their spouses or against the "system," nor, unlike the women in Barbara Molony's study in this volume, did they ever consider seeking assistance or recognition from public officials: they did not need to. That their husbands—who were more like business partners with whom they divided the work of family survival—had provided reliably (and entrusted them with their money) was sufficient cause to feel satisfied. They strenuously asserted themselves only when their husband's involvement with another woman threatened the marriage. For entertainment, sympathy, help, or companionship, they turned to one another.

The family network was thus a safety net and an escape valve for its members—especially its female members—and it made women's public roles on behalf of themselves or their families unnecessary. On the other hand, we may need to broaden our notion of what public or societal activities meant for women of this class and generation. Rather than engaging in political activity, the women's way of reaching out beyond their households, and thereby sustaining valuable connections and human interactions, was to create numerous ties, imbedded in the larger family, that served many vital needs.

Relatives shared contacts, information, and resources useful to first-generation urban dwellers in a rapidly changing environment. They engaged in the frequent give-and-take of favors that extended their range of acquaintances even beyond the family to the friends and associates of family members. *Shinseki*, after all, included influential men related by marriage—in-laws who, before their marriage, had been strangers. By harnessing their cooperation, women in the family network gained access, albeit limited and indirectly, to the public or outside "men's world"—to brothers and brothers-in-law who, among other things, lent them money, found them husbands, interceded on behalf of their children, and provided them with medical care. Similarly, a woman could elevate herself in her husband's family by using her influence with her blood kin to help him and his relatives.[41]

Family ties, especially among the women, also eased the strains of women's married lives. The women's association with one another often proved more emotionally gratifying than their relationships with their husbands, and in later years socializing with female kin provided relief for widows from the tensions of living with married children. Instead of seeking to influence politics in behalf of their family's welfare or in the interests of feminist causes, as many other women did in Japan and elsewhere, the sisters sustained a family network that helped them meet the social expectations of them as newly arrived, urban middle-class wives and mothers and that gave them assistance, recognition, sympathy, and social ties outside the male-dominated, but male-absent nuclear family.

Voluntary transactions among urban nuclear families, especially those related on the female side, replaced some of the basic functions associated with rural kindred organizations (*dōzoku*) or with

---

41. There is even a special word, *keibetsu*, to express the network of influential matrimonial alliances established through a wife; see Hamabata, *Crested Kimono*, p. 147.

groupings of close neighbors who often were also relatives (*kumi*) in agricultural villages. We cannot necessarily assume, therefore, that industrialization and urbanization resulted in the complete isolation of the urban, middle-class Japanese nuclear family. The frequent contacts seen among the sisters demonstrate their reworking and flexible adaptation of several types of Japanese family institutions to meet the demands of modern, urban life and, in particular, to meet the needs of women in the family.[42] Although the nuclear family and the *ie* may have remained male-dominated, the network of the modified extended family had a woman-centered character.

---

42. Ties among sisters seem to be declining in contemporary Japan. Given the smaller size of families, fewer women have sisters, and women in the current generation probably rely more on their mothers than on their sisters. Women living in cities, apart from extended families, may also seek advice on such matters as gift giving and proper attire for social events like weddings from tea ceremony teachers, according to Barbara Lynne Rowland Mori, "The Traditional Arts as Leisure Activities for Contemporary Japanese Women," in *Re-imaging Japanese Women*, ed. Anne Imamura (Berkeley: University of California Press, 1996), pp. 117–34.

PART IV

Empire and Its Consequences

CHAPTER TEN

Rethinking Japanese-Chinese Cultural Relations in the 1930s

See Heng Teow

In view of the Japanese military invasion of China and the protracted war there, it is not surprising that the literature on Japanese-Chinese relations in the 1930s focuses largely on political, strategic, military, diplomatic, and economic issues. Significant as these issues are, it is also important to explore the cultural dimensions of Japanese-Chinese relations. This chapter studies Japan's cultural policy toward China as manifested in the activities of the Cultural Affairs Division (Bunka jigyōbu; CAD) of the Ministry of Foreign Affairs (Gaimushō) from the outbreak of the Manchurian Incident in 1931 to the eve of the Marco Polo Bridge Incident of 1937. It discusses the Japanese government's perception of cultural relations with China, particularly its handling of the question of "learning" from China versus "teaching" China and its management of issues that surfaced in its attempt to "import" and "export" ideas, values, education, scholarship, medicine, science, and technology.

Much of the scholarship on this topic stresses Japanese cultural imperialism toward China, which is seen to have begun in the 1890s with Japan's establishment of cultural and educational institutions, hospitals, and newspapers in China. Scholars argue that this cultural offensive intensified in the 1920s with the establishment of the China Cultural Affairs Bureau (Tai-Shi bunka jimu-kyoku) in May 1923 and its restructuring as the CAD in December

1924 and that in the 1930s the CAD served primarily as an instrument for the military invasion of China.[1] Although the issue of cultural imperialism is relevant, it is a complex concept that requires many levels of analysis, from the intent of policy to its implementation to its consequences, a task beyond the scope of a short essay. Instead, this chapter explores one facet of the complex mix of elements characterizing relations in this period. By highlighting the wide range of activities carried out by the CAD, it illustrates the multitude of perspectives needed to understand Japanese-Chinese cultural relations during this period of escalating military, political, and economic tensions.

Origins and Development of the Cultural Affairs Division

The CAD originated in the Law for the Creation of a Special Account for Cultural Work Directed Toward China (*Tai-Shi bunka jigyō tokubetsu kaikeihō*), passed by the Japanese Diet in March 1923. Funding for the Special Account was to be derived from the remaining principal and interest on Japan's Boxer indemnity (¥72 million) and the income and interest derived from the settlement of rights pertaining to Shantung railway properties (¥14.5 million), salt enterprises (¥5.3 million), and mining ventures (¥2.33 million), for a total of ¥94.13 million. The Special Account was to finance activities in the areas of education, scholarship, public health, relief work, and other cultural undertakings both in China and among Chinese citizens residing in Japan, as well as scholarly research on China in Japan. Annual expenditures from the Special Account were initially set at ¥2.5 million and then at ¥3.0 million, beginning in 1926. Any surplus was to be kept as a reserve fund to enable the continuation of activities following the cessation of the Shantung Treaty in 1938 and the Boxer Protocol in 1945. The government

---

1. See, e.g., Huang Fuqing, *Jindai Riben zai-Hua wenhua ji shehui shiye zhi yanjiu* (Japanese social and cultural enterprises in China) (Taibei: Academia Sinica, 1982); and Wang Shuhuai, *Gengzi peikuan* (The Boxer indemnity) (Taibei: Academia Sinica, 1974). For my evaluation of the issue of cultural imperialism, see See Heng Teow, *Japan's Cultural Policy Toward China, 1918–1931: A Comparative Perspective* (Cambridge, Mass.: Harvard University Asia Center, 1999), pp. 124–62.

was responsible for presenting annual estimates of revenues and expenditures to the Diet.[2] In May, the China Cultural Affairs Bureau was created within the Ministry of Foreign Affairs to administer and oversee the programs of the Special Account.

The creation of the account and the establishment of the bureau were landmark events. They represented the Japanese government's first effort at cultural diplomacy through the institutionalization of cultural policy toward China. The long-term focus of the policy was clear: at an annual expenditure of ¥2.5 million, the total of ¥94.13 million would finance the proposed cultural programs for 37 years.

With the emergence of Manchukuo in March 1932, Japan added a program of cultural work toward Manchuria (*Tai-Man bunka jigyō*) under the CAD. As part of this effort, the Japan-Manchuria Cultural Association (Nichi-Man bunka kyōkai), a semigovernmental

---

2. The Boxer indemnity was compensation for damages incurred during an antiforeign uprising in 1900 by members of a secret society known as the Boxers. According to the Boxer Protocol signed in 1901, China had to pay a total of 450 million silver taels to the foreign powers involved. The United States was the first nation that remitted a portion of its share of the indemnity, allocating it strictly for educational purposes. Japan was the next to do so, followed by France, the Soviet Union, Belgium, Italy, Great Britain, and the Netherlands. The information presented here is extracted from the Special Account Bill. For an English translation, see Sir C. Eliot to the Marquis Curzon of Kedleston, Apr. 13, 1923, in Great Britain, *China Confidential Print*, Foreign Office Publication 405 Series (microfilmed series), FO 405/240, pp. 155–59; and for the original Japanese version, see Dai Nihon teikoku gikai shi kankōkai, comp., *Dai Nihon teikoku gikai shi* (Records of the Imperial Diet of Japan) (Tokyo, 1930), 14: 1031. For secondary sources regarding the Special Account, see Wang, *Gengzi peikuan*; Huang, *Jindai Riben*; Abe Hiroshi, "*Tai-Shi bunka jigyō*" no kenkyū: kindai Nit-Chū gakujutsu bunka kōryūshi no ichidanmen (Research on "Japanese cultural work toward China": one aspect of the history of Sino-Japanese cultural interchanges in modern times) (Tokyo: Ajia keizai kenkyū-jo, 1976); Kawamura Kazuo, "Tai-Shi bunka jigyō kankei shi: kanseijō yori mitaru" (A history of Japanese cultural work toward China: a bureaucratic perspective), *Rekishi kyōiku* 15, no. 8 (Aug. 1967): 80–95; Yamane Yukio, *Kindai Nit-Chū kankei no kenkyū: tai-Ka bunka jigyō o chūshin to shite* (Research on Sino-Japanese relations in modern times: focusing on Japanese cultural work toward China) (Tokyo: Tōkyō joshi daigaku tōyōshi kenkyūshitsu, 1980); Sophia Lee, "The Foreign Ministry's Cultural Agenda for China: The Boxer Indemnity," in *The Japanese Informal Empire in China, 1895–1937*, ed. Peter Duus et al. (Princeton: Princeton University Press, 1989), pp. 272–306; and Teow, *Japan's Cultural Policy*.

organization, was established in October 1933. Following Japan's withdrawal from the League of Nations in 1933, the Foreign Ministry found it even more important for Japan to maintain links with the international community. To this end, in 1934, an "outside agency" of the Foreign Ministry, the Society for International Cultural Relations (Kokusai bunka shinkōkai), was created to strengthen cultural ties with nations in the West. By August 1935, the CAD had been reorganized into three departments. The First Department oversaw the implementation of cultural work. It had three sections: the first handled China-related institutions and students' affairs; the second was responsible for Japanese-Chinese cultural exchanges and a plethora of cultural projects and events; the third managed new cultural enterprises. The Second Department, responsible for general and miscellaneous matters, focused on the financial aspects of cultural programs. The Third Department supervised Japan's cultural relations with countries other than China and Manchuria and worked in tandem with the Society for International Cultural Relations to promote cultural diplomacy. Under its auspices, Japan engaged in cultural exchanges with, among other countries, the United States, Great Britain, France, Brazil, Mexico, Germany, Italy, Hungary, Austria, Iran, Iraq, Afghanistan, India, Siam, and the Philippines. A total of twenty people staffed the CAD. This organizational structure persisted until the eve of the Marco Polo Bridge Incident.[3]

---

3. On the restructuring of the CAD, see Gaimushō hyakunenshi hensan iinkai, comp., *Gaimushō no hyakunen* (A hundred years of the Foreign Ministry) (Tokyo: Hara shobō, 1969), 1: 1039–48; *Bunka 18: Shōwa jūichi nendo shitsumu hōkoku* (Official report, 1936), Dec. 1, 1936, in "Chōsho: Bunka jigyōbu" (Reports: Cultural Affairs Division), Japanese Foreign Ministry Archives (hereafter JFMA); and "Bunka gaikō sasshin ni Gaimushō iyoiyo nodasu" (The Gaimushō embarks on reforming cultural diplomacy), *Asahi shinbun*, May 30, 1935, in H.2.2.0.2-4: Nihon no taido (Japan's attitude), JFMA. On Diet discussions on cultural diplomacy, see "Ippan taigai bunka jigyō jisshi sokushin ni kansuru Gikai no tōgi ni kansuru ken" (Materials pertaining to Diet discussions on promoting and implementing general aspects of cultural diplomacy), in H.0.0.0.1: Tōhō bunka jigyō kankei zaryō (Miscellaneous materials pertaining to Oriental cultural work), II, JFMA; and "Bunka 24: Kokusai bunka jigyō ni kansuru dai rokujūshichi teikoku gikai jijutsu kiroku shōroku" (A summary of the records of the 67th Imperial Diet's discussion of matters pertaining to international cultural work), in "Chōsho: Bunka jigyōbu,"

Motivations and Concerns

International cultural rivalries, pragmatic interests, and a blend of ethnocentrism, moralism, and idealism motivated the Japanese state to initiate a cultural policy toward China in 1923. The government was perturbed by the increase in Western influence in China, as seen in the proliferation of Western educational institutions and the growing number of Chinese students in Western countries. At the same time, it was concerned about the rising anti-Japanese sentiments among the Chinese. These concerns convinced the Foreign Ministry that the education of Chinese students was particularly important because, it was believed, many of these students would later rise to positions of authority and play decisive roles in Chinese relations with Japan. In addition, many Diet members and intellectuals felt that Japan had a responsibility to "civilize" China because of the historical ties between the two countries and their position as close neighbors that shared the same culture and were of the same race (*dōbun dōshu*). Some, influenced by Wilsonian ideals of universalism and global goodwill, held that by helping to civilize China, Japan would contribute to world peace and civilization.[4]

These same motives also explain the continuation and expansion of the state's cultural policy toward China in the 1930s. The Japanese government was concerned to protect its national interests and aspirations in China, especially Manchuria and North China. It saw its legitimate interests threatened increasingly by the Guomindang government and Chinese nationalism. Japanese military leaders regarded Manchuria and North China as buffer zones

JFMA. For details on the Kokusai bunka shinkōkai and Japan's international cultural diplomacy, see Shibasaki Atsushi, *Kindai Nihon to kokusai bunka kōryū: Kokusai bunka shinkōkai no sōsetsu to tenkai* (International cultural relations and modern Japan: History of the Kokusai bunka shinkōkai, 1934–45) (Tokyo: Yūshindō kōbunsha, 1999); Kokusai bunka shinkōkai, comp., *Honpō kokusai bunka dantai benran* (A handbook of international cultural organizations in Japan) (Tokyo: Kokusai bunka shinkōkai, 1934); and the collection of documents in I.1.1.0.1: *Honpō kakkoku kan bunka kokan kankei zakken* (Miscellaneous materials on Japan's cultural relations with other countries), JFMA.

4. For details, see Teow, *Japan's Cultural Policy*, pp. 32–51, 174–80.

against Russian power and Soviet communism; Japanese businesses also had much at stake in this region.[5] In the 1930s, the government gradually developed a new concept of regionalism, first by advocating an autonomous and self-sufficient empire comprising Japan, Manchuria, and North China. In April 1934 it enunciated the Amau Doctrine, which claimed China as Japan's sole responsibility; this was reaffirmed in August 1936 when the Hirota cabinet called for the increased military and economic integration of Japan, Manchuria, and North China. These policy statements eventually led to the declaration of Japan's New Order in East Asia in November 1938 and the Greater East Asian Co-prosperity Sphere in 1940.

Government officials also considered cultural factors important in the promotion of Japanese political and economic interests in China. For instance, a May 1937 Foreign Ministry report advocated that the CAD perform a variety of roles, such as improving understanding between the people of China and Japan, bringing stability to the lives of the Chinese people, promoting the mutual survival of China and Japan, collecting intelligence, creating Japanese-Chinese political organizations under the guise of culture, and investigating the patterns of Chinese thought and education.[6] Two years earlier, in 1935, another Foreign Ministry proposal on reforming Japan's cultural work toward China had noted that since Chinese students in Japan would likely be the future pillars of Japanese-Chinese amity, close attention should be paid to grooming them. More student exchanges were needed, and the research facilities at the graduate schools of Japanese imperial universities should be expanded to absorb more Chinese students.[7]

Others outside the Foreign Ministry shared this goal of developing cultural ties with China. For example, Doihara Kenji, a China expert in the Japanese army, contended that the idea of culture should not be limited to the realm of arts and scholarship but be

---

5. John K. Fairbank et al., *East Asia: Tradition and Transformation* (Boston: Houghton Mifflin, 1973), pp. 705–7, 714.

6. See "Bunka jigyōbu jigyō oyobi Bunka jigyōbu ni kansuru shiken" (The Cultural Affairs Division and personal views on the Cultural Affairs Division), May 1937, in H.o.o.o.1, II, JFMA.

7. See "Tai-Shi bunka jigyō kaizen an" (Proposal to reform Japan's cultural work toward China), 1935, in H.2.2.0.2-4, JFMA.

broadened to encompass economics. It was important for Japan to respond to the rising tide of communist ideology in the East and to finish establishing the economic bloc encompassing Japan, Manchuria, and China. Nakayama Natsumi, a staff member of the Pan-Asiatic Association (Dai-Ajia kyōkai), which was established in March 1933 by Japanese right-wing nationalists to promote unity among Asians, similarly argued that the CAD had withstood the test of time and should be continued, but its budget should be increased so that it could undertake experimental, economic, and industrial ventures to promote bilateral economic cooperation.[8]

Foreign Ministry officials were equally wary of the increasing international cultural rivalries in China. Other countries had also been remitting their Boxer indemnities for cultural programs, and, from 1931 to 1937, they could be said to be more successful than Japan since their programs had the endorsement of the Chinese government. The programs of the British and the Americans were especially popular. The British had been investing the bulk of their Boxer funds in industrial projects such as railway rehabilitation and water control, with the profits used for educational and other cultural purposes. Many Chinese viewed this emphasis on industrialism as more beneficial than purely cultural projects. Like the Japanese, the Americans focused on culture, with grants to students and various educational and cultural bodies, but their efforts were seen as less politically motivated than those of the Japanese.[9] Not surprisingly, voices within the government urged that Japan counteract the perceived surge of Western influence in China. One reform proposal saw China as being overwhelmed by Western cul-

---

8. See Doihara Kenji, "Kōdō bunka no hatten to Nichi-Man-Shi teikei" (The development of the culture of the imperial way and the cooperation of Japan, Manchuria, and China); and Nakayama Natsumi, "Bunka teki Nihon no sōzō" (The creation of a cultural Japan), both in "Tai-Shi bunka jigyō ni kansuru kaku hōmen no hihan oyobi iken" (Various criticisms and opinions pertaining to Japan's cultural work toward China), Jan. 1937, in H.o.o.o.1, II, JFMA. On the Pan-Asiatic Association, see Lydia N. Yu-Jose, "Japanese Organizations and the Philippines, 1930s–1941," *Journal of International Studies* (Sophia University, Tokyo), 33 (Apr. 1994): 91–96.

9. For details on the American and British remissions, see Teow, *Japan's Cultural Policy*, pp. 92–123.

ture and advocated greater efforts to attract the brightest Chinese
students to Japan instead of the United States, Great Britain, and
France, which was the prevailing trend.[10]

Other sentiments motivated Japan's cultural policy toward
China during this period. The Great Depression had not only
plunged many liberal-democratic nations in the West into an economic abyss but also created political and ideological uncertainties.
Many Western intellectuals and policymakers started to doubt that
liberal democracy could save their nations, and alternative ideologies such as fascism, Nazism, and communism rapidly gained
ground. Since Japan recovered from the economic depression earlier than the West, right-wing nationalists increasingly felt that the
Japanese cultural approach might be the solution to the social ills
of the day, particularly for Asian countries. Japan, as the predomi-
nant Asian power, could help restore the cultural heritage of China,
which had long been the cradle of Oriental (Tōhō) civilization, and,
together, the two nations could then promote Oriental civilization
at the global level. For Nakayama Natsumi, the phrase "light
emerges from the East" was particularly apt. Ishii Fumio, a com-
mentator on cultural issues whose articles were published in the
journal *Shina* (China), argued that whereas China had represented
the Orient in the past, Japan had now assumed that role; Japan had
become the elder brother and parent, and China, the younger
brother and child.[11] Likewise Nakatani Takeyo, a publications of-

---

10. See "Tai-Shi bunka jigyō kaizen an." For other accounts, see the collection
of documents in H.2.2.0.2-2: Beikoku no taido (America's attitude), III, JFMA;
H.2.2.0.2-3: Eikoku no taido (Britain's attitude), II, III, JFMA; and H.2.2.0.2-5:
Kakkoku no taido (The attitudes of various countries), II, III, IV, JFMA. See also
Bunka 62: Ōshū shokoku ni ikeru Shina ryūgakusei ni kansuru chōsa (Investigation
on Chinese students in the various countries of Europe), July 1933; *Bunka 66:
Eikoku no danpi baishōkin shobunpō* (The management of Britain's Boxer indem-
nity), July 1936; *Bunka 69: Tōhō shokoku ni ikeru kakkoku no bunka jigyō* (The cul-
tural work of various countries in the countries of Asia), Apr. 1936; and *Bunka 71:
Kakkoku no danpi baishōkin shobun mondai* (The matter of the management of the
Boxer indemnities of the various countries), Oct. 1932, all in "Chōsho: Bunka jigyōbu," JFMA.

11. See Nakayama, "Bunka teki Nihon no sōzō"; Ishii Fumio, "Shina jikyoku to
Nis-Shi bunka teikei" (The situation of China and Sino-Japanese cultural cooperation), both in "Tai-Shi bunka jigyō ni kansuru kaku hōmen no hihan oyobi iken";

ficer of the Pan-Asiatic Association, maintained that, for better or worse, Japan, Manchuria, and China had a common destiny, an East Asian destiny. Yet, before there could be an Asian renaissance, he held, there had to be a Chinese renaissance, and to bring this about, Japan had to share with its neighbors the culture that it had preserved, accumulated, digested, and refined. In a similar vein, Nakayama contended that to regard Manchukuo as merely another manifestation of imperialism would be to distort the truth, since the underlying reason for Japan's action there was the promotion of culture.[12]

These approaches can be seen as an attempt to stress Japan's role as cultural leader of East Asia, provide the appropriate cultural justification for Japan's status as the only major Asian power, and enhance Japan's national prestige on the international scene. At the same time, right-wing nationalists saw the promotion of an Oriental cultural order in East Asia as a means of countering the cultural approach of the Western powers toward China, which they regarded as aimed at promoting Western values and thus as inimical to China's as well as Japan's interests.

Others emphasized the idealist premises of cultural interaction. They highlighted the significance of culture in the realm of ideas and ideals and attached importance to intellectual and cultural pursuits for their own sake. They further contended that cultural policy should be divorced from politics, economics, and other materialistic concerns and that the elements of reciprocity, educational benefits, and long-term commitments should be stressed.

Members of the medical community were among the most active advocates of this stance. One key example was the Universal Benevolence Association (Dōjinkai). Founded in 1902, it received partial support from CAD to promote medicine and public health

---

and Teow, *Japan's Cultural Policy*, pp. 175–76. For a similar view by a Chinese professor, see Jiang Kanghu, "Tōhō bunka no fukkō" (The revival of Oriental culture), in "Tai-Shi bunka jigyō ni kansuru kaku hōmen no hihan oyobi iken."

12. See Nakatani Takeyo, "Hoku-Shi shisō kōsaku no jūyōsei o ronzu" (A discussion of the importance of ideological work in North China), in "Tai-Shi bunka jigyō ni kansuru kaku hōmen no hihan oyobi iken"; and Nakayama, "Bunka teki Nihon no sōzō." See also Akira Iriye, *China and Japan in the Global Setting* (Cambridge, Mass.: Harvard University Press, 1992), pp. 66–83.

in Asian countries. The association operated four hospitals in China, one each in Beijing, Hankou, Qingdao, and Ji'nan. Despite the impression of many Chinese that these hospitals served primarily Japanese residents in China, during the period 1931 to 1937, three of the four hospitals had more Chinese (630,383) than Japanese (358,650) patients; only the hospital in Qingdao served more Japanese (469,753) than Chinese (266,053) patients. [13] Various members of the association argued for further altruistic activities in this area. Iwanari Ishihito suggested that more hospitals be set up in China, free medicine be dispensed through Chinese provincial governments, family medical books and kits be popularized, and medical textbooks translated. Terazaki Yoshitarō, a doctor who worked at the hospital in Hankou, hoped that Japanese and Chinese doctors would form a China Medical Association, which would be an ideal organization to promote Japanese-Chinese culture and for Japan to learn more about Chinese medicine, as well as to ensure the position of Chinese doctors in China. Likewise Katayomi Sanehito, another member of the Dōjinkai, argued that profit considerations could not be part of cultural work; only when activities were done for the sake of humanity and society, such as the practice of medicine to save lives, could they be regarded as cultural work. [14] In an article published in the May 1936 issue of the association's journal, Ishibashi Toshi, an eye doctor who had worked in Beijing, urged Japan to set up more schools in China and to support and maintain ties with Chinese graduates of Japanese institutions. He argued that Japan ought to catch up with the Western powers, which had not only established schools with comprehensive facilities but also provided free medical treatment to the sick and offered assistance to Chinese alumni of their schools. [15]

---

13. See Huang, *Jindai Riben*, pp. 80–92.

14. See Iwanari Ishihito, "Dōjinkai no Chūgoku shidō seishin o ronsu" (A discussion of Dōjinkai's guiding spirit in China); Terazaki Yoshitarō, "Shokan e fu" (Impressions); and Katayomi Sanehito, "Bunka jigyō no igi" (The meaning of cultural work), all in "Tai-Shi bunka jigyō ni kansuru kaku hōmen no hihan oyobi iken."

15. See Ishibashi Toshi, "Chūgoku ni gakkō o" (Schools in China), in "Tai-Shi bunka jigyō ni kansuru kaku hōmen no hihan oyobi iken."

A review of Japanese efforts published in 1935 in *Igai jihō* (Medical news) maintained that due to Japan's clumsy diplomacy, its cultural activities had not promoted closer relations but instead encouraged anti-Japanese feelings and resulted in the withdrawal of Chinese participation and the misperception that Japan was practicing cultural imperialism. The article advocated a thorough review of Japanese cultural work in China.[16] Others outside the medical field took a similar view. To Gotō Asatarō, a professor of humanities at Nippon University, the tone of Japanese-Chinese relations should be neighborly love; only by recognizing the strong consciousness of the Chinese masses and respecting their feelings could warmhearted relations be deepened. Gotō further argued that Japanese in China should move out of the concession areas and that Japanese should treat Chinese students in Japan with warmth. For Akaji Tadano, a member of the House of Peers, Japan should promote Oriental culture to deepen the friendship between the two countries. To encourage Confucianism, he advocated conducting more research on the Confucian classics. Japanese-Chinese cultural interchanges depended mainly on scholarly exchanges, and these, he felt, should also be broadened to exchanges among the common people.[17]

Cultural Programs

The wide range of motivations and concerns behind Japan's continuation and expansion of its cultural policy toward China in the 1930s were reflected in the variety of cultural programs carried out by the CAD. One important difference, however, is that in contrast to the 1920s, when there was Chinese input into the policy-making processes, Japan's cultural policy from 1931 on was decided unilaterally by the Japanese government. The Manchurian incident ended all official Chinese participation in Japanese cultural ven-

---

16. See "Tai-Shi bunka jigyō" (Japan's cultural work toward China), *Igai jihō*, June 23, 1935, in H.2.2.0.2-4, JFMA.

17. See Gotō Asatarō, "Nis-Shi hito kōyū no kyōchō" (An emphasis on friendship between the people of Japan and China); and Akaji Tadano, "Tōyō bunka no shinzui" (The essence of Oriental culture), both in "Tai-Shi bunka jigyō ni kansuru kaku hōmen no hihan oyobi iken."

tures in China.[18] Nevertheless, this did not mean that all cultural activities were undertaken solely to advance Japan's immediate political and economic goals. Such motives were less discernible in some ventures. Below I briefly survey the multitude of programs sponsored by the CAD in the 1930s, starting with those most concerned with promoting Japan's immediate interests.

One new initiative undertaken by the CAD in the 1930s was the North China Industrial Science Research Institute (Kahoku sangyō kagaku kenkyūjo). Established in December 1936 in Qingdao, it promoted research primarily on agriculture, animal husbandry, water control, and mineral ores so as to facilitate the economic development of North China. This emphasis gave the institute a role in promoting the effective Japanese exploitation of the economic resources of North China. A February 1936 Foreign Ministry intelligence report noted that Japanese agricultural and scientific technology could help resuscitate Chinese villages; this would contribute to peace and stability in China, leading to an increase in Chinese purchasing power and increased trade between Japan and China. Special mention was made of cotton cultivation and wool production. The report expressed the hope that the institute's research would help to promote Japanese-Chinese economic cooperation in North China, and this would also be the basis for consolidating and deepening ties between the people of Japan and China.[19]

Another institute supported partly by the CAD, the East Asia Common Culture Institute (Tō-A dōbun shoin), could also be viewed as furthering Japan's immediate interests in China. Established by the East Asia Common Culture Association (Tō-A

---

18. For Chinese input in the 1920s, see Teow, *Japan's Cultural Policy*, pp. 63–91.

19. See "Tai-Shi bunka jigyō no dōkō" (The direction of Japanese cultural work toward China), *Kanpō shūhō*, no. 10 (Feb. 1936), in H.o.o.o.1, II, JFMA; Takafusa Nakamura, "Japan's Economic Thrust into North China, 1933–1938: Formation of the North China Development Corporation," in *The Chinese and the Japanese: Essays in Political and Cultural Interaction*, ed. Akira Iriye (Princeton: Princeton University Press, 1980), pp. 220–53; and *Bunka 36: Shantung menka chōsa fukumeisho* (Investigative report on raw cotton in Shantung), Apr. 1937, in "Chōsho: Bunka jigyōbu," JFMA.

dōbunkai) in Shanghai in 1901, this institute provided Japanese students with a firm grounding in the Chinese language and in the political and economic conditions of contemporary China in the hope that its graduates could better promote Japanese interests. Because its students were fluent in Chinese and regularly undertook extensive field research in various parts of China, the Common Culture Institute was regarded by many Chinese as a Japanese "spy school." In 1938, 1,487 (55.4 percent) of its graduates worked in Manchuria and China, many as "labor managers, negotiators, cultural brokers, and general troubleshooters," in such major organizations as the Central Bank of Manchukuo, the South Manchurian Railway Company, and the East Hopeh Autonomous Government. Others were employed as interpreters for the Japanese military establishment. Because of such activities, the institute has been quite correctly characterized as "an enabling arm of Japanese imperialism in China" that trained "the advance guard of Japanese imperialism in China."[20]

The CAD also provided financial assistance to Japanese residents' associations in Qingdao, Shanghai, and Tianjin to support activities that benefited Japanese residents of those communities. The Qingdao Japanese Residents' Association received support for its management of four primary schools, the Qingdao Japanese Middle School, and the Qingdao Japanese Girls' High School. The four primary schools, the Shanghai Japanese Girls' High School, the Shanghai Japanese School of Commerce, and the Shanghai Japanese Business School benefited from similar support to the Shanghai Japanese Residents' Association. And the association in Tianjin received funding for the local Japanese Girls' High School.[21]

20. See Douglas R. Reynolds, "Training Young China Hands: Tōa Dōbun Shoin and Its Precursors, 1886–1945," in *The Japanese Informal Empire in China*, ed. Peter Duus et al., pp. 210–71, esp. pp. 263–64, 270.

21. In Qingdao in 1933, the primary schools had a combined enrollment of 2,080 students; the middle school, 395 students; and the high school, 409 students. In Shanghai in 1933 the high school had an enrollment of 327 students; the school of commerce, 257 students; and the business school, 107 students. (No figures are known for the primary schools.) In Tianjin in 1933, the high school had an enrollment of 163 students. See *Bunka 64: Bunka jigyōbu jigyō gaiyō* (A summary of

Other cultural programs aimed to develop Chinese and Manchurians as "intermediaries" and "collaborators" to assist in the administration of Manchuria. From September 1935 to August 1936, twenty teachers, recommended by the Ministry of Education of Manchukuo, attended Japanese normal schools for a year. Between February 1935 and March 1938, five Mongolian students, selected by the Mongolian Political Division of Manchukuo, underwent training at four Japanese agricultural schools. From December 1935 to November 1936, 325 Chinese and 121 Manchurians took courses at Japanese military, navy, police, and railway institutes.[22]

Despite the Japanese state's interest in grooming intermediaries and collaborators, participation in these programs seems to have been more voluntary than coercive. The study and training institutes were not "brainwashing" centers, but institutions open to Japanese as well. They were quite different in this regard from the programs associated with the People's Renovation Society (Xinmin hui), an organization set up in December 1937 to promote a new ideology to justify Japan's actions in China. Managed by Japanese military personnel, the society acted as the ideological wing of the Provisional Government of China based in Beijing. It publicized its ideas through a finely orchestrated system of propaganda, utilizing mandatory educational policies, radio broadcasts, songs, plays and films, newspapers and periodicals, libraries, and teahouses, as well as special training institutes to groom a core of Chinese leaders.[23] In contrast, the programs of the CAD were more diffuse, displaying no such disciplined and rigorous pursuit of specific agendas. This suggests that the issue of collaboration should be analyzed in a more complex fashion rather than simply tying it to the conspiratorial machinations of the Japanese occupiers. Similarly,

---

the work of the Cultural Affairs Division), Dec. 1934, in "Chōsho: Bunka jigyō-bu," JFMA, 35–38.

22. See *Bunka 18: Shōwa jūichi nendo shitsumu hōkoku*, pp. 19–20, 24–25.

23. See Akira Iriye, "Toward a New Cultural Order: The Hsin-min Hui," in *The Chinese and the Japanese*, ed. idem, pp. 254–74; and Beijing Records Office, comp., *Riwei Beijing Xinmin hui* (The Xinmin hui in Japanese-occupied Beijing) (Beijing: Records Office, 1989). On other "cultural" aspects, see Louise Young, *Japan's Total Empire: Manchuria and the Culture of Wartime Imperialism* (Berkeley: University of California, 1998).

there was no monolithic anti-Japanese response among the people of China but, instead, a diversity of responses to the Japanese conquest and occupation of Manchuria and North China, a circumstance that helps to explain the continuing participation by Chinese and Manchurians in Japanese cultural programs.[24]

Much the same can be said of the CAD's provision of Boxer indemnity scholarships. Grants had been awarded to Chinese students to pursue studies in Japan since 1924, and 26,846 Chinese students studied in Japan from 1931 to 1937, with the number reaching a peak of 18,096 in the years 1935 to 1937. This surge in numbers is explained partly by the depreciation of the Japanese currency, which made it cheaper for Chinese to study in Japan, as well as the poor employment conditions prevailing in China during this period.[25] Yet the continuous flow of Chinese students to Japan even after the Manchurian Incident suggests that Chinese students still saw Japanese educational institutions as offering beneficial training. An analysis of the Boxer indemnity scholarship holders in 1931, 1932, and 1936 reveals that recipients came from all parts of China, although there was a relatively larger representation from Manchuria and North China in 1936. The Chinese students pursued a variety of studies—law, medicine, engineering, the natural and applied sciences, social sciences, and humanities. Beginning in November 1930, grants were also awarded to Japanese students to study in China; in 1936 there were 66 recipients.[26]

The CAD also provided financial assistance to Chinese students through its support of the Japan-China Association (Nikka gakkai). Established in 1918 in Tokyo to improve the life of Chinese stu-

---

24. See, e.g., David P. Barrett and Larry N. Shyu, eds., *Chinese Collaboration with Japan, 1932–1945: The Limits of Accommodation* (Stanford: Stanford University Press, 2001); Rana Mitter, *The Manchurian Myth: Nationalism, Resistance, and Collaboration in Modern China* (Berkeley: University of California, 2000); Wen-hsin Yeh, ed., *Wartime Shanghai* (London and New York: Routledge, 1998); and Poshek Fu, *Passivity, Resistance, and Collaboration: Intellectual Choices in Occupied Japan, 1937–1945* (Stanford: Stanford University Press, 1993).

25. See Sanetō Keishū, *Chūgokujin Nihon ryūgakushi* (A history of Chinese students in Japan) (Tokyo: Kuroshio, 1960), pp. 544–45; and Lee, "The Foreign Ministry's Cultural Agenda," p. 296.

26. See Huang, *Jindai Riben*, pp. 131–42; and *Bunka 18: Shōwa jūichi nendo shitsumu hōkoku*, pp. 8–17; and *Bunka 64: Bunka jigyōbu jigyō gaiyō*, pp. 39–44.

dents in Japan, the association continued to provide an array of services to Chinese students in Japan in the 1930s. These included dormitory facilities, language training, academic counseling, and other social services. It also provided financial aid to such organizations as the Chinese Students' Christian Youth Association in Japan, the Manchurian Students' Association in Japan, and the Harbin Institute managed by the Japanese-Russian Association. Beginning in 1925, the association also assumed management of the East Asian Higher Preparatory School (Tō-A kōtō yobi gakkō), a preparatory school founded in 1914 for Chinese students and later renamed the East Asian School (Tō-A gakkō).[27]

CAD funding for cultural exchanges also continued into the 1930s. Travel grants were awarded for cultural visits. For example, from December 1935 to November 1936, 113 Japanese and, from 1932 to 1936, 248 Manchurians and 243 Chinese received travel grants. Other forms of CAD aid in 1936 were the 3,023 volumes of books donated to a number of educational institutions in Manchuria and China, financial grants to thirteen schools and hospitals in Manchuria and China to purchase equipment and other resources, and financial assistance to 24 scholarly projects in the field of Chinese studies.[28]

Parallel to programs that might be considered as promoting Japanese interests in China, the CAD also underwote cultural programs that had no immediate political or economic benefits for Japan. For example, in Manchuria the CAD sponsored research on Manchurian-Mongolian culture in the humanities and natural sciences, especially in the fields of history, language, ethnology, ethnography, geography, religion, and archaeology; it also supported the establishment of cultural institutions such as research centers, libraries, and museums. To promote research on Manchurian-Mongolian culture, the Investigation Committee on Manchurian Cultural Work (Tai-Man bunka jigyō shinsa iinkai) was set up in April 1933. It proceeded to endorse such research projects as the history of the Khitans during the Liao-Jin era, the races and relig-

---

27. See Huang, *Jindai Riben*, pp. 188–93; and Wang, *Gengzi peikuan*, pp. 522–25.
28. See *Bunka 64: Bunka jigyōbu jigyō gaiyō*, pp. 48–58; and Huang, *Jindai Riben*, pp. 179–82.

ions of Manchuria and Mongolia, the archaeology of the eastern capital of Jilin province, and the compilation of a Manchurian-Japanese dictionary. The Japan-Manchuria Cultural Association undertook similar projects. These included establishment of the Manchurian National Museum, the compilation of Ming and Qing archival materials, the repair and restoration of the temples and detached palaces of Rehe, and the publication of the *Qingchao shilu* (Records of the Qing dynasty), which ran to 3,500 volumes.[29]

In China the research carried out by the Beijing Humanities Institute (Pekin jinbun kagaku kenkyūjo) and the Oriental Cultural Academy (Tōhō bunka gakuin), both supported by the CAD, likewise reflected Japanese interest in the classical scholarship of East Asia. The Beijing Humanities Institute, opened in December 1927, undertook the compilation of a sequel to the *Siku quanshu tiyao* (Summaries and annotations of the complete library of the four treasuries, a project initiated in the eighteenth century by the Qianlong emperor). Having completed, at the end of 1930, an index of materials to be included in the compilation, the scholars proceeded to undertake summaries and annotations of the original *Siku* project categorized under the four headings of Classics, History, Philosophy, and Belles Lettres.[30] The Oriental Cultural Academy, established in 1929, opened two research centers to promote sinological studies in Japan: one in Kyoto in November 1930 and another in Tokyo in September 1933. With twelve researchers and two assistants, the Kyoto institute worked on such topics as the archaeology of the plastic arts of the Six Dynasties, the archaeology of ancient bronze utensils, ancient rhyming tones, and the local administrative structures of the Tang dynasty. The Tokyo institute had fourteen researchers and fifteen assistants, who worked on subjects such as Han dynasty music, paintings of the Six Dynasties, the history of Chinese coinage during the medieval age, and the intellectual history of the Wei-Jin and Northern

---

29. See *Bunka 64: Bunka jigyōbu jigyō gaiyō*, pp. 58–63; and *Bunka 18: Shōwa jūichi nendo shitsumu hōkoku*, pp. 101–6.

30. See *Bunka 18: Shōwa jūichi nendo shitsumu hōkoku*, pp. 60–62; Yamane, *Kindai Nit-Chū kankei no kenkyū*, pp. 14–33; and Huang, *Jindai Riben*, pp. 159–61.

and Southern dynasties. The Oriental Cultural Academy also undertook the reproduction and reprinting of Chinese classics; by 1936, twelve such works had been reproduced and reprinted.[31]

Besides research on East Asian classical studies, another focus of Japanese research was the natural sciences. Such research was undertaken, among other places, at the Shanghai Natural Sciences Institute (Shanhai shizen kagaku kenkyūjo), established in April 1931, under the auspices of the CAD. The institute consisted of a medical faculty with departments of pathology, bacteriology, and Chinese pharmacology; and a science faculty with departments of physics, chemistry, biology, and geology. The institute's emphasis on basic research differentiated it from the applied research of the North China Industrial Science Research Institute. In 1936, 28 Japanese and fourteen Chinese researchers undertook a total of 152 research projects. These included studies of the hydrography of the Yangzi River, the geophysics of the Yellow River, the chemical composition of the yellow loess of North China, the histology of insects, the classification of freshwater fishes in Shantung province, and the chemistry of the causative agents of smallpox.[32] The CAD also established the Beiping Japanese Modern Science Library (Peipin Nihon kindai kagaku toshokan) and the Shanghai Japanese Modern Science Library (Shanhai Nihon kindai kagaku toshokan). Opened in 1936, both libraries were intended to promote Japanese-Chinese scientific and economic cooperation. Besides housing collections on agriculture, industries, commerce, medicine, and the natural sciences, the libraries also screened films and conducted lectures on scientific developments.[33]

---

31. See *Bunka 18: Shōwa jūichi nendo shitsumu hōkoku*, pp. 79–100; and *Bunka 64: Bunka jigyōbu jigyō gaiyō*, pp. 15–23. Regarding other research on classical scholarship of East Asia, see *Bunka 14: Kō-Mō no iseki to sono kōei ni tsuite* (Regarding the relics and descendants of Confucius and Mencius), Jan. 1932; *Bunka 22: Shina jikan no genjō ni tsuite* (Regarding the present state of temples in China), Aug. 1934; and *Bunka 58: Chengde no koseki* (The ancient relics of Chengde), June 1935, all in "Chōsho: Bunka jigyōbu," JFMA.

32. See *Bunka 18: Shōwa jūichi nendo shitsumu hōkoku*, pp. 66–79; *Bunka 64: Bunka jigyōbu jigyō gaiyō*, pp. 7–15; and Huang, *Jindai Riben*, pp. 167–77.

33. See *Bunka 18: Shōwa jūichi nendo shitsumu hōkoku*, pp. 130–34.

Many of the Japanese participants in these activities were sinologists who understood Chinese history and culture and were sympathetic to the Chinese cause. They included Hashikawa Tokio, the director of the Beijing Humanities Institute from 1933 to 1945, and highly regarded sinologists such as Takeuchi Yoshimi and Imahori Seiji, who had studied in China on Boxer indemnity grants. There were also dedicated scholars in other fields, such as Toyama Ichirō and Komiya Yoshitaka of the Shanghai Natural Sciences Institute, who attempted to pursue their studies despite the deterioration in Japanese-Chinese relations. A number of these Japanese participants blamed Japanese militarism for hindering the pursuit of their scholarly work in China.[34]

Chinese Responses

As the preceding discussion shows, from 1931 to 1937 the CAD did little to advance Japan's immediate political or economic interests or to marginalize and dominate Chinese culture. In fact, the emphasis on the classical aspects of East Asian culture could be seen as promoting the cause of sinology and the stress on the natural sciences as furthering the cause of modern science in China. Nevertheless, they elicited Chinese criticisms of Japanese cultural aggression. For instance, in a book on China's proper response to Japanese imperialism, published in Shanghai in 1931, Gong Wu rebuked Japan for using Chinese money to finance Japanese cultural imperialism. He accused the Japanese of being hypocritical, of couching their imperialist designs under the guise of "sweet phrases" such as "working for the welfare and benefits of the Chinese people." He believed, however, that the Chinese people could not be fooled, since they had clearly seen through the "wicked" actions of the Japanese.[35] Similarly, the proliferation of Japanese cul-

---

34. Lee, "The Foreign Ministry's Cultural Agenda," pp. 284–86, 291–92, 297, 305. For a comparison with Japanese scholars associated with the research work of the South Manchuria Railway Company, see Joshua A. Fogel, *The Cultural Dimension of Sino-Japanese Relations: Essays on the Nineteenth and Twentieth Centuries* (Armonk, N.Y.: M. E. Sharpe, 1995), pp. 118–36.

35. See Gong Wu, "Chūgoku wa ika ni shite Nichi teikokushugi ni taifu subeki ya" (How China should respond to Japanese imperialism), in *Bunka 13: Han-Nichi*

tural and educational institutions in Manchuria since 1907 was cited
in books as evidence of Japan's cultural aggression toward China
and of Japanese efforts to train collaborators and traitors and to use
culture as a tool to destroy China. Japan's cultural efforts were
perceived to have intensified in order to counter the more successful American cultural efforts in China.[36] Such sentiments reinforced the popular notion that through its cultural work Japan had
hoped to "soften" and "enslave" the Chinese, benumb and manipu-
late them into obedient masses, exploit their weaknesses, and distort the world's perceptions of China.[37]

Articles and editorials in Chinese newspapers and journals also
characterized Japan's cultural policy toward China as cultural co-
lonialism. According to Chinese writings gathered by the CAD,
the Chinese saw Japan's sponsorship of Chinese students as an attempt to buy Chinese goodwill, although the authors of these publications held that goal had not been realized. "Pro-Japanese" students might have either proceeded to Manchuria to become
officials or become traitors, but many of the more capable students,
upon returning home, had become anti-Japanese, thwarting the
goal of Sino-Japanese "amity."[38] Similar criticisms were raised in an
editorial in the *Tianjin yishibao* on May 15, 1936. The editorial argued that Japan was pursuing both a cultural and a military policy
toward China. For example, besides constructing libraries and research institutes in North China, Japan had also established air-
ports and military camps. If the goal was to promote understanding, Japan should diminish its militarization efforts in China. The
editorial concluded that although China generally welcomed and

---

teikokushugi sōsho no gaiyō (A summary of materials on anti-Japanese imperialism),
Feb. 1932, "Chōsho: Bunka jigyōbu," JFMA.

36. See "Nihon teikokushugi to Chūgoku" (Japanese imperialism and China);
and Hsueh Ti, "Nihon teikokushugi Man-Mo shinryaku gaikan" (A general view
of Japanese imperialist aggression in Manchuria and Mongolia), both in *Bunka 20:
Manshū mondai sono hoka zatcho tekiyō* (A summary on the problem of Manchuria
by various authors), in "Chōsho: Bunka jigyōbu," JFMA.

37. See Gong Wu, "Chūgoku wa ika ni shite Nichi teikokushugi ni taifu subeki
ya."

38. See "Nihon no tai-Shi bunka seisaku ni taisuru zakkan" (Miscellaneous
views on Japan's cultural policy toward China), 1933, in H.2.2.0.2-4, JFMA.

was grateful to foreign countries for their cultural work, the country opposed Japan's use of cultural works as the vanguard of its militarization effort.[39]

When Okada Kanekazu, chief of the CAD, visited Beijing University in July 1935, he encountered a lukewarm reception from the Chinese professors he met. Although they acknowledged the value of promoting traditional Chinese culture, they also voiced the need for China to absorb foreign cultures in order to cope with the changing times. Since China possessed neither the financial nor the human resources to do this alone, it would welcome cultural cooperation with foreign nations. They emphasized, however, that such cooperation should address the needs of China and not be undertaken for other political agendas; otherwise it would be like "a butcher hanging a sheep's head but actually selling dog's meat," and all Chinese would oppose it. Indeed, China had on occasion refused to undertake "cultural cooperation" with foreign countries. The activities of agencies associated with the CAD, they felt, reflected Japan's perspective more than genuine cultural cooperation between the two countries. The Chinese professors reiterated that Sino-Japanese cultural cooperation should not (1) be behind the times; (2) forget Asian ancestry and be enslaved to Western culture; (3) be dominated by the cultural policies of other countries; or (4) be decoration only and not based on reality. Rather, it should (1) incorporate social science and be based on modern science; (2) allow Asians to do things in a distinctively Asian manner and spirit, taking into consideration Asian natural and societal relations; and (3) encourage the participation of Chinese scholars, with space for expressing their talents.[40]

Japan-educated Chinese students also articulated various criticisms. Some found that Japanese higher education, like that in European and American countries, stressed economics and political science. Consequently Chinese students who studied Japanese

---

39. See "Nihon tai-Shi bunka jigyō no sekkyokuka" (The progression of Japanese cultural work toward China), *Tianjin yishibao*, in "Tai-Shi bunka jigyō ni kansuru kaku hōmen no hihan oyobi iken."

40. See the dispatch from the Japanese embassy to the Japanese foreign minister, July 12, 1935, in H.2.2.0.2-1: Shina no taido (China's attitude), III, JFMA.

culture were often inadequately prepared and had to drop out; to rectify this situation, this group called for more discussion of Japanese culture and more organizations to support Chinese students. Others commented that, given the great progress of Japanese medicine in recent years, more could be done to improve the practice of medicine in China. Still others asked for more effort to alleviate the frustrations faced by Chinese students studying in Japan.[41]

On the whole, it appears that most Chinese perceived Japan's cultural efforts from 1931 to 1937 in terms of Japanese cultural aggression, an emphasis that has continued to the present day in Chinese scholarship on modern Japanese-Chinese cultural relations.

Conclusion

From 1931 to 1937, Japan continued its cultural policy toward China through the CAD, a policy that began in 1923. Besides perpetuating existing cultural programs, Japan also introduced new programs. This expanded cultural policy was motivated by several factors: pragmatism, international cultural rivalries, and sentiments of ethnocentrism, moralism, and idealism. Japan's policy in turn elicited Chinese charges of Japanese cultural imperialism. Given Japanese acts of aggression and domination in various parts of China during this period, such criticisms are understandable. The fact that Chinese had no input into the policymaking process after 1931 could only have intensified their distrust of Japanese motives. Nonetheless the wide range of activities carried out by the CAD highlights the complex mix of elements characterizing Japanese-Chinese cultural relations. Although some cultural activities were pursued primarily to further Japan's political and economic agenda

---

41. See Tan Juezhen, "Nihon bunka o ika ni shite sen'yō suru" (How Japanese culture can be enhanced); Shen Zhijian, "Igaku ryūgakusei hakken ni tsuite" (Regarding the dispatch of medical students overseas); Chen Lin, "Shinrai ryūgakusei no me ni eitta Tōkyō" (Tokyo as reflected in the eyes of the newly arrived students); and Wang Boyi, "Ryū-Nichi Chūgoku gakusei no risshū zakkan" (Miscellaneous thoughts of a Chinese student in Japan with the arrival of fall), all in "Tai-Shi bunka jigyō ni kansuru kaku hōmen no hihan oyobi iken."

in China, others had few such intentions, even if they were generally perceived by the Chinese as part of Japanese imperialism and aggrandizement. What should we conclude from this situation?

Although a nation's foreign cultural policy is often closely connected with the other components of its diplomacy (strategic, political, and economic), this does not mean that cultural matters cannot be pursued independently of the dictates of politics and economics. In the context of CAD activities from 1931 to 1937, this possibility was recognized by a number of Chinese participants. For instance, at the Beijing Humanities Institute, scholars defended themselves against charges of collaboration and disloyalty by asserting that culture and politics represented two different spheres of activities and that cultural matters transcended national boundaries.[42] On this same premise, the Shanghai Natural Sciences Institute maintained ties with individual Chinese scholars and participated in conferences of Chinese bodies, such as the China Science Society, the China Institute of Engineers, the China Zoological Society, and the China Botanical Society.[43] Likewise the Universal Benevolence Association remained in contact with various Chinese medical associations and took part in seminars and lectures involving Chinese medical practitioners.

Within the government, the Foreign Ministry, despite being pressed by military leaders to assume a more nationalistic and militarist direction, still attempted to chart a moderate course for Japan's foreign relations in the 1930s.[44] With the Marco Polo Bridge Incident in 1937 and Japan's expanded war effort in China, however, the Foreign Ministry came under greater pressure to toe an ultranationalistic line. Japan's cultural policy toward China came under the control of the Asia Development Board (Kō-A-in) in 1938 and then the Greater East Asia Ministry (Daitō-A-shō) in 1942. The Foreign Ministry retained some control over Japan's cultural relations with other countries until 1940, when the CAD was dis-

---

42. Lee, "The Foreign Ministry's Cultural Agenda," p. 285.

43. Ibid., p. 290.

44. For an analysis of the Gaimushō's roles in China, see Barbara J. Brooks, *Japan's Imperial Diplomacy: Consuls, Treaty Ports, and War in China 1895–1938* (Honolulu: University of Hawai'i Press, 2000).

banded.[45] By then the Japanese-Chinese conflict had become part of the global conflagration between the Allied and the Axis powers, and Chinese leaders such as Chiang Kai-shek and Mao Zedong were portraying the conflict as one of democracy versus totalitarianism, culture versus barbarism, and good versus evil.[46]

The activities of the CAD from 1931 to 1937 should be seen in all their complex dimensions. Caught in a tangled web of suspicions, fears, miscalculations, and tragedies, it is understandable that Japanese-Chinese relations in modern times have sometimes been painted in the contrasting monotones of black and white, right and wrong. This certainly does not do justice to the many intricate threads that constituted the fabric of modern bilateral relations.

---

45. See *Gaimushō no hyakunen*, 1: 1048; and Lee, "The Foreign Ministry's Cultural Agenda," p. 283.

46. See Iriye, *China and Japan*, pp. 83–88.

CHAPTER ELEVEN

Mocking Misery: Grass-Roots Satire in Defeated Japan

John W. Dower

On January 17, 1947, a clever letter published in the *Asahi shinbun* under the title "What's Fashionable in the Capital Now" offered a snapshot of life in Tokyo less than a year and a half after Japan's defeat. The vignette was simultaneously lively and bleak—a nice mirror, in every way, to the ambience of the time.

Those who peopled this cityscape bore little resemblance to the "hundred million" whose hearts had supposedly beat as one a few years earlier, when the militarists controlled the scene and the emperor's soldiers and sailors were engaged in a mad campaign to create a new "Greater East Asia" imperium. *Ichioku isshin* (one hundred million, one heart) was surely the most overworked slogan of the war years. The *Asahi*'s letter writer, by contrast, portrayed a society in which a myriad hearts seemed to be working at cross-purposes. Japan's vaunted social harmony was nowhere to be seen.

Pistol-wielding robbers, gangs of thieves, pickpockets, swindlers, runaway prisoners, kidnappers, murderers, and "fake police detectives" prowled these streets, alongside prostitutes, black market operatives, purged ex-officials, and a horde of functionaries who had totally reversed their expressed views about right and wrong. Dark deeds took place in bright daylight. Prices were rising so fast that postcards with the postage printed on them quickly became out of date. (What to do? Buy a sheet of supplemental stamps, cut them with scissors, paste them on with glue.) Disruptive strikes and demonstrations were erupting everywhere. People played the lottery, looking like cheerful Ebisu, the god of good luck, when they won—and like Enma, the scowling guardian at hell's gate, when they lost.

The transportation system was a horror. Robbers worked the railways as they worked the streets. The trains ran late or were canceled entirely, largely because of the shortage of coal. They broke down and had dreadful accidents. ("Don't let your beloved child travel," the writer warned.) Deliveries did not arrive on time. Fake edibles—pickled garnishes with misleading labels, "imitation cakes without sugar, saké and soy sauce diluted with water"—were being sold. Consumers were confronted with "light bulbs with short lives, pencils that break when sharpened, knives that don't cut even when sharpened, screws that bend when turned." This was but a fraction of what could be told. Japanese society, alas, threatened to "go on descending, descending, into a bottomless pit."[1]

What made this satire particularly droll was that it was a takeoff on a famous fourteenth-century parody of the same title—an anonymous lampoon that ridiculed the sorry state into which the capital city of Kyoto had fallen during the so-called Kenmu Restoration, when civil war plagued the land. Times changed and did not change, and the possibility of ransacking the past for language and precedents usable in the present made the sting of defeat more bearable. Past, present, and future were inextricably linked in defeated Japan.

"What's Fashionable in the Capital Now" is a small example of what I have characterized elsewhere as the "bridges of language" that enabled many Japanese to navigate the transition from war to peace with a certain sense of continuity—even, indeed, with a sar-

---

1. Asahi shinbunsha, ed., *Koe* (Voice) (Tokyo: Asahi bunko, 1984), 1: 264–65. This is a selection of letters to the editor originally published in the "Koe" section of the *Asahi shinbun*: vol. 1 covers 1945 through 1947. See also the lengthy "Picture of Tokyo" printed in the Feb. 20, 1947, issue of the *Asahi* and quoted in Tōkyō yakeato yamiichi o kiroku suru kai, ed., *Tōkyō yamiichi kōbō shi* (Tokyo: Sōfūsha, 1978), pp. 55–57.

donic sense of humor.[2] Wartime Japan tolerated homespun jokes alongside satire of the enemy, and periodicals such as the monthly magazine *Manga* (Cartoon) kept a substantial cadre of housebroken humorists and cartoonists employed right up to (and through) the surrender. In the crushing sanctimony of the holy war, however, it was taboo—and seriously hazardous to one's health—to openly mock such targets as the state and "national polity," or the ruling groups, or the vaunted "Yamato spirit" that purportedly made every Japanese an obedient subject tingling with patriotism, loyalty, and filial piety. The fragile but venerable tradition of public satire and self-mockery that had taken root in late feudal Japan and carried over to the early twentieth century was one of the more minor casualties of the war. It was also one of the first "traditions" to recover.

At an elemental level, this recovery involved little more than the inventive reapplication of proverbs and catchphrases. "Thanks to our fighting men" (*heitaisan no okage desu*), one of the most pious expressions of the war years, for example, became almost overnight a caustic allusion to how the country had fallen into such miserable circumstances. Other well-known sayings proved similarly adaptable to explaining the national disaster. "The frog in the well doesn't know the ocean" (*i no naka no kawazu taikai o shirazu*), a hoary old saw, now was evoked to belittle the militarists and nationalists and their fatuous wartime proclamations about "spiritual strength" and "certain victory." Merchants, politicians, and other opportunists who quickly swallowed the bitterness of defeat and began catering to the U.S. occupation forces confirmed the old saying that "the burning sensation is forgotten once things pass your throat" (*nodomoto sugureba atsusa o wasureru*).

"Proof surpasses theory" (*ron yori shōko*, a rough equivalent to "the proof of the pudding is in the eating") found ubiquitous application amid the rubble. One magazine, for instance, used this as a caption for a photograph of burned-out buildings. In its New Year

---

2. Examples of the search for a usable past appear throughout John W. Dower, *Embracing Defeat: Japan in the Wake of World War II* (New York: W. W. Norton & The New Press, 1999). "Bridges of Language" is the title of chapter 5 in that study.

issue of 1946, the pictorial weekly *Asahi gurafu* (Asahi graphic) made grim use of another familiar expression by printing a photo of the mushroom cloud over Hiroshima with the caption "truth that emerged out of lies" (*uso kara deta makoto*). "Sailing with the wind" (*ete ni ho o ageru*), a phrase with counterparts in every culture, was used to characterize everything from a commitment to democracy to the most crass opportunism.[3]

Even the rapacious black market, which constituted much of the "real" economy from the time of surrender until around 1949, contributed to the humorous redirection of pious set phrases. While Emperor Hirohito spent an inordinate amount of time agonizing over the sanctity and preservation of the regalia associated with his dynastic line (the sequestered mirror, sword, and jewel), black-market toughs made a stab at charisma by flaunting their own "three sacred regalia": aloha shirts, nylon belts, and rubber-soled shoes. This was a witty, irreverent appropriation of imperial pretensions indeed—an irreverence that indirectly said something about the throne's waning mystique.[4]

The black market also inspired a suggestive revision of the lyrics of one of the country's most popular and sentimental children's songs, "Big Sunset, Little Sunset" ("Yūyake koyake"). In this instance, moreover, we can see the seeds of postdefeat cynicism in the war years themselves, for "Yūyake koyake" had also inspired at least one subterranean presurrender parody. The original song (dating from 1923) opens as follows:

Yūyake koyake de	Big sunset, little sunset—
hi ga kurete	the day draws to a close.
Yama no otera no	From the mountain temple
kane ga naru	sounds the bell.
Otete tsunaide	Hand in hand,
mina kaero	let's all head home.

---

3. For a good sample of such "reapplication" of old proverbs and clichés, see the series of photographs accompanied by satirical captions in *Asahi gurafu*, Jan. 1946. This clever graphic commentary is another early example of the *iroha* associations discussed in this essay. The captions alone are reproduced in *Iroha karuta*, a Winter 1974 special volume (*bessatsu*) of the elegant magazine *Taiyō*, p. 102 (hereafter cited as *Iroha karuta*).

4. Tōkyō yakeato yamiichi o kiroku suru kai, *Tōkyō yamiichi kōbō shi*, p. 52.

| Karasu mo issho ni | Let's go home together |
| Kaerimashō | with the crows. |

During the war, however, as Japan's leaders continued to spout the rhetoric of ultimate victory while the country's plight became more and more palpably desperate, even children gave voice to disillusion. Apparently inspired by the fact that many temple bells had been melted down to feed the war machine and thus were no longer to be heard, the lyrics to "Big Sunset, Little Sunset" underwent such mocking revision as this:

Yūyake koyake de	Big sunset, little sunset—
hi ga kurenai	the day doesn't come to a close.
Yama no otera no	From the mountain temple
kane naranai	no bell sounds.
Sensō naka naka	The war doesn't seem
owaranai	to ever end.
Karasu mo ouchi e	Even the crows
kaerenai	cannot go home.[5]

---

5. Tongoe Shin, *Kodomo no kaeuta kessakushū* (Tokyo: Heibonsha, 1998), pp. 109-11. This was by no means the only wartime song subjected to mockery before the defeat. The same fate, for example, befell the lyrics of the "Patriotic March" ("Aikoku kōshinkyoku"), a song that appeared shortly after the initiation of war with China in 1937 and enjoyed explicit government support. The tasty flavor of this particular parody is suggested by the metamorphosis of the march's opening line, where "Look, dawn comes to the Eastern Sea" (*Miyo Tōkai no sora akete*) became "Look, Tōjō's head is bald" (*Miyo Tōjō no hage atama*). Another patriotic song, in this instance dating from 1940 and celebrating the purported founding of the Yamato state 2,600 years previously, inspired several parodies. Entitled "Twenty-six-hundred Years Since the Founding" ("Kigen wa nisen roppyaku nen"), the song dwelled on mythical birds and glorious radiance and concluded with heartfelt evocation of "ah, the pounding heart of the hundred million" (*aa, ichioku no mune wa naru*). In the parody, the names of cigarette brands replaced the nouns in the original, and the song became a lament about inflation driving up the price of tobacco. The lyrics concluded with the sad observation that "ah, the hundred million has no money" (*aa, ichioku wa kane ga nai*)—or, in a slightly different rendition, "ah, the hundred million weep" (*aa, ichioku no tami ga naku*). Most shocking (and surely most intriguing for the practitioner of psychohistory to ponder) were the parodies of a 1930s children's song entitled "I Love Soldiers." The first verse of the original lyrics ran as follows: "I love soldiers / When I grow up / I'll put on medals and don a sword / Mount a horse and gallop off" (*Boku wa gunjin daisuki yo / Ima ni ōkiku nattaraba / Kunshō tsukete ken sagete / Ouma ni notte hai dōdō*). Children sang several variations of this, all appar-

A third stage in this lyrical metempsychosis appeared in the form of a letter to the *Asahi* in 1947, a week before "What's Fashionable in the Capital Now," under the title "Big Black Market, Little Black Market" ("Ōyami koyami"). The new lyrics, a pithy mix of cynicism and idealism perfectly in tune with the times, ran as follows:

> Big black market, little black market—
> the day draws to a close,
> and honest men are made out to be fools.
> Skimpy dinner, out of firewood,
> trembling in a house where rain leaks in.

> The small black marketeer is chastised
> and finds himself in jail,
> while out in a mansion, drinking and eating,
> the big black marketeer is laughing.

> When I become a grown-up,
> Mister Big Round Moon,
> let's make a really bright country
> where honest men aren't made out to be fools.[6]

One of the more popular and ritualized forms of mocking misery in defeated Japan derived from the annual New Year's practice of playing "syllable card" (*iroha karuta*) games. Dating from around 1800 as a children's game, this originally involved associating the elements of the cursive hiragana syllabary with the opening syllable of well-known proverbs or sayings. This quickly evolved into a game in which a set of 96 cards—half with the sayings written on them (each beginning with a different syllable), the other half decorated with illustrations of each particular saying (with the opening kana syllable itself appearing in one corner)—was scattered

---

ently beginning with essentially the same first three lines. Here is one such version: "I hate soldiers / When I become small / I'll be held by Mother and drink her milk / Get a coin and go buy candy" (*Boku wa gunjin daikirai / Ima ni chisaku nattaraba / Okāsan ni dakarete chichi nonde / Issen moratte ame kai ni*). In other versions, children sang about drinking Mother's milk, after which "I'll disappear into her stomach" (*Onaka no naka e kiechau yo*)—or "I'll sleep soundly on her lap" (*Ohiza de suyasuya nenne suru*). For these examples, see ibid., pp. 183–94.

6. Asahi shinbunsha, *Koe*, 1: 253. This appeared in the Jan. 9, 1947, issue of the *Asahi*.

on the floor. The textual cards were picked up at random and read aloud, and participants competed to find and pick up the illustrated card that corresponded to what had been read. This was a literate and frequently raucous amusement, and it encouraged many variations. Since there was no fixed collection of proverbs or sayings that had to be used, the makers of *iroha* sets were free to introduce their own associations, and even to create their own catchy phrases.

The game apparently originated in the Kansai area (Kyoto and Osaka) and was quickly adopted (and adapted) in Edo, where the feudal lords congregated in homage to the shogun. It reflected the culture and inventiveness of the townspeople rather than the samurai, however, and, among other things, revealed how widely and *vertically* literacy had spread during the long era of warrior domination. Many proverbs used on the cards were Chinese in origin, and introducing them to children's play obviously served a certain didactic or hortatory educational purpose. As a product of commoner culture, however, the early card sets often revealed a certain detachment from the pious platitudes and moral injunctions of the ruling groups. Contrary to what one might expect, the virtues of loyalty and filial piety (*chū* and *kō*) that so obsessed the chattering ruling classes were most conspicuous by their absence from Edo-period *karuta* sets.[7]

---

7. The *kana* syllabary consists of 48 "syllables," but the symbol read as "n" is omitted from the game (since it never begins a word), giving a total of 47. However, the syllable *kyō* (from Kyoto, where the game may have originated) was commonly included in the old card games, thus accounting for the conventional total of 48 cards (doubled to 96). The appearance of the initial *kana* syllable on the picture cards made the game appropriate for teaching children the syllabary itself (and not just proverbs). The order in which the *kana* appear in the card set derives from the famous "iroha poem" (*iroha uta*) that dates from the late tenth century and is made up of the 47 syllables (again excluding *n*) of the syllabary. (This *iroha* order was the most common way of "alphabetizing" lists, entries, and the like until 1889, when the *a-i-u-e-o* order familiar today became conventional.) The term *karuta* itself comes from the Portuguese for "card" and entered the native vocabulary in the sixteenth century, when the Japanese first encountered and began to copy the foreigners' illustrated playing cards. The original name for the children's game introduced at the turn of the nineteenth century was *iroha-tatoekaruta*, with *tatoe* meaning "proverb." See *Iroha karuta*, pp. 57–68, and for the observations and examples about commoner attitudes that follow here, pp. 72–75.

By and large, the early nineteenth-century *iroha* cards produced in the Kansai area appear to have featured short and sweet aphorisms about wasting time and energy. Typical examples are "driving a nail into rice bran," "putting a clamp on bean curd (*tofu*)," "shooting a gun in the dark," "giving a gold coin to a cat," "looking over a fence when blind," "putting in eye drops from the second floor" (a Kansai gem indeed!). *Iroha* cards in Edo, by contrast, were apparently strongest on exhortations to be sharp and wary—such as "inattentiveness is the great enemy" and "look around three times before having a smoke." Confucian pieties—or, more precisely, the pieties of Confucianists—sometimes received decidedly oblique acknowledgment. For example, "reading the *Analects* but not knowing the *Analects*" (*"Rongo" yomi no "Rongo" shirazu*)—one way of referring to "a learned fool"—was the saying chosen for the syllable *ro* in one late-feudal set of "syllable cards." While commoner children in the waning decades of warrior rule apparently were spared indoctrination about filial piety in their little card game, they did on the other hand learn about "old people who ought to know better" (*toshiyori no hiyamizu*).

What did these youngsters learn about the venerable samurai from their *iroha karuta*? Not a great deal, it seems, although they did encounter the well-known observation that "the samurai uses a toothpick even though he hasn't eaten" (*bushi wa kuwanedo taka-yōji*). This does not exactly seem to have been designed to promote awe of the ruling class. Similarly, it is doubtful that card-playing greatly enhanced religious piety among youngsters. On the contrary, their New Year's Day play reminded them that "even a sardine's head seems precious if you believe in it" (*iwashi no atama mo shinjin kara*) and that Buddhist priests were inclined to give "inept and long-winded sermons" (*heta no nagadangi*). At the same time, however, under *ko* they might encounter the harsh Buddhist injunction that "a child is an encumbrance in all three stages of existence" (*ko wa sangai no kubikase*). Other aphorisms offered these young people a very hard-nosed and pragmatic mixture of the sacred and profane. Under the syllable *chi* (here read *ji*), for example, the card game might remind them that "money can affect your fate even in hell" (*jigoku no sata mo kane shidai*).

Inherent ambiguity sometimes sharpened the potential double edge of these "educational" games. This is suggested by the famous saying that (since it begins with the syllable *i*) opens many of the earliest sets: *inu mo arukeba bō ni ataru*, or "if even a dog moves around, it will encounter a stick." What exactly did this mean? Apparently, one thing at one time, another and quite contrary thing at another time. Originally, the saying seems to have been intended as a warning that anyone who got out of line would find trouble (that is, be hit with a stick). The sanguine spin came in thinking of the dog happily finding a stick by wandering around. In this case, going out of bounds might bring good fortune.[8] When cartoonists picked up the *iroha karuta* as a vehicle for satire in defeated Japan a century later, they obviously had an established but extremely flexible "tradition" to play with. As we shall see, they even reintroduced their own version of the wandering dog.

In the "modern" era that followed the Meiji Restoration, the *iroha karuta* spread throughout the country. Sometimes they were even popularly called "dog-stick cards" (*inubō karuta*) from that best-known of opening sayings. In the Meiji and Taishō periods, card sets were sometimes attached to children's books as a merchandising bonus. Pithy phrases were cleaned up and rendered more "wholesome." By the 1930s, when the cards became vehicles for patriotic exhortation, soldiers (*heitai*) marched in where an earlier generation might have found farts (*he*) more entertaining as an opening syllable. In a typical card set from 1940, for example, the association for *he* was "Playing soldier, don't cry even if you fall" (*heitaigokko korondemo nakuna*).[9]

The convention of associating *kana* syllables with illustrated graphics had obvious attractions for cartoonists addressing adult audiences. It was natural and easy, that is, to transfer the multiple "card" format to the printed pages of periodicals as an extended sequence of single-panel illustrations with witty *iroha* captions.

---

8. Ibid., pp. 6, 79.

9. Ibid., pp. 79, 87. One of the unwholesome early flatulence "sayings" for *he* was "tightening the buttocks after passing a fart" (*he o hette shiri tsubomeru*). *Iroha karuta*, which contains many excellent full-color reproductions of card sets, includes a good one from the war years on p. 87.

Among other things, this provided a clever format through which
to kick off each new year with a wry, impressionistic commentary—sometimes by turning old phrases to new uses, sometimes by
bending or cleverly altering an old proverb, sometimes by coining a
sharp new aphorism or wedding a barbed graphic to a pithy and
newly fashionable phrase. For several years following the defeat,
such cartoons in the form of "new edition syllable cards" (*shinpan
iroha karuta*) provided an ironic magazine commentary on the contemporary scene.

Although these graphic little jokes certainly constitute one of the
most modest and ephemeral forms of social commentary and cultural expression imaginable, in retrospect they capture the flavor of
the times with remarkable pungency. At the same time, they also
convey a sense of grassroots cynicism and iconoclasm that (in one
way or another) tells us quite a bit about the transition to "democracy" in postwar Japan. There is even, perhaps, a small sense of coming full circle—in that public discourse was regaining the more detached, ironic, even sacrilegious tone that had been present in earlier
times. In a wonderful little example of
this reinvented tradition, one of the
first postdefeat cartoon adaptions of the
syllable card motif opened (almost)
with that hoary dog-and-stick proverb.
The illustration portrayed a trembling
dog staring at a boiling pot of stew. This
was a commentary on the acute food
shortage that Japanese in all walks of
life confronted in the wake of defeat,

and the accompanying revised caption read: "If a dog walks around,
it may well become soup" (*inu mo arukeba nabe ni sareru*).[10]

---

10. *Kyōryoku shinbun*, Jan. 1946. A nastier variation on this most famous of
opening *karuta* proverbs was offered in the *Asahi gurafu* issue of the same date.
Here virtually the identical classic saying (given as *inu ga* [rather than *mo*] *arukeba
bō ni ataru*)—that is, "If a dog walks around, it will encounter a stick"—was accompanied by a photograph of three GIs accompanied by three young Japanese
women. Readers were left to speculate on their own who was the dog and who
the stick, but the sarcasm was unmistakable.

Until 1949, the Japanese media were subjected to formal censorship by the American-led occupation authorities. All media expression thus took place in a box. Although the parameters of permissible expression were much greater than had been the case under the presurrender Japanese regimes, certain logical targets of satire were formally taboo. The victors and their entire early agenda of "demilitarization and democratization" were by and large off-limits to criticism—hardly an elegant or admirable model of democracy in action. As a consequence, the postsurrender cartoonists, like everyone else in the media, practiced self-censorship as a matter of course. During the war years, they had ridiculed and demonized the "devilish Anglo-Americans." Now they mocked themselves and the sorry plight into which their "holy war" had led them.[11]

Such mockery tended to zero in on several targets. The most immediately striking were the folly of the recent war and the deservedly humiliating fall from grace of the country's erstwhile leaders. Yesterday's holy war was now more than just profane. It was a joke, an act of profound stupidity, a stain on the nation's honor. And yesterday's heroes, both military and civilian (but almost always excluding the emperor), had become today's goats. An incisive early example of this new cynicism and ridicule—and, indeed, of the *iroha karuta* as a vehicle for postwar political commentary—is an exuberant sequence of 47 "New Edition Syllable Cards" by Saji Takashi and Terao Yoshitake (see Fig. 11.1) that appeared in the 1946 New Year issue of a labor-oriented periodical named *Kyōryoku shinbun* (Cooperative press). Here is a close-up selection of Saji and Terao's vignettes of the new Japan (their *i-ro-ha* panels run top to bottom, right to left).[12]

---

11. See Dower, *Embracing Defeat*, chap. 14 on "Censored Democracy."

12. *Kyōryoku shinbun*, Jan. 1946. See also *Shōwa manga shi*, a special volume (*bessatsu*) of the engaging multivolume illustrated collection *Ichiokunin no Shōwa shi* (Shōwa history of the hundred million) (Tokyo: Mainichi shinbunsha, 1977). This unpaginated volume devoted to Shōwa-era cartoons (up to 1977) includes the opening 23 entries of the *Kyōryoku shinbun* feature by Saji and Terao, plus the full reproduction (47 "cards") of another sequence discussed at length below: Ogawa Takeshi's "Voice of the People: New Edition Syllable Cards" (hereafter cited as Ogawa, "Voice of the People"). Many of the phrases or "captions" on these cards involved ironic twists on well-known clichés or catchphrases that are impossible to convey in English.

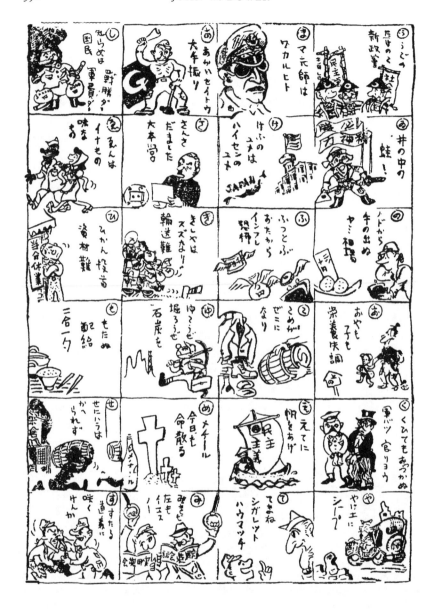

Fig. 11.1 "New Edition Syllable Cards for 1946" (Saji Takashi and Terao Yoshi-taka, "Shinpan iroha karuta," *Kyōryoku shinbun*, New Year issue, 1946).

NI
"Despised fellow being kicked out"
(*nikumarekko yo o hijikaru*)
Graphic: foot stomping a uniformed officer

HO
"Much pain for a lost war"
(*bone ori zon no makeikusa*)
Graphic: white flag of surrender above a stack
of rifles

HE
"Thanks to our fighting men"
(*heitaisan no okage desu*)
Graphic: distressed faces of a mother, father,
and child

TO
"Even old men are breaking out in cold sweat"
(*toshiyori mo hiyaase*)
Graphic: three trembling men, one in military cap,
with one of them thinking "war crimes"[13]

CHI
"Vowing to build a new Japan"
(*chikatte kinzuku shin Nippon*)
Graphic: repatriated soldier holding hands
with a smiling woman

---

13. This is a good example of the subtle, clever, historically resonant (and thoroughly untranslatable) wordplays that were so often involved in these graphic jokes. *Toshiyori mo hiyaase* is very close to the mocking phrase that appeared in the Edo-period *iroha karuta* and was translated earlier in this chapter as "old people who ought to know better" (*toshiyori no hiyamizu*). *Hiyamizu* is literally "cold water," and the connotation of imprudent old people derives from the notion that they might carelessly imperil their health by drinking cold water. *Hiyaase*, "cold sweat"—the term used in the 1946 *iroha* cartoon—is a wonderfully vivid characterization of the old-guard leaders who were trembling in fear of being convicted of war crimes. At the same time, whether consciously or subconsciously, *hiyaase* is layered over *hiyamizu*. The "cold sweat" of these men in defeat is inseparable from their imprudence in leading Japan into hopeless war and miserable defeat.

RI
"Army general in a cage"
(*rikugun taishō ori no naka*)
Graphic: former General and Prime Minister
Tōjō Hideki behind bars

O
"Women entering the election wars"
(*onna noridasu senkyosen*)
Graphic: newly enfranchised woman campaigning
for office

WA
"Me too, me too—black market dealings"
(*ware mo ware mo no yami shōbai*)
Graphic: man with black-market goods

KA
"The Divine Wind didn't blow"
(*kamikaze mo fukisokone*)
Graphic: crowded houses in flames, with bombs
falling on them[14]

YO
"Thanks for quitting [the war]"
(*yoku koso yamete kudasatta*)
Graphic: seven smiling faces of ordinary people

TA [DA]
"Even cabinet ministers do the black market"
(*daijin mo yami*)
Graphic: elderly official with black-market fish

---

14. This is not only a supremely ironic deflation of the wartime "divine wind" mystique but also another example of a subject—the wartime U.S. air raids—that subsequently rarely passed the censor's screening. This is also true of the associations given for the syllables *so* and *ya* that follow.

RE
"Great Asia War" that stained history
(*rekishi o kegasu Dai Tōa Sen*)
Graphic: military boot tromping on the pages of
an open book

SO
"The sky is blue, the ground in ruins"
(*sora wa aozora chi wa haikyo*)
Graphic: bombed-out building against the sky

NE
"No bedding or house to sleep in"
(*neru ni ie nashi futon nashi*)
Graphic: shivering mother, father, and child

MU
"Making trouble and losing rationality"
(*muri o tōshite dōri ni maketa*)
Graphic: man holding a bamboo spear being hit on
the helmet with a sledgehammer labeled "reason"

KU
"Militarists and bureaucrats—too late for regrets"
(*kuitemo ottsukanu gunbatsu kanryō*)
Graphic: officer and top-hatted bureaucrat
in handcuffs

SA
"Imperial Headquarters, which deceived all
the way"
(*sanza damashita Daihon'ei*)
Graphic: wartime military officer broadcasting
a speech

Probably because its 1946 New Year special appeared so soon after the defeat, at a time when the occupation's censorship operation was still cranking up, the *Kyōryoku shinbun* also included several direct references to the conquerors and, in some instances, transgressed the subsequent bounds of permissible expression. The conquerors entered the *iroha* tradition thusly.

MA
"General MacArthur, an understanding man"
(*Ma gensui wa wakaru hito*)
Graphic: the general's face, wearing his familiar cap and sunglasses

KE [KYŌ]
"The capital's dreams are defeat dreams"
(*kyō no yume wa haisen no yume*)
Graphic: the Stars and Stripes flying over a Japanese building, and a small map of the archipelago with JAPAN written in English[15]

YA
"Jeep on burned land"
(*yaketsuchi ni jeep*)
Graphic: the ubiquitous American jeep driving through ruins

TE
"Hand signal—cigarette, how much?"
(*temane—shigaretto hau maachi*)
Graphic: Japanese man communicating with a GI

E
"The ties that bind are strange and wonderful"
(*en wa ina mono aji na mono*)
Graphic: a black GI and Japanese woman walking arm in arm[16]

---

15. For reasons maddening to delineate, *kyō* is actually written *kefu* in the old writing style, and so this particular *iroha* association is given for the syllable *ke*. "Dreams of the capital" was an old phrase referring to Kyoto. Here, of course, the allusion is to "dreams in Tokyo." Since *kyō* also can mean "today," the clever pun has even further connotations.

16. See also note 10 above concerning the comparably disdainful treatment of fraternization in the *Asahi gurafu* issue of January 1946. This same "photo-*karuta*"

While the *Kyōryoku shinbun* was ushering in the first new year of the era of defeat with these indelicate observations, readers of another publication were offered a different but complementary set of *kana* associations in a "new edition syllable cards" cartoon sequence by Ogawa Takeshi titled "Voice of the People" (see Fig. 11.2) Here, for example, the graphic for *me* depicted a Tōjō-esque figure wearing dark glasses, with the simple caption "blind leader." The holy war was trashed in the rendering for *se*, which depicted a military sword discarded in a garbage bin, accompanied by the caption "fed up with war." A splendid little evocation of popular sentiment was conveyed in the rendering for *mo*, which portrayed a determined-looking peasant leaning on a hoe in a field. The caption read: "Not going to be deceived any more."

ME
"Blind leader"
(*mekura shidōsha*)
Graphic: Prime Minister Tōjō as blind man giving a speech

SE
"Fed up with war"
(*sensō wa korikori*)
Graphic: military sword in a trash bin

---

feature in *Asahi gurafu* also used the syllable *e* to highlight the presence of blacks in the U.S. occupation force. In this instance, a photograph of an old Japanese man lighting the cigarette of a black GI was accompanied by the same proverb ("The ties that bind are strange and wonderful"). Japanese commentators reasonably speculate that such taboo observations probably made it into the media at this early stage because the censors simply did not pick up on or pay attention to these clever, insider word games. See, e.g., *Iroha karuta*, p. 102. For the duration of the occupation, verbal or graphic treatment of black Americans was negligible, although Japanese racial responses to their presence were not negligible at all.

MO
"Not going to be deceived any more"
(*mō damasarenu*)
Graphic: determined farmer leaning on a hoe

The attraction of this last entry for the cultural and political historian is that it captured in a few swift strokes what was surely the most popular of all explanations among Japanese as to how they had become embroiled in such a disastrous war. They had, it was said time and again, "been deceived" (*damasareta*). From this, it followed that the people as a whole had to take care never again to be misled by their leaders. And from this observation, in turn, it was but a natural step to argue that the best way to do away with irresponsible leaders was to create a genuinely open, rational, democratic" society. Seen from this perspective, the scowling cartoon farmer was saying a great deal indeed. He represented (whether he fully realized it or not) a potentially solid "grassroots" basis of support for a drastically liberalized national polity.

The "Voice of the People" sequence also included a few wryly obsequious genuflections to the occupation force. Thus, the drawing for *re* depicted the entry to General MacArthur's headquarters, with the sidebar "Doubly Honorable Allied Force." For *na*, readers were offered an American sailor engaged in friendly conversation with a little Japanese girl. The caption read "Friendly Advancing Force"—picking up a familiar euphemism for the occupation force that, in itself, could be used as a point of departure for a disquisition on the Japanese penchant for weasel words. During the war, for example, it had been military gospel that the imperial army and navy always advanced and never retreated. Thus, when they *did* withdraw from a confrontation, this was rarely acknowledged by plainly speaking of "retreat" (*taikyaku*). Rather, the emperor's soldiers and sailors were said to be engaged in *tenshin*, literally "turning around and advancing." In a similar manner, the

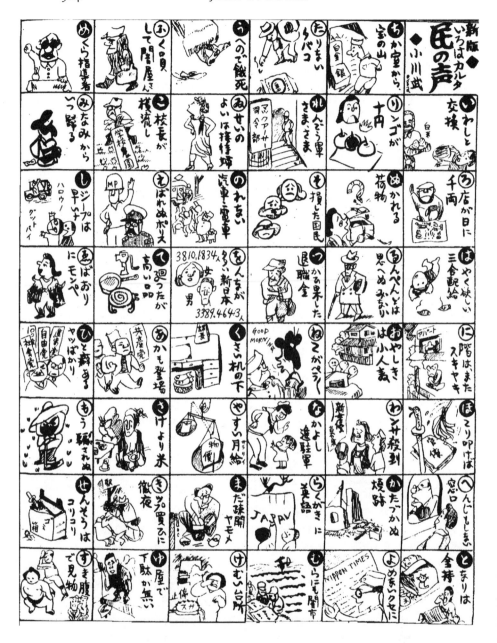

Fig. 11.2   "Voice of the People: New Edition Syllable Cards" (Ogawa Takeshi, "Tami no koe: shinpan iroha karuta," *Manga to yomimono*, New Year issue, 1946).

RE
"Doubly Honorable Allied Force"
(*rengōgun samasama*)
Graphic: entrance to "MacArthur
General Headquarters"

NA
"Friendly Occupation Force"
(*nakayoshi Shinchūgun*)
Graphic: American sailor with
Japanese child

country's defeat (*haisen*) was most often referred to in official pronouncements (much less so in popular discourse) as the "termination of the war" (*shūsen*), a far more gentle construction. Much the
same linguistic aversion was involved in denaturing the occupation
force (*senryōgun*) by referring to it as the "advancing force" (*shinchūgun*).

The cartoon *karuta*, in any case, went far beyond these renditions of conquered and conqueror. They were also, in their way, a
more literally graphic counterpart to the word pictures of chaos
and confusion conveyed in parodies such as "What's Fashionable
in the Capital Now" and "Big Black Market, Little Black Market."
From 1946 to 1949, a good many of these graphics focused on an
aspect of the defeat that virtually every Japanese encountered on a
daily basis: the black market. Rampant egoism prevailed here, as
already seen in some of the mocking entries in *Kyōryoku shinbun*.
Ogawa's cartoon *karuta* for *fu* observed that many of the millions

FU
"Repatriated and now in the black market"
(*fukuin shite yamiyasan*)
Graphic: Ex-serviceman, still wearing his military cap

of servicemen and civilians who had been overseas when the war ended made ends meet as black market operatives after they were repatriated.[17]

Over two years after the surrender, a humor magazine ushered in 1948 by inviting well-known cartoonists to contribute *karuta*-style graphics and found many of them still obsessed with the centrality of the black market in everyday life. For *chi*, for example, Katō Etsurō pointed out the relationship between the dynamism of the illegal market and the incompetence of the government with a drawing of a sturdy man in gaiters, carrying a huge bundle on his back. The caption read, "delay in rations makes the black marketeer fat" (*chihai de futoru yami shōnin*). Ogawa Tatsuo satirized the lucrative gains farmers made by diverting their produce from the official distribution system to the black market. His graphic for the syllable *wa* (involving a subtle wordplay) depicted a gloating farmer seated in his house with foodstuff behind him and paper currency spread all over the floor in front of him. Tanaka Hisao used the syllable *ya* to belittle the big operatives who were "getting fat on the black market, forgetting one's place" (*yamibutori mi no hodo shirazu*). His drawing depicted an obese man in a suit picking up paper money with chopsticks. Katō Etsurō then re-entered this collaborative card set with an unusually scathing riff on *fu*. His drawing offered a woman in kimono giving a speech, while a fat, grinning man in dark glasses stood behind her. What was this slice of life all about? Simple: "Wife is Diet member, husband is black marketeer" (*fujin wa daigishi teishu wa yamiya*).[18]

Beyond these conquered/conqueror vignettes, and beyond the black humor of the market, the *iroha* satires captured the sheer chaos of everyday life as well as any other mode of popular expression in these years. Saji and Takao captured this most vividly in

---

17. See the 1946 *iroha* cartoon entries reproduced in *Shōwa manga shi*.

18. This interesting "collaborative" *iroha* cartoon sequence appears in the Jan. 1948 issue of *Nippon yūmoa* (Japan humor). A more common postsurrender mockery of the two-income couple had the husband being a black market operative and the wife a "panpan prostitute" (the "panpan" catered primarily to the foreign personal affiliated with the occupation); see, e.g., the unillustrated *iroha* witticisms in *Manga*, Jan. 1947, p. 23.

U
"Starved to death in Ueno Station"
(*Ueno de gashi*)
Graphic: feet of a corpse protruding from
a covering

MI
"When will he return from the south?"
(*minami kara itsu kaeru*)
Graphic: woman weeping over the failure of a
loved one to return

O
"More women in New Japan"
(*onna ga ōi shin Nippon*)
Graphic: Numbers indicating how Japanese
women now greatly outnumbered men due to
heavy fatalities in the war

their rendering of a shivering family with "no bedding or house to sleep in." Ogawa's "Voice of the People" went further. His grim offering for *u*, for example, depicted the feet of a corpse sticking out from under a blanket, a common scene in railway stations and other underground public facilities where the homeless congregated for several years after the surrender. The wives, parents, and children who waited, often for years, for word of whether their overseas loved ones were still alive provided the subject for *mi*, a woman brushing away tears. In a "syllable card" for *o*, Ogawa offered a woman's face with the figure 38,101,834 and a man's face by the number 33,894,643—picking up statistics that revealed the demographic imbalance caused by the war deaths of young men, a loss that meant many Japanese women of marriage age were deprived of potential spouses.

In a lighter vein, the prevalence of petty theft became a man leaving a public bath house and discovering someone had stolen one of his wooden clogs. Shortage of decent clothing emerged in "Voice of the People" as a woman wearing the *haori* coat worn

YU
"Clog missing at the public bath"
(*yuya de geta ga nai*)
Graphic: Man leaving a bathhouse and
staring at a single wooden clog

E
"Formal coat and pantaloons"
(*ebaori ni monpe*)
Graphic: Woman wearing a formal overgarment for
kimono along with the unglamorous cotton pants
worn during the war and often for several years after

TA
"Not enough tobacco"
(*tarinai tabako*)
Graphic: picking up a discarded
cigarette butt

with kimono along with the decidedly unglamorous *monpe* pantaloons common during the war and, for many poor women, for
many years after. Another vignette of daily vexations offered a
white-collar worker picking a cigarette butt off the ground. "Not
enough tobacco" was the concise legend.

Other illustrators and wordsmiths used the syllable-card format
in comparably pointed ways. Thus, the *desirability* of being sent to
prison (where one was at least guaranteed food and lodging) inspired, for the syllable *tsu*, a prisoner singing happily as a policeman led him off to the slammer. The accompanying text read
"volunteering to go to prison by committing a crime" (*tsumi o oka-
shite keimusho shigan*). Another card set picked up on the postsurrender efflorescence of messianic new religions, several of which
were founded by women who claimed to have had ecstatic visions.
The graphic here offered a cross-eyed woman kneeling in front of a
Shinto pendant with her hands clasped in prayer and tiny figures
prostrating themselves before her. Playing on the syllable *ki*, the
caption called less than reverential attention to "new religions

where an insane person becomes a deity" (*kichigai ga kamisama ni naru shinshūkyō*).[19]

Such barbed observations went on and on. The once prized virtue of frugality was ridiculed with aphorisms (here for the 1947 New Year) to the effect that, in the midst of runaway inflation, it was "foolish to make a plan for the year" (*ichinen no hakarigoto suru dake yabo*). The best one could do was "steal when poor, spend madly when prosperous" (*kasshite wa dorobō, uruoeba ranpi*). It was a rare cartoonist who could resist a grim (or sick) reference to the prevalence of blindness caused by drinking the cheap methyl alcohol popular among the down-and-out. "Stoned and blind" (*yoi shirete me ga tsubure*) was the blunt association for the syllable *yo* that accompanied a cartoon of a disoriented man with a bottle labeled "methyl" before him. A drawing of a man in the berth of a railway sleeper car was turned into a joke by contrasting his comfortable accommodation with the "fourth class" status to which—in General MacArthur's own humiliating words—Japan had fallen as a nation. "A first-class sleeper in a fourth-class country" (*yontō koku ni ittō shindai*) was the caption here. Although Emperor Hirohito generally escaped the barbs of the humorists just as he evaded almost every other sort of substantive criticism, his unprecedented post-defeat decision to tour the country and mingle with common people prompted one publication to enlarge a famous old saying. "A crane in the dump" became "crane in the dump, emperor in the crowd" (*hakidame ni tsuru, hitonami ni tennō*).[20]

The postwar spread of commercialized sex drew attention with renderings of nude shows and old men reading pornography. "Showing thighs is a business" (*momo o miseru ga shōbai*) was one

---

19. These last two examples, as well as those that follow in the text, have been selected from the various cartoon sets previously cited, plus a Dec. 1948 sequence in *Shin Osaka* (New Osaka) that is reproduced in *Iroha karuta*, pp. 103–4.

20. The emperor reference, regrettably, appeared as an *iroha* witticism without illustration (in *Manga*, Jan. 1947). Ono Saseo drew the emperor removing a huge mask-like head capped with traditional Heian court headgear, and emerging as an ordinary man in Western suit, as an association for *te*. "Even the emperor is a human being" (*tennō mo ningen*) was his caption, referring to the Jan. 1, 1946, imperial rescript in which Emperor Hirohito more or less renounced his "divinity"; see *Nihon yūmoa*, Jan. 1948.

dignified new association for *mo*. The difficulties of true romance during the acute food shortage that lasted for three or four years after the defeat was conveyed in a 1948 graphic of a couple on a park bench trying to have a "rendezvous while carrying sweet potatoes" (*imo motte rendezvous*). The postwar phenomenon of seeking a marriage partner at public meetings devised solely for that purpose was captured in the notion that "the ties that bind come from a group marriage meeting" (*en wa shūdan miai*).

Struggling to survive day to day by selling personal possessions such as clothing piece by piece, just as one peeled and ate the edible bamboo shoot, inspired one of the most famous coinages of the postsurrender period—"bamboo-shoot existence." From this came, in 1948, a predictable cartoon *karuta* depicting a woman standing before an empty bureau, with the caption "already three years of bamboo-shoot existence" (*takenoko gurashi mo sannen*). In another syllable-card sequence for 1948, hunger for a touch of glamour prompted the observation that "women can be caught by a dress" (*onna wa ishō de tsurareru*). The accompanying illustration clearly slipped by the occupation's American censors: it depicted a young woman reaching for a dress dangled by a male figure with a gigantic nose in silhouette—a decidedly uncomplimentary rendering of the Caucasian conquerors who exchanged luxury gifts for sexual favors.

What the new freedoms associated with "democracy" might mean for old virtues such as filial piety inspired the talented cartoonist Ono Saseo to offer, also in 1948, a drawing of a little boy giving a speech to his trembling father. "Child humbles parent" (*ko wa oya o hekomasu*) was Ono's association for *ko*. In the same issue in which this cartoon appeared, however, Miya Shigeo offered hope that some old customs were still being preserved. His rendering for *re* introduced "a cultured person who knows manners" (*reisetsu o shiru bunkajin*)—but it was not, in fact, intended to put traditionalists' hearts at rest. Miya's "cultured person," depicted bowing before a Shinto shrine, was a young American GI.

And how did young Japanese emerge in these *iroha* sallies (when not engaged in the black market or in personal and family relationships)? University students worked part-time jobs instead of attending classes or spent their time waving red flags in front of their old professors. Workers celebrated May Day under hammer-and-sickle flags. A young woman with high and "westernized" aspirations was sure to end up an old maid because "her ideals are too high" (this particular graphic offered a kimono-clad woman brushing off men with her elbow while holding a book with the English title "Love Is Best"). Alternatively, young people could enjoy another of democracy's great attractions, the boogie-woogie—or attend auditions held by movie studios looking for "new talent" (here the unkind graphic portrayed a young would-be female star with a nose like a potato).

Much of this was frivolous, of course. While the satirists were poking fun at the postwar confusion, a great many other Japanese were seriously searching for "bridges of language" that would provide them with usable traditions for the present and future. The Shōwa emperor, guided by advisers like the career diplomat Shigemitsu Mamoru (soon to be indicted as a war criminal) and ever intent on preserving the sanctity of his dynasty, rediscovered the 1868 Charter Oath of the Meiji founding fathers. His mission, like that of his grandfather, the Meiji emperor, he declared on New Year's Day 1946, had always been to throw off the evil customs of the past and seek knowledge throughout the world. (He did not explain how this cosmopolitan search had led to Nazi Germany.)[21] Less rhetorically but more dramatically, the emperor's postwar decision to become a "crane in the dump" and mingle with the hoi polloi had its most obvious precedent in the imperial tours his grandfather, the Meiji emperor, had carried out in various parts of the country in the 1880s. On both occasions, these carefully choreographed royal excursions were undertaken to stabilize popular support for the throne at a time of political agitation and uncertainty.

---

21. A diary entry by Tokugawa Yoshihiro, dated Apr. 24, 1968, and disclosed in the Japanese media in 1999, is the most recent revelation of the emperor's obsession with the regalia and preservation of his family line; see *Asahi shinbun*, Jan. 6, 1999. On Shigemitsu and the emperor's belated appreciation of the Charter Oath, see Dower, *Embracing Defeat*, pp. 287–89, 313–15; examples of all the other "uses of tradition" mentioned in these concluding paragraphs appear scattered throughout this same source.

Within days after the emperor announced Japan's capitulation, millennial rhetoric about "changing the world" (*yonaoshi*) that had been popular in the late feudal period was resurrected as an appropriate way of thinking about the challenges now posed by defeat. Closer in time, liberals rediscovered "Taishō democracy." Progressives and leftists called attention to the aborted ideals of the "freedom and people's rights movement" (*jiyū minken undō*) of the early Meiji period and to the proletarian and labor movements that had emerged (and been crushed) after the turn of the century. The celebration of "May Day" resumed in 1946, after having been suppressed for ten years—the seventeenth such celebration in Japan. Popular protests against the government's woefully inept rationing system, which culminated in a tumultuous "Food May Day" a few weeks later, were in certain ways a striking replication of the most dynamic occasion of popular protest in prewar Japan—the 1918 "rice riots." In both instances, the impetus to nationwide demonstrations derived from spontaneous local protests by housewives. The birth of a radical postwar university student movement (beginning with Student May Day in 1946) was explicitly linked to the anniversary of a notorious prewar incident involving suppression of academic freedom (the Takigawa incident of 1937).

Marxists quickly revived the acrimonious but intellectually stimulating *Rōnō-kōza* theoretical debates suppressed in the 1930s. Libertines, hedonists, and exhausted escapists resurrected the *ero-guro-nansensu* vogue that had embraced the "erotic, grotesque, and nonsensical" in the early 1930s in a thinly sublimated expression of protest against the rising tide of militarism. Scientists talked about returning to "our peaceful research." Conservative philosophers like Kōsaka Masaaki criticized the absence of Western-style "objectivity" in Japanese culture but saw hope for the future in the "sacred power" and estimable state-centered and family-centered "morality" that supposedly characterized Japanese culture. Writers as diverse as the austere "Kyoto School" philosopher Tanabe Hajime and the enormously popular writer of historical epics Yoshikawa Eiji turned to the thirteenth-century evangelist Shinran for wisdom concerning both repentance (*zange*) and ecstatic conversion (*ōsō*). Outcast thinkers of "dangerous thoughts" from the war years, such as Kawakami Hajime, Miki Kiyoshi, Ozaki Hotsumi, and Miyamoto Yuriko became postwar (and, for Miki and Ozaki, posthumous) heroes and heroines.

Industrialists and other leaders of big business quickly called attention to the many usable "pasts" on which postwar economic reconstruction could and should be built. Predictably, these included the rehabilitation of a *zaibatsu*-dominated capitalist system and the restoration of intimate commercial and personal ties with the United States and Great Britain. At the same time, business leaders and economic planners also called attention to the dramatic advances in applied science and technology that the long war itself had stimulated. This, they argued—coupled with continued strong state input into economic planning—would provide the foundation for the country's future development as an advanced economic power. Indeed, in technocratic as well as technological ways, the very mobilization for "total war" that had led to miserable defeat soon proved to be an unexpectedly dynamic and adaptable "past" on which to construct a more democratic and peacefully oriented Japan.[22]

Even the Japanese post office took part in the business of reinventing tradition and building bridges from the old to the "new" Japan. There was no place for a Meiji-era hero like General Nogi Maresuke on postage stamps any more, but who could take his place? From early on, it was clear that the country's new indigenous heroes had to be modern "cultural" figures, but it took a long time to decide who these should be. It was not until 1949 that the postal service inaugurated its Cultural Leaders Series with a stamp honoring the medical researcher Noguchi Hideyo. Between 1950 and 1952, sixteen eminent prewar men and one distinguished woman (the writer Higuchi Ichiyō) were similarly commemorated as prewar models for the new postwar era.[23]

---

22. I have summarized some of the literature on the legacies of Japan's so-called Fifteen-Year War in "The Useful War," an essay reprinted in John W. Dower, *Japan in War and Peace: Selected Essays* (New York: The New Press, 1993), pp. 9–32.

23. For postage stamps, see the popular annual catalogs issued by Nihon yūbin kitteshō kyōdō kumiai (Japan stamp dealers' association), *Nihon kitte katarogu*. The 1949–52 Cultural Figures Series is reproduced on p. 12 of the 1998 catalog. Individuals honored in 1950 were the educator Fukuzawa Yukichi, writer Natsume

The bridges that linked past, present, and future were many and various indeed.

Sōseki, writer Tsubouchi Shōyō, Kabuki actor Ichikawa Danjurō, and educator Niijima Jō. In 1951, stamps honored the painter Kanō Hōgai, theologian Uchimura Kanzō, writer Higuchi Ichiyō, writer Mori Ōgai, poet Masaoka Shiki, and painter Hishida Shunsō. The series concluded in 1952 with stamps commemorating the philosopher Nishi Amane, legal scholar Ume Kenjirō, astronomer Kimura Sakae, educator Nitobe Inazō, scientist Terada Torahiko, and artist and aesthetic critic Okakura Tenshin. Presurrender Japanese stamps did not, in fact, commemorate many "cultural heroes," apart from General Nogi.

Index

Index

Harvard East Asian Monographs
(* out-of-print)

Harvard East Asian Monographs

Harvard East Asian Monographs

Harvard East Asian Monographs

Harvard East Asian Monographs

Harvard East Asian Monographs